D0940268

CHANGING THE RULES:
CANADIAN REGULATORY REGIMES AND INSTITUTIONS

After more than a decade of deregulation and privatization in Canada, the time is ripe for an examination of the regulatory institutions that were reshaped, rebuilt, or newly created in the process. At the same time as internal factors were affecting changes, new international agreements such as NAFTA and global telecommunications were also having a major impact on both regulators and the communities being regulated.

This book examines changes to key institutions and argues for a greater breadth of institutional analysis. It also examines particular regulatory bodies, such as the Canadian Radio-Television and Telecommunications Commission, the National Energy Board, and the Canadian Transport Agency. Furthermore, the analysis extends to civic regulation, the regulation of privacy, internal trade regulation, and international trade and finance.

Although the individual authors focus on federal regulation, some reference is made to federal–provincial developments. The book is structured such that regulation is cast as an interplay among four regimes: sectoral, framework or horizontal, intrastate and cabinet, and international. These regimes both converge and collide but their basic internal attributes allow them to function independently as well.

The editors and authors also explore themes such as the lessons learned in the theory and political arts of Canadian regulation, the regulatory capacity of the Canadian state, regulatory accountability, and the Canadian regulatory culture in a comparative context. The result is a book that brings a vitality to the ever more complex subject of government regulation in Canada.

G. BRUCE DOERN is a professor in the School of Public Administration at Carleton University and joint chair in Public Policy in the Department of Politics at Exeter University.

MARGARET M. HILL is a policy analyst in Strategic Planning and Policy Coordination in the Policy and Communications Directorate of Environment Canada and is a visiting professor in the School of Public Administration at Carleton University.

MICHAEL J. PRINCE is the Landsdowne Professor in the Faculty of Human and Social Development, University of Victoria.

RICHARD J. SCHULTZ is a professor in the department of Political Science, McGill University.

Edited by G. Bruce Doern, Margaret M. Hill,
Michael J. Prince, and Richard J. Schultz

Changing the Rules: Canadian Regulatory Regimes and Institutions

UNIVERSITY OF TORONTO PRESS
Toronto Buffalo London

© University of Toronto Press Incorporated 1999
Toronto Buffalo London
Printed in Canada

ISBN 0-8020-4163-9 (cloth)
ISBN 0-8020-8025-1 (paper)

Printed on acid-free paper

Canadian Cataloguing in Publication Data

Main entry under title:

Changing the rules : Canadian regulatory regimes and institutions

Based on a conference held in Ottawa, Ont., May 1997.
Includes bibliographical references.
ISBN 0-8020-4163-9 (bound)   ISBN 0-8020-8025-1 (pbk.)

1. Administrative agencies – Canada.   2. Independent regulatory commissions –
Canada   I. Doern, G. Bruce, 1942–   .

JL75.C48 1999   352.8'0971   C98-932530-X

University of Toronto Press acknowledges the financial assistance to its publishing
program of the Canada Council for the Arts and the Ontario Arts Council.

Contents

List of Tables and Figures

Preface

This book is the product of a co-operative effort between the School of Public Administration at Carleton University and the Centre for the Study of Regulated Industries at McGill University. Twenty years ago these two institutions sponsored two conferences that resulted in the book *The Regulatory Process in Canada* (Macmillan 1978). This initial collaboration occurred at a time when the study of regulation was in its infancy. A burst of research was also underway in the late 1970s at the Law Reform Commission of Canada, the Economic Council of Canada, and the Institute for Research on Public Policy. In the case of the latter two bodies, a large part of the research was carried out and coordinated by Professor W.T. Stanbury.

Twenty years on, in May 1997, another conference was held, because it was felt that a broad review of regulatory institutions was long overdue. This most recent conference has resulted in the present account of Canada's regulatory institutions in the late 1990s. Canada's rules have been changed; this book examines how, and what choices and challenges have accompanied the change. We also needed new and broader ways to study regulation. Thus the book builds on a companion comparative study organized by Bruce Doern and Stephen Wilks at Exeter University in the United Kingdom. Some of the authors who contributed to this volume were also involved in the Exeter project and its resulting book, *Changing Regulatory Institutions in Britain and North America* (University of Toronto Press, 1998).

Initial drafts of the chapters were presented at the May 1997 conference in Ottawa. We were also very fortunate in securing the involvement of leading practitioners, including George Hariton, Bell Canada; Harvey Romoff, transportation consultant; Michel Elias, Gaz Metropolitain; Terry Rochefort, National Energy Board; Ian Scott, Cable Television Association; Andrei Sulzenko, Val Traversy, and Kernaghan Webb, Industry Canada; and John McBride,

Treasury Board Secretariat. Several prominent academics specializing in the field also acted as commentators, including Stephen Wilks, Exeter University; Susan Phillips, Carleton University; and Gilles Paquet, University of Ottawa. We are grateful to all these participants, who helped enhance the quality of the final product. Special thanks are also due to two anonymous University of Toronto Press academic reviewers who offered useful comments on the manuscript.

In revising the papers and developing the final book, we have been especially conscious of the need to relate this work to two audiences. One is the general student of the politics of regulation who is seeking a reasonably orderly understanding of what Canada's regulatory institutions consist of as the century ends and how they have changed over time. The other audience is our fellow regulatory academics and practitioners, for whom we think the book can offer some new ways of visualizing the Canadian regulatory state of the late 1990s. The academic and practitioner community for this book will tend to be centred in political science, public administration, and law, but we have also drawn, where appropriate, on the economics literature and on the role that economists play in the design of regulatory institutions.

Institutional approaches have become more influential in recent years, especially in political science and public administration, the home base of the editors and the majority of the authors in the book. But an adequate approach to the study of regulation must be multidisciplinary. Economists W.T. Stanbury and W.G. Waters II bring an economic perspective, and scholars such as Hudson Janisch, Michael Trebilcock, and Robert Howse bring a legal perspective to the book.

This enterprise would have been impossible without the generous financial assistance of several bodies and we would like to thank the Social Science and Humanities Research Council of Canada, the Bureau of Competition Policy, Industry Canada, the Canadian Radio-television and Telecommunications Commission, Environment Canada, the Treasury Board Secretariat, Bell Canada, Nortel, Stentor, and Gaz Metropolitain.

We greatly appreciate the support and encouragement of our publisher, the University of Toronto Press. Special thanks are also due to Kristin Doern and Joan Doern for excellent and tenacious editorial and computer services.

G. BRUCE DOERN, MARGARET M. HILL,
MICHAEL J. PRINCE, AND RICHARD J. SCHULTZ

Abbreviations

ACA	Australian Communications Authority
ACCC	Australian Competition and Consumers Commission
AIT	Agreement on Internal Trade
BCNI	Business Council on National Issues
BCP	Bureau of Competition Policy
CAC	Consumers' Association of Canada
CCME	Canadian Council of Ministers of the Environment
CDIC	Canada Deposit Insurance Corporation
CEAA	Canadian Environmental Assessment Act
CEPA	Canadian Environmental Protection Act
CHST	Canadian Health and Social Transfer
CRTC	Canadian Radio-television and Telecommunications Commission
CTA	Canadian Transportation Agency
CTC	Canadian Transport Commission
EC	European Community
EU	European Union
FCC	Federal Communications Commission (U.S.)
FISC	Financial Institutions Supervisory Committee
FTA	Free Trade Agreement (between the U.S. and Canada)
FTC	Federal Trade Commission (U.S.)
GATS	General Agreement on Trade in Services
GATT	General Agreement on Tariffs and Trade
NAFTA	North American Free Trade Agreement
NBFI	Non-Bank Financial Institutions
NEB	National Energy Board
NEP	National Energy Program
NTA	National Transportation Agency

NTARC   National Transportation Act Review Commission
OECD   Organization for Economic Cooperation and Development
OPC   Office of the Privacy Commissioner of Canada
OPRA   Office of Privatization and Regulatory Affairs
OSC   Ontario Securities Commission
OSFI   Office of the Superintendent of Financial Institutions
RAD   Regulatory Affairs Division (of Treasury Board Secretariat)
RIAS   Regulatory Impact Assessment Statement
RIP   Regulated Industries Program
SBD   Second Banking Directive (of the European Union)
TRIMs   Trade-Related Investment Measures
TRIPs   Trade-Related Intellectual Property (rights)
UNCTAD   United Nations Conference on Trade and Development
WTO   World Trade Organization

CHANGING THE RULES:
CANADIAN REGULATORY REGIMES
AND INSTITUTIONS

1

Canadian Regulatory Institutions: Converging and Colliding Regimes

G. BRUCE DOERN, MARGARET M. HILL, MICHAEL J. PRINCE, and RICHARD J. SHULTZ

Canadian regulatory institutions have changed greatly since the last burst of concerted regulatory analysis occurred two decades ago. At the time that the American airline deregulation initiative began in 1978, Canada's regulatory system, built gradually over the previous decades and consolidated in the 1960s and 1970s, seemed relatively stable and familiar. Although it had not been immune to change and there had certainly been early signs of criticism, the Canadian regulatory state was, in relative terms, leading the quiet life, captured as much by apparent normalcy as by the industries it was regulating (Economic Council of Canada 1979, 1981; Stanbury 1980; Doern 1978).

The basic contours of the regulatory state were familiar but not always well known. At the centre of the system stood the small set of major federal independent regulators – the Canadian Radio-television and Telecommunications Commission (CRTC), the National Energy Board (NEB), and the Canadian Transport Commission (CTC) – each with a nation-building mandate of one sort or another. Environmental and consumer regulation had emerged but had also already suffered their first decline in political salience. Competition policy and regulation were scarcely discussed in polite company. Within the government, the vetting of regulation was minimalist, consisting merely of rudimentary cost-benefit analysis of regulations made under some health and safety statutes and a Department of Justice review of 'the regs' that did not yet have to consider the Charter of Rights and Freedoms. Internationally, there were sectoral issues to be sure, mainly regarding the United States, but as late as 1982 free trade was not even on the federal policy radar screens (Doern and Tomlin 1991). Financial regulation was still ensconced behind its comfortable four 'pillars' (institutional types), nationally and internationally (Coleman 1996; Harris 1995).

As a new century fast approaches, the study and practice of Canada's regulatory institutions differ from those of the late 1970s in several ways. Globalization and international factors have radically altered the picture and a more concerted body of regulatory theory and analysis is affecting practice and reform through liberalization and incentive-based regulation. Deregulation in key industrial sectors, in concert with the telecommunications revolution, has changed markets. Expanded regulation has occurred in some areas of framework business and environmental regulation; and 'civic regulation,' which produces rules governing communities, morality, and the welfare state, has also grown. In the 1990s, an era of government cutbacks, there is far greater interest in and concern about regulatory compliance and service delivery. The Charter of Rights and Freedoms and other central vetting criteria have also had a considerable impact. Finally, in the late 1990s, citizens, interest groups, and interests are much more suspicious of government regulation in some respects, but continue to seek the protection of the state in others.

This book examines the causes and effects of these various changes in Canadian regulatory institutions and regimes, and assesses possible future patterns of choice and change. Concerned primarily with the politics of Canadian regulatory institutions, the focus of this collection is on the federal government but reference is made to broad federal–provincial developments as well. It also links changes in Canada to international regulation and to comparative change in other countries and jurisdictions, such as the United States, the United Kingdom, and the European Union (Eisner 1993; Francis 1993; Doern and Wilks 1998).

To facilitate an understanding of regulatory institutional change, both this chapter and the book as a whole are structured around a framework in which modern regulation is cast as an interplay among four regimes: a sectoral regime, a framework or horizontal regime, a cabinet-executive regime, and an international regime (Doern 1998). These regimes converge and collide but basic internal attributes cause them to function independently as well. This four-regime framework is described, utilized, and evaluated as a schema later in this chapter, drawing on the analysis of the contributing authors as well as other literature. In the concluding observations made in Chapter 17, we look at other, complementary themes that arise throughout the book. These centre on the lessons that have been learned in the theory and political arts of Canadian regulation, the regulatory capacity of the Canadian state, and the Canadian regulatory culture in a comparative context. However, before proceeding to these large tasks, we need to examine what it means conceptually and practically to speak of Canada's regulatory institutions.

Taking Stock of Canada's Regulatory Institutions

To take stock of Canada's regulatory institutions, three analytical steps are necessary. The first involves a discussion of definitions of regulation. Then the basic patterns of change in the regulatory outputs of government must be identified. Finally, the four-regime framework must be introduced as a way of making sense of Canada's regulatory institutions writ large.

Broadening the Definition of Regulation

There is no escaping the need for a broader view of regulation than has been customary. Despite the tendency to cast the last two decades as an era of deregulation, it is evident that, overall, the density and extent of rule making by, or on behalf of, the state has increased. If regulations are, generically, rules of behaviour backed up by the sanctions of the state (Doern and Phidd 1992; Brown-John 1981) then they can be, in the view of different political interests, rules expressed

- as constitutional or quasi-constitutional rules (e.g., the Charter of Rights and Freedoms and the 1994 Internal Trade Agreement);
- in statutes (e.g., The Canadian Environmental Protection Act);
- in delegated legislation or 'the regs' (e.g., eligibility rules regarding benefits under welfare or workfare laws);
- as guidelines (e.g., the merger guidelines under the Competition Act); or
- as standards and codes (e.g., for shipping refrigerated products, or for professional ethics).

As one moves across these modes and levels of regulatory expression, the extent and nature of the state's sanctions (from strong to virtually non-existent) vary widely and the range is itself fought over by interests. To some people, the expression 'there ought to be a law' means that there should be a statute or a regulation; for others, a flexible guideline will do. Still others may believe that no rules at all would be even better.

In this collection we have erred on the side of breadth in defining regulation, largely because political reality also errs on the side of breadth. There is some comfort in confining one's view of the regulatory state to rules governing the marketplace or other delimiting features, but this means excluding important areas of regulation. For example, we have included civic regulation, a realm in which rules are forged to affect behaviour in the community, morality, and the welfare state. For some these rules are just social policy writ large, but for those on the front lines of the social economy, this is a regulatory world of a most intrusive and life-defining kind. We have also chosen to include the state's regulation of the behaviour of its own ministers and officials.

Though we err on the side of breadth, it is important to realize that a logical conundrum eventually arises. The wider the definition provided for regulation, the more it becomes equated with government and governance as a whole. But at some point governance is not merely regulation, and government is more than just a regulatory state. It also involves taxation, spending, and ensuring that diverse policy goals and values are implemented in democratic life (Doern and Phidd 1992; Pal 1997).

Considerable breadth is also needed when conceptualizing the regulatory process. Analytically and in practice two main features of the process can be highlighted: regulation making, and compliance and enforcement (Doern 1978; Schultz and Alexandroff 1985; Ogus 1994; Meier 1985). Basic regulation-making processes include defining representation and accountability. The statutory base of the regulatory system and the various aspects of accountability are clearly crucial starting points. The concerns here are not only the actual statutory details but also the regulatory compromises enshrined in the parent laws. In other words, in any regulatory system there is a hierarchy of norm or goal-setting modes, which starts, as we have seen above, with law or statutory expressions, extends to framework principles and duties, and continues into regulations (e.g., delegated legislation passed through regular review processes), as well as guidelines and codes. It also includes the processes through which the regulator addresses the interests it is regulating or must otherwise deal with.

The second element of any regulatory system is the compliance and enforcement process. In most conceptions of regulatory systems, the compliance and enforcement process would include all the previously mentioned aspects of the decision-making process but also the processes for handling licence applications and renewals (or equivalent activity). It would also cover the handling of consumer and citizen complaints and appeals and the development of service standards (Sparrow 1994; Grabosky 1995; Doern 1994). Such 'case-handling' processes are at the centre of implementing regulations. However, especially in an era of efforts to 'reinvent' government, implementation also involves both softer compliance activities and approaches and economic-incentive-based regulation (Hood 1986; Grabosky 1995). Compliance activity can be seen to include aspects of education and training at several levels (e.g., within regulated firms and within the regulatory body). Compliance turns also on actual scientific or technical capacity (and its demonstrated objectivity) and whether that knowledge base is up to date in a fast-changing economy.

Direct enforcement activity is also a crucial part of the regulatory process. In some areas of regulation more than others, enforcement will depend on access to the courts and on the size and consequences of penalties in law. Legal action to ensure enforcement may also come from or simply be threatened by various players and competitor firms and consumer and public interest groups, as well as the regulators and governments themselves (Ayres and Braithwaite 1992).

Some care must also be taken in using the term 'regulatory agency' or regulatory body or mode (Hill 1994). The regulatory body can be an independent collective commission, such as the CRTC; a single statutory person, such as the Director of Investigation and Research under the Competition Act; or a government department headed directly by a minister, such as the Health Protection Branch in Health Canada. As several chapters indicate, however, it is rare for a single regulatory body to have total control of the entire system of regulation in a given subject field. The fact that one-stop regulatory shopping is unusual is also a key part of the politics of regulation.

Regulatory Outputs

Interpreting trends in regulatory outputs must be approached with caution, owing to the definitional issues discussed above. How can one determine whether regulation in Canada is increasing or declining as a basic output of government? Keep in mind that we are speaking here only of outputs, not outcomes. Outcomes refer to actual effects and proven compliance and, hence, an even bigger analytical world. But even outputs present problems. Efforts are made to 'count the regs,' in the sense of counting delegated legislation subject to the federal Regulatory Impact Analysis System (RIAS) process and published in the *Canada Gazette* or in an equivalent provincial government publication. Fazil Mihlar's work, both in this book (see Chapter 12) and elsewhere, indicates that by this measure regulation is still growing, although probably at a reduced rate compared to a decade ago (Mihlar 1996).

But such counts do not include rule making through statutes themselves or through the use of numerous guidelines or codes. The latter realm is probably growing in recent years precisely because of the search for reinvented and flexible government approaches, but no one is counting these kinds of rules. Nor is it clear that merely counting rules is a useful exercise (Cohen and Webb 1998). The 'count' has also to deal with the problem of weighing the import of some rules compared to others.

Given the diverse world of regulatory outputs, what can be said about trends? First, regulation in a general sense has continued to grow. Deregulation and liberalization have undoubtedly occurred in areas such as transportation, energy, telecommunications, and banking; the evidence lies in statutory change and, in some areas, simply in decisions by regulators not to act (e.g., so-called regulatory forbearance in the telecommunications field). However, marketplace framework regulation, defined broadly, has increased in the last decade (see the discussion of Regime II below). International regulation has also increased, but in ways that we reserve for later discussion in this chapter. Because the relationships among key regulatory regimes are changing, there is greater demand for transitional regulation. Finally, there is probably an increase in regulation of the state by the state, a point to which we return below.

Regulatory Regimes

The final task in our 'stock taking' of regulation in Canada is to examine the nature of regulatory regimes, how authors have used the regime concept, and why our four-regime framework is utilized to partially overcome some of the problems involved in coming to terms with Canada's regulatory institutions. There are varying usages of the term 'regime' and differences between its use in domestic versus international politics and policy.

For example, Harris and Milkis define a regime as 'a constellation of (1) new ideas justifying governmental control over business activity, (2) new institutions that structure regulatory politics, and (3) a new set of policies impinging on business' (Harris and Milkis 1989, 25). They then use this concept to examine the changes in health and safety regulation in the United States by the Reagan administration, compared to the earlier progressive era of American regulatory politics. A regime shift is seen to occur that affects the two regulatory agencies examined: the U.S. Federal Trade Commission and the Environmental Protection Agency. In this sense, a regime has a temporal dimension and is seen to extend beyond a single regulatory agency.

In their separate and joint work Hoberg and Harrison (including the latter's chapter in this volume) use the term regime to describe a number of characteristics and relationships, including ideas, processes, and players; statutory mandates; organizational capacity; and intergovernmental context (Hoberg 1993; Harrison and Hoberg 1994; Harrison 1996). This even more complex constellation has been used to characterize the environmental regulatory and policy regimes of the United States and Canada. Similarly, the language of regimes has been used to examine Canadian competition regulation (Doern 1995), where core and noncore players, ideas, statutes, organizations, processes, and clusters of interests are mapped and examined. Again, the analytical terrain is cast beyond any single regulatory body, although the regime may well be centred on one main regulatory agency. For example, a study of the Canadian telecommunications regime would certainly focus on the CRTC, but it would extend well beyond that agency. On the other hand, an effort to examine the Canadian biotechnology regulatory regime has to start without a single agency 'home base' (Doern and Sheehy 1997). This particular regime is spread across at least six regulatory bodies.

Economists often refer to 'rate of return' or 'price-capping' as different regimes for public utility regulation (Crandall and Waverman 1995). Here regime is equated with basic systems of thought and analysis that might anchor certain types of regulation. In this way distinctions between 'command-and-control' and 'incentive-based' regulation may be made to distinguish regimes of regulation.

In the study of international relations, 'regime' is frequently used to convey softer arrangements and agreements among countries, where any real organizational centre is lacking (Krasner 1983; Cutler and Zacker 1992; Zacker 1996). Thus there are regimes for whaling or for Arctic pollution or for any number of problems or issues of discussion and action. Competition policy and regulation at the international level has been characterized as being more regime-like in this sense, because relationships tend to fall largely in the realm of notifications and information sharing rather than in the realm of institutionalized dispute settlement through a core international organization (Doern and Wilks 1996).

Finally, the term regime can be equated with 'systems and subsystems' of regulation, with 'arenas and subarenas' of regulation, and with interacting 'policy communities' and 'networks' (Pross 1992; Pal 1997). Perhaps what this discussion indicates is that although there is a genuine need for middle-level ways of classifying and ordering the regulatory world, it is difficult to achieve agreement on terminology and boundaries. The problem in part is that the middle realm between the microworld of one regulatory agency or body and the macroworld of 'all regulation' is vast.

Despite these difficulties, the wider scope of regulatory change in the last two decades renders an effort to map and understand regimes more necessary. In keeping with some of the analytical uses described above, we view a regulatory regime to be an interacting set of organizations, statutes, ideas, interests, and processes engaged in rule making and implementation. In other words, the first test of the existence of a regime is the presence of some inner core of such features and characteristics that warrants the designation for analytical purposes. Building on earlier comparative work (Doern 1998) we examine Canada's regulatory institutions in this chapter, as indicated above, as an interplay among four regimes: Regime I, the sectoral regime; Regime II, the horizontal framework regulatory regime; Regime III, the overall governmental executive regime for making and managing regulation; and Regime IV, the international regime, embracing global, regional, and bilateral rules-based approaches or de facto codecision making by national or international bodies. Each of these regimes has features that deal with both the purposes of regulation and the processes of achieving them.

Each regime is first profiled in terms of its core features (see Table 1.1). In this sense each regime is an analytical ideal type, but also has strong empirical reference points. But we are ultimately interested in the interplay among them and the ways in which convergence and conflict occur among regimes over the period as a whole. In this latter sense, the regimes are a prism through which some aspects of change can be seen over the past two decades. The framework is also used to draw out a few of the key points made by the various authors about regulatory institutions in Canada. Not all the contributing authors, however, employ the full range of the four-regime framework. And some use the concept of regimes in the other ways discussed above, such as an environmental regulatory regime or a regime for regulating privacy.

TABLE 1.1
A Synopsis of Regulatory Regime Characteristics and Changes

Regime	Characteristics	Changes & Issues
Regime I – Sectoral	Monopoly or utility regulation Control of entry and exit Profit or 'rate of return' regulation Vertical sectors but with 'nation-building' mandates Multifunctional status as 'governments in miniature' Significant policy powers E.g., CRTC, NEB, CTC Command-and-control regulation	Significant decline of monopoly features due to techological change, deregulation and liberalization Competitive convergence of various kinds among sector's erstwhile 'pillars', 'modes,' and 'fuels' Sectors seen as means of production and thus decline of nation-building task Competition mandates given or asserted Move toward incentive regulation, 'price-capping,' and flexible regulation, No longer 'governments in miniature,' especially CTA and NEB; reduced size But assumption of newer environmental roles and negotiating approaches Reassertion of cabinet powers over policy

TABLE 1.1 *(continued)*
A Synopsis of Regulatory Regime Characteristics and Changes

Regime	Characteristics	Changes & Issues
Regime II – Framework	Intent is economy- and society-wide 'horizontal' rules that do not unduly discriminate against or in favour of sectors Regulator is often a line department headed by minister Three clusters of regulators • health and safety • marketplace framework • civic Key aspects of competition, environment, and consumer framework rules seen as truncated and weak Horizontal reach but not grasp De facto sectoral preferences still present	Increased demand for Regime II regulation Some due to 'regulatory shift' and new forms of rent-seeking Greater attention paid to framework rules as a whole due to trade and global pressures Competition and environment regulation strengthen but still dispute about its actual enforcement Pressure to use incentive regulation and compliance Civic regulation increasing and probably more punitive Numerous kinds of dense accountability relations and greater use of special operating agencies
Regime III – Cabinet/ Executive	Needed to manage regulation within the state as complement to the way spending and taxation are managed Difficult to aggregate the totality of regulatory decisions partly because costs show up mainly in private budgets of firms, citizens, and interests Initial rudimentary vetting of 'the regs' at the centre of cabinet (Justice Department review and limited cost-benefit of some health and safety laws) Early focus on managing 'up' to ministers and thus	Sequence of efforts to manage regulation 'down and in' and then 'out and across' as diverse values and criteria were advanced and advocated Some reforms intended to be regulation-focused but others simply had often unintended effects on regulatory system within the state Reform values and criteria include: • Charter of Rights • Cost-benefit • RIAS process • Competitiveness

12   Doern, Hill, Prince, and Schultz

TABLE 1.1 *(continued)*
A Synopsis of Regulatory Regime Characteristics and Changes

Regime	Characteristics	Changes & Issues
	traditional accountability concepts	• Flexibility • Reinventing of government Broadened basis on which state regulates itself: • privacy • freedom of information • commercial secrets The more contracting-out occurs and quasi-market service delivery is promoted, the more the state must regulate itself
Regime IV – International	International obligations and discussion (with other governments, especially U.S., and with international bodies always a part of some regulatory sectors (e.g., energy and codecisions by U.S. regulators) International rules not as 'authoritative' in the sense that there is no world government with full compliance and enforcement capacity GATT rules growing in importance but dispute settlement still sluggish and necessary reliance on persuasion and diplomacy	Globalization (world product) sourcing; telecommunications revolution; massive increase in mobility of financial capital, ecological interdependence) greatly reinforces internationalization FTA, NAFTA, EU, and WTO agreements and continuous trade negotiations affects all areas of regulation as whole systems of regulation are examined and negotiated Trade rules deal with 'over the border' issues and rules previously seen as 'domestic' Dispute-settlement processes become more institutionalized Trade norms exert pressure to promote performance-based regulation, harmonization, and mutual recognition of rules Banking and financial services 'regulation' becomes greatly internationalized Social and environmental interests seek international protection and recognition through social charters of various kinds

Regime I and the Transformation of Major Sectoral Regulators

Regime I consists of sectoral regulators which, historically, have been characterized as monopoly or public utility sectors in which the regulator regulates a monopoly supplier or quasi-monopoly set of suppliers (Armstrong and Nelles 1986; Brander 1990; Strick 1990). The regime is seen as covering separate vertical sectors of the economy and thus in Canada embraces bodies such as the previously mentioned CRTC, NEB, and CTC (now the CTA). At its historic core, Regime I regulates entry to and exit from the industry and has preferred to regulate broadly through some form of profit and/or 'rate of return' regulation. Regulation is often developed as a substitute for competition, which normal markets would otherwise supply. But other purposes are frequently deemed to be more important, including in some sectors the prevention of excessive competition.

These well-known regulators have also been charged with managing industrial sectors that have been cast variously as nation-building and nation-binding industries. Accordingly, the regulators have been characterized as bodies that function like 'governments in miniature,' by which it is meant that they have been granted an array of policing, promoting, and planning functions (Schultz and Alexandroff 1985). These include direct policy roles and subsidy functions that go beyond the narrower notions of regulation. In Canadian history, these regulators have also had rationales and mandates intended to protect Canada from undue American influences, cultural and economic, and to promote Canadian-owned and based development (Tupper and Doern 1988).

Chapters 2, 3, and 4 bring out these early features of Regime I regulators but, in their coverage of more than two decades of development, the authors also clearly demonstrate the nature of their transformation. One way of initially capturing this change is to observe how each sector has undergone a process of 'convergence' in different guises. Convergence is a term used in the broadcasting and telecommunications sector to refer to the manner in which digital technologies are allowing broadcasters and telephone companies to move into each other's business. The dual pillars are converging. The language of 'pillars' is used in the financial services sector as well. The separate pillars of banking, insurance, securities, and trusts are becoming, to a much greater extent, one merged sector. In energy, the analytical equivalents are the fuels or energy sources – coal, oil, gas, and electricity – and the evidence of conversion lies in the increasing degree to which technology allows considerable and continuous 'interfuel' substitution. Finally, in transportation, the evolution of the transport regulators shows that the transport pillars were once cast as modes of transport: rail, road, air, and shipping. For years policy centred on a form of managed intermodal competition, rather than competition among firms, regardless of mode. But again technology and deregulation philosophies have seen the collapse of such distinctions, at least when defining what kind of competition is being sought.

What this means is that the heretofore vertical sectors have become much less vertical and resemble instead an odd array of tilting or leaning regulatory 'towers of Pisa.' In an era of liberal economics it also means that national policy makers increasingly see these 'sectors' as simply factors of production, each a crucial input into the economic functioning of every other sector of the economy. This means not only that the sectors are visualized more as 'means' rather than ends in themselves, but interest-group politics around each sectoral regulator are also affected. For example, one of the key changes in all three realms is the emergence of much stronger 'industrial user' group lobbies.

But these regulators remain sectoral to some extent, for three reasons. First, some aspects of monopoly still exist. Second, there are fears about exactly how the politics and economics will work out in the transition phases of convergence. These fears are usually expressed via various conceptions of what 'competition' ought to be: free and comprehensive, workable, fair, and socially responsible (e.g., for vulnerable or low-income users of a utility). Third, the regulatory body at the centre of each sector fights for its own survival while adapting or being forced to adapt. The adaptive responses include moving from profit and 'rate of return' regulation to more flexible incentive-based and 'price-cap' regulation; the open advocacy of competition within the regulatory mandate through practising regulatory forbearance; and the acquisition of other tasks even while budgets and staff are shrinking. Each of the three regulators examined in Part I of the book have different histories and are examined in different ways, but each author captures some of the politics of institutional transformation that Regime I is undergoing.

Both Hill's analysis of the transport sector leading to the recently renamed Canadian Transportation Agency and Doern's account of the National Energy Board reveal the transformation of the regulators in the face of new competitive paradigms and pressures. Structurally, both agencies have seen their range of powers and functions reduced and their membership and staffs greatly reduced. Both have also adapted themselves to take on and perform newer or resultant functions in that they have assumed negotiated approaches to problem solving and, especially in the case of the NEB, new environmental functions have been absorbed to become part of the mandate.

The analysis by Schultz of the CRTC focuses on the struggle over policy-making powers between the CRTC and the government, and demonstrates a somewhat paradoxical outcome. While the broadcasting-telecommunications sector has arguably witnessed the most dynamic set of changes and competitive turbulence among the three sectoral regulators, the CRTC is 'still standing' in much the same structural and outward form as before. It retains a considerable range of powers and has largely successfully defended itself to date against many efforts by successive governments to claw back policy control from it.

Regime II: Framework Regulators and the Extent of Horizontal Reach

Regime II captures a cluster of regulators whose inner logic is centred on the fact that the broad intent of rule making is to fashion horizontal or framework-oriented regulations. In short, these rules are not intended to discriminate among sectors of the economy or society but rather, in principle, to treat all sectors equally. In other words, the intention is not to create a whole host of sectorally specific rules precisely because, if such was the result, the economy would be pock-marked with regulation-induced internal barriers. The focus here is on broad intent because a key question is the extent of horizontal reach that is actually achieved and how the nature of the reach has changed in the last two decades.

Arguably, there are two traditional clusters of Regime II regulators. One cluster consists of 'health and safety' regulators and, if defined broadly, would encompass drug, food, product safety, occupational health, and environmental regulators (Dewees 1983). The regulators within Regime II are also often spoken of as 'science-based' regulators, whose rules deal with issues of risk. Broadly speaking, these have tended to be regulated by departments headed directly by ministers. Another cluster incorporates 'marketplace framework' regulators and includes laws and rules governing consumer matters, competition, company law, bankruptcy, and intellectual property (patents, trademarks, and copyright). Most of these framework regulators have been based in one federal department, the Department of Consumer and Corporate Affairs (until 1993) and now Industry Canada. A third cluster that we deliberately add in this book is civic regulation, which, in a different way, establishes rules about morality, welfare, and the social economy.

Regime II regulators, largely ignored twenty years ago, are, in the latter part of the 1990s, in the ascendancy. This book deals with only a small sample of Regime II activity, but reference to both environmental regulation and the regulation of competition is illustrative of important features of Regime II evolution. Environmental regulation was initially framework oriented, largely because its regulatory intent focused on elements such as water and air. An initial burst of successful regulatory activity (Doern and Conway 1994; Harrison 1996) was followed by decline from the mid-1970s to the mid-1980s. A second burst of activity centred on general legislation, such as the Canadian Environmental Protection Act (CEPA) and legislation on environmental assessment.

Competition law and regulation have also been strengthened, but the pattern here is different. Competition law prior to 1986 was notoriously weak, in part because it was centred on criminal law provisions. The 1986 Competition Act sought to make competition regulation not only more clearly framework oriented but also to recast offences as civil matters (Khemani and Stanbury 1991; Doern 1995).

Compared to the situation twenty years ago, both environment and competition regulation can be considered to be much more framework oriented, but hardly perfectly so. Their reach has been extended but not necessarily their grasp. In the case of environmental policy, as the Harrison chapter demonstrates, the number of sectors actually covered remains small and enforcement is still weak or problematical. In the case of competition regulation, as the Janisch chapter indicates, there are still several exemptions from competition law. Moreover, tensions regarding the jurisdiction of competition regulators on the one hand, and Regime I regulators on the other, over just what competition means or ought to mean and who should decide, are also evident.

A general effort to move from command-and-control regulation to more flexible incentive-based forms of regulation, including guidelines, codes, and standards is also discernible within Regime II. There are many reasons for this attempt to change the approach to regulation (e.g., business pressure, budget cutbacks) but there is also a sense in which such change must be an inherent part of the logic of Regime II. If the approach is too command-and-control oriented, it is likely to become more and more sectoral and pock-marked. If it is kept flexible, the odds are that, while its framework nature will be maximized, concerns will be raised about the accountability and enforcement of such mechanisms (Cohen and Webb 1997).

The transformation of Regime II has varied roots. Certainly, citizens and voters still demand regulation in this area. Waters and Stanbury capture some of this in their analysis of 'regulatory shift,' as new health, safety, and fairness values and pressures impinge on various regulators in the telecommunications and transportation fields, as well as in other realms. Globalization and the need for competitive industries has also caused governments and business to turn their attention to the broader features of the whole set of marketplace framework laws (Doern 1995). The health and safety regulators have been less often viewed as comprising a subset of Regime II regulators, but they may become so as citizens and voters not only become more aware of different concepts of risk but also begin to question the adequacy and objectivity of the science that underpins this kind of framework regulation (Dewees 1983).

The changing role of consumer interests has also been influential. Consumer interests are in a general sense horizontal and cross-economy, but their organized expression through a national association is clearly problematical and now changing. Schultz's analysis of the Consumers' Association of Canada (CAC) shows tensions both in the relations between the CAC and telecom regulators and within the association itself. In the former relationship, the CAC had to secure legitimacy regarding expertise and was dependent on state funding for its interventions. In its early days the CAC challenged the entrenched monopoly regulated firms but, as competitive forces emerged, it often found itself defending the status quo as consumer interests shifted. Within the CAC there were conflicts over priorities engendered by the skewed nature of the funding received and by the rapidly changing nature of consumer issues that found voice in other ways or were seeking different outlets of expression, such as industrial user groups and free trade policies.

As argued above, in our view Regime II regulatory institutions must include the realm identified as civic regulation. Prince's analysis in Chapter 9 takes stock of this crucial realm, suggesting a complex layering of rules not only in the welfare and workfare state, but also in justice and corrections, the Charter of Rights, and rules on morality. This is a growth area of regulation and many such rules are often advocated by the same interests which, on the economic front, have advocated a non-interventionist state.

Finally, we conclude this section of the book with a broad look in Chapter 10 at accountability systems, or what Prince labels 'Aristotle's benchmarks.' Prince discusses not only the most basic array of accountability provisions which have long been a part of regulatory democracy in Canadian parliamentary government, but also key newer features, such as the Charter of Rights. The very notion of accountability has become densely pluralistic and extends well beyond executive-bureaucratic arrangements to involve the courts much more than twenty years ago.

Regime III: Managing Regulation within Government, the State as Regulator of Itself?

Regime III is a set of regulators and regulatory processes that manage regulation in the state, especially within the executive-bureaucratic arena, but extending beyond it as well, ultimately to Parliament and the courts. It is a regime because, regardless of what is happening in Regimes I and II, the government must somehow manage the totality of its own regulatory decisions in terms of both purposes and processes. This is not a difficult concept to understand when one thinks of the other two main instruments of policy making that the government seeks to manage. Taxation and spending both have regular rhythms and cycles of decision making that are well known, the former centred on the annual Budget Speech process and the latter on the annual budget process leading to the passage of the Estimates (Doern and Phidd 1992).

Regulation as a policy instrument and activity has always presented more problems for the central agencies of the government, largely because of two key features of regulation (however defined). The first is that the costs of regulation do not tend to show up in the budget of the state: they appear in the private budgets of citizens, interests, and corporations. The state has some costs to bear but these are small compared to those that affect the private sector. The second reason is that regulations are not easily aggregated (at the centre of the political executive and also at the centre of regulatory departments) and converted into the common denominator of dollars.

These problems have not, however, stopped governments, especially in the last two decades, from trying to devise ways in which they could manage the regulatory function within the state (Stanbury 1992). The problem has always been determining what criteria and values should be used to structure such a management effort, how it might be organized as a series of decision processes, and whose behaviour (e.g., ministers, senior officials, front-line officials) would have to change. We have already, in the opening paragraphs of this chapter, mentioned a few initiatives (e.g., the early requirements for very limited vetting by the Department of Justice and for a truncated form of cost-benefit analysis in the late 1970s). Subsequent changes reveal a search for the elusive holy grail of regulatory virtue. Indeed, the picture seems to be one in which there are simply a series of 'add-ons' to criteria and processes, with no one knowing whether those that already exist are being applied and work, or how new criteria will alter the mix.

Thus, regulatory management has been informed since 1982 by desires to 'Charter proof' the regulatory state, which means ensuring that regulations do not violate or deny fundamental rights and freedoms. Cost-benefit processes have evolved to the full RIAS process, but the analytical terrain has also been joined in the 1990s by concerns for competitiveness criteria, the former pushed by central agencies such as the Treasury Board and the latter by economic departments such as Industry Canada. Central pressures for and initiatives on 'reinventing' government, special operating agencies, and the development of service delivery standards have also emerged (Doern 1994). So too have program review and efforts to decentralize government in the interests of a renewed federalism (Swimmer 1996).

The point about these initiatives is that some were intended to be primarily about regulation in a Regime III sense, while others have partially unintended effects on the coherence and efficacy of regulatory management. They reflect the fact that the state is a pluralist 'they' and not an integrated 'it' and is manoeuvring through a changing policy/political agenda in a complex environment. In regulatory matters these features are exacerbated by the fact that regulations are less quantifiable than spending and taxation and less capable of being aggregated.

The three chapters in Part III of the book capture some of the range of issues that have, in a very real sense, 'loaded up' Regime III.

Margaret Hill's analysis in Chapter 11 shows how the intent and focus of the management of regulation has shifted over the last two decades from concerns about accountability 'up' to ministers to 'in and down' accountability, with an emphasis on getting regulatory departments to improve their analysis and to practice better stakeholder consultation. The latest 'out and across' phase has attempted to manage regulation more strategically, taking account of economic competitiveness and other macroglobal trade demands and needs. It also involves a form of institutional 'rediscovery' of the simple fact that regulation must somehow be integrated with broader policy debates, where it is inevitably joined to other taxation and expenditure choices and trade-offs.

Fazil Milar's examination of the federal record in many of these aspects reveals federal practice to be seriously flawed. For example, the key provisions of the RIAS process are often not carried out. In his discussion of risk assessment and health and safety regulation, Milar concludes that the government simply has no way of strategically assessing what risks as a whole warrant regulatory intervention and what forms of intervention, if any, should be used.

Chapter 13 provides a more particular example of systemwide initiatives, where the state is in a very real sense trying to regulate itself. Colin Bennett's examination of the regulation of privacy shows not only the intricacies of defining what privacy means but also how officials are induced to obey the rules. Various officials throughout the apparatus of the state are 'the regulated' in privacy laws, but often we know little about what values and incentives they understand in this regard. After all, officials (often the same ones) are also asked simultaneously to obey other systemwide values and policies, such as freedom of information, rules about commercial privilege, and cabinet secrecy.

While the main pattern of change in Regime III is the growing complexity of competing rationales, the regime is not oblivious of the changes that have been traced in the other regimes examined above. In some cases, Regime III is trying to adjust to changes in Regime I, where deregulation is more endemic, and also to Regime II, where expansion is still underway. It is also having to take in and absorb international trade rules and their imperatives. But in other respects, Regime III simply continues on under its own steam, searching for the more perfect but highly elusive sense of the state's need to manage probably the most difficult of its three main policy instruments.

Regime IV: International and Cross-Jurisdictional Regulation

Regime IV can, in one sense, be seen as a virtual commonplace reflection of contemporary globalization and of the internationalization of most areas of public policy, including regulation (Doern, Pal, and Tomlin 1996). Regulators are increasingly constrained by, or must interact with, a potential array of international agencies (regulatory and otherwise) and other countries' national regulatory bodies, international coalitions of interest groups, and the existence of international rule-based dispute settlement processes or prescribed cross-boundary consultation processes (Taylor and Groom 1988; Trebilcock and Howse 1995). Regulation also quickly becomes cross-jurisdictional in other ways that defy national boundaries and arrangements within states. We see this below in the case of Canada's Agreement on Internal Trade (AIT), but it also occurs in particular sectoral ways, such as between Canadian and American energy or transport regulators.

However, the central feature of this regime is that traditionally, international regulation is for the most part not 'authoritative,' in the sense that there is no world government to supply compliance through direct enforcement. The international system has typically had to rely more on persuasion and diplomacy, in short, on softer instruments of governing. Thus, many policy fields are influenced by obligations but the array of mechanisms available for ensuring compliance in domestic regulation does not exist.

This does not mean that particular regulators have not had to face the realities of international bodies or other countries' regulators. For example, Canadian energy regulators in the oil, gas, and hydro-electric sectors have for decades had to deal with the codecision-making powers of the American set of national regulators before projects and sales could proceed or be expanded, or indeed contracted in emergency situations (Doern and Toner 1985). However, in the telecommunications sector, there was for a long period a mutual recognition of each other's national monopoly arrangements. This has obviously changed in the past decade and hence Regime IV for the telecommunications sector in North America and elsewhere more clearly involves a globalization-influenced process (Lee 1996; Drake 1994; Globerman et al. 1992; Schultz and Brawley 1996).

In the late 1990s Regime IV must in particular be tied to the Uruguay Round agreement of the GATT and to the establishment of a strengthened and broadened World Trade Organization (WTO). On a regional basis Regime IV is also tied to the rules and decision-making processes of the European Union and NAFTA. Not only are fundamental trade rules crossing borders and affecting practices in various 'domestic' regulatory realms, but newer 'crosswalk' institutions are being negotiated between heretofore separate international realms, such as competition, the environment, intellectual property, and investment (Trebilcock and Howse 1995; Wiener 1995). In the European Union and NAFTA contexts, the degrees of harmonization and integration vary both sectorally and horizontally and thus crosswalks take many forms.

Many of these realms involve processes and change whereby largely national fields of regulation, such as environment and competition, are seeking to become working international systems. For competition policy these changes range from limited progress toward the international harmonization of antitrust laws at the world level to quite extensive integration at the level of the European Union (Doern and Wilks 1996). For environmental regulation, internationalization has taken the form of many binational cross-border agreements and some regional institutional experiments, such as the NAFTA environmental commissions. At the global level there are fewer, but still very important, protocols on particular pollutants (Vogel 1995; Doern 1993).

When dealing with Regime IV it is vital in the institutional mapping process to know whether a particular international regime has 'rule-based' dispute-settlement processes at hand or whether it remains, at this stage, a looser set of arrangements with more subtle influences. Again, this is because there is no world government as such, but rather an array of relationships in general and functional areas of international relations centred more on diplomacy and persuasion than on the sanctions of a non-existent world governing authority. And yet, the greater incursions of Regime IV suggests that, overall, it is becoming more 'authoritative' than it was twenty years ago.

A final glimpse into the interplay among regimes can be seen by considering briefly a process of learning between Regime III and IV. As we have seen, Regime III refers to the process for managing regulation within the executive. While many vetting criteria have been used in these processes, in a sense they have always been seen as domestic criteria. To put it more specifically, regulatory managers typically had little to do with their own country's foreign affairs departments. And, because of the historical characteristics of Regime IV, foreign policy departments did not see themselves as being in the regulatory business. Now they do and now they must, especially since interests play one regime off against another, in that if they cannot succeed in obtaining favourable rules domestically, they will lobby internationally to try to win concessions.

Thus governments that are signatories to the Uruguay agreement and to other regional pacts must be capable of determining whether they are complying not only with particular provisions but with whole systems of law and regulation. The general and specific ways in which this is occurring are discussed in the three chapters in the final section of the book.

Doern's analysis of the Internal Trade Agreement in Chapter 14 shows some of the immediate cross-jurisdictional spillovers as a larger, international-trade-centred regulatory regime takes hold. In the first instance the AIT seeks to require ministers and officials to behave differently than they have in earlier decades, especially with regard to their instincts to regulate in a variety of ways and in a variety of sectors. In the case of internal trade, the behaviour to be restrained is mainly that of provincial governments and the goal is to promote free trade internally within the Canadian economic union. Doubts about the agreement centre on whether ministers and officials (especially in provincial governments) will in fact obey the AIT and whether appropriate sanctions can be brought to bear.

But in an even larger sense, the AIT absorbed and sought to transplant key concepts derived from international trade. These included aspects of harmonization and mutual recognition and the greater use of performance-based rather than procedurally based rules in health and safety regulation. Importantly, it also brought the realities of macromultipolicy field negotiations to the realm of federal-provincial relations, which broke up some traditional sectoral arenas of regulatory decision making (Doern and MacDonald 1999).

The Howse and Trebilcock chapter shows even more broadly the extent to which pressures for harmonization of rules are increasingly institutionalized, not only within the actual terms of trade agreements such a NAFTA, but also through co-operation among functional regulators across boundaries. The latter operate through processes for continuous review among governments and, increasingly, among international coalitions of interests groups. The chapter by Harris on banking and financial services also demonstrates the extent to which international forces and realities have always been a part of regulation in this sector. But it conveys even more the escalation of external regulatory influence as the underlying dynamics of global finance have revolutionized world commerce, producing both the collapse of the traditional four pillars of the industry and raising new combinations of problems in which prudential regulation becomes a concern and requires intensive international cooperation among regulatory authorities.

Conclusions

The scope and nature of Canada's regulatory institutions have changed greatly in the past two decades. Set in the context of trends that show deregulation in some sectors but greatly expanded regulation in other realms, this introductory chapter has argued the need for a much broader conception of regulation and regulatory institutions than has been customary. It has also sought to provide a broadened basis for understanding the causes of regulatory change.

Our four-regime framework has been advanced not only to indicate the continuing importance of each regime – sectoral, framework, cabinet-executive, and international – but also to indicate some of the ways in which the four regimes are converging and colliding. Portraying regulatory institutions, politics, and development as an interplay among these regimes is obviously not the only way to examine regulatory phenomena, but we believe it has basic analytical value in helping to understand Canada's regulatory world as a new century emerges.

Between the macroworld of regulation as a whole and the microworld of the individual regulatory body, both students of regulation and regulatory practitioners need a more complete middle-level mapping of the Canadian regulatory terrain. Regimes as used above are not exact categorizations, but they exhibit sufficient internal characteristics to be useful in locating regulation of different kinds. They also raise questions about why change is occurring and why Canadians view regulation in many different ways, in a democracy that is arguably more open and undoubtedly more complex than in the past.

REFERENCES

Armstrong, Christopher, and H.V. Nelles. 1986. *Monopoly's Moment: The Organization and Regulation of Canadian Utilities, 1830–1930.* Philadelphia: Temple University Press.
Ayres, Ian, and John Braithwaite. 1992. *Responsive Regulation: Transcending the Deregulation Debate.* Oxford: Oxford University Press.
Brander, James A. 1990. *Government Policy towards Business.* 2nd ed. Toronto: Butterworths.
Brown-John, C. Lloyd. 1981. *Canadian Regulatory Agencies.* Toronto: Butterworths.
Cohen, D., and K. Webb. 1998. *The Role of Voluntary Codes.* Ottawa: Government of Canada.
Coleman, William C. 1996. *Financial Services, Globalization and Domestic Policy Change.* London: Macmillan.
Crandall, R.W., and L. Waverman. 1995. *Talk Is Cheap: The Promise of Regulatory Reform in North American Telecommunications.* Washington: Brookings Institution.
Cutler, A.C., and M.W. Zacher, eds. 1992. *Canadian Foreign Policy and International Economic Regimes.* Vancouver: UBC Press.

Dewees, Donald, ed. 1983. *The Regulation of Quality*, ch. 1. Toronto: Butterworths.

Doern, G. Bruce, ed. 1978. *The Regulatory Process in Canada*. Toronto: Macmillan of Canada.

Doern, G. Bruce. 1993. *Green Diplomacy*. Toronto: C.D. Howe Institute.

– 1994. *The Road to Better Public Services: Progress and Constraints in Five Federal Agencies*. Montreal: Institute for Research on Public Policy.

– 1995. *Fairer Play: Canadian Competition Policy Institutions in a Global Market*. Toronto: C.D. Howe Institute.

– 1998. The Interplay Among Regimes: Mapping Regulatory Institutions in Britain and North America. In G. Bruce Doern and Stephen Wilks, eds., *Changing Regulatory Institutions in Britain and North America*, ch. 2. Toronto: University of Toronto Press.

Doern, G. Bruce, and Tom Conway. 1994. *The Greening of Canada: Federal Institutions and Decisions*. Toronto: University of Toronto Press.

Doern, G. Bruce, and Mark MacDonald. 1999. *Free Trade Federalism: Negotiating the Canadian Agreement on Internal Trade*. Toronto: University of Toronto Press.

Doern, G. Bruce, Les Pal, and Brian Tomlin, eds. 1996. *Border Crossings: The Internationalization of Canadian Public Policy*. Toronto: Oxford University Press.

Doern, G. Bruce, and Richard Phidd. 1992. *Canadian Public Policy: Ideas, Structure, Process*. Toronto: Nelson Canada.

Doern, G. Bruce, and Heather Sheehy. 1997. The Federal Biotechnology Regulatory System: A Commentary on an Institutional Work in Progress. Paper presented at the Conference on Biotechnology, the Consumer and the Canadian Marketplace, Ottawa, 24–25 September 1997.

Doern, G. Bruce, and Brian Tomlin. 1991. *Faith and Fear: The Free Trade Story*. Toronto: Stoddart.

Doern, G. Bruce, and Glen Toner. 1985. *The Politics of Energy*. Toronto: Methuen.

Doern, G. Bruce, and Stephen Wilks, eds. 1996. *National Competition Policy Institutions in a Global Market*. Oxford: Clarendon.

– 1998. *Changing Regulatory Institutions in Britain and North America*. Toronto: University of Toronto Press.

Drake, W.J. 1994. Asymmetric Deregulation and the Transformation of the International Telecommunications Regime. In E. Noam and G. Pogorel, eds., *Asymmetric Deregulation: The Dynamics of Telecommunications Policy in Europe and the United States*. Norwood, N.J.: Ablex Publishing.

Economic Council of Canada. 1979. *Responsible Regulation*. Ottawa: Economic Council of Canada.

– 1981. *Reforming Regulation*. Ottawa: Economic Council of Canada.

Eisner, M.A. 1993. *Regulatory Politics in Transition*. Baltimore: Johns Hopkins University Press.

Francis, John. 1993. *The Politics of Regulation: A Comparative Perspective*. Cambridge, Mass.: Blackwell.

Globerman, S., H. Janisch, R.J. Schultz, and W.T. Stanbury. 1992. Canada and the Movement Towards Liberalization of the International Telecommunications Regime. In A.C. Cutler and M.W. Zacher, eds., *Canadian Foreign Policy and International Economic Regimes*. Vancouver: UBC Press.

Grabosky, Peter N. 1995. Using Non-governmental Resources to Foster Compliance. *Governance* 8, no. 4: 527–50.

Harris, R.A., and S.M. Milkis. 1989. *The Politics of Regulatory Change*, ch. 3. New York: Oxford University Press.

Harris, Stephen. 1995. *The Political Economy of the Liberalization of Entry and Ownership in the Canadian Investment Dealer Industry*. Unpublished PhD thesis, Department of Political Science, Carleton University.

Harrison, Kathryn. 1996. *Passing the Buck: Federalism and Canadian Environmental Policy*. Vancouver: UBC Press.

Harrison, Kathryn, and George Hoberg. 1994. *Risk, Science and Politics*. Montreal: McGill-Queen's University Press.

Hill, Margaret. 1994. The Choice of Mode For Regulation: A Case Study of the Canadian Pesticide Registration Review 1988–1992, ch. 3. Unpublished PhD thesis, Department of Political Science, Carleton University.

Hoberg, George. 1993. *Pluralism By Design: Environmental Policy and The American Regulatory State*. New York: Praeger.

Hood, Christopher. 1986. *Administrative Analysis*. London: Harvester Wheatsheaf.

Jacobs, Scott. 1992. *Regulatory Management and Reform: Current Concerns in OECD Countries*. Paris: OECD.

Khemani, R.S., and W.T. Stanbury, eds. 1991. *Canadian Competition Policy Law and Policy at the Centenary*. Halifax: Institute For Research on Public Policy.

Krasner, David, ed. 1983. *International Regimes*. Ithaca, N.Y.: Cornell University Press.

Law Reform Commission. 1986. *Policy Implementation, Compliance and Administrative Law*. Ottawa: Law Reform Commission of Canada.

Lee, Kelly. 1996. *Global Telecommunications Regulation: A Political Economy Perspective*. London: Pinter.

Meier, K.J. 1985. *Regulation: Politics, Bureaucracy, Economics*. New York: St Martins.

Mihlar, Fazil. 1996. *Regulatory Overkill: The Cost of Regulation in Canada*. Vancouver: Fraser Institute.

Ogus, Anthony I. 1994. *Regulation: Legal Form and Economic Theory*. Oxford: Clarendon.

Pal, Leslie. 1997. *Beyond Policy Analysis*. Toronto: Nelson.

Pross, Paul. 1992. *Group Politics and Public Policy*. 2nd ed. Toronto: Oxford University Press.

Schultz, Richard J., and Alan Alexandroff. 1985. *Economic Regulation and the Federal System*. Toronto: University of Toronto Press.

Schultz, Richard J., and R. Brawley. 1996. The Internationalization of Telecommunications Policy. In G. Bruce Doern, Leslie Pal, and Brian Tomlin, eds., *Crossing Borders: The Internationalization of Canadian Public Policy*, ch. 5. Toronto: Oxford University Press.

Sparrow, Malcolm K. 1994. *Imposing Duties: Government's Changing Approach to Compliance*. London: Praeger.

Stanbury, William T., ed. 1980. *Government Regulation: Scope, Growth, Process*. Montreal: Institute for Research on Public Policy.

–   1992. *Reforming the Federal Regulatory Process in Canada, 1971–1992*. Published as Appendix to House of Commons Standing Committee on Finance, Subcommittee on Regulations and Competitiveness, ch. 5. Issue No. 23. Ottawa: Supply and Services Canada.

Strick, John. 1990. *The Economics of Government Regulation: Theory and Canadian Practice*. Toronto: Thomson.

Swimmer, Gene, ed. 1996. *How Ottawa Spends, 1996–97: Life under the Knife*. Ottawa: Carleton University Press.

Taylor, Paul, and A.J.R. Groom, eds. 1988. *International Institutions at Work*. London: Pinter.

Trebilcock, Michael J., and Robert Howse. 1995. *The Regulation of International Trade*. London: Routledge.

Tupper, Allan, and G. Bruce Doern, eds. 1988. *Privatization, Public Policy and Public Corporations in Canada*. Montreal: McGill-Queen's University Press.

Vogel, David. 1995. *Trading Up: Consumer and Environmental Regulation in a Global Economy*. Cambridge: Harvard University Press.

Wiener, Jarrod. 1995. *Making Rules in the Uruguay Round of the GATT: A Study of International Leadership*. Aldershot: Dartmouth.

Zacher, Mark W. (with Brent A. Sutton). 1996. *Governing Global Networks: International Regimes for Transportation and Communications*. New York: Cambridge University Press.

PART I
MAJOR FEDERAL SECTORAL REGULATORY BODIES

2

Still Standing: The CRTC, 1976–1996

RICHARD J. SCHULTZ

Twenty years ago, the Canadian regulatory agencies in the energy, transportation, and communications sectors dominated their respective fields, not only through their comprehensive regulatory decision-making powers, but equally in their capacity as the primary public policy advisers, indeed developers, in those sectors. The combination of their wide-ranging functions, their considerable autonomy within the federal government and, not insignificantly, the relative weakness of any bureaucratic rivals at the time meant they truly merited the designation 'governments in miniature' (Schultz and Doern 1998). Today, only the Canadian Radio-television and Telecommunications Commission (CRTC) retains its traditional status and power. Its counterparts, the National Energy Board and the Canadian Transport Commission, are more 'miniatures' than governments; they have become mere shells of their former selves as the result of dramatic reductions over the past ten years in roles, powers, and personnel.

The paradox of the diminished status for the energy and transportation regulators is that the CRTC has maintained its status despite the fact that, arguably, it has encountered far more organizational turbulence as a result of technological, economic, and political forces than were experienced by its sister agencies. Technological forces have necessitated a re-examination of the rationales for regulation, whether in the broadcasting or the telecommunications sectors. The economic consequences flowing from the technological potentials have been enormous, as different actors sought to have the regulatory policies entrenched or radically altered, as the case may be, to reflect their stakes in the outcomes. The result has been unending, intense, political conflicts involving a vast array of domestic and international societal and state interests.

In the telecommunications sector, for example, the past two decades have seen the following embroiled in continuous, overlapping battles: incumbent telephone companies; new or would-be entrants; residential and corporate consumers; unions; federal and provincial governments, including competing departmental bodies; and, finally, foreign governments with their own sets of state and societal interests (Buchan et al. 1982; Stanbury 1986; Globerman et al. 1992; Surtees 1994; Janisch and Romaniuk 1995; Schultz and Brawley 1996). The situation in the broadcasting sector has been similar, as traditional and novel broadcast media; their industrial and artistic communities; consumers; different levels of governments; and international actors, especially those based in the United States, sought to protect or advance their interests (Collins 1990; Raboy 1990, 1995a, 1995b; Ellis 1992; Meisel 1989). Moreover, there is no sign that the conflicts will diminish as a result of the convergence of the telecommunications and broadcasting sectors, particularly since that convergence is linked to the evolving 'information highway' (Information Highway Advisory Council 1995; Globerman et al. 1996).

In the energy and transportation sectors, the replacement of the traditional regulatory regime, that is, 'the system of ideas, institutions and policies' (Harris and Milkis 1989, 23), has been almost complete, as deregulatory ideas and policies have largely swept away the agencies in their wake. In the communications sector, on the other hand, the changes have been more limited. In particular, while the regime ideas and policies have been, or are in the process of being, transformed, the governing institutions still remain, largely unaltered. More specifically, the CRTC has been able, notwithstanding the policy turmoil and the emergence of powerful challengers, in both markets and governments, to resist and rebuff demands for any major institutional change that would challenge its role and powers as the lead actor in the communications regulatory regime. The staying power of the CRTC is all the more remarkable given the priority that other governmental actors, political and bureaucratic, have placed on institutional change.

The CRTC, established in 1968 as the Canadian Radio-Television Commission, was the most significant institutional development in the broadcasting regulatory regime since the creation of the CBC in the 1932–6 period. The new agency was necessary, in part, to resolve the internecine conflicts between the Board of Broadcast Governors, the first institutionally separate regulator for Canadian broadcasting, and the Canadian Broadcasting Corporation (Stewart and Hull 1994; Peers 1979). An equally compelling rationale for the new agency was to bring under public control a new technology, cable distribution of broadcasting signals, which threatened the most fundamental ideas and policies of the traditional broadcasting regulatory regime through its ability to deliver American television signals directly to Canadian viewers (Bartley 1990).

The result was the broadcasting 'government in miniature,' the CRTC. It was the first independent regulator with decision-making capacity in the broadcasting sector, responsible for licensing broadcasting undertakings, now defined to include cable systems, and developing, through regulations and policy statements not subject to political control, the appropriate public policies to give effect to the objectives of the Broadcasting Act. That legislation gave the CRTC a virtually open-ended mandate, as reflected in the statement that the Canadian broadcasting system should 'safeguard, enrich and strengthen the cultural, political, social and economic fabric of Canada.' That the CRTC was to be much more than a regulatory policeman was reflected in its dual roles of 'regulation and supervision of the Canadian broadcasting system.' Finally, unlike its sister agencies, the CTC and the NEB, whose decisions were subject to more positive and extensive political controls, CRTC decisions could only be referred back to the agency by cabinet for reconsideration or ultimately set aside. They could not be altered by cabinet (Schultz 1977). The only major change in the CRTC's mandate came in 1976, when responsibility for telecommunications was transferred to it from the CTC. Although the statutory basis for telecommunications regulation remained the Railway Act of 1905, the transfer included more direct cabinet control over its telecommunications regulatory decisions than the CRTC was used to, as the cabinet could vary, in whole or in part, such decisions on its own initiative or on appeal.

For the past twenty years, successive ministers of communications have placed a priority on changing the distribution of power within the federal government so as to reduce the CRTC to more of a policy-implementation role, through its regulatory responsibilities, and concomitantly enhance their own role, and that of their department, as the primary policy makers. In part, this reflected a series of conflicts over both individual regulatory decisions and underlying public policies which, in the absence of statutory change, continued to be under the control of the CRTC (Hall 1990). As a result, ministers insisted that elected political authorities, not appointed regulators, were to control the selection of regulatory ideas and the development of policies for their attainment. The following statement from the minister of communications in 1985 (Masse 1985a) is typical of ministerial ambitions since 1976 and represents the importance and the rationale that such actors have placed on fundamentally altering the dominant institutional relationship in which the CRTC was the lead governmental actor while ministers and their officials played mere supporting roles: 'The purpose of the provisions concerning the government's power of direction is to establish clearly and unequivocally that only the government, which is accountable to parliament for its actions, is empowered to develop major telecommunications policies. This responsibility should not be borne by the CRTC since it is a quasi-judicial organization that does not have to answer to the public for its actions.'

Although considerable effort was expended over the past twenty years to redesign the institutional system, little fundamental institutional change has occurred. Attempts to claw back policy powers from the CRTC, while numerous, have been largely unsuccessful. Compared to the situation in 1976, especially in comparison with the decline of its sister regulatory agencies, the CRTC still dominates the communications regulatory regime. Although many institutional aspects of the CRTC as a regulatory body could be explored, such as its composition over the years, especially its leadership; its regulatory processes and compliance systems; and its relationships with regulated interests, given the centrality of the institutional conflicts to its history and performance, this chapter examines how the CRTC has been able to maintain its primacy vis-à-vis other governmental actors, political and bureaucratic.[1]

The chapter consists of three sections, all of which focus on the central institutional issue facing the CRTC over the past twenty years: protecting its roles and responsibilities as an independent regulatory agency. In the first section, we review two of the major CRTC-governmental conflicts in the broadcasting sector that illustrate the thesis that the CRTC successfully defended itself. The second section will focus on the telecommunications sector. Finally, in the third section we analyse the evolution of the development of new legislation for both the broadcasting and telecommunications sectors, legislation that left the CRTC's status as primary actor largely intact.[2]

The CRTC and the Broadcasting Policy Issues

In 1976, near the close of the first decade of its existence, the CRTC was aggressively assertive of its role as the primary actor in the institutional complex responsible for the Canadian broadcasting sector. Conflicts with departmental and political officials over policy initiatives largely date from this year, particularly in the cable sector. Two specific conflicts are representative of the policy issues that confronted the broadcasting sector over the past twenty years and demonstrate how the CRTC exercised and protected its territory from challengers.

The first conflict, which involved specifically the introduction of pay television and, more generally, the role of the cable industry in the broadcasting system, would take almost a decade to resolve. This seemingly interminable battle in which the regulatory agency refused to relinquish any authority to successive ministers of communications was largely responsible for the demands from departmental officials and ministers for a reassessment of the role of the CRTC and a reduction in its independence from political direction. Although the Department of Communications eventually won the particular battle with the CRTC on this set of issues, this victory required protracted effort and underscored the fact that, under the existing institutional arrangements, the CRTC had considerable autonomy to ignore governmental policy wishes. That the same set of issues would emerge in the first half of the 1990s in a dispute over the introduction of direct-to-home (DTH) satellite broadcasting distribution suggests the staying power of the CRTC as both independent actor and primary decision maker, notwithstanding the introduction of new instruments of constraint.

Conflict over Pay Television

In 1976 the CRTC still clearly interpreted its mandate to 'regulate and supervise' the Canadian broadcasting system in a manner reflecting the original intentions of the architects of the 1968 Broadcasting Act. Contrary to the Task Force on Broadcasting Policy, which maintained that regulation of the cable industry was an afterthought in the development of that legislation, the CRTC considered cable regulation to contain the threat posed to the policy objectives of the legislation was one of the main, if not the primary, purposes of its legislation (Bartley 1990). It had taken that responsibility seriously and, through its policies on simultaneous substitution and community programming, the CRTC's quota on the distribution of foreign signals (the 3+1 formula) and especially its attempt, in 1969, only one year into its mandate, to prohibit the use of microwave systems to extend cable's reach, had sought to ensure that cable was a decidedly subordinate and nonthreatening component of broadcasting as a 'single system.'

During the first half of the 1970s the CRTC rejected repeated calls from the cable industry to introduce pay television services, on the grounds that such services would be deleterious to the health of the Canadian broadcasting system (Woodrow and Woodside 1982; Henderson 1989; Hall 1990). Specifically, in 1975, after an extensive public hearing, the CRTC ruled against licensing pay systems at that time, particularly because the off-air broadcasters, public and private, then the 'chosen instruments' for the attainment of the broadcasting policy objectives, were unprepared or incapable of becoming the primary actors in the development of pay services. If the broadcasters would not assume such a responsibility, the CRTC concluded that the Canadian broadcasting system was not ready for the challenges of pay television and it was opposed to having '... the system's resources and creative energies diverted into new endeavours' (CRTC 1975, 10).

Recognizing that the CRTC was not going to be particularly responsive to demands for pay services, advocates of pay television, primarily the cable industry, turned their sights on a new lobbying target, the Department of Communications, which had been established the year after the formation of the CRTC and was clearly in pursuit of a mission. Only six months after the CRTC's rejection of pay television, in a speech crafted by one of her senior officials and the chief lobbyist for the Canadian Cable Television Association, the new minister of communications, Jeanne Sauvé, announced in June 1976 that the department intended to play an active role in developing pay television (Hall 1990, 241). Furthermore, she declared her belief that 'the establishment of pay television on a large scale is inevitable.' To this end, she stated that the government would be issuing a policy statement on pay television and that she expected the CRTC to call for licence applications. In short, the minister was insisting that the department and not an independent agency would be responsible for the development of public policies. The agency's role, as far as the minister was concerned, was confined to implementing such policies.

The commission, however, proved to be far less accommodating than the minister expected. All that it was prepared to do was revisit the issue through a second public hearing, the result of which was an implicit statement that, contrary to the minister's statements, the CRTC, and not the minister of communications, would determine when the 'inevitable' would take place, and that was not going to be in the near future. Two years after the ministerial speech, the CRTC rejected all applications on the grounds that 'it would be premature and impossible to endorse the introduction of a national pay-television system at this time' (CRTC 1978, 54).

There appeared to be little that the government could do to force the commission to follow its preferred policy course. The commission's enabling statute did not yet permit the government or the minister to issue an order by means of a policy directive to the commission on this type of policy matter and the commission appeared to be unwilling to accede voluntarily to the government's wishes. Ironically, the Conservative government elected in 1979 had greater success in forcing the resignation of the chair of the CRTC, who had been only recently appointed by the previous Liberal government, than in getting the commission to accept the Communications Department's pay television policy. The policy stalemate was, in fact, only resolved as a result of a fortuitous set of circumstances, largely the result of the government-induced resignation of the chair and the appointment of an acting chair.

The acting chair, confronted with a new government ill-disposed toward the commission, a department that continued to press for the introduction of pay television, and perhaps thinking that a successful resolution to the dispute might make the government more receptive to appointing him chair of the commission for a full term, agreed to a face-saving initiative proposed by the minister of communications. A special committee consisting of four CRTC members and four provincial representatives was appointed over the objections of some of the full-time members of the CRTC (Murray 1983, 64) to investigate a complex set of issues relating to unlicensed access to satellite services and the extension of television service to northern and remote communities as well as pay television. Following the report of this committee and the return of the Liberals to power in 1980, the commission issued a call for applications for pay television licences. The first licences were issued in 1983. After seven years, the Department of Communications had prevailed, although it is worth noting that the commission decision, which embraced a 'competitive model' rather than monopoly provision of pay services, was probably not what either the department or the primary advocates for pay television, the cable industry, had in mind when the exercise began.

The DTH Conflict

The very public conflict between the CRTC and the federal cabinet over the licensing of direct-to-home satellite television services between 1994 and 1995 symbolizes the struggles over policy determination in the broadcasting sector and the extent of the deterioration in the relationship between the federal government and the regulatory agency determined to protect not only its independence but its preferred policy outcomes. Although it would appear in the end that, as in the case of pay television ten years earlier, the government successfully asserted its primacy as policy maker, reality is much more complicated. While the commission did have to endure a policy directive that challenged some of the specifics of its original licensing decision, most of the policy framework developed by the CRTC alone to govern the provision of DTH services remained in force.

The DTH conflict had its roots in the development of the second generation of high-powered satellites, combined with the development of digital video compression, which would enable consumers to bypass both the over-the-air broadcasters and, most significantly, the cable systems which, since the mid-1980s, had been transformed from 'public enemy number one' to the 'chosen instrument' for both the government and the CRTC for the implementation and protection of Canadian broadcasting policy. Viewers would be able to receive these overwhelmingly American signals directly and economically. The significance of the presumed threat posed by DTH services is reflected in the depictions of such services as 'death stars' or the 'ultimate deregulator' (Ellis 1992). If Canadian consumers were to access such services beyond the purview of the CRTC, DTH promised to challenge fundamentally both the traditional ideas or rationale for regulating broadcasting in Canada and the current beneficiaries of that regulation: broadcasters, cable companies and, not insignificantly, the CRTC itself. The *Globe and Mail* suggested in 1991 that the availability of DTH services meant that 'the Canadian television industry as we have come to know it, the whole symbiotic ecosystem of politicians, regulators, broadcasters, specialty services, cable carriers, producers and various hangers-on ha[d] two years to live' (Ellis 1992, 163).

The first stage of the conflict began when the CRTC held what it called 'a structural hearing' in March 1993 (CRTC 1993). Ostensibly the purpose was to review 'the evolving communications environment, and its impact on the existing and future structure of the Canadian broadcasting system' (p. 1). The commission's public response to the new technologies was somewhat ambivalent. On the one hand, the commission appeared to appreciate the transformative effect of the new technologies for traditional regulation, which may 'become increasingly ineffective in sheltering the Canadian broadcasting system from expanding competition from non-Canadian service providers'(p. 4). Consequently, the commission appeared to be highly realistic when it concluded that, in the new environment, 'any attempt to impose protectionist measures as a means to safeguard the Canadian broadcasting system would only prove counterproductive and impracticable' (p. 5). Notwithstanding these statements, the CRTC promised on the other hand to apply 'the appropriate enforcement tools' should non-Canadian service providers seek to enter 'the Canadian market without making contributions to the Canadian system as required of all broadcasting undertakings' (p. 8).

Subsequent actions by the CRTC belied the initial rhetoric of its 'new realism' and the claim that it favoured 'consumer-driven tv.' In 1993 the commission undertook to encourage the development of a 'strong Canadian DTH industry ... [to] form an effective part of the overall response by the Canadian broadcasting system to non-Canadian DBS [Direct-Broadcast-Satellite] services' (CRTC 1993, 45). More importantly, it proposed to exempt Canadian DTH service providers from licensing and detailed regulation (CRTC 1994a). The purpose of such an exemption was to encourage 'the growth of this alternative source of programming delivery [and] also help the Canadian broadcasting system as a whole to compete with foreign Direct-Broadcast-Satellite services.'

An exemption would be granted only if the applicant met the following criteria:

- the DTH satellite service distributes the programming services of radio, television, specialty, and pay television (including pay-per-view) undertakings that are licensed or authorized by the commission, and distributes those programming services locally, regionally, or nationally to subscribers on a DTH basis, with or without fee, using Canadian satellite facilities;
- programming services provided by the DTH satellite service may also be distributed indirectly to subscribers through cable television, radiocommunication, or satellite master antenna television (SMATV) undertakings;
- the DTH distributor does not originate any programming itself;
- only foreign programming services formally authorized by the CRTC are distributed;
- there are more channels devoted to distributing Canadian programming services than foreign services; and
- all technical requirements of the Department of Communications have been met.

In August 1994 the CRTC announced (CRTC 1994b) that only one applicant, subsequently known as ExpressVu, met the conditions and would therefore be the only one licensed under the exemption power. The one major potential competitor to ExpressVu, Power DirectTv, jointly owned by Power Corp of Montreal and Hughes DirecTv, which is controlled by General Motors, was not given an exemption because it planned to use American and Canadian satellites and consequently did not meet the requirement for exclusive use of Canadian satellite facilities for all programming.

The political uproar that greeted the CRTC licensing decision was unlike anything that had been previously experienced in Canadian communications regulation. Critics (Corcoran 1994; *Globe and Mail* 1995a) charged that the CRTC, through its criteria of exclusive use of Canadian satellite facilities, was deliberately seeking to limit competition between DTH providers and, more importantly, favouring a specific firm over others. The CRTC (*Globe and Mail* 1995c) defended its decision on the grounds that it was not granting an exclusive licence to ExpressVu, but only exempting it from the licensing system because it met the all-Canadian criterion. Other applicants, according to this argument, could eventually be licensed but they would have to go through the more rigorous and time-consuming public licensing process. CRTC critics, including the federal cabinet, were not placated by these arguments. In particular, the government announced a public review of DTH policies and established a three-man panel to undertake such a review. It is important to note that, although the government initially stated that the CRTC exemption order 'reflects existing policy', a senior official subsequently maintained that the CRTC appeared to have underestimated the impact that DTH services would have on the Canadian broadcasting system.

Following the review, the committee (Policy Review Panel 1995) criticized the CRTC for its use of the exemption power and the resulting noncompetitive situation. It recommended that competition be permitted and, to this end, that the cabinet issue a directive to the CRTC ordering it to license all qualified DTH applicants. Equally important was the recommendation that all services should be subject to the same Canadian content conditions required of other licensed broadcasting entities. The panel also recommended that the CRTC requirement for exclusive use of Canadian satellite facilities be eliminated.

The government decision to issue a directive to the CRTC to implement the major recommendations of the review panel caused an unprecedented public dispute between the chair of the CRTC and the government. According to some reports (*Financial Post* 1995), fear of such a dispute apparently led departmental officials to make a failed attempt to persuade the CRTC to implement the government's policies without recourse to a formal policy directive. The CRTC, however, was not prepared to be so accommodating. The chair, Keith Spicer, in testimony that apparently reflected the views of all members of the commission (*Globe and Mail* 1995b) before both the House and Senate Committees reviewing the directive complained that it was 'retroactive regulation' and as such 'intrinsically unfair and destabilizing.' Furthermore, as the government's action, in the CRTC's opinion, was 'overstepping its legitimate authority,' the CRTC threatened to challenge the directive in court. Spicer contended that the proposed directive was an abuse of the power: The government's power of direction was never meant to usurp the commission's exclusive role in implementing broadcasting policy for Canada. It was plainly and unmistakably meant only as an instrument to guide broadcasting policy in a general orientation.' The result, he argued, was that the 'Commission's independence and integrity are at stake.'

Neither the government nor the parliamentary committees that reviewed the directive were persuaded by the CRTC's arguments and objections. In the end, the government issued a directive to the CRTC ordering it to license DTH on a competitive basis. The only other major change ordered to the original CRTC decision, which the CRTC could not take issue with, was the requirement that licensed DTH systems would have to make a financial contribution, based on a percentage of gross annual revenues, to production of Canadian programming.

The CRTC had indicated in its earlier structural hearing that it intended to impose such a requirement, although it had not included it in its original criteria for exempting licensees.

In retrospect, while it would be erroneous to say that this particular dispute was ultimately 'much ado about nothing,' the highly public nature of the dispute led most observers to ignore the core of this particular instance of regulatory policy making. The fact is that the CRTC, while unsuccessful in favouring its preferred licensee, was able to establish the most important dimensions of the public policy to govern the provision of DTH services. In all the debates, it is important to note that there was little controversy about the CRTC requirements then applicable to cable companies being extended to DTH companies in order to promote Canadian content and, just as importantly, to reduce competition from American programming. Such requirements, which could be described as transforming DTH service into 'cable in the sky' systems, diminished the competitive threat DTH was assumed to pose to monopoly cable companies. Both delivery systems, cable and DTH, will offer essentially the same product, the same range of channels, in order to implement what surely was the essential goal of CRTC policy: to continue policies that seek to promote and protect Canadian content and, not incidentally, the current chosen instrument for those ends, the cable industry.

Under the CRTC policy, a policy subsequently endorsed, indeed extended by the government, the revolutionary potential of DTH services to transform the broadcasting system has been, at least in the short term, significantly diluted. Far from being 'increasingly ineffective' as the CRTC had feared, traditional regulation was deployed to shelter 'the Canadian broadcasting system from expanding competition from non-Canadian service providers' – and the CRTC was the primary agent in arranging that deployment. The DTH conflict disrupted but did not spell, as had been predicted, the end of the 'whole symbiotic ecosystem' of Canadian broadcasting, in which the CRTC remains, albeit somewhat bruised, the dominant institutional actor in the broadcasting sector.

Transforming Telecommunications

In 1975, the basis for a fundamental transformation in the telecommunications regulatory regime began with the transfer of responsibility for telecommunications from the transport regulator, where it had been located since 1906, to the communications regulatory agency, which was renamed the Canadian Radio-television and Telecommunications Commission. Although the government described the move as simply 'housekeeping,' that was clearly an understatement. Whereas its predecessor only a few years earlier had been self-effacing in describing its responsibilities as limited to 'toll jurisdiction' and repeated its long-standing philosophy of regulatory purpose as being to 'regulate, not initiate' and corrective, not managerial, the CRTC had a decidedly different regulatory approach. Drawing on its ten years as a broadcasting regulator, where its statutory mandate was less to police and more to manage or plan the broadcasting sector through its powers of 'regulation and supervision,' the CRTC clearly interpreted its mandate very differently.

This became evident within a few months of the transfer taking effect, when the commission issued what was ostensibly a statement of its proposed procedures. The CRTC indicated that it would not be bound by the Canadian Transport Commission's traditional, very narrow, interpretation of its statute. It proclaimed that: 'The principle of "just and reasonable" rates is neither a narrow nor a static concept. As our society has evolved, the idea of what is just and reasonable has also changed, and now takes into account many considerations that would have been thought irrelevant 70 years ago, when regulatory review was first instituted. Indeed, the Commission views this principle in the widest possible terms and considers itself obliged to continually review the level and structure of carrier rates to ensure that telecommunications services are fully responsive to the public interest (CRTC 1976, 3).

Two aspects of the commission's radically different statement of regulatory purpose are noteworthy. The first is that it occurred just as the United States was in the throes of transforming its telecommunications regulatory regime (Temin and Galambos 1987; Crandall 1991; Brock 1994). The traditional principles were being re-examined and found wanting and new policies were consequently being put in place. The second is that there was no statutory basis for the new regulatory philosophy espoused by the CRTC. The legislation transferring jurisdiction to it had been 'housekeeping' only in the sense that no other provisions of the enabling legislation were changed. In exercising its responsibilities for telecommunications regulation, the CRTC was to be guided by the same limited sections of the 1905 Railway Act requiring 'just and reasonable rates' and no 'undue discrimination' in the interconnection of telephone systems, which the CTC and its predecessors had interpreted in a very narrow manner.

How radical the new era in telecommunications would be was very quickly established, not simply by the CRTC's statement of new regulatory purpose, but by its regulatory actions. Within less than four years, the CRTC had changed the scope of telephone rate regulation in federal jurisdiction by expanding it to include quality of service of the telephone companies and especially by subjecting, for the first time, the interprovincial rates of Bell Canada and the

British Columbia Telephone Company to regulatory scrutiny. Equally important, it radically interpreted the provision stipulating no 'undue discrimination' so as to prohibit Bell Canada from giving itself a benefit over companies that might want to compete with it through the interconnection of services (CRTC 1977).

If the CRTC had simply expanded the scope of its regulation of the aspects of the pricing conduct or service behaviour of federally regulated telephone companies, that, while significant, would not merit the description of transforming the telecommunications regulatory regime. What does merit that description is the CRTC's interpretation between 1976 and 1996 of the essential structural premises and ideas governing telecommunications regulation. In these years the CRTC did not simply preside over the transformation of Canadian telecommunications from a system based on the monopoly provision of telecommunications services; more than any other single public actor it was responsible for the extension of competitive provisioning of such services. When the CRTC assumed jurisdiction, monopoly was the norm and presumed to be natural. Today, as a result of CRTC decisions, competition is the norm and monopoly decidedly most 'unnatural.' What has occurred under CRTC guidance, and often initiative, has been a regime transformation, at least insofar as ideas about government regulation of the sector and policies for the advancement of those ideas are concerned.

When the CRTC acquired jurisdiction and immediately asserted its responsibilities, the stage was set for conflicts between the commission and its political 'masters' similar in nature to those that were experienced in the broadcasting sector. This was most clearly the case in 1977, when the federal cabinet overturned one of the first CRTC telecommunications decisions, namely, the rejection of Telesat Canada's application to join the consortium of telephone companies then known as the TransCanada Telephone System (now Stentor). The CRTC, already demonstrating its concern for structural aspects of the industry, ruled that such membership would not be in the public interest. The cabinet disagreed, justifying its decision simply by stating in a press release that the government had to consider a range of 'broad issues of public policy ... far wider than that which the CRTC could reasonably have been expected to consider. Many of these issues lie well beyond the purview of the Commission' (Kane 1980, 69). It would not be the last time that the government would both fail to enunciate publicly the policy factors that it thought should guide CRTC decision making and lament the absence of a policy directive mechanism.

Notwithstanding this particular intervention, for the purposes of this chapter the argument that the CRTC was the primary public institutional actor in the transformation of the telecommunications regulatory regime can be proven through a review of the structural decisions it made, decisions that fundamentally changed the basic ideas and policies then governing the telecommunications system. On these issues, involving first private and second, public network competition, and customer attachment of terminal equipment, the government played a secondary role. Rather than providing direction and setting the goals for the CRTC, political authorities were reduced to a supporting, noninitiating, and nondirecting role that limited them simply and solely to indicating agreement with the basic decisions and the larger policy framework developed by the CRTC. The one major exception in the series of transformative decisions, where the government played the primary role, involved the resale of telecommunications services. The four decisions will be discussed in turn.

Public and Private Network Competition

One of the central traditional premises of telecommunications policy, in Canada as elsewhere, was that telephone service was a natural monopoly. This premise was challenged first in the United States over several decades and then, in 1976, in Canada, immediately after the CRTC acquired jurisdiction. The challenger was CNCP Telecommunications, which applied to the CRTC for permission to interconnect its private voice and public data network to the local switched networks of Bell Canada. Such an application, which called into question the traditional monopoly of Bell Canada, challenged not only its presumed corporate power in governmental circles, but the interests of provincial governments, which owned, in the case of the three Prairie provinces, or regulated, in four others, the telephone companies in their respective territories. After a lengthy and controversial public hearing, the CRTC approved the application in 1979 (CRTC 1979). Although Bell Canada appealed the decision to the federal cabinet, the appeal was denied. Within two years the decision was made applicable to British Columbia Telephone, the other primary company regulated by the CRTC.

In 1983, CNCP applied to the commission for interconnection with the federally regulated companies to provide full public long-distance telephone competition. The incumbent firms, joined by consumer groups and unions, opposed the application on the grounds that if permitted it would threaten the universal affordability of telephone service through the erosion of cross-subsidies from long-distance to local service. In this instance, although it deemed that the benefits of such competition would be very positive for Canada, the commission (CRTC 1985) denied the application, ostensibly on the grounds that the applicant had a questionable business plan and would probably be unable to provide service economically.

For the purposes of this chapter, the significance of this decision is not the result per se but the fact that the decision was taken primarily because of opposition from commissioners to the principle of competition. It is worth noting that no policy statement by the government had been issued on the merits of public long-distance competition. Furthermore, although the minister of communications in the Liberal government at the time of the application had taken credit for CRTC decisions that promoted competition, neither the Liberal government nor the Conservative government that replaced it in 1984 had a public policy on competition, as opposed to the specific application before the commission. On the other hand, the Conservative minister of communications did indicate in a speech in 1985, around the time that the CRTC was preparing its decision, that he was opposed to 'dereglementation brutale,' which would presumably follow competition (Masse 1985b).

When the restructured CNCP, now known as Unitel, applied once again for interconnection with all telephone companies under federal jurisdiction to provide long-distance public voice competition, the commission approved the application (CRTC 1992). This time it is possible that the CRTC was taking heed of indirect signals from the cabinet that the time had come to permit full long-distance competition. The signals, if indeed they were signals, would have come as a result of the role of the cabinet in the conflict over competition through the resale of public long-distance services (see below). Even if the 1992 approval by the CRTC of the principle of public long-distance competition reflected a willingness to follow political direction on the matter, the CRTC's role as prime actor was still apparent because of the specific nature of the decision.

The commission had before it the application from Unitel as well as a more regional application. Rather than simply approving such applications, the CRTC, on its own initiative, turned the public hearing process into a generic proceeding. As a result, it then approved a radical form of competition, which was unexpected by all observers (Surtees 1994). It approved both national and regional competition, as well as facilities-based and resale competition, for all companies under its jurisdiction. In addition, it approved a system of discounts for the new entrants for the initial period of entry. In a single decision, the CRTC had not only reversed its original opposition to public voice competition but profoundly transformed the structure of the telecommunications industry (Globerman et al. 1993).

Liberalization of Terminal Attachment Policies

The independence and determinative role of the CRTC was also demonstrated in the commission's decisions on the attachment of customer-owned or supplied terminal equipment to the telephone network. Although this was permitted in the United States as early as 1968, Bell Canada rigorously fought any attempts by customers to win the right in Canada and obtained permission from the CRTC's predecessor to terminate service because of the attachment of a 'foreign device,' an answering machine. Bell was still opposed to liberalizing the terminal attachment policies after the CRTC acquired jurisdiction but, recognizing the procompetitive approach the commission was adopting in its early decisions, the company attempted to pre-empt the commission. It applied to change its rules to permit individuals to attach all but the primary telephone set to its network. The CRTC, however, demonstrated that it was as independent of the telephone companies, the presumed dominant force in the traditional regulatory regime, as it was of political direction. In 1980 (CRTC 1980) the commission required Bell to permit any customer, business or residential, to permit the attachment to its network of virtually any type of terminal equipment, from faxes to answering machines and telephones to PBXs, provided that independent specified technical standards for the equipment were met. In 1981, this decision was made applicable to the British Columbia Telephone Company (CRTC 1981). Although appealed to cabinet, the decision was upheld and another major premise of the regulatory regime had been changed by the regulator.

Resale of Long-distance Telecommunications

The one major case where the CRTC was not able to control the policy process involved the resale of public long-distance services. The CRTC had originally approved a limited form of resale in 1985 but specified that such resale could only involve so-called enhanced services and not the equivalent of public long-distance services. This was to prevent the introduction of long-distance competition indirectly, after the commission had refused to permit such competition directly in the 1985 CNCP decision discussed above. In 1987, the CRTC approved requests from Bell Canada to terminate the services of a company on the grounds that it was offering what were essentially non-enhanced services and was therefore in violation of the CRTC policy (CRTC 1987).

The company in question, however, fought back, not only through the CRTC but also by means of a comprehensive lobbying effort directed at departments and officials other than the Department of Communications. These other departments were able to prevail by winning a series of reprieves from the cabinet that prevented Bell Canada from withdrawing service to the company. Although the CRTC, supported by the Department of Communications, fought vigorously to persuade cabinet to uphold its position, it was unable to win such a decision. It is important to note that at no time did cabinet indicate that it favoured liberalization on this issue in principle but could only agree with some temporary relief. Nevertheless, after three years the CRTC decided that cabinet was indeed sending it a message, however garbled and muted, and announced that it would permit full resale of long-distance services.

Legislation and Political Direction: In Search of the Holy Grail

This chapter has argued that the CRTC has been the dominant public actor in shaping and directing the transformation of the communications institutional regime. This has clearly been the case in the telecommunications sector. In the broadcasting sector, where change has been less pronounced, the CRTC has also been assertive in protecting both its independence and its policy role. The irony, of course, is that while the CRTC has asserted its dominance, political authorities, regardless of political party, have over the past twenty years reiterated the priority of establishing an appropriate relationship between the regulatory agency and themselves. In the words of the minister quoted above, the government's objective was to 'establish clearly and unequivocally that only the government ... is empowered to develop major telecommunications policies. This responsibility should not be borne by the CRTC.'

Yet this responsibility has indeed been borne, aggressively and often self-confidently, by the CRTC. The failure of successive governments to rearrange the relationship between the government and the agency is one of the more fascinating aspects of the past two decades. In this section we review the attempts by the government to reassert its authority and, in particular, the specific proposals and instruments that it presumed would accomplish this objective.

As early as 1968, when the Department of Communications was established, the government of the day acknowledged that existing statutory instruments had lost their effectiveness as guides for the emerging telecommunications era. The first minister of communications promised 'a national plan and a national communications policy to integrate and rationalize all systems of communications whether those of today such as telephones, microwave relays, telex, TWX, telegraph and the Post Office, or those of tomorrow: communications satellites; sophisticated information retrieval systems linking computers which exchange and store information of all kinds; lasers, and on up to the "wired city" of tomorrow' (Keirans 1969).

Consequently the minister would embark on the course that would be followed by so many of his successors: establish a task force or something similar. In 1969, the instrument was the Telecommission. In the early seventies there were various policy papers followed by reports from advisory bodies such as the Clyne Committee; the Applebaum–Hébert Committee; a departmental task force on telecommunications policy in 1984, which did not issue a report; the Task Force on Broadcasting Policy in the late 1980s; and two major intergovernmental regulatory investigations, not to mention numerous federal-provincial conferences.

Finally, in the 1990s the original objective appears to have been met, although not in the form of a single 'national plan' or communications policy. In 1991 a new Broadcasting Act was passed and this was followed by the Telecommunications Act in 1993. For our purposes three aspects of these legislative initiatives are particularly germane to the central issue of establishing the appropriate institutional relationship between political authorities and the regulatory agency (i.e., one that confines the latter to a subordinate role): the statement of policy objectives to guide and structure regulatory decision making; the inclusion of a 'policy directive' power as an aid to such structuring; and, finally, the political appeal mechanism as a fall-back device to ensure that the regulator has acted appropriately from a policy perspective. Before turning to the recently enacted statutes, it is appropriate to comment on the legislative history of earlier attempts to address these questions.

In 1977, the first attempt to legislate a new policy and institutional framework was made when the Liberal government introduced a telecommunications bill in the House of Commons. Neither this bill nor the subsequent two versions went beyond first reading. One of the more notable features of these legislative proposals is that they contained a single statement of telecommunications objectives for both the telecommunications and broadcasting sectors, the last time this would be attempted. The policy statements were virtually identical, with one major exception. In the original version (Bill C-43, given first reading 22 March 1977), the final paragraph of section 3, in terms reminiscent of the 1968 Broadcasting Act, stated that 'the telecommunications policy for Canada enunciated in this section can best be achieved by providing for *the regulation and supervision* of the Canadian broadcasting system and of telecommunication undertakings over which the Parliament of Canada has legislative authority by a single independent public body' (emphasis added). The next version (Bill C-24, 26 January 1978) distinguished between 'the regulation and supervision of the Canadian broadcasting system and the regulation of telecommunication undertakings,' while the third version (Bill C-16, 9 November 1978) dropped all reference to 'supervision'. Inasmuch as Pierre Juneau, chairman of the CRTC until 1976, had energetically and effectively opposed any attempts to remove a reference to 'supervision' in the first version, subsequent changes may reflect both a shift in the relative relationship between the CRTC and the department and an attempt by the latter to reinforce, through the omission of the managerial role suggested by the word 'supervision,' the emphasis on the CRTC's policy implementation role sought by the department.

This point is supported by the second major feature of the proposed statutes, namely, the inclusion of an expanded 'policy directive' power for the cabinet. The 1968 Broadcasting Act contained such a power but it was limited to three very specific issues. It will be recalled that the issue of policy direction, other than through statute, emerged in both the conflict over the introduction of pay television in 1976 and, in the following year, over Telesat Canada's membership in the TransCanada Telephone System. In the latter case, the minister lamented the lack of an 'adequate statutory mechanism through which the government could have provided clear policy guidance to the CRTC' (Kane 1980, 69). One of the more interesting aspects of the proposed directive power in its original versions in 1977–8 ,which suggests that the objective was to establish that the minister and the Department of Communications were the lead policy actors, is that there was no provision for either consultation with the CRTC prior to issuance of a directive or review by Parliament before the directive would take effect.

Given the far-reaching decisions that the CRTC made in the first seven years after it had received its telecommunications mandate, not to mention the ongoing conflicts over pay television, it is perhaps surprising that between 1978 and 1987 there was no attempt to introduce comprehensive telecommunications legislation. Indeed, as we shall see, 1978 was the last time that a single statute was proposed for the regulation of both telecommunications and broadcasting. The government was still concerned, however, about the independent, insufficiently constrained policy-making capacity of the CRTC. Consequently, a bill was introduced in 1984 to permit the cabinet to issue policy directions to the CRTC. Unlike earlier proposals, a role for both the commission and Parliament in the development of any directive was to be established. But the bill died when Parliament was prorogued in 1984.

In 1987, the government chose to focus its energies on broadcasting legislation to the exclusion of telecommunications. This time the legislation was passed by the House of Commons but died in the Senate when the election was called in 1988 (Meisel 1991). As this bill was similar in all but one respect to the legislation ultimately enacted in 1991, there is no need to comment on its specific provisions. The most significant aspect of this attempt was the active lobbying by the then chair of the CRTC, André Bureau, against a provision that he found highly objectionable. The provision in question would have created an incentive system to supplement the existing regulations governing Canadian content. The chair's efforts further embittered the relationship between the government – especially the Department of Communications – and the commission and reinforced the department's determination to bring the agency under control.

The 1991 Broadcasting Act was the culmination of more than a decade of effort. It contained a statement of broadcasting policy objectives, supplemented by a statement of 'regulatory policy,' although the distinction between the two and the necessity for the latter may be questioned. The legislation also granted the government the long-sought power to issue binding policy directives to the commission, subject to the procedural requirements originally outlined in the 1984 bill. Finally, the Act contains a revision to the traditional political appeal mechanism. In the 1968 statute, the cabinet override power was fairly unconstrained. Under the new legislation, cabinet must provide reasons, based on the policy objectives identified in the statute, when it orders a reconsideration of a licensing decision and, if it decides to set aside a decision, it must provide written reasons for its action (Conklin 1992).

Separate legislation to govern the telecommunications industry was passed in 1993. The 1993 Telecommunications Act, which replaced the 1905 Railway Act, includes a statement of policy objectives (found in the Appendix) and provides as well for cabinet policy directives to the CRTC, subject to the same constraints found in the broadcasting legislation. The statute continues the traditional power of the cabinet to 'vary or rescind' telecommunications regulatory decisions, a power that is considerably broader than that contained in the broadcasting statute. There is also a significant difference between the two appeal mechanisms. The Broadcasting Act requires the cabinet to justify its action by stipulating where 'the decision derogates from the attainment' of the statutory policy objectives. The Telecommunications Act is more open-ended, in that the cabinet need only 'set out the details of any matter [it] considers material.' The statute does not contain a power for the minister of communications to grant licences for telecommunications firms, although the original version of the legislation included such a provision.

The very long gap between aspiration and fulfilment may render the legislation ineffective, most especially that for telecommunications. Most of the major decisions for transforming the regulatory regime have largely been taken (decisions announced in May 1997 (CRTC 1997) addressed the last bastion of monopoly, the local network, by permitting local competition.) Second, assuming some major issues remain outstanding or emerge, the statement of policy objectives in either statute is unlikely to prove an onerous constraint on the regulatory agency: the oft-claimed objective of 'establishing clearly and equivocally' the respective policy relationship between the regulator and the government has not been met. When the legislation was before the Senate Committee (Canada, Senate 1992) for prestudy in 1992, this was a major criticism of many witnesses and their concern was shared by the committee itself. But it is worth asking, given that the CRTC fashioned 'a silk purse from the sow's ear' of the minimalist 1905 statutory injunctions requiring 'just and reasonable rates' and 'no undue discrimination,' whether any statement of policy could provide a meaningful constraint.

A similar point can be made about the legislative attempts to link cabinet appeals to the statutory policy objectives found in the Broadcasting Act. If these objectives will not structure agency discretion in anything more than a symbolic fashion, it is equally doubtful that they will prove any more of a constraint on a cabinet determined to change a regulatory decision. Finally, after two decades of recommendations from a wide range of sources that the policy directive be adopted as an intermediate policy tool for governments to structure regulatory decision making, it remains to be seen if this instrument will satisfy either its advocates or political authorities. A policy directive mechanism was premised on a reasonably clear statement of objectives which might still require some ranking of priorities or clarification in the case of conflicts. For reasons stated, neither of the two statutes would appear to satisfy that objective. In the case of political authorities, the conflict over the DTH licensing decision may discourage subsequent use of the tool. In short, it is clearly an open question whether passage of the new statutes and conferring new powers on political authorities in an era in which the major policy decisions have already been taken by the regulator will challenge the dominant role of the regulatory agency or constitute the significant institutional realignment long sought by political authorities.

Conclusions

The argument of this chapter is that, unlike its sister agencies in the energy and transportation sectors, the CRTC has been able, in the face of formidable challenges, to protect its status as the primary institutional actor in the communications regulatory regime. The CRTC has acted, and continues to act, as the primary agenda setter for the sector and, where policy conflicts ensue, its preferences usually dominate the policy outcomes. I have attempted to support this argument through the analysis of several major institutional conflicts involving both broadcasting and telecommunications issues. Other examples, such as the introduction of specialty services in cable television or the deregulation of cable rates attempted in the latter half of the 1980s, could have been adduced to reinforce the argument.

This is not to suggest, of course, that the CRTC has been 'out of control' or that it has won all its battles. The cabinet, when it has been committed to a course of action, has been able to persuade the commission to respect its preferences, as the cases of the introduction of pay television or the licensing of direct-to-home satellite television illustrate. Most recently, through its appeal powers, the cabinet was able to delay local telephone rate increases. But in these and other cases, when the commission has had to bend or submit to external direction, the CRTC nevertheless placed its imprint on the regulatory outcomes, either through its capacity to delay decisions with which it disagreed, such as the licensing of pay television, or its ability to shape, through its various powers, the specifics of those outcomes. The policy on direct-to-home satellite television is perhaps the best example of the latter process, notwithstanding the conventional view that the cabinet successfully imposed its policy on the commission.

The success of the CRTC in defending its institutional role is all the more impressive in light of the long-standing objective of successive ministers of communications to radically reorder the institutional relationship between the agency and cabinet so as 'to establish clearly and unequivocally that only the government ... is empowered to develop major policies.' In view of my argument that almost all such policies developed over the past twenty years bear the very significant imprint of the CRTC, how can the staying power of the CRTC be explained?

One possible explanation is that the oft-proclaimed ambition of political authorities for policy dominance has been little more than an exercise in symbolic politics. Cabinet, according to this interpretation, had no intention of actually ruling, but sought the perception of being 'in control.' This was undoubtedly a factor in the late 1970s, when the federal government was involved in a series of intergovernmental conflicts over communications issues that were linked with larger issues, such as constitutional reform. As the CRTC was perceived to be largely unresponsive to provincial concerns, especially compared to other regulatory agencies (Schultz 1979), and the government did not want the CRTC to contaminate larger issues, the government's insistence that it would establish clearer lines of control could be seen as a signal to assuage provincial concerns.

The fact that it took more than fifteen years for the government to fulfil (apparently) its commitment – through new legislation and, particularly, the inclusion of an expanded policy directive power – can be attributed in part to the relative junior status of successive ministers of communications within the federal hierarchy. Communications, until the department disappeared in 1993, was never a primary position within the federal cabinet and was for twenty-five years, with few exceptions, an introductory appointment. Not surprisingly, therefore, ministers of communications – except perhaps for Gerard Pelletier in Trudeau's administrations and Marcel Massé and Flora Macdonald in

Mulroney's governments – normally possessed little political clout within Ottawa. Consequently, while individual ministers would regularly invoke the need for political control, they were unsuccessful in persuading their colleagues to go beyond an almost ritualistic introduction of the appropriate legislation, as in 1977–8 and 1984, to commit the necessary parliamentary time to act on the issue.

A final explanation for the CRTC's influence rests in the relative competence and expertise of the respective bureaucracies and leadership in the Department of Communications and the CRTC. While successive ministers were relatively junior, the CRTC's first decade, in which much of the institutional dynamics between the rival bodies was established, was characterized by the very aggressive and politically well-placed leadership of Pierre Juneau. Subsequent chairs of the CRTC were able to build on that leadership and assert and augment the independence of the commission and, particularly, its policy-making responsibilities. The appointment of Charles Dalfen as the first vice-chair for telecommunications in 1976 is regarded as comparable to the appointment of Juneau in setting the tone and the authority of the CRTC for its expanded responsibilities. The relative imbalance of the two bureaucracies was particularly pronounced, according to both governmental and industry participants, by the concentration of telecommunications expertise in the CRTC. Departmental telecommunications personnel suffered both in comparison with the CRTC staff and within their own department, where cultural officials and issues predominated. Consequently, in competition with the commission, which was eager to assert its independence and its ability to set the agenda for both the government and the telecommunications industry, the department was largely relegated to a reactive, distinctly secondary role.

In view of the oft-repeated objective of political control over policy making, the limitations of the Department of Communications are most apparent in the 1991 Broadcasting Act and the 1993 Telecommunications Act. Despite the profound changes and continuing challenges facing both sectors, these statutes largely reflect the priorities identified in the 1970s. In fact, the policy statements are very similar to those contained in the three bills that did not go beyond first reading in 1977 and 1978. Critics of the telecommunications legislation proposed in 1992, including the Conservative-dominated Senate Committee (Canada, Senate 1992; Janisch and Romaniuk 1995), faulted the department for the open-ended, almost vacuous, nature of the policy statement and asked for more defined and ranked policy goals. The fact that the department sought a new power for the minister to grant telecommunications licences rather than provide clearer policy direction to the CRTC was but another sign of the weakness of that department as a rival to the commission. When witnesses before the Senate Committee examining the proposed legislation almost universally condemned this proposal and the committee supported this position, the minister was forced to backtrack and delete the provision from the legislation that was subsequently enacted. The result, as indicated above, was that the new legislative policy provisions should not act, any more than the 1968 Broadcasting Act, as a significant constraint on the CRTC's discretion.

The CRTC has to date been largely successful in fending off political and bureaucratic rivals to its status as the primary institutional actor in the communications regulatory regime. More than any other participant in that regime, it has established the pace and the direction for changes in regulatory policies and instruments for both the broadcasting and telecommunications sectors, notwithstanding legislative and other attempts to constrain its powers. The issue that confronts the CRTC, as it enters the millennium, however, is whether it will have as much success in deflecting technological and economic forces as it has political rivals. Its ability to 'stay standing' will surely be tested in the coming years.

Appendix

CANADA: 1993 NATIONAL TELECOMMUNICATIONS ACT POLICY STATEMENT (SECTION 7)

It is hereby affirmed that telecommunications performs an essential role in the maintenance of Canada's identity and sovereignty and that the Canadian telecommunications policy has as its objectives

(a) to facilitate the orderly development in Canada of a telecommunications system that serves to safeguard, enrich and strengthen the cultural, social, political and economic fabric of Canada;
(b) to render reliable and affordable telecommunications services of high quality accessible in both urban and rural areas in all regions of Canada;
(c) to enhance the efficiency and competitiveness, at the national and international levels, of Canadian telecommunications;
(d) to promote the ownership and control of Canadian carriers by Canadians;
(e) to promote the use of Canadian transmission facilities for telecommunications within Canada and between Canada and points outside Canada;
(f) to foster increased reliance on market forces for the provision of telecommunications services;

(g) to stimulate research and development in Canada ... And to encourage innovation in the provision of telecommunications services;
(h) to respond to the economic and social requirements of users of telecommunications services particularly the privacy of individuals.

NOTES

I would like to thank Bruce Doern, George Hariton, Hudson Janisch, and Ian Scott for their comments on the first draft of this chapter.

1 For discussion and analysis of other aspects of the CRTC over the years see, for example, Raboy (1995a, 1995b); Doern (1997).
2 In this chapter I concentrate exclusively on relations between the CRTC and political authorities to the exclusion of public-private sector relationships. Although it could be argued that the former were epiphenomenon and that the real power to direct the development of both the broadcasting and telecommunications sectors was in private sector hands, I reject such a thesis. While there have been private sector 'winners' in both the broadcasting and telecommunications sectors, these have changed over time and without predictable consistency. The subject of public-private relationships and relative power in the telecommunications sector is the subject of an ongoing project, tentatively entitled 'A World Turned Upside Down: The Politics of Telecommunications 1976–1996,' by Richard J. Schultz and Hudson Janisch.

REFERENCES

Bartley, A. 1990. Ottawa Ways: The State, Bureaucracy and Broadcasting, 1955–1968. PhD thesis, McGill, Department of Political Science.
Brock, G.W. 1994. *Telecommunication Policy for the Information Age*. Cambridge, Mass.: Harvard University Press.
Buchan, R.J., et al. 1982. *Telecommunications Regulation and the Constitution*. Montreal: Institute for Research on Public Policy.
Canada. Senate. 1995. *Report on the Governor in Council Direction Orders to the Canadian Radio-Television and Telecommunications Commission*, First Session Thirty-Fifth Parliament, June 1995.
Canada. Senate Committee on Transport and Communications. 1992. *Report on the Subject Matter of Bill C-62, An Act Respecting Telecommunications*, Third Session, Thirty-Fourth Parliament, June 1992.
Collins, R. 1990. *Culture, Communications and National Identity: The Case of Canadian Television*. Toronto: University of Toronto Press.

Conklin, D.B. 1991. The Broadcasting Act and the Changing Pathology of Cabinet Appeals. *Media and Communications Law Review* 2:297–333.

Corcoran, T. 1994. Canadian Roadblock to Telecommunications Competition. *Globe and Mail*, 1 September, B2.

Crandall, R.W. 1991. *After the Breakup*. Washington, D.C.: Brookings Institution.

CRTC. 1975. *Policies Respecting Broadcasting Receiving Undertakings*. Ottawa: CRTC Public Announcement, 16 December.

– 1976. *Telecommunications Regulation – Procedures and Practices*. Ottawa: CRTC, 20 July, Notice of Public Hearing, CRTC 1976–2.

– 1977. *Challenge Communications v. Bell Canada*. Telecom Decision CRTC 77–16.

– 1978. *Report on Pay Television*. Ottawa: Minister of Supply and Services.

– 1979. *CNCP Telecommunications, Interconnection with Bell Canada*. Telecom Decision CRTC 79–11.

– 1980. *Bell Canada – Interim Requirements Regarding the Attachment of Subscriber-Provided Terminal Equipment*. Telecom Decision CRTC 80–13.

– 1981. *British Columbia Telephone Company – Interim Terms and Conditions Regarding the Attachment of Subscriber-Provided Terminal Equipment*. Telecom Decision CRTC 81–19.

– 1985. *Interchange Competition and Related Issues*. Telecom Decision CRTC 85–19.

– 1987. *Tariff Revisions Related to Resale and Sharing*. Telecom Decision CRTC 87–2.

– 1992. *Competition in the Provision of Public Long Distance Voice Telephone Services and Related Resale and Sharing Issues*. Telecom Decision CRTC 92–12.

– 1993. *Structural Public Hearing*. Ottawa: Public Notice CRTC 1993–74.

– 1994a. *Call for Comments – Proposed Exemption Order Respecting Direct-to-Home Satellite Distribution Undertakings*. Ottawa: Public Notice CRTC 1994–19.

– 1994b. *Exemption Order*. Ottawa: Public Notice CRTC 1994–111.

– 1997. *Local Competition*. Ottawa: CRTC 97–8.

Doern, G. Bruce. 1997. Regulating on the Run: The Transformation of the CRTC as a Regulatory Institution. *Canadian Public Administration* 40, no. 3: 516–38.

Ellis, D. 1992. *Split Screen: Home Entertainment and the New Technologies*. Toronto: Friends of Canadian Broadcasting.

Financial Post. 1995. 29 April, p. 9.

Globe and Mail. 1995a. 12 January, Editorial, p. A18.

– 1995b. 7 June, pp. B1, B14.

– 1995c. 17 June, p. D7.

Globerman, S., H.N. Janisch, R.J. Schultz, and W.T. Stanbury. 1992. Canada and the Movement Towards Liberalization of the International Telecommunications Regime. In A.C. Cutler and M.W. Zacher, eds., *Canadian Foreign Policy and International Economic Regimes*. Vancouver: UBC Press.

Globerman, S., H.N. Janisch, and W.T. Stanbury. 1996. Convergence, Competition and Canadian Content. In W.T. Stanbury, ed., *Perspectives on the New Economics and Regulation of Telecommunications.* Montreal: Institute for Research on Public Policy.

Globerman, S., H. Oum Tae, and W.T. Stanbury. 1993. Competition in Public Long Distance Markets in Canada. *Telecommunications Policy,* 17 (May/June): 297–310.

Globerman, S., W.T. Stanbury, and T.A. Wilson, eds. 1995. *The Future of Telecommunications Policy in Canada.* Toronto: Institute for Policy Analysis, University of Toronto.

Hall, R. 1990. The CRTC as Policy-Maker, 1968–1992. PhD thesis, McGill Graduate Program in Communications.

Harris, R.A., and S.M. Milkis. 1989. *The Politics of Regulatory Change.* New York: Oxford University Press.

Henderson, J. 1989. Decade of Denial: The CRTC, the Public Interest and Pay Television, 1972–1982. MA thesis, McGill Graduate Communications Program.

Information Highway Advisory Council. 1995. *Connection, Community, Content: The Challenge of the Information Highway.* Ottawa: Information Highway Advisory Council.

Janisch, H.N., and B. Romaniuk. 1995. Canada. In E. Noam, S. Komatsukzai, and D.A. Conn, eds. *Telecommunications in the Pacific Basin.* New York: Oxford University Press.

Kane, T.G. 1980. *Consumers and the Regulators.* Montreal: Institute for Research on Public Policy.

Keirans, E. 1969. In *Canada. House of Commons. Debates,* 27 February, p. 6016.

Masse, M. 1985a. Minutes of Proceedings and Evidence of the Standing Committee on Communications and Culture, Issue 10, 6 May, p. 10.4.

– 1985b. Looking at Telecommunications – The Need for Review: Notes for an Address. Electrical and Manufacturers' Association, Montabello, 20 June.

Meisel, J. 1989. Near Hit: The Parturition of a Broadcasting Policy. In K. Graham, ed., *How Ottawa Spends: 1989–90,* 131–63. Ottawa: Carleton University Press.

Murray, C. 1983. *Managing Diversity.* Kingston: Institute of Intergovernmental Relations, Queen's University.

Peers, F.W. 1979. *The Public Eye: Television and the Politics of Canadian Broadcasting, 1952–1968.* Toronto: University of Toronto Press.

Policy Review Panel. 1995. *Direct-to-Home Satellite Broadcasting.* Ottawa: Canadian Heritage.

Raboy, M. 1990. *Missed Opportunities: The Story of Canada's Broadcasting Policy.* Montreal: McGill-Queen's University Press.

– 1995a. Influencing Public Policy on Canadian Broadcasting. *Canadian Public Administration,* 38, no. 3: 411–32.

– 1995b. The Role of Public Consultation in Shaping the Canadian Broadcasting System. *Canadian Journal of Political Science* 28, no. 3: 455–78.

Schultz, R.J. 1977. Regulatory Agencies in the Canadian Political System. In K. Kernaghan, ed., *Public Administration in Canada*. 3rd ed. Toronto: Methuen.

– 1979. *Federalism and the Regulatory Process*. Montreal: Institute for Research on Public Policy.

Schultz, R.J., and M.R. Brawley. 1996. Telecommunications. In G.B. Doern, L.A. Pal, and B.W. Tomlin, eds. *Border Crossings: The Internationalization of Canadian Public Policy*, 82–107. Toronto, Oxford University Press.

Schultz, R.J., and G.B. Doern. 1998. No Longer 'Governments in Miniature.' Canadian Sectoral Regulatory Institutions in a North American Context. In G.B. Doern and S. Wilks, eds., *Changing Regulatory Institutions in Britain and North America*. Toronto: University of Toronto Press.

Stanbury, W.T., ed. 1986. *Telecommunications Policy and Regulation*. Montreal: Institute for Research on Public Policy.

Stewart, A., and W.H.N. Hull. 1994. *Canadian Television Policy and the Board of Broadcast Governors, 1958–1968*. Edmonton: University of Alberta Press.

Surtees, L. 1994. *Wire Wars*. Scarborough: Prentice-Hall.

Temin, P.W., and L. Galambos. 1987. *The Fall of the Bell System*. New York: Cambridge University Press.

Woodrow, R.B., and K.B., Woodside, eds. 1982. *The Introduction of Pay Television in Canada*. Montreal: Institute for Research on Public Policy.

3

Recasting the Federal Transport Regulator: The Thirty Years' War, 1967–1997

MARGARET M. HILL

This chapter examines the evolving role of regulation in Canada's national transportation system in the thirty years from 1967 to 1997. There were huge changes in the rail and air industries during this period and the overall structure of the regulatory system was equally unsettled. The Canadian Transport Commission (CTC) regulated the rail and air sectors under the regulatory regime established by the 1967 National Transportation Act. Regulatory jurisdiction was handed over to the newly created National Transportation Agency (NTA) two decades later, when the Transportation Act was rewritten and a more market-oriented regulatory philosophy was inaugurated.[2] In 1996, the legislation was revised yet again through the Canada Transportation Act[3] and a third regulatory body, the Canadian Transportation Agency (CTA), assumed responsibility for achieving 'a safe, economic, efficient and adequate network of viable and effective transportation services.'[4]

The 1967–97 period amounted to a three-decade-long struggle over the scope of rail and air regulation and the role of the federal regulatory body. The CTC-centred regime exemplified what Schultz and Alexandroff (1985) call planning regulation. The post-1996 CTA era marks a return to classic policing regulation and, in particular, a retrenchment from the regulator's role as policy maker. Two hybrid forms of regulation – serving a promoting-policing function on the rail side and a policing-promoting function on the air side – characterized regulation under the NTA in the intervening years. As Schultz and Doern (1998) have recently contended, the federal transport regulator was transformed during this period from a 'government in miniature' to a shell of its former self.

The chapter begins with a discussion of the origins of the independent regulatory agency and the dilemmas this mode of organization poses for the modern administrative state. In the latter regard, special attention is paid to Schultz and Alexandroff's concept of policing, promoting, and planning regulation, which can provide a basis for examining the range of regulatory approaches in a particular regulatory regime, such as Canada's regime for air and rail regulation. The policing-promoting-planning framework is then used to analyse three distinct periods in the recent history of federal regulation in the rail and air sectors.

Background

In the post–Second World War era, Canadians have increasingly found themselves in a regulated society. The growth of regulation has been reflected in – and has necessitated – changes in the machinery of government. Where the dominant mode for regulation was once the traditional ministerial department, government regulation is now also performed through independent regulatory agencies and self-regulation. Each of these modes poses special administrative and political dilemmas (Hill 1994). The focus in this section is on independent regulatory agencies, since this mode of organization has long been the preferred arrangement for Canada's transport regulatory regime.

Regulation by Independent Agency: Origins and Dilemmas

The independent regulatory agency model is an outstanding example of the successful borrowing of regulatory innovations developed elsewhere. Its origins lie in the nineteenth-century commission model first developed at the state level in the United States (e.g., the Massachusetts Board of Railroad Commissioners) and later perfected at the federal level, with the establishment of bodies such as the U.S. Federal Trade Commission, the Securities and Exchange Commission, and the Inter-State Commerce Commission (Armstrong and Nelles 1986; Eisner 1993; Baldwin 1989). The commission model sat uncomfortably in a political system like Canada's, which is founded on British principles of responsible government and judicial independence. Nevertheless, the model's guiding principles of separating policy development from regulatory administration and achieving efficiency through an appointed collective body operating at a distance from the executive branch of government found sympathy among those involved with designing the machinery of government for Canada's emerging regulatory state. The American commission model subsequently took shape in Canada as the independent regulatory agency (Cruikshank 1991).

The Canadian independent regulatory agency model is defined and distinguished from other modes of regulation by where it locates responsibility for regulatory authority. The conventional departmental mode vests responsibility in an elected minister while the self-regulation mode grants responsibility to an industry or a profession. In the agency mode, on the other hand, responsibility resides in an appointed body, usually a collective board. The architects of Canada's regulatory agencies have always been mindful of the traditions of cabinet and parliamentary government and the related principles of individual and collective ministerial responsibility. As a result, Canadian regulatory agencies have never enjoyed the same degree of independence as their American counterparts.

The rise of the regulatory agency in Canada has been an important phenomenon of the twentieth century, with the model enjoying particular proliferation in the years between the end of the Second World War and the 1980s (Law Reform Commission of Canada 1980; Mullan 1985). The preference for regulation by independent agency was not a planned development in the administrative state. Instead, it was a pragmatic response to the emerging challenges of good government. Independent regulatory agencies were embraced on the grounds that they met the desire of elected officials to depoliticize highly contentious and divisive issues, that they improved the efficiency of public administration through a clear division of labour between elected officials and expert regulators and tailor-made operating practices, that they enhanced opportunities for public participation in important areas of government decision making, and that they injected, with their board structure, an element of representation.

Regulatory commentators are quick to point out, however, that these so-called 'principles of organization' have never been followed with any consistency in Canada, at either the federal or provincial level (Canada 1986, 9). They also emphasize that the independent agency is, as Hodgetts puts it, a 'structural heretic' and poses a series of significant administrative and political dilemmas in Canada's system of government (Hodgetts 1973). The dilemmas arise because agencies tend to be delegated wide discretion to make choices between competing demands and to make decisions that have an impact on the authoritative allocation of resources in society. Moreover, the discretion is often not appropriately constrained because the agencies operate outside the normal channels of political control and accountability mechanisms, while present, are indirect and often ineffective.

Canada's various kinds of independent regulatory agencies have been the subject of much critical attention since the 1970s. The criticism originated with the realization by the Economic Council of Canada, the Law Reform Commission of Canada, and others that agencies were awarded powers with tremendous political significance, in areas of vital economic activity. The powers were regulatory in the first instance. Often, however, agencies also exercised nonregulatory powers, including subsidy allocation, quasi-judicial decision making, and arbitration. This led some commentators to conclude that the federal landscape had come to resemble a family of mini-Leviathans. Moreover, Janisch (1978, 1979) and others were impressed by the ease with which certain regulatory agencies were drawn into the policy-making process and, indeed, became powerful political actors.

Many solutions were proposed, both in the regulatory literature (Thomas 1984; Vandervort 1979) and in government (Canada 1986). Most focused on strengthening accountability through mechanisms such as policy directives; appeals to the courts or cabinet; more precise statutory drafting, which would leave less discretion in the hands of agencies; closer parliamentary scrutiny of agency budgets and proposed changes in regulations; revised appointment procedures for agency members; and fixed terms of office and post-employment conflict of interest guidelines for agency staff. At bottom, however, the need for arm's-length regulatory expertise to assist in the administration of modern government was rarely questioned.

Policing, Promoting, and Planning Regulation

The dilemmas posed by regulation by independent regulatory agency are brought to the fore through Schultz and Alexandroff's (1985) policing-promoting-planning framework. The concept of policing, promoting, and planning regulation was originally developed to shed light on the inherently multifunctional nature of the regulatory instrument. But it can also provide a basis for examining the range of regulatory approaches in a particular regulatory regime.

Schultz and Alexandroff argue that there are three types of regulation, each differentiated by purpose and scope. The three types – policing, planning, and promoting – all lie between the market and public ownership as forms of government intervention.

Policing regulation is classic government regulation according to Schultz and Alexandroff, and is properly associated with natural monopoly or public utility regulation. Policing regulation has limited objectives related to the participants in a single sector of the economy and applies to a narrow range of industry behaviour. The standard approach is to prevent unacceptable behaviour from occurring by setting rates or prices. Policing regulation is mainly reactive, responding to grievances only once unacceptable behaviour has taken place. It is not concerned with industry structure.

Promoting regulation is more intrusive and proactive. The goal is to protect or enhance the economic well-being of entities subject to regulation through the imposition of public obligations regarding, for example, entry and exit, accounting practices, depreciation, and corporate structures. Public firms are often favoured over their private sector counterparts in a promoting regulatory regime. The regulation of Canada's airline industry from 1938 to the late 1960s conformed to Schultz and Alexandroff's promoting regulation.

Planning regulation 'involves a much more ambitious, positive role for economic regulation' (Schultz and Alexandroff 1985, 6). The goals are both endogenous and exogenous and are explicitly designed to affect industry structure (e.g., through prescribing priorities for companies). The scope of planning regulation is wide, with regulation trying to affect a broad mix of behaviour. Moreover, a planning regulatory regime typically involves public obligations being imposed on entities in both the public and private sectors. The regulator in a planning regime is a problem solver and, in Redford's terminology, performs an adjustive role (Schultz 1982). Schultz and Alexandroff consider that the regulation of Canada's broadcasting sector epitomizes planning regulation.

Given the foregoing descriptions, it should be apparent that policing, promoting, and planning regulatory regimes present increasingly large challenges for political control and accountability. An independent regulatory agency that is involved in policing firm behaviour in a single sector is, in principle, least offensive. A planning-style agency, on the other hand, is similar to what Schultz and Doern (1998) term a government in miniature. With the extent of power this entails, such an agency is most susceptible to the charge that it violates essential principles of democratic government through its arm's-length relationship with the political executive.

Policing, promoting, and planning regulation are not mutually exclusive. In addition, as Schultz and Alexandroff's (1985) analysis of airline, telecommunications, and capital market regulations shows, detectable shifts often occur over time in the nature and scope of regulation in a given sector of the economy. Shifts from policing to promoting and especially planning regulation – or any combination thereof – have a significant impact on the linkages between the lead regulatory authority and the policy community of actors that surrounds it.

The remainder of this chapter relies on the policing-promoting-planning framework to examine the recasting that has taken place within Canada's transport regulatory regime from 1967 to 1987, from 1987 to 1996, and in the post-1996 period. The discussion is comparative and focuses on the mandate of the regulatory agency at the centre of the air and rail regulatory regimes in each of the three periods, the agency's structure and regulatory and policy roles, and the structure of the surrounding policy community.

1967–1987: The Canadian Transport Commission and
Planning Regulation

Transportation has had political, economic, and social significance in Canada from the earliest days. Transportation, as an industry and a service, was central to laying the foundation for an economically viable Confederation. Transport policy has always included important political objectives (McLean 1902; Langford 1976; Reschenthaler and Roberts 1979).

It was not until 1967, however, that Parliament established a comprehensive legislative and regulatory framework for transportation. The National Transportation Act, which took effect in September of that year in response to the recommendations of the MacPherson Royal Commission on Transportation, provided a statement of policy applicable to air, rail, motor vehicle, and water transport, as well as commodity pipelines. An independent regulatory agency, the Canadian Transport Commission, was established to oversee the regulatory system prescribed by the Transportation Act and its supporting legislation, mainly the Railway Act[5] and the Aeronautics Act.[6]

Given the historic importance of transportation in the building of Canada, it is perhaps not surprising that the CTC was cast in the role of planning regulator. The commission's planning role was not left unchallenged over the subsequent two decades. Nonetheless, on the whole, the CTC-centred regulatory regime amounted to what Lowi (1979) has termed 'unregulated regulation.' This is true for both the air and rail sides of the commission's responsibilities.

Mandate

The National Transportation Act created a single, integrated federal regulatory agency for all modes of transportation. The CTC was charged with implementing the regulatory system set out under the Act and, in particular, the statement of national transportation policy contained in section 3. Section 3 declared that: 'an economic, efficient and adequate transportation system making the best use of all available modes of transportation at the lowest total cost is essential to protect the interests of the users of transportation and to maintain the economic well-being and growth of Canada, and that these objectives are most likely to be achieved when all modes of transport are able to compete ... having due regard to national policy and to legal and constitutional requirements.'

The national transportation policy was plainly riddled with competing objectives. The central thrust was toward competition, but competition with limits. The Transportation Act assigned responsibility for settling on the appropriate trade-offs between, say, efficiency and the economic well-being of Canada to the CTC. This challenge of interpretation – and the associated challenge of ensuring that trade-offs were reflected in regulatory decisions – would prove to be the principal source of the CTC's planning role in the air and rail regulatory regime (Janisch 1978).

The limited nature of competition under the 1967 Transportation Act was best seen in the Act's residual rate regulation provisions. Section 23, for example, permitted anyone to challenge rates established by a carrier or carriers pursuant to the National Transportation Act or the Railway Act where there was reason to believe that the effect of the rate might 'prejudicially affect the public interest.' A series of rate decisions sorted out the inherent ambiguities of this public interest test (Janisch 1978, 10–19). At the same time, the decisions showed the full extent to which the CTC was involved in planning the development of Canada's rail system.

It is equally important to recognize that the National Transportation Act promoted only intermodal competition (e.g., between air and rail) and not also the intramodal variety (e.g., between rail carriers). This was reflected in the mode-by-mode approach in the wording of section 3 and reinforced by the commission's organizational structure and operating procedures (see below).

Finally, the CTC was formally established as a multifunctional government in miniature. The commission was empowered to review, rescind, change, alter, or vary any of its orders or decisions; to apply sanctions where breaches of regulations occurred; to undertake research necessary to achieve Canada's national transportation policy and to support the CTC in its duties; and to manage the system of subsidies created under the Maritime Freight Rates Act.[7] Regulatory responsibilities were therefore only part of a larger bundle of governing functions exercised by the CTC.

Structure

The basic structure of Canada's new transport regulator was defined under the National Transportation Act. The commission's board consisted of seventeen full-time members, each appointed by cabinet for a maximum ten-year term during good behaviour. Members could be reappointed, but a commissioner would cease to hold office upon reaching age seventy. The Act called for one board member to be appointed as president and two others as vice-presidents (legal and research).

The Transportation Act also required the establishment of modal committees. These committees – for instance, for air transport and rail transport – conducted the work of the commission in their respective areas. Each committee consisted of three commissioners and the commission's president acting in an *ex officio* capacity. Subsection 24(3) of the Act authorized the committees to exercise any of the commission's powers and duties and confirmed that a committee's orders, rules, or directions had effect 'as though they were made or issued by the Commission.' The substructure of modal committees meant that, while the CTC had taken over the staffs and responsibilities of three agencies (i.e., the Board of Transport Commissioners for Canada, the Air Transport Board, and the Canadian Maritime Commission), an integrated approach to transport regulation was still somewhat illusory.

Internally, the CTC was fragmented as well. Staff were organized along modal lines, mirroring the committee structure. There was also a research division. When it began operation in September 1967, the CTC had a staff of approximately 335 person years. This number had escalated to over 1,000 person years by 1986.

Regulatory Role

As discussed above, the goal of the National Transportation Act was to achieve an economic, efficient, and adequate transportation system for Canada. The market, and, in particular, intermodal competition, was one tool. The main tool under the Act, however, was the CTC and its role in regulatory planning. To discharge its responsibilities in relation to the national transportation policy in section 3 of the Act, the CTC was compelled to take a systemwide view and to coordinate and harmonize the operations of all transport carriers. The commission also had access to a number of important mode-specific regulatory powers.

On the rail side, the National Transportation Act and the Railway Act granted the CTC important residual controls over rates. These included the public interest test established by section 23 of the Transportation Act (see above). The commission was also involved in ensuring rail rates were compensatory[8] and in setting ceilings on rates for captive shippers.[9] The planning nature of the CTC's mandate was reinforced by section 106 and related sections of the Railway Act, which gave the commission responsibility for approving carriers' proposals for line abandonment and rationalization. Rail safety (e.g., accident investigation) also fell within the CTC's jurisdiction.[10]

On the air side, the principal source of the CTC's planning role was its authority to allow (or prevent) market entry through the licensing of carriers based on the public convenience and necessity test set out in subsection 16(3) of the Aeronautics Act. The statutory criteria were extremely broad and, according to Janisch (1978, 32), encouraged ad hoc decision making by the Air Transport Committee. The CTC was also empowered under subsections 45(1) and (2) of the Act to ensure that the tariffs and tolls proposed by air carriers were just and reasonable.

The CTC's planning role with respect to air transport was, on paper at least, less than it was in the rail area. The commission's discretion to award licences to air carriers had the significant limitation that approval could not be denied to Air Canada (or one of its subsidiaries) if it was necessary to allow the carrier to satisfy an agreement it had entered into with the federal minister of transport. Moreover, in contrast to the case with rail, the CTC had no jurisdiction over the safety of air carrier operations, nor over the equipment acquired or used by air carriers.

Finally, it should be noted that the National Transportation Act, 1967 gave the commission authority under subsections 46(1) and 26(1) to make orders and regulations for exercising any jurisdiction conferred on it by an Act of Parliament. Neither these orders nor regulations were subject to approval by Parliament, cabinet, or the minister of transport. Such orders or regulations could have a profound impact on the content and process of agency decision making, especially in view of the range of objectives to be pursued. The Act did, however, permit cabinet in its discretion to vary or rescind any of the CTC's orders, rules, or regulations.[11] Cabinet intervention in this respect was binding upon the commission and all parties.

Policy Role

A strong policy role, as Schultz and Alexandroff (1985) note, is one of the principal manifestations of a planning function for regulation. In the case of the CTC, there were a number of ways in which the regulator became intertwined in policy. The first was through its regular public interest determinations, for example, on rail rates and carrier licensing. The CTC could also be called upon under section 22 of the Transportation Act to provide policy advice to the minister of transport on measures for developing the various modes, the criteria for federal investment, and other matters. The CTC had an extensive research program to support its own activities and this sometimes led it on a collision course with policy controversies.[12]

The National Transportation Act offered next to no guidance on the relationship between the commission and the federal Department of Transport. Not surprisingly, this lacuna in the regulatory regime was a primary source of contention in the 1967–87 period. It lay at the heart of a power struggle between the lead actors in the federal transport policy community, which would culminate in a formal retrenchment of the CTC's regulatory role in 1987.

The independent regulatory agency model rests on an organizationally based separation of responsibility for policy and regulatory administration. The model's differentiation of roles is artificially neat, however, and the relationship between policy and regulatory administration is in reality highly symbiotic. For one thing, regulatory frameworks must be updated to take account of new policy directions originating from Parliament or the responsible minister. At the same time, difficulties in administering a regulatory system often suggest the need for changes in the enabling legislation. Janisch (1978, 110) makes the additional point that there is no need for a regulatory agency to 'decide absolutely everything all over again with each application,' provided its policy making is sufficiently transparent. The close interconnection of policy and regulation was certainly recognized in early thinking about independent agencies. Its importance had been downplayed, however, in the design of the CTC-centred regime and no provision had consequently been made for binding policy directives from the government.

The history of the CTC during the period 1967–87 was dominated by tensions over the proper scope and nature of the commission's involvement in air and rail policy. In principle, the federal air and rail portfolio was divided between the CTC and the minister (and department) of transport, with the former allocated regulatory jurisdiction and the latter given jurisdiction over policy matters. In practice the division was not so clear cut. The lack of clarity surfaced in exchanges before the House of Commons Standing Committee on Transportation over how ministerial policy should be applied in commission decision making, in a series of ministerial reversals of decisions of the Air Transport Committee, and elsewhere (Janisch 1978, 114–24). Conflict came to a head in the late 1970s, with the proposal in Bill C-33 for binding policy directives, and again in the early 1980s, with Minister Axworthy's unilateral development and announcement of a new air transport policy for Canada (Axworthy 1984; Hill 1988).

Structure of the Policy Community

The policy community surrounding the CTC for the 1967–87 period was, for the most part, the classic iron triangle. The regulator and the regulated (i.e., carriers) worked together to dominate the regulatory process. Consumer groups were on the periphery, agitating for wider consultation and improved representation, as they did in the case of the CRTC (see Chapter 8).

The added element in the policy community was federal-provincial conflict. This was particularly true with respect to air transport. The provinces became significant actors in the air transport sector as of the 1970s, using acquisitions or contractual arrangements with existing carriers as policy instruments for achieving provincial goals. Conflicts ensued with the federal regulatory regime. The provinces, for instance, demanded standing before the CTC in recognition of their new presence in the air sector and became more aggressive in seeking ministerial review of CTC decisions.

Intergovernmental conflict was central to the demise of the commission's planning role as the 1967–87 period came to an end (Schultz and Alexandroff 1985, 47–60). Federal-provincial battles had combined with other developments to produce a fundamental rebalancing of power in the air and rail regulatory regimes. Ultimately, as the next section goes on to explain, a planning role for the CTC was no longer sustainable.

1987–1996: The National Transportation Agency and Planning and Policing Regulation

The 1970s and early 1980s witnessed a number of separate but related developments that led to significant change in the role of Canada's transport regulator. The CTC itself had begun the process of change through a series of decisions increasingly sympathetic to market forces. There were other drivers of change as well, such as the gradual coalescing of expert opinion in favour of regulatory reform and liberalization; transport deregulation in the United States, which caused substantial short-hauling of Canadian routes; and the coming to power of a government determined to increase competition in the air and rail industries under the auspices of its policy White Paper, *Freedom to Move* (Mazankowski 1985; Hill 1988).

Another factor that contributed to the demise of the regulator's planning role was the transformation that had taken place in air and rail transportation during the preceding two decades. Much of this evolved naturally from developments in the industries and the larger international economy. Carriers consolidated their markets. Technological advances made innovative new services possible (e.g., container-based intermodal services) and altered the economics of transportation. Furthermore, an emergent resource sector, dependent in large measure on shippers in remote areas of the country, posed new problems for achieving efficiency in the national transportation system.

The regulator had been able to direct the course of air and rail transportation through the seventies and eighties but this became increasingly impossible in the new environment of the mid-1980s. The end of planning regulation was cemented when actors from across the policy community began to reconsider the old paradigms for air and rail regulation and to question what transportation was all about and whether a public utility approach to regulation was still appropriate.

Against this backdrop, the Mulroney government identified the complete overhaul of Canada's national transportation as one of its first priorities when it came to power in September 1984 (Schultz 1988, 1995). This was to be a pillar in the government's agenda for economic renewal. Extensive consultation took place with industry actors, academics, public officials, and interest groups. In July 1985, the minister of transport, the Honourable Don Mazankowski, tabled its White Paper, *Freedom to Move*.

Freedom to Move never mentioned 'deregulation' per se, but its direction was clear: 'The [National Transportation Act, 1967] and other transportation legislation represent a philosophy of regulation that has become outmoded ... reliance on competition and market forces rather than regulations, is clearly the wave of the future' (Mazankowski 1985, 1–3). In response, the White Paper recommended that the explicit statement of transportation policy objectives in section 3 of the existing Transportation Act be revised to promote both inter- and intramodal competition, greater efficiency, and less government intervention in transportation. *Freedom to Move* also made specific suggestions about how the 1967 regulatory framework ought to be amended to reflect the new objectives, for instance, by replacing the old public convenience and necessity test for entry to the air market with a fit, willing, and able requirement and, on the rail side, by allowing shippers to negotiate confidential contracts with individual railways.

The Mulroney government's approach to transport regulation was symbolized in its proposal for a new regulatory agency. The agency's primary functions would be to conduct hearings on matters of public importance, resolve disputes between shippers and carriers, and review major mergers and acquisitions of federally regulated transportation companies – not review tariffs, as the CTC did.

The House of Commons Standing Committee on Transport held hearings on *Freedom to Move* in the autumn of 1985. Legislation was introduced the following summer and again, with a new Parliament, in November. A revised National Transportation Act, which mirrored all the main elements of *Freedom to Move*, including a new regulatory agency, received Royal Assent in August 1987 and came into effect 1 January 1988. The role of the National Transportation Agency was fully consistent with the agency's roots in a White Paper that favoured greater reliance on market forces. There were still remnants of a planning function, for both air and rail. In each case, however, planning was now combined with a policing role.

Mandate

The objective in 1967 had been a national transportation system that was economic, efficient, and adequate. Twenty years later, the Transportation Act's statement of objectives was revised. Section 3 of the 1987 legislation declared that the policy goal was for a transportation system that was not only economic, efficient, and adequate, but also safe and viable.

The National Transportation Act, 1987 ushered in a general relaxation of regulatory control over the air and rail sectors. A 'fit, willing, and able' requirement replaced the old 'public convenience and necessity' test for entry to any class of domestic commercial air service. Air carrier licences were no longer subject to conditions on routes, destinations, flight schedules, fares, or equipment and it was easier for airlines to discontinue service on unprofitable routes. With respect to rail regulation, shippers could now negotiate confidential contracts with individual railways, although rail rates were still required to be compensatory and collective rate setting was still prohibited. Restrictions on rail line abandonment were eased.

There was a stark contrast with the mandate and role of the CTC. The commission had been charged with planning the development of Canada's air and rail sectors through regulation. The central purpose of the agency, on the other hand, was to regulate the transition to less regulation. The NTA was to be 'more an overseer of market forces than a regulator of transport' (Canada 1993, vol. 1, 184). This fundamental change in the nature of the mandate of Canada's transport regulator automatically reduced the political significance of the functions its performed.

Structure

The structure of the federal air and rail regulator changed under the 1987 Transportation Act in accordance with the intended shift in the NTA's role from policy maker to catalyst for dispute resolution. As outlined in sections 6 through 8 of the Act, the new agency had a board with just nine full-time and six part-time members and members were appointed for five-year renewable terms rather than the ten-year terms that had existed at the CTC. The Act's abandonment of regional representation requirements for the board's composition provided further evidence of the retreat from a political role for regulation in the new regime.

The CTC's system of modal committees had no place in the NTA-centred regime. Instead, the NTA was organized along functional lines mirroring the responsibilities assigned to it under the 1987 legislation: dispute resolution, market analysis, transportation subsidies, legal services, corporate management and human resources, and secretariat and regional operations. The logic was that this type of organizational structure was best suited to facilitating harmonization across different modes and promoting both inter- and intramodal competition.

The CTC had ballooned to gigantic proportions by the mid-1980s. Its successor was a much smaller organization. In 1992–3, the agency operated with 508 person years and a budget of $35 million.

Regulatory Role

The National Transportation Act officially clipped the regulatory wings of the federal transport regulator. Whereas the CTC had performed a planning role, the new agency was confined to policing activities, with only a few exceptions. But these exceptions were not insignificant. As a result, the NTA's regulatory role in the 1987–96 period was most accurately described as a policing-promoting hybrid. On the air side, there was relatively pure policing. On the rail side, policing was combined with a dose of more assertive, proactive regulation.

Domestic air service in southern Canada was for all intents and purposes fully deregulated under the 1987 Transportation Act and related amendments in the Aeronautics Act. There was complete freedom to enter the market, provided a carrier was controlled by Canadians and met the 'fit, willing and able' requirement in section 72 of the Transportation Act. The latter test was passed if the carrier had adequate insurance and a safety certificate from Transport Canada. Carriers were also free to exit the market, subject only to advance public notice of their intention to discontinue service.[13]

The only significant holdover from the previous period of planning regulation in the air sector was in the designated Northern region, where the agency retained a regulatory role.[14] Northern markets were still considered to be fragile. As a result, market entry was only permitted if the agency was satisfied that a new service would not 'significantly decrease or destabilize existing air services in the area.' Even then, however, the burden of proof rested with opponents of a proposed service and the carrier was not required to demonstrate market demand. Furthermore, the NTA in practice adopted a light-handed approach to regulating the Northern region.

On the rail side, the NTA lost all of the responsibilities that the CTC had exercised over confidential rates and safety, confirming that the direction of the new regulatory regime was clearly toward policing. In contrast to what had happened with air regulation, however, the agency still performed a strong regulatory role in two areas. The first concerned ensuring that shippers were protected from rail rates and services that were not commercially reasonable. The NTA accomplished this through its determination of competitive line rates (CLRs),[15] interswitching orders,[16] and dispute resolution activities (i.e., mediation and final offer arbitration).[17] The agency's second area of ongoing regulatory responsibilities, rail line abandonment and rationalization, was covered under sections 157 through 181 of the National Transportation Act.

In addition to recasting the scope of regulation, the 1987 amendments to the Transportation Act introduced a number of changes in the procedural aspects of the agency's regulatory functions. The most significant was a narrowing of the broad power enjoyed by the CTC to make rules, orders, and regulations. Any rule, order, or regulation made pursuant to the 1987 Act that was directed to more than one person or body and was made in exercise of one of the NTA's legislative powers required the approval of the governor-in-council.[18] This gave cabinet a new way to have *ex ante* impact on regulatory processes and decisions at the NTA.

Policy Role

The granting of broad, ambiguous power to the CTC – and the agency's willingness to act upon its mandate – had been attacked from all sides since 1967. The 1987 amendments to the Act attempted to address these concerns. For one thing, the National Transportation Act, 1987 explicitly restricted agency responsibility to deciding specific cases, and the right to formulate general policy was left firmly in the hands of elected officials. Moreover, the NTA was only entitled to take action in response to problems or on request. Resolving private disputes between shippers and carriers and reviewing major mergers and acquisitions in the transport sector was a decidedly different role than making decisions about tariffs and equipment and regulation routes. The NTA's role was inherently less political than that of its predecessor.

The provision for policy directives in the 1987 Transportation Act represented an attempt to correct a key shortcoming in the earlier legislation. Under sections 23 to 26, policy directives could be issued by the governor-in-council, at the request of the NTA or on the governor-in-council's own motion, on any matter within the NTA's jurisdiction. The Act stipulated in subsection 23(1) that policy directives were binding, that 'every such direction shall be carried out by the Agency.'

Cabinet's authority to issue policy directives was not completely unchecked, however. The Act required the minister of transport to consult the agency in advance about any proposed policy directive. The Act also specified that a particular process must be followed in Parliament before a policy directive could take effect. Ultimately, too, the NTA had a certain degree of freedom owing to its responsibility to apply a policy directive to the facts of any particular case before it.

The emasculation of the active policy role played by the CTC was incomplete for other reasons as well. The Transportation Act still provided, for instance, for public interest investigations regarding rail rates and line abandonment.[19] These were considered to be part of the Act's overall approach for ensuring a level playing field between shippers and the railways. In practice, the agency's authority to conduct public interest investigations did not translate into active policy making, since these investigations were used primarily as a bargaining tool in negotiations between shippers and carriers.[20]

Structure of the Policy Community

The 1987 revisions to the National Transportation Act struck a new balance in the distribution of power in the policy community surrounding Canada's air and rail regulator. The new Act took systematic steps to strengthen the NTA's accountability to the minister of transport, cabinet, and Parliament and thereby adjusted power and influence within the federal transport portfolio. The Act also redrew the overall landscape of the policy community by casting old actors in new roles and expanding the size of the cast.

Although the 1987 Act was most noteworthy for lessening regulatory controls and facilitating competition, it also addressed some of the technical and procedural problems often associated with the operation of independent regulatory agencies. First and foremost among these were problems of accountability. The architects of the 1987 legislation sought to improve accountability in several ways: by carefully circumscribing the agency's discretion; by including provision for policy directives; by requiring cabinet approval for the agency's rules, orders, and regulations; by retaining cabinet's power to override agency decisions; by amending the terms of appointments to the NTA; and by providing for regular monitoring of the implementation and effects of the Transportation Act. Strengthening accountability relationships was another way in which the Mulroney government sought to reassert political control over what it considered to be an inappropriately activist air and rail regulator.

In the larger policy community, the key development was the fragmentation of power that the 1987 regulatory framework both recognized and fuelled. The change in the regulator's role from planning to combined policing and promoting and the enlarged policy role assumed by Transport Canada have already been discussed. The new regime also greatly expanded the influence of travellers and shippers, those whom the transportation system was supposed to serve. In the case of shippers, their ascendant status in the policy community was reflected in the Act's competitive access provisions, but also in the very notion that air and rail transportation was seen as a service and as an input to costs and therefore a determinant of competitiveness of the economy (Hill 1988).

Post-1996: The Canadian Transport Agency and Policing Regulation

One of the checks and balances inserted into the 1987 Transportation Act was a compulsory five-year review. Section 266 of the Act required the governor-in-council to appoint a special National Transportation Act Review Commission (NTARC) to assess the impact of the Act after five years, evaluate the state of competition in the transport sector, examine implementation issues, and determine whether the 1987 legislation was equipped to deal with present and future challenges in Canada's transport sector.

The NTARC was appointed in January 1992. Under the chairmanship of Mr Gilles Rivard, the commission consulted widely with industry actors and other stakeholders and financed a number of research studies. The NTARC submitted its final report to the minister of transport in January 1993. It concluded that 'the regulatory reforms contained in the *NTA, 1987* [had] been successful in achieving their established objectives' (Canada 1993, vol. 1, 18). Significantly, however, the commission's main recommendation was for further withdrawal of the federal government from direct management of the transportation sector and from the business of balancing economic interests through regulation. The commissioners wrote that, in contrast to the past, regulation of the transport sector was no longer 'intended as an instrument to protect, to develop and to balance various interests' (Canada 1993, vol. 1, 18).

Consistent with this view, the NTARC concluded that 'a fundamental reassessment of [the NTA's] tasks and operations [was] appropriate' (Canada 1993, vol. 1, 194). The commissioners advised the minister of transport to establish a review process to examine the agency's programs, organization, and financial and human resources to determine their suitability for its existing and recommended mandate and to assess the extent to which the agency employed the most appropriate, efficient, and cost-effective methods in meeting its objectives. The suggestion from the NTARC was clear: the ever-shrinking role for regulation ought to be reflected in regulatory structures.

A number of other developments had also taken place since 1987 that ensured that the NTA would be lightened of its remaining regulatory burdens. The old public utility paradigm had been superseded in the eyes of many policy makers and key segments of industry by a global competitiveness and service-based paradigm. The gradual embedding of a market philosophy in the regulatory regime had led to a major restructuring of both the shipper and rail sectors. In the latter instance, concerns began to surface in the 1990s about the extent to which the remaining constraints on carriers' freedom to move threatened their financial viability. Outside the immediate regulatory arena, a transformation was underway in thinking about the public sector. Managerialist-inspired ideas about regulatory reform reasserted the old politics-administration dichotomy and staked a strong claim on behalf of elected officials for controlling the policy levers of government, leaving regulators with strictly administrative functions.[21]

The minister of transport, Doug Young, responded by introducing a package of amendments to the 1987 National Transportation Act and the Railway Act in March 1996. Bill C-14 received quick parliamentary approval and the re-named Canada Transportation Act took effect on Canada Day of the same year.[22] The Act replaced the NTA with a new Canadian Transportation Agency (CTA). The CTA's role and mandate exemplify policing regulation. On both the rail and air sides of the regulator's jurisdiction, the retreat from planning regulation is now essentially complete.

Mandate

The statement of national transportation policy remains relatively intact in the Canada Transportation Act. The new legislation does, however, update the statement's language to take into account changes in the underlying paradigms for transport policy and regulation. Section 5 of the Act declares that the objective for Canada's transportation system is 'a safe, economic, efficient and adequate network of viable and effective transportation services.'

The major development in the 1996 Canada Transportation Act is the even more pared down role it creates for the regulator. The focus of the agency remains on its core quasi-judicial functions (i.e., mediation and final offer arbitration). In some areas, the NTA's limited role in regulation continues. The agency is mandated, as was the NTA, to adjudicate licensing disputes in the air sector, to set regulated rail rates, and to determine the location of rail lines and crossings and rail level of services obligations. The Canada Transportation Act also continues the NTA role of administering the fitness tests for both air and rail.

In other areas, the CTA's regulatory responsibilities are greatly reduced compared to those of its predecessor. The new agency no longer has authority to review proposed mergers between transportation companies, to control entry to the Northern air market, or to review confidential railways contracts or tariffs.[23] The CTA also has no investigation or inquiry powers that it can activate on its own motion and then use as a basis for ordering parties to take certain actions.

In other ways, too, the CTA is anything but a government in miniature. The agency has lost its role as administrator of the Western Grain Transportation Act subsidy program. Moreover, ministerial announcements and documentation from the CTA itself regularly stress that the 'renewed' agency is a policy taker and will simply implement and interpret Canada's transportation policy.[24] This latter point is developed more fully below.

Structure

The CTA is a shell of its former self from an organizational point of view. The agency's board consists of just seven full-time members and a maximum of three temporary members.[25] There is no requirement for regional representation, nor does the CTA maintain regional offices.

The contrast between the CTA and its predecessors is perhaps most striking with regard to the size of its staff. The CTA operates with 200 person years, less than the CTC enjoyed at its inception. The number of person years is expected to fall still further as the agency settles into its new role and becomes more adept at using the management tools at its disposal (e.g., cost recovery).[26]

Regulatory Role

As noted above, the CTA has been relieved of the wide scope of regulatory powers enjoyed by the CTC and, to a much lesser degree, the NTA. The change to a policing role is most pronounced on the rail side, where the last vestiges of a proactive promoting role have disappeared. The 1987 National Transportation Act had deregulated most prices in the rail sector but retained important restrictions on rail rationalization. This incongruity was resolved through the 1996 package of amendments. Sections 140–6 of the new legislation permit uneconomic lines to be taken over by new owners or operators, for instance through their transference to a short-line operator. The regulatory incentives under the old system had instead encouraged the discontinuance of service when a line was uneconomic.

The agency's role in regulating the rail sector is confined in the post-1996 period to the Canada Transportation Act's provisions regarding competitive access (i.e., dispute resolution, competitive line rates, and interswitching). Even here, however, the agency's wings have been clipped. The 1996 amendments provide far greater direction to the agency about how the provisions should be implemented, for example by setting out, in subsection 27(2), a 'substantial harm' test.

On the air side, a policing role for the regulator has been confirmed. The 1996 Canada Transportation Act deregulated the previously protected Northern area and the agency's role is therefore minimal at best. The only significant function that remains with the agency is consumer protection. The latter flows from sections 59, 60, and 61 of the Act, relating to the sale of tickets, minimum financial requirements to obtain a domestic licence, and carriers' statutory obligations to disclose the true operator of an air service, respectively.

In both the air and rail sectors, then, the CTA is a true policing regulator. A small condition applies to this characterization. The 1996 Act created a new area for regulatory activity for the agency. This is to ensure that there are no 'undue obstacles to the mobility of persons with disabilities' in relation to all federally regulated modes of transportation and facilities.[27] To date, the CTA has discharged this added responsibility mainly through the issuance of codes of practice and other soft regulatory techniques.[28]

It is worth noting that Canada's transport regulator has become not just a police officer but also a regulatory manager in the post-1996 period. The 1996 Act introduces the concept of fixed timelines for agency decision making. The agency must normally render decisions within 120 days.[29] The other managerial dimension of the CTA's regulatory activities is cost recovery. Under section 34 of the Act, the agency is entitled to cost recovery on most matters brought before it, including licensing fees and licence renewal or amendment fees.

Policy Role

Perhaps the principal idea underlying the Canada Transportation Act, 1996 is that setting transportation policy is a job for the minister of transport and for government more generally. The Act wholly returns responsibility for making determinations about the public interest in the rail and air sectors to the minister and Transport Canada. This is consistent with – and indeed reinforces – the larger strategy at Transport Canada to return to core activities in the wake of the early 1990s federal government wide program review exercise.

As observed earlier in the chapter, the 1987 National Transportation Act remedied a gaping hole in the CTC-centred regulatory regime, by subjecting the regulator's decision-making authority to binding policy directives issued by the governor-in-council. This provision continues in the 1996 Act. Moreover, the Canada Transportation Act removes the agency's power to investigate at its own motion. This means that there is even less room for the agency to be a significant policy actor. Nonetheless, it must be noted that, at the working level, there continues to be close collaboration between the regulator and Transport Canada at all stages of the policy process.[30]

The new division of work between the agency, as policy taker, and Transport Canada, as policy maker, resonates with current public management theory. The post-1996 model for the regulatory regime is based on a portfolio- and systemwide view of the transport policy domain. Rather than concentrating on regulatory functions alone and in isolation from the other levers through which the federal government can influence the transportation sector, the new approach considers the policy domain writ large. Sets of functions, with the attendant responsibilities and accountabilities, have been assigned to organizational actors in accordance with the belief that policy making is properly in the hands of elected ministers and their departments, not appointed collective boards. The second guiding principle in the post-1996 period is that administration of a regulatory regime, no matter how narrow the scope of that regime, is separate and distinct from the task of designing the regulatory regime and the broader policy context of which it is part.

Structure of the Policy Community

The array of political actors surrounding Canada's air and rail regulator continues to expand in the post-1996 period. Expansion has been especially pronounced on the rail side, where new sets of interests have emerged within the shipping community. A gradual differentiation of small and large shippers is well underway as we near the end of the 1990s. Early signs of this development were evident in the House of Commons Standing Committee on Transport's hearings on Bill C-101 (which was later to become C-14).[31] The politics of rail regulation have also become more complex, with the emergence of a nascent short-line industry in Canada.[32]

Other interests are likely to come to the fore as well. On both the air and rail sides, there may be more opportunity in the post-1996 regulatory regime for consumer interests to have influence, not only with the regulator but also with carriers. Moreover, with the new policy leadership role assigned to Transport Canada, we might expect to see a higher profile for other federal departments in the policy community, if only because of the working linkages they have with Transport.

The structure of the transport policy community has been overhauled in the 1990s. If there is a government in miniature in the regulatory regime, it is Transport Canada rather than the CTA. From its origins as an aggressive, proactive planning regulator and its middle years as the wielder of significant tools for promoting regulation, the agency has been recast as the policer of Canada's rail and air sectors.

Conclusions

This chapter has tracked the evolution of Canada's federal transport regulator from the creation of the Canadian Transport Commission in 1967 through to the establishment of the Canadian Transportation Agency in the summer of 1997. The 1967–97 period has been characterized as a three-decade long struggle over the nature and scope of rail and air regulation and the role of the federal regulatory body. There are striking parallels with the *real* Thirty Years' War, a battle which engaged most of Europe between 1618 and 1648 and ended with the signing of the Treaty of Westphalia.

The Thirty Years' War began when the future emperor of the Holy Roman Empire, Ferdinand II, attempted to impose a system of regulation on his domains. The regulatory regime in this case was religious based – Roman Catholicism – rather than air and rail regulation. As was the case with transport regulation in Canada, however, the ensuing battle in Europe was fought by various actors, for various reasons, including territorial and commercial rivalries. Rousseau wrote in 1761 that the key issue in the Thirty Years' War was finding the appropriate balance of power. As this chapter has demonstrated, the same can be said for the 1967–97 period in Canadian air and rail regulation.

Moreover, neither the Thirty Years' War nor the 1967–97 period ended with the settling of all outstanding problems. It is open to question whether the recasting of Canada's federal transport regulator over the past thirty years is 'the outstanding example in history of meaningless conflict,' as the British historian C.V. Wedgwood described the Thirty Years' War in a classic book published in 1938. The past three decades of federal air and rail regulation have been anything but a period of meaningless conflict. The changes during that time have reflected an important evolution in the goals ascribed to regulation and the role of the federal regulator. At least for those interested in the emergence and subsequent maturing of the Canadian regulatory state, the history of the CTC, the NTA, and the CTA offers manifold opportunities for lesson drawing, especially in a comparative context.

NOTES

1 R.S.C. 1970, c. N-17, as amended.
2 S.C. 1992, c. 21.
3 S.C. 1996, c. 10.
4 Ibid., s. 5.
5 R.S.C. 1970, c. R-2.
6 R.S.C. 1970, c. A-3.
7 R.S.C. 1970, c. M-3.
8 Railway Act, s. 262(1).
9 Ibid., s. 262(3).
10 Ibid., s. 225(1).
11 National Transportation Act, 1967, s. 64(1).

12 The potential for collision diminished in 1970 with the creation of the Canadian Transportation Development Agency. The CTDA, funded by the federal Department of Transport, assumed many of the CTC's research responsibilities.
13 National Transportation Act, 1987, s. 76.
14 The designated area was defined in s. 27(1) of the Act, and the NTA had authority to pass regulations applicable to this area as per s. 102.
15 National Transportation Act, 1987, ss. 134–43.
16 Ibid., s. 152.
17 Ibid., ss. 46–57.
18 Ibid., s. 27.
19 Ibid., ss. 59–63.
20 Based on confidential interviews conducted by the author during the course of work for the NTRAC.
21 On the rise of managerialism, see Aucoin (1990), Hood and Dunleavy (1994), Pollitt (1988), and Savoie (1994).
22 Bill C-14 had been introduced originally as Bill C-101, in the Thirty-Fifth Parliament, and was virtually identical.
23 The loss of jurisdiction covers other modes as well (e.g., licensing of interprovincial bus and truck companies, commodity pipelines, and carrier entry into northern marine resupply markets).
24 See Canada (1995) as well as the Notes on Controversial Issues prepared by the NTA for the House of Commons Standing Committee on Transport in its hearings on Bill C-14 (available through the CTA's website on the Internet). The mission statement of the CTA also focuses on 'administ[ering] transportation legislation and government policies.' The view that the CTA is, for all intents and purposes, a policy taker was confirmed in a number of confidential interviews conducted by the author.
25 Canada Transportation Act, 1996, ss. 7–9.
26 Confidential interviews.
27 Canada Transportation Act, 1996, Part V.
28 See, e.g., Code of Practice: Aircraft Accessibility, issued by the CTA in November 1996.
29 Canada Transportation Act, 1996, s. 29.
30 Confidential interviews.
31 It was made evident, for example, that Canada's small shippers were increasingly aggressive in their pursuit of niche markets.
32 The short-line industry was examined by the NTARC in 1992–3 (see vol. 2, 177–9). The industry includes new entrants such as the Central Western Railway (in Alberta), Rail Tex (which operates short-line services in Ontario and Nova Scotia), and Algoma Central Railway (which operates in northern Ontario).

REFERENCES

Armstrong, Christopher, and H.V. Nelles. 1986. *Monopoly's Moment: The Organization and Regulation of Canada's Utilities, 1830–1930*. Philadelphia: Temple University Press.

Aucoin, Peter. 1990. Administrative Reform in Public Management: Paradigms, Principles, Paradoxes and Pendulums. *Governance* 3, no. 2 (April): 115–37.

Axworthy, Lloyd. 1984. *New Canadian Air Policy*. Ottawa: Department of Transport.

Baldwin, John R. 1989. *Regulatory Failure and Renewal: The Evolution of the Natural Monopoly Contract*. Ottawa: Economic Council of Canada.

Canada. 1993. National Transportation Act Review Commission. *Competition in Transportation: Policy and Legislation in Review*, vols. 1 and 2. Ottawa: Minister of Supply and Services.

Canada. 1988. National Transportation Agency. *Annual Review*. Ottawa: Minister of Supply and Services.

Canada. 1986. Task Force on Program Review. Study Team on Regulatory Agencies. *Regulatory Agencies*. Ottawa: Minister of Supply and Services.

Canada. 1995. Transport Canada. 1995. *The Canada Transportation Act*. Ottawa: Minister of Supply and Services.

Cruikshank, Ken. 1991. *Close Ties: Railways, Government and the Board of Railway Commissioners*. Montreal: McGill-Queen's University Press.

Eisner, M.A., 1993. *Regulatory Politics in Transition*. Baltimore: Johns Hopkins University Press.

Hill, Margaret M. 1988. Freedom to Move: Explaining the Decision to Deregulate Canadian Air and Rail Transportation. Unpublished research paper, School of Public Administration, Carleton University.

– 1994. The Choice of Mode for Regulation: A Case Study of the Federal Pesticide Registration Review, 1988–1992. Unpublished PhD thesis, Carleton University.

Hodgetts, J.E. 1973. *The Canadian Public Service: A Physiology of Government*. Toronto: University of Toronto Press.

Hood, C., and P. Dunleavy. 1994. From Old Public Administration to New Public Management. *Public Money and Management* 14, no. 3 (July-Sept.): 9–16.

Janisch, Hudson N. 1978. *The Regulatory Process of the Canadian Transport Commission*. Ottawa: Law Reform Commission of Canada.

– 1979. Policy Making in Regulation: Towards a New Definition of the Status of Independent Regulatory Agencies in Canada. *Osgoode Hall Law Journal* 17, no. 1: 46–106.

Langford, John. 1976. *Transport in Transition*. Montreal: McGill-Queen's University Press.

Law Reform Commission of Canada. 1980. *Independent Administrative Agencies.* Working Paper No. 25. Ottawa: Minister of Supply and Services.

Lowi, Theodore J. 1979. *The End of Liberalism: The Second Republic of the United States.* 2nd ed. New York: W.W. Norton.

Mazankowski, Don. 1985. *Freedom to Move: A Framework for Transportation Reform.* Ottawa: Minister of Supply and Services.

– 1986. *Freedom to Move: The Legislation.* Ottawa: Transport Canada.

McLean, S.J. 1902. Reports upon Railway Commissions, Railway Rate Grievances and Regulative Legislation. In Canada, *Sessional Papers*, Sessional Paper 20A.

Mullan, David J. 1985. Administrative Tribunals: Their Evolution in Canada from 1945 to 1984. In Ivan Bernier and Andrée Lajoie, eds., *Regulations, Crown Corporations and Administrative Tribunals.* Toronto: University of Toronto Press.

Pollitt, Christopher. 1988. *Managerialism and the Public Service: The Anglo-American Experience.* Oxford: Basil Blackwell.

Reschenthaler, G.B., and B. Roberts, eds. 1979. *Perspectives on Canadian Airline Regulation.* Montreal: Institute for Research on Public Policy.

Savoie, Donald J. 1994. *Thatcher, Reagan, Mulroney: In Search of a New Bureaucracy.* Toronto: University of Toronto Press.

Schultz, Richard J. 1979. *Federalism and the Regulatory Process.* Montreal: Institute for Research on Public Policy.

– 1982. Regulatory Agencies and the Dilemmas of Delegation. In O.P. Dwivedi, ed. *The Administrative State in Canada.* Toronto: University of Toronto Press.

– 1988. Regulating Conservatively: The Mulroney Record 1984–88. In Andrew B. Gollner and Daniel Salee, eds., *Canada Under Mulroney.* Montreal: Véhicule Press.

– 1995. Paradigm Lost: Explaining the Canadian Politics of Deregulation. In C.E.S. Franks, ed., *Canada's Century: Governance in a Maturing Society.* Montreal: McGill-Queen's University Press.

Schultz, Richard J., and Alan Alexandroff. 1985. *Economic Regulation and the Federal System.* Toronto: University of Toronto Press.

Schultz, Richard J., and G. Bruce Doern. 1998. No Longer 'Governments in Miniature': Canadian Sectoral Regulatory Institutions in a North American Context. In G. Bruce Doern and Stephen Wilks, eds., *Changing Regulatory Institutions in Britain and North America.* Toronto: University of Toronto Press.

Thomas, Paul G. 1984. Administrative Law Reform: Legal Versus Political Controls on Administrative Discretion. *Canadian Public Administration* 27: 120–8.

Vandervort, Lucinda. 1979. *Political Control of Administrative Agencies.* Ottawa: Minister of Supply and Services.

4

Moved Out and Moving On:
The National Energy Board as a
Reinvented Regulatory Agency

G. BRUCE DOERN

The National Energy Board (NEB) has quite literally 'moved out' and 'moved on' from its regulatory roots. It moved out and away from Ottawa to the oil patch heartland of Calgary in 1991, a movement of considerable distance geographically but arguably even greater in terms of its impact on organizational culture. It is moving on as well, not only in its full acceptance of deregulated commodity markets and flexible, market-sensitive regulatory approaches, but also in its institutional tilt toward enhanced environmental and health and safety roles. In the terminology of this book, it is still at its core a Regime I regulatory body, because energy facilities still exhibit significant (though reduced) monopoly features, but it has also taken on Regime II regulatory functions.

While transformation is the central theme of this chapter, there is also evidence of stability and of a return to the way in which the NEB was viewed in its earliest days from 1959 on, which was badly disrupted in the conflictual 'energy crisis' years of the late 1970s and early eighties. First, it has had leadership stability since 1985, in the person of Roland Priddle, a consummate non-political energy expert and professional. Second, the NEB is seen, in the relative political calm of deregulated oil and gas markets, as a regulator of technical competence and minimal politics. And third, its status as the centre of energy expertise in the federal government has in many respects been restored, not only by its own competence but also by the major downsizing of the lead federal energy department, National Resources Canada (Doern 1995).

There are many potential ways of examining the transformation of sectoral regulatory bodies such as the NEB. The account of the CRTC provided in Chapter 2 focuses on the issue of the preservation of policy powers by the CRTC in relation to its home departments and the cabinet. The analysis of the CTC, NTA, and CTA in Chapter 3 utilizes the Schultz and Alexandroff 'planning, promoting, and policing' framework to trace thirty years of change in the transportation sector. To complement those approaches, the focus in this chapter is on the NEB as a regulatory body itself, including changes in its basic organizational culture, the nature of its regulatory processes, and its acquisition of newer framework regulatory roles in the environmental and safety fields.

The chapter is organized into four parts. First, the political-economic imperatives of Canadian energy regulation writ large, and of earlier eras in the NEB's history, are reviewed. The second section highlights the key features of the current NEB mandate and its organizational transformation prior to and after its move to Calgary. Third, the operation of the NEB's reinvented incentive-based regulation is examined mainly through exploring how the monopoly aspects of energy regulation in the pipeline sector have been altered through the adoption of a more flexible negotiated 'settlement process,' but also through a brief discussion of how the export review function has been liberalized and market tested. Finally, we look at key features of the NEB's environmental and safety mandates.

Political-Economic Imperatives and NEB History

The regulation of energy in Canada is a function of four political-economic imperatives which, in the 1990s, are joined increasingly by a fifth (Canada 1988; McDougall 1982; Bregha 1980). The four imperatives that have prevailed over all of Canada's post-war energy development are: a rich and diverse energy endowment of oil and gas, hydro-electric, coal, and nuclear fuels; Canadian dependence on American continental markets to make feasible most major energy developments; divided constitutional jurisdiction over energy matters between the federal and provincial governments, with significant resource ownership powers residing in the hands of the latter; and the pan-Canadian spatial reality of energy resources in regions distant from consumer population centres, triggering not only transportation problems but also entrenched political-economic divisions among Canada's regions – especially between the producer regions of western Canada and the heavily populated consumer regions of Ontario and Quebec. The fifth imperative, present in the past but more evident in the 1990s, is the desire for a better marriage between energy and the environment.

The broad evolution of the National Energy Board can also be described in relation to three basic periods of energy development since the Second World War: 1945 to 1972, 1973 to 1983, and 1984 to the present (Lucas 1977, 1978; McDougall 1982; Doern and Toner 1985; Butt 1986). These periods correspond roughly to different levels of reliance on markets versus state intervention to influence the pace and nature of energy and resource development. The first and last periods have been very market oriented, while the middle period, greatly influenced by the two world oil crises of 1973 and 1979–80, witnessed a surge of government intervention, regulatory and otherwise. Each period can also be seen as embracing the emergence of a new 'ascending' or dominant fuel (from coal and hydro to oil and nuclear power to natural gas). But cumulatively a situation has evolved in which there are currently more economic opportunities for interfuel substitution in industrial production and consumer use (Canada 1988, Vollans 1995).

The NEB was established in 1959, largely to advise the government on broad energy matters (there was no federal energy department as such at that time) and to regulate oil and gas pipelines and the export of oil, gas, and electricity. Nuclear power is regulated by the Atomic Energy Control Board (Doern 1977). The NEB emerged as the energy industry was becoming more national in nature, in that west-to-east pipelines were being planned or built, but Canada-U.S. issues and markets were also relevant. Thus, as a sectoral regulator, the NEB was concerned with public interest regulation of monopoly pipeline carriers but also with the level of exports (and imports) of oil and gas in the longer-term national interest (Lucas 1977 1978).

National energy regulation almost from the outset was multifunctional in that it had both to police a monopoly pipeline sector and to plan energy expansion. Indeed, by the time there was an acknowledged need for a National Energy Board, energy issues had become highly politicized as a result of a series of conflicts arising from federal-provincial and Canada-U.S. relationships, particularly regarding the building of the TransCanada Pipeline. In particular, industrywide issues, such as long- and short-term domestic supply and foreign exports, rather than firm-specific actions, were the primary concern.

The NEB's primary function from the beginning was to be a sectoral planner that would use its powers to regulate interprovincial pipeline construction and especially the levels of exports of oil, natural gas, and electricity in order to protect Canada's long-term energy needs. The board, because of the limited policy guidance in its authorizing statute, was expected to become the primary draftsman of Canadian energy policy. Underscoring this responsibility, and establishing the precedent that would shortly be followed in the transportation and broadcasting sectors, the NEB was made the federal government's primary policy adviser. It was mandated to monitor the current and future supply of and demand for Canada's major energy commodities and to recommend to its minister such measures that it considered necessary or advisable in the public interest for the control, supervision, conservation, use, marketing, and development of energy and sources of energy.

It is perhaps not surprising that the first disputes over the roles and powers of independent agencies should arise with respect to the youngest agency, the National Energy Board. This agency had no institutional history of either independence or centrality of function compared to its counterparts in the transportation and communications sectors that could have protected it from the challenges it confronted very early in its operation.

Within a few years of its creation in 1959, the NEB emerged as a powerful, independent regulatory body. In the words of its second chair, the NEB was perceived to be 'the smallest shop with the biggest clout in town' (quoted in Dewar (1980), 30. In only its first decade of operation the NEB appeared to have successfully carved out an exclusive policy and regulatory space, an outcome that reflected both its power and technical competence to make regulatory decisions and its role as the primary policy adviser to the federal government on energy issues. One measure of its power was the fact that it quickly developed as a closed regulatory shop that 'decided energy issues almost exclusively in response to the representations of the provincial governments and private companies which participated in its proceedings' (Doern and Toner 1985, 83). Other interested parties had greater difficulty gaining effective access and the federal government appeared to be content both with how the NEB operated and the quality of its policy advice.

Although the ramifications did not appear to be appreciated at the time, the decline of the NEB as the primary regulatory and policy actor within the federal government can be dated from 1966, for it was in this year that a bureaucratic rival and eventual successor emerged. The rival was the Department of Energy, Mines and Resources (EMR), a department that brought together a number of technical units within Ottawa but, more importantly, was assigned a policy adviser role to its minister on energy issues. In the first five years of its existence, EMR did not appear to pose much of a challenge to the dominance of the NEB, in part because of its limited policy expertise. One sign of the potential conflicts emerged in the early 1970s, however, when the department began to lobby the government to restrict funds for the NEB for policy advisory personnel on the grounds that this was unnecessary duplication (Doern and Toner 1985).

Within a decade, however, the NEB had been displaced as the primary bureaucratic agent in both the regulatory and policy sectors. One factor was the growing concern, played upon by officials within EMR, that the NEB was too close to the industry and consequently Ottawa was too dependent on industry information, which was channelled through the NEB (Doern and Toner 1985, 85). Another was that the quality and indeed the accuracy of the NEB's advice

and information were suspect. The energy crises, international and intergovernmental, that ensued after the 1973 oil embargo brought the dissatisfaction with
the NEB to a head.

Within less than five years not only had the Department of Energy, Mines
and Resources displaced the NEB as primary policy adviser but the government had assumed some of the NEB's regulatory functions for itself and hived
off other responsibilities for other agencies (Doern and Toner 1985, ch. 11;
Desveaux 1995). In addition, rather than delegating new responsibilities to the
NEB as a consequence of the energy conflicts, the federal government opted
instead to create new regulatory instruments. In 1973, for example, using its
power to approve NEB regulations, the cabinet transferred the power to issue
export permits from the NEB to the cabinet itself, but the board was still
required to advise on the level of export price for gas and oil. In 1975 Parliament passed the Petroleum Administration Act, which gave cabinet, not the
NEB, the power to regulate oil and gas prices. The same year saw the creation
of a state-owned oil company, Petro-Canada, which was the result of governmental dissatisfaction with its existing 'windows' on the industry, especially
the NEB, which now appeared to be, if not captured by, then far too sympathetic to the industry.

The displacement of the National Energy Board as primary regulatory agency
and policy adviser was completed in 1980, with the announcement of the
National Energy Policy (NEP). Although the NEB had lost its monopoly status
as policy adviser, it retained some status and role in the policy process throughout
the 1970s. In 1980, however, it was completely isolated and excluded from the
development of the NEP. Neither its chair, board members, nor its staff were
consulted by the political and bureaucratic officials in the drafting of the NEP,
despite the fact that this was the most comprehensive set of regulatory initiatives in Canadian energy history. It was only with the demise of the NEP and
the deregulation of oil and gas under the Mulroney Conservative government
from 1984 on that the NEB re-established itself at the heart of the Canadian
energy regulatory regime.

The NEB Mandate and a Profile of Key Changes since 1985

Since our concern in this chapter is with recent regulatory evolution, it is best
to sketch out the current mandate and dynamics of the NEB's role and then to
trace how and why it has changed from its earlier roles.

The NEB is an independent federal regulatory tribunal that reports to Parliament through the minister of natural resources. The up to nine-member board
(there are currently seven members) functions as a court of record and thus has

powers regarding attendance at hearings, the swearing in and examination of witnesses, the production and inspection of documents, and the enforcement of its orders. The NEB's regulatory decisions and the reasons for them are issued as public documents. Under the National Energy Board Act the NEB grants authorizations for:

- the construction and operation of interprovincial and international oil and gas and commodity pipelines, international power lines, and designated interprovincial power lines;
- the setting of tolls and tariffs for oil and gas pipelines under its jurisdiction;
- the export of oil, natural gas, and electricity; and
- the import of natural gas (National Energy Board 1994).

The NEB also recently acquired powers regarding the regulation of oil and gas exploration and production activities on Canada's federally owned frontier lands (the Canada Oil and Gas Operations Act), outside of areas subject to federal-provincial accords. The board also has a duty to monitor the current and future supply of and demand for Canada's major energy commodities. Finally, the NEB acts in an advisory function and may, on its own initiative, hold inquiries and conduct studies on specific energy matters and prepare reports for the information of Parliament, the federal government, and the general public.

At the core of its business are the NEB's approximately 750 applications per year from energy firms. The great majority of these seek routine orders for export licences, pipeline tolls, and certificates for construction of new facilities. But larger pipeline expansions are also included. Larger projects typically involve an oral public hearing but the majority of total projects are governed by internal processes of examination or written public proceedings (National Energy Board 1996).

In the latter years of the 1990s, the NEB describes itself in ways that reflect the new realities of economic deregulation, expanded social regulation, budgetary cutbacks, and internationalization and globalization. For example, in early 1995 it described itself as:

- 'a leader in the implementation of policies which now provide a comprehensive framework for the free functioning of oil and gas markets, nationally and internationally';
- an efficient and economical regulator whose staff has 'declined from about 550 (in 1985) to 282' (in 1994) and whose expenditures have been reduced by about 14 per cent in the same period;

- a regulator that distinguishes between the 'deregulation of markets for energy and proper regulation of energy facilities,' in the latter case involving 'considerations of the natural environment (and) human safety';
- a regulator which, in 1994, carried out 'environmental assessments' of more than 160 projects';
- a regulator that has improved ability and authority to take 'immediate action when the safety of company employees and the public is at risk' (this includes the designation of its own officers as designated inspection officers);
- a regulator committed to the introduction of electronic filing for its key regulatory activities, with expected further savings and efficiency for the NEB and for the firms involved;
- a regulator whose approximately $34 million cost of operation is now 85 per cent paid for by cost-recovery charges from industry, whereas its work had previously been entirely paid for from budgetary appropriations (National Energy Board 1994a, 1–5).

In Calgary it has functioned in a close daily interaction with the heart of the Canadian oil and gas industry. International and regional energy regulation has also been altered by the provisions of the Canada–U.S. Free Trade Agreement and NAFTA. The free trade deals made it more difficult for federal energy authorities to interfere with the free flow of energy commodities across the Canada–U.S. border, as they had in the energy crisis era, especially from 1980 to 1984, under the federal Liberal's interventionist National Energy Program (NEP) (Doern and Tomlin 1991).

Each of the features of the NEB and its milieu described above can be contrasted to its earlier phases of operation as a regulator. First, in 1985 the policy and regulatory approach was changed to facilitate the deregulation of gas. The changes allowed more direct buy-sell relationships between gas producers and gas users, with the consequent weakening of some of the previous monopoly powers of the pipelines and distribution companies. Gas deregulation eventually extended to the ending of the NEB-administered rule that had established surplus reserve tests for exports. These provisions had required a twenty-five to thirty-year domestic supply cushion before exports were allowed (Lucas 1978; Doern and Toner 1985; Canada 1988).

As the NEB issues its export licences and orders, it must take into account section 118 of the National Energy Board Act, which requires the board to satisfy itself that the quantity of gas or oil to be exported does not exceed the surplus remaining, after due allowance has been made for the reasonably foreseeable requirements for use in Canada. As mentioned above, export licences and orders are a key part of the NEB's business and thus there is little doubt that this aspect of its work has been deregulated relative to its earlier history (Watkins 1991).

With respect to overall regulatory efficiency, there is no doubt that the NEB is a leaner institution, both in terms of its staff composition and in its approach to other regulatory matters and procedures. Following a discussion of 'industrial irritants' in 1987, the NEB gradually moved toward a process of 'negotiated settlements' for resolving disputes over tolls between pipeline companies and their customers (see below). NEB membership was reduced from thirteen to its current size of a maximum of nine board members. The number of economists employed by the board has been significantly reduced, in part because there is less need for 'cost-benefit' analysis of export applications. Indeed, there was concern that the mere fact that such analysis was being done would be evidence that the NEB was not practising proper free market approaches.

Both the relocation of the NEB to Calgary in 1991 and the funding of the board through cost recovery are seen by many within the board and in the industry as positive, promarket steps. An NEB staff member in Calgary is likely to have lunch with an energy businessperson rather than another bureaucrat, as was the more probable case in an Ottawa location. Cost-recovery funding has resulted in the need for annual discussions to discuss the level of charges. This has produced, because of the kinds of information shared, a greater in-depth appreciation by both regulator and business of each other's practical world.

There is also a partial link between the Calgary move and the eventual 1996 restructuring of the internal organization of the NEB from ten functional branches to five 'process-based business units' (National Energy Board 1997b). When the move to Calgary occurred, the NEB was being reduced in size but it also lost a large number of staff who decided not to move. This cadre of staff was largely replaced by Alberta-based persons, who brought with them the business-oriented culture of the Calgary milieu. When the senior management of the NEB decided in 1994 to review the NEB's organization and strategic objectives it faced a barrage of criticism about the organization's style of management. The 1994 review was conducted on a broad, participative basis through the ranks of the staff and it brought out a strong call for a different, less hierarchical, way of doing things. Other organizational modes were canvassed, which ranged from awareness of the general 'reinvented government' modes of restructuring service delivery (Doern 1994) to practical examples of change being put in place in some U.S. state energy regulatory bodies and also in the Alberta government.

The resulting change is centred on a leadership team approach that includes, in addition to the chair, vice-chair, and executive director, five 'business leaders' for corporate services, information management, commodities, applications, and operations (including environment and safety areas of the mandate). What this means in practical terms is that knowledge experts such as economists, environmental experts, engineers, and financial staff are no longer lodged in separate functional branches, but are dispersed throughout the organization in teams. Some of the teams then focus on key regulated firms. For example, there are teams for TransCanada Pipelines (by far the largest regulated gas pipeline) and for other large pipelines. The environmental aspects of this team approach are discussed below, but in the meantime it is important to note that the NEB was altered by its move to Alberta and by related developments.

The 'flip side' of this deregulatory picture is found in the evident addition to the NEB of new framework or social regulatory tasks in both the environmental and occupational health and safety fields (see below). Indeed, in the jargon of the new NEB 'business plans,' this is seen as one of the NEB's growing 'lines of business.' In the 1970s and 1980s, the NEB was not known as a bastion of proenvironmentalism (Bregha 1980). It had always been concerned with the safety of energy facilities but the NEB, along with other energy players, had also fought environmentalists tooth and nail in some extremely high-profile projects, both in the southern reaches of Canada and in the frontier areas of the north (Bregha 1980; Doern and Toner 1985).

The NEB as Incentive Regulator: Negotiated Pipeline-toll Incentive Settlements and Export Review Processes

The NEB has gradually moved its system of regulation toward an incentive-based system and also toward the use of a negotiated settlement process. The latter process is used beyond the pipeline toll area of regulation and, in general, is intended to provide an alternative to the adversarial process that otherwise flows from the NEB's statutory provisions and role as a court of record. An adversarial public hearing process was commonly used until the mid-1980s. In the pipeline monopoly sector, the traditional mode of regulation was a 'cost of service' concept, which is similar to 'rate of return' regulation. The process required the submission of elaborate cost information to the NEB and expensive hearing processes. Under such a system there was little incentive for pipeline companies to economize on costs, because cost savings were passed on to shippers. Under incentive regulation achieved through negotiated settlements (which typically are for four or five years' duration) there are incentives to be more efficient, since the gains are shared between the pipeline company and shippers.

Much depends then on the nature of the settlement process, and on the role of the NEB. In 1988 the NEB issued guidelines on the settlement process, which provided that all interested parties had to be involved in the settlement negotiation and that the agreed settlement had to be unanimous. The concern of the NEB was that these processes could not usurp the NEB's overall public interest role. The process did not involve any provision for mediation by NEB staff or outside mediators. NEB staff were present at a couple of the first processes but the NEB felt that this practice had to stop in case there were later court challenges to an agreement or a failure to achieve an agreement and later action was needed by the board.

The early steps to incentive regulation took time and reflected the evolution of thinking in the board and within the industry (Rochefort 1997). A 1987–8 consultation occurred on the NEB's public hearing process, where the issue of negotiated settlements was raised as an alternative to traditional regulation. Bilateral task forces composed of pipeline companies and their shippers were also meeting and were functioning in such a way that they were reducing the number of tariff issues that had to be dealt with at NEB hearings. A January 1993 workshop on incentive regulation was held and led to, among other things, a generic cost of capital hearing, which in turn led to greater regulatory efficiency and flexibility.

By 1994 the NEB was able to publish an updated set of guidelines regarding what constituted an acceptable settlement. These criteria are that:

1 all parties having an interest should have a fair opportunity to participate;
2 the board's ability and discretion to take into account any public interest considerations that may extend beyond the immediate concerns of the negotiating parties must not be fettered;
3 the settlement process must produce adequate information on the public record for the board to understand the basis for the agreement and to assess its reasonableness;
4 board staff may attend task force meetings upon invitation and solely for the purposes of information exchange and discussion of procedural matters; and
5 the board will not accept a settlement that contains provisions that are illegal, or contrary to the NEB Act (Rochefort 1997, 3).

Several negotiated incentive settlements have been successfully concluded which, board staff argue, have met the initial tests of producing lower toll rates, more efficiency incentives, and better agreement and consensus. Multiyear agreements have been negotiated and approved for Interprovincial Pipeline in 1995 and, in 1996, for TransCanada Pipelines, the Trans Mountain Pipe Line Company, and Trans-Northern Pipelines.

Other issues that might be raised about the settlement process fall outside the scope of this chapter. For example, once agreements have been reached and approved, the NEB cannot easily track whether the agreement is fully implemented, in part because it no longer has a post-agreement information trail. In addition, the views of shippers are hard to discern. Groups of shippers may sign agreements and thus indicate support, but smaller shippers may feel that the bilateral settlement process gives them no more de facto choice or influence than the earlier system of regulation.

While all of the above regulatory reinvention was occurring, the NEB was still dealing with a pipeline sector that was largely a monopoly. However, in the latter half of the 1990s proposals are emerging that would convert parts of the energy pipeline market into more genuine competitive markets. These would establish competitors for existing pipelines. Thus the NEB has approved Express Pipeline, an oil export pipeline, whose shareholders 'will bear the risk of under-utilization' (National Energy Board 1996, 2). As other pipelines are built the incumbent will increasingly resist the new entrants, in much the same way that Bell Canada was able to do in the telecom sector, albeit only for a few years. The likelihood is strong that re-regulation or transitional regulation will also occur in the wake of such struggles.

While the focus in this section is on the settlement process in pipeline regulation, brief mention must also be made of the processes for reviewing and approving energy exports, especially natural gas. The NEB Act requires the NEB to ensure that long-term exports of natural gas are surplus to reasonably foreseeable Canadian requirements. Oil exports are not a problem in this respect, because crude oil is only bought and sold on a short-term basis. As mentioned earlier, the political concern about security of supply was so sensitive that, prior to 1987, this aspect of the NEB's mandate was backed by the legal requirement to ensure that there were proven reserves for twenty-five years. There were several reasons for the elimination of this provision, among which was the view in western Canada that this was a subsidy cost paid by western producers to support eastern consumers and industrial users of gas.

With the Mulroney government's agreement, the NEB in 1987 moved to a market-test-and-review process (called the 'market-based procedure') to ensure long-term supply. It is important to stress that this export approval function is still anchored by the NEB's own estimating and monitoring of Canada's energy reserves. But the export licence process is now a far simpler two-step process involving assessment (in effect, the monitoring function noted above) and a challenge process. When proposed export contracts are filed publicly with the NEB, any Canadian industrial user can use the challenge process if it believes, and can demonstrate in a public hearing, that it cannot obtain the gas from a supplier on similar terms and conditions. This mechanism has not been used and thus the NEB is satisfied after ten years of gas deregulation that the market-based approach is working and is more efficient than the pre-1987 export regime (National Energy Board 1997a).

The NEB as Joint Environmental and Safety Regulator

As highlighted above, one of the key transformations of the NEB is its assumption of a greater, and more integrated, role in environmental regulation. The NEB had been considering environmental matters related to its activities prior to 1995, but in that year the Canadian Environmental Assessment Act (CEAA) took effect and provided a further legal imperative for the NEB's role (Sato 1997). The environmental assessment process of the federal government as a whole had itself been transformed, largely by court rulings that had determined that the federal 'guidelines' previously in existence were in fact lawlike in their nature (Doern and Conway 1994). As a result of the CEAA, the NEB (as a 'responsible authority' under the CEAA) has to work closely with Environment Canada's Canadian Environmental Assessment Agency to ensure that their joint required processes are efficient and avoid duplication but at the same time are effective regarding environmental assessment.

The NEB's process operates in three phases: first, an evaluation is made of potential environmental effects of proposed projects; the second phase involves the monitoring and enforcement of terms and conditions attached to the project approval; the third phase consists of continuous, longer-term monitoring of operations. The NEB's application process can involve different types and levels of review, depending on the amount of public interest and the size of the project. These reviews can include a public hearing, a written hearing, or an internal board process, with or without public involvement. A further dimension of the environmental assessment process is found in the provisions of the CEAA itself, which set out four types of assessment processes: screening, comprehensive study, mediation, and panel review. Given this array of potential processes, there has been a considerable learning curve for the NEB, affected companies, and interveners.

One of the generic institutional issues centres on the differences between quasi-judicial versus administrative approaches to regulatory decision making (Ratushny 1987). The NEB is by statute anchored to a quasi-judicial role, whereas the CEAA processes and the approaches of other departments that might be involved in a joint process are more administrative. As we have already seen above, in the discussion of the toll 'settlement process,' the NEB has evolved its own more flexible approaches, but it must always be conscious of the quasi-judicial role mandated by its statute, including the fact that its decisions may be appealed to the courts.

Since 1995, the NEB has had four proposals that required a CEAA comprehensive study report. One was subsequently suspended, but three projects (the Express Pipeline Project, the Sable Island Project, and the Alliance Pipeline project) have each proceeded in a variety of ways through to the review panel. While considerable co-operation has occurred between the NEB and Environment Canada, there are bound to be differences of view as to how to proceed in different case situations. For example, in the Express project, the NEB requested that, to avoid duplication, the CEAA provisions for 'substitution' be used. The minister of the environment 'decided that a joint panel would be more appropriate' than a single NEB process (Sato 1997, 5).

Given that there are now several new pipelines being proposed, the NEB will probably acquire more environmental business. The NEB's members have typically been engineers and technically trained persons, but one of the new appointees has more direct environmental experience as an academic and consultant and all board members are becoming more familiar with their environmental mandate, in part as a result of the length of the hearings in the cases noted above. For example, the Express hearing involved thirty-four hearing days, including eleven devoted to environmental aspects, and its panel (two NEB members and two environmental scientists) made thirty-nine recommendations (Sato 1997, 5).

A final aspect to the environmental mandate of the NEB deserves emphasis in terms of regulatory organizational culture. The restructuring of the NEB into a 'business leader' and team model of organization has resulted in the dispersal of its environmental professionals throughout other team groups. Rather than being concentrated in one functional staff advisory group, they are now found in all business groups. It is too early to judge the efficacy of this approach, but there is one aspect that warrants mention. In the larger debate on environmental and sustainable development regulation, the case has often been made that for environmental policy to succeed, all federal departments have to become their own regulators. In short, environmental issues have to be every department's business. In a broad sense that is the intended impact of the CEAA across the government, while the dispersal of the environmental professionals across the NEB business teams is the attempted institutionalization of the same concept within the board. Whether either works in practice is another subject. It should be noted, however, that the dispersal of environmental and other professionals is compensated for by the concept of 'professional leaders' in the new organization. The professional leaders (in environment, economics, engineering, and energy resources) provide a focal point and offer coaching and mentoring for members of particular disciplines.

While the focus thus far has been on environmental regulatory roles, mention must also be made of the NEB's growing safety regulation mandate. The NEB regulates approximately 40,000 kilometres of pipelines, many of which are aging. Issues surrounding stress corrosion cracking are among the problems that have had to be examined in recent years, with further regulatory vigilance needed to ensure the 'integrity of existing pipeline infrastructure' (National Energy Board 1996, 4).

Conclusions

Between 1959 and the mid-1970s the National Energy Board was a classic sectoral public utility regulator, known for its technical competence and relatively non-political nature. From the late 1970s to 1984 it was institutionally marginalized in political, policy, and regulatory terms, primarily because of the ill-fated juggernaut known as the Liberal National Energy Policy. Since 1985 the NEB has, in one sense, gone 'back to the future' by reasserting its dominance as the main centre of energy regulatory expertise in the federal government.

The NEB has also 'moved out' and 'moved on.' The move to Calgary had important effects in terms of organizational culture and milieu, although of course this move by itself does not explain the reinvented nature of the NEB as a regulatory institution. The pressures to deregulate after 1984 came from an angry industry and a supportive Conservative government with strong western Canadian cabinet representation. The NEB has also moved to incentive-based regulation, in part because of real concerns in the industry about competitive costs, but also in response to the demonstrated effect of reinvented regulation among some American energy regulators and as the result of receptivity within the NEB to the ideas both of reinvented government and incentive-based regulation. The recourse to incentive-based approaches and negotiated settlements undoubtedly has both merits and drawbacks. Some efficiency gains have been made, but questions about the accountability and transparency of the negotiated settlement process remain.

As for its acquisition of greater environmental and safety roles, the causes are also mixed. In part they are due to environmental politics which, unexpectedly, sent the issue of environmental assessment first into the courts, then into new federal law, and finally onto the lap of the NEB. Expanded safety roles are a product of the ageing of the pipeline system. Regardless of the exact mix of causes, the NEB is now both an economic and social regulator in a way that it was not in any previous decade of its history.

NOTE

I wish to thank the several NEB officials and industry spokepersons who kindly agreed to interviews for this research and some of whom also commented on earlier drafts and offered constructive suggestions.

REFERENCES

Bregha, François. 1980. *Bob Blair's Pipeline*. Toronto: Lorimer.
Butt, Roger. 1986. Regulating Deregulation: The National Energy Board and Tory Energy Policy. Unpublished research essay, School of Public Administration, Carleton University.
Canada. 1988. *Energy and Canadians into the 21st Century*. Ottawa: Minister of Supply and Services.
Desveaux, James A. 1995. *Designing Bureaucracies: Institutional Capacity and Large-Scale Problem Solving*. Stanford: Stanford University Press.
Dewar, Elaine. 1980. Groping in the Dark. *Canadian Business* (May): 13–16.
Doern, G. Bruce. 1977. *The Atomic Energy Control Board*. Ottawa: Law Reform Commission.
– ed. 1978. *The Regulatory Process in Canada*. Toronto: Macmillan.
– 1994. *The Road to Better Public Services: Progress and Constraints in Five Federal Agencies*. Montreal: C.D. Howe Institute.
– 1995. The Formation of Natural Resources Canada: New Synergies or Old Departmental Fiefdoms? Paper presented to the Workshop on the 1993 Federal Reorganization, Canadian Centre for Management Development.
Doern, G. Bruce, and Tom Conway. 1994. *The Greening of Canada: Federal Institutions and Decisions*. Toronto: University of Toronto Press.
Doern, G. Bruce, and Brian W. Tomlin. 1991. *Faith and Fear: The Free Trade Story*. Toronto: Stoddart.
Doern, G. Bruce, and Glen Toner. 1985. *The Politics of Energy*. Toronto: Methuen.
Lucas, A.R. 1977. *The National Energy Board*. Ottawa: Law Reform Commission.
– 1978. The National Energy Board. In G. Bruce Doern, ed., *The Regulatory Process in Canada*, 259–313. Toronto: Macmillan.
McDougall, John N. 1982. *Fuels and the National Policy*. Toronto: McClelland and Stewart.
National Energy Board. 1994. *Annual Report 1993*. Ottawa: National Energy Board.
– 1996. *National Energy Board Annual Report 1995*. Ottawa: National Energy Board.

- 1997a. *Long-term Canadian Natural Gas Contracts: An Update*. Ottawa: National Energy Board.
- 1997b. *Welcome to the Transformation*. Ottawa: National Energy Board.

Ratushny, Ed. 1987. What are Administrative Tribunals? The Pursuit of Uniformity in Diversity. *Canadian Public Administration* 30, no. 1: 1–13.

Rochefort, Terry. 1997. Reforming the Regulation of Canadian Pipelines. Paper presented to the Regulatory Reform Program of the Conference Board of Canada, 7 May, Calgary.

Sato, Ken. 1997. Integration of Environmental Assessment with the Regulatory Process. National Energy Board, Calgary. Presentation to CAMPUT 97, Whistler, BC.

Schultz, Richard J., and Alan Alexandroff. 1985. *Economic Regulation and the Federal System*. Toronto: University of Toronto Press.

Toner, Glen. 1986. Stardust: The Tory Energy Program. In Michael J. Prince, ed., *How Ottawa Spends 1986–87*, 119–48. Toronto: Methuen.

Vollans, Garry E. 1995. The Decline of Natural Monopolies in the Energy Sector. *Energy Studies Review* 7, no. 3: 247–61.

Watkins, G. Campbell. 1991. Deregulation and the Canadian Petroleum Industry: Adolescence or Maturity. In Walter Block and George Lermer, eds., *Breaking the Shackles: Deregulating Canadian Industry*, 215–52. Vancouver: Fraser Institute.

PART II
THE CHANGING NATURE OF FRAMEWORK
REGULATION

5

Competition Policy Institutions: What Role in the Face of Continued Sectoral Regulation?

HUDSON JANISCH

In light of the general trend over the last two decades toward greater reliance on competition in many sectors of the Canadian economy, we should have witnessed a flowering of competition policy institutions as they came into their own. This chapter seeks to explain why such a phenomenon has not occurred. In so doing, the focus will be on the adequacy and appropriateness of institutional arrangements during a period of transition. Were the competition authorities ever placed, or ever able to place themselves, in such a strategic position as would allow them to play an increasingly influential role in the past twenty years? Did other institutions, particularly old-line sectoral regulatory agencies, adapt to the changing environment with sufficient alacrity to maintain their predominance, thereby keeping the competition authorities at bay? What would be the significance of the form of the move toward greater reliance on competition? Would an incremental shift (under regulatory supervision) inevitably limit, or even prevent, any significant direct role for competition law and policy? Might there be an indirect role by way of participation in the regulatory process? Might the espousal of 'competition' by the regulators not turn the issue from being a stark choice between competition and regulation into the more subtle issue of whose form of 'competition' was to prevail? Before moving to explore these and related issues, we should first consider whether it is at all appropriate to address competition policy issues in any general re-examination of regulatory institutions.

The Threshold

Unlike economic regulation, competition law does not involve prior approval of business conduct, nor is it interested in regulating levels or quality of service, prices, or profits. Moreover, unlike regulation, it seeks to stay away from micromanagement and is not concerned with outcomes, or with who wins or loses. Indeed, the exclusive goal of competition policy is usually considered to be economic efficiency, that is to say, the achievement of competition unadorned by currently fashionable regulatory adjectives such as 'sustainable' and 'fair.'

While the primary focus of regulation (*ex ante*) and competition policy (*ex post*) are thus in theory quite different, it must be recognized that, in practice, the actual goals of competition policy and the institutions designed to implement them bring competition policy well within the ambit of regulation, broadly conceived. Thus a close look at Canada's legislation (the Competition Act 1986) reveals, for example, that it is concerned to ensure that small and medium-sized enterprises have an 'equitable' opportunity to participate in the economy. As well, considerable discretion (a hallmark of regulation) has been built into the Act itself, while implementation of competition policy has involved a perennial debate over the respective roles of compliance and enforcement, another fundamental theme in regulation.

Most importantly, a wide range of institutions are involved in competition policy, including:

- a government ministry, Industry Canada;
- lawyers from the Department of Justice, who take applications to the Competition Tribunal and prosecute criminal matters;
- courts of law dealing with criminal prosecutions and appeals from the Competition Tribunal;
- an independent statutory authority, the Director of Investigation and Research;
- an investigatory and inquiry agency, the Competition Bureau; and
- a hybrid, lay-judicial, multimember independent agency, the Competition Tribunal.

This complex mix of (in)consistent government actors inevitably raises the very sort of intractable legal, political, and institutional decisions that lie at the heart of regulation (Doern 1996, 68). And there can be no denying the importance of institutional design when even economists have come to recognize that they have to be attuned to the importance of design of policy and institutions. As Donald Hay succinctly put it, 'the appropriate design of policy and policy institutions is crucial to a successful competition policy' (Hay 1993).

The 1986 Compromise

After protracted debate, a new competition law was enacted in 1986. In essence it took the form of a compromise between business interests, which were adamantly opposed to any strengthening of competition law, and those who dismissed the existing criminal-law-based, court-enforced competition law as entirely ineffectual. As a result, there was a partial shift away from criminal to civil law and a new hybrid, judicial-lay Competition Tribunal (the tribunal) was established (Doern 1995). However, the director of investigation and research (an independent government official) was (ironically) given a monopoly on enforcement, there being no provision for private enforcement or treble damages, which could have created an incentive for non-governmental initiative. Unlike in the U.S., no strict liability, per se, offences were created, it being a central requirement of the Act that a 'substantial lessening' of competition had to be shown before a breach could be established.

For our purposes three aspects of the compromise need to be examined. First, how effective has the tribunal proven to be? Has it lived up to the expectations of its creators? Second, how has the grant of exclusive enforcement power to a government official worked out? Can a case be made for private enforcement? Would such an initiative revitalize Canadian competition law and policy? Third, and most importantly, how has the interface between competition policy and regulation been dealt with? Has the 'regulated conduct defence' inhibited more extensive application of competition law during a period of transition toward greater reliance on competition?

A Design-flawed Tribunal?

It had been widely assumed in the debate leading up to the 1986 legislative compromise that the tribunal would become the central locus of authoritative expertise in the interpretation and application of the Competition Act, especially with respect to the reviewable practice provisions governing mergers. Yet since its creation the tribunal has heard only two merger cases, four abuse of dominance/exclusive dealing cases, two refusal to deal cases, and one contested variation of a consent order. This amounts to only nine cases in ten years in which the tribunal has been called on to make an authoritative ruling on a disputed set of legal or factual issues. That there were only two merger cases is particularly striking, because this was a period characterized by a surge of mergers. Despite one of the largest merger waves in Canadian history in the late 1980s, and despite the fact that the director of investigation and research (the director) and officials at the Competition Bureau (the bureau) reviewed literally thousands of mergers, only two cases were presented to the tribunal for authoritative adjudication. By contrast, the bureau was very active in achieving negotiated remedies. In those relatively few cases in which a negotiated resolution could not be obtained, merging parties were six times more likely to abandon the transaction than to defend it in a contested proceeding before the tribunal (Campbell, Janisch, and Trebilcock 1996, 2).

The tribunal has thus become a relatively minor institutional player in the competition policy process relative to the bureau. Why has this marginalization of the tribunal occurred? An appropriate starting point for analysis must be to recognize that, whatever the initial expectations had been, the mere existence of the tribunal will not in and of itself ensure its continued use if it 'does not respond effectively to the concerns of those who can initiate proceedings be-fore it' (Grover and Quinn 1991, 230). Indeed, it would appear that the tribunal's composition and formalized procedures have caused it to operate in a fashion very similar to the courts. 'The resulting costs and delays involved in Tribunal proceedings have caused firms, and the Director, to substitute the locus of decision-making, even in difficult cases, away from the Tribunal toward the Bureau where process values such as transparency, accountability and rea-soned public decision-making are much diminished' (Campbell, Janisch, and Trebilcock 1996, 3).

An ideal regime for adjudicating 'reviewable practices' under the Competi-tion Act would minimize the aggregate of three broad categories of 'costs' (Stanbury 1992; Campbell 1993):

• Type I error costs (i.e., interfering with procompetitive transactions or conduct);
• Type II error costs (i.e., allowing anticompetitive transactions or conduct); and
• transaction costs (public or private, broadly defined).

The challenge here is that no single category of costs can be minimized without affecting the others. A focus on Type I errors will tend to increase the risk of Type II errors, and vice versa. Somewhat similarly, Type I and Type II errors could be reduced by employing a more thorough and finely tuned adju-dicative process, but only at the expense of increased transaction costs. Over time, experience may improve the ability of adjudicators and enforcement agencies to discriminate between pro- and anticompetitive activities (thereby reducing Type I and Type II errors) and to operate decision-making processes more effectively (thereby reducing transaction costs).

There is a wide variation in the level of formality involved in procedures adopted by administrative tribunals. At one end of the spectrum is a courtlike approach, characterized by extensive and formal procedures; strict rules of evidence; passive, impartial, and detached decision makers; and a heavy (or even exclusive) reliance on the adversary process. This approach might well minimize Type I and Type II errors, but the transaction costs involved will be very high. At the other end of the spectrum are to be found simplified procedures tailored to respond to particular needs; much less emphasis (perhaps even none at all) on the restrictive rules of evidence; the use of expert decision makers, who are proactive in defining issues and in requesting parties to provide relevant information; and a deliberate attenuation of the full adversarial process by way of limitation, for example, on time-consuming discoveries and protracted and unhelpful cross-examination. In general, this informal approach seeks to lower transaction costs while maintaining Type I and Type II errors at tolerable levels.

What is particularly striking with respect to the tribunal is that this very danger of too high a level of formality had been anticipated in the debate leading up to the 1986 legislative compromise, and firm steps had been taken to guard against it. Thus subsection 9(2) of the Competition Act specifically provides: 'All proceedings before the Tribunal shall be dealt with as informally and expeditiously as the circumstances and consideration of fairness permit.' As a matter of administrative law, this reference to 'fairness' is significant because it mandates a lower level of formality than that required to meet the older 'natural justice' standard. However, it has also to be recognized that the tribunal was created as a 'court of record' staffed by judges as well as lay persons and possessed of at least some of the powers of a superior court. Nevertheless, the tribunal could have chosen to give greater weight to subsection 9(2), but has instead adopted highly formalized procedures that give rise to extensive and time-consuming litigious steps comparable to those in any other contested commercial case.

A courtlike approach is not at all well suited to merger and other reviewable practice proceedings, for a variety of reasons:

- issues of credibility (the prime justification for formal procedures such as cross-examination) are not as important as documentary and expert economic industry evidence;
- the adjudicator's task is not merely to determine past events, but to apply judgment to the best available information about what is likely to happen in the future if the transaction or conduct proceeds;
- high levels of procedural protection are most appropriate where punitive measures are taken; the tribunal's powers are remedial rather than punitive; and
- merger cases are often extremely time sensitive; full natural justice procedures are neither necessary nor desirable in this type of decision making.

The fundamental cause of excessive procedural formality lies in the design of the tribunal itself. As part of the 1986 compromise, it was created as a unique, hybrid body made up of judges and lay members in an attempt to combine the benefits of judicial impartiality with economic and business expertise. Unfortunately, the balance struck in the legislation relegates the lay experts to the status of second-class citizens, in that the tribunal's chair must always be a judge, each panel must be presided over by a judicial member, and all questions of law are reserved exclusively for judicial members. In practice, judicial members have comprised the majority of the tribunal's membership throughout much of its history and all but one of the lay members have been part-time appointees. As well, the influence of the judges dominated in the initial formulation of the tribunal's rules and has continued to do so in subsequent individual decisions on procedural matters.

It has been argued that the design fault here is so profound that only the entire elimination of judicial members will suffice to both reduce unnecessary transaction costs and refocus the tribunal on substantive economic and business issues, not legal niceties (Campbell 1994). Should this not be done, then two major reforms need to be undertaken (Campbell, Janisch, and Trebilcock 1996, 12–23).

First, the judicial members' monopoly over questions of law should be eliminated, as it serves no useful purpose and invites unnecessary litigation in view of the great difficulty involved in distinguishing questions of law from mixed questions of law and fact. Moreover, any attempt to carve out questions of law for exclusive judicial scrutiny would be highly counterproductive, as questions of law that arise in the context of competition policy are likely to involve fundamental economic issues in which the involvement of expert lay members would be just as relevant as on factual matters.

Second, under the Competition Act each tribunal panel must include at least one judicial and one lay member. Although it is the lay members who are expected to bring critically important economic and business expertise to the tribunal, judicial members have formed the majority on several recent cases. The more appropriate balance would be to have two lay members on every three-member panel, and three or four on any five-member panel.

As well, moves could be undertaken within the present legal framework to streamline tribunal proceedings. These could include, for example, the adoption of a case management approach (especially with respect to the delineation of key issues), limits on interventions and discovery in favour of the director's inquiry powers, prefiling of all evidence (not just that of experts), and restrictions on the tribunal's highly interventionist approach to consent proceedings.

Most importantly, there must be an improvement in the quality of tribunal decisions, which have thus far been characterized by undue emphasis on lengthy recitations of evidence with only minimal analysis of relevant economic theory or general principles (Campbell and Rowley 1992; Graham 1993). As a result, 'the Director has relied almost exclusively on his own interpretation of the new legislation whose most important terms and trade-offs are undefined' (Stanbury 1992, 446). The most striking example of the lack of impact of tribunal decisions may be seen in the way in which the director ignored them in developing his own merger enforcement guidelines in 1991. The most prominent example was the director's decision (Wetston 1992) to ignore the consumer welfare interpretation of the efficiency defence suggested by the tribunal (Hillsdown 1992). Even though commentators have tended to support the director's substantive positions (Schwartz 1992; Crampton 1993), ignoring the tribunal undermines its credibility, usurps the law interpreter function assigned to it by Parliament, and diminishes crucial process values such as transparency, accountability, and reasoned public decision making (Campbell Janisch, and Trebilcock 1996, 27).

Until very recently, the courts tended to reinforce the tribunal's propensity to judicialize its procedures by treating it virtually as an inferior court. This approach ignored the essential character of the tribunal as an expert administrative body, which should be more concerned with economics and business structure than points of law. This judicial misperception of the role of the tribunal was in contrast with the general trend in administrative law for generalist courts to defer to the decisions of expert tribunals.

At one time, administrative tribunals, boards, commissions, and agencies in all their diversity were assimilated to the 'general law' administered by the 'ordinary courts' on the assumption that the courts should approach the review for legal error of an administrative agency's interpretation of its enabling statute as they would when hearing an appeal from a court occupying a lower position in the same judicial hierarchy. It followed that if the administrative tribunal adopted an interpretation different from that of the court, it thereby committed an error of law and its decision would be set aside. In more recent times, there has been a shift from what had been a positivist legal tradition to a functionalist approach, in which it came to be recognized that specialized agencies are more likely than any reviewing court to be in a position to make informed assessments of the interpretation of their enabling statutes that will allow for the most effective implementation of programs created by the legislature.

From a functionalist perspective, considerations of limited institutional competence suggest that courts should have only a highly constrained, residual role in reviewing matters that are more accurately characterized as issues of public policy and administration rather than questions of law and legality. While still insisting on procedural openness and a minimum standard of rationality in the interpretation of legislation, contemporary administrative law requires that a reviewing court afford a wide measure of deference to the reasoned choices of a specialized agency (Evans et al. 1995, 28–31).

This approach was finally applied to the tribunal by the Supreme Court of Canada in the Southern case in March 1997. The issue before the tribunal had been whether the acquisition by a large daily newspaper of surrounding community newspapers 'substantially lessened competition,' thereby violating the Competition Act. The tribunal concluded that it had not, on the grounds that daily and community newspapers operated in different markets. The director successfully appealed this decision to the Federal Court of Appeal, which concluded that the tribunal had applied a wrong legal test. The standard of review applied was one of 'correctness,' i.e., was the tribunal's decision the same one the reviewing court itself would have arrived at? A further appeal to the Supreme Court of Canada was successful, and the original decision of the tribunal was restored. Most significantly, the standard of review now adopted was that of 'reasonableness,' i.e., was it within a zone of reasonableness, although not necessarily the same result the court itself would have arrived at?

Contextual, functionalist considerations favouring judicial deference included that what was at issue was a mixed question of law and fact; that the purpose of the Competition Act was broadly economic, and that the case involved the application of competition law principles falling squarely within the tribunal's sphere of expertise. These considerations were said to outweigh the existence of an unfettered right of appeal to the courts or the role played on the tribunal by its judicial members.

The Supreme Court of Canada's determination that the tribunal should be treated not as a court but as an expert administrative agency strongly supports reconsideration of overly judicialized procedures which, as we have seen, have gone some way to marginalize the tribunal and to minimize its role when compared to that of the director. The prospects for such reconsideration will be assessed in the concluding section of this chapter.

Private Party Access to the Tribunal?

If a faulty initial design (subsequently exacerbated by a limited vision of the potential role for an expert administrative agency) has gone far to marginalize the tribunal, it may be that a restrictive view of who should have access to the tribunal has isolated it yet further.

Private enforcement could supplement public resources with private initiatives and information, especially where public resources devoted to enforcement are modest or diminishing (Stanbury 1997) and there is urgent need for cases to flesh out the general standards contained in public law (Campbell, Janisch, and Trebilcock 1996). Private enforcement can also be an effective means of holding public enforcers accountable for decisions not to prosecute. As well, private enforcement allows plaintiffs to achieve corrective justice by way of remedies for past and future harm. However, it has to be recognized that public enforcers may enjoy comparative advantages over private enforcers in terms of economies of scale and investigative tools. Moreover, private enforcement may result in overdeterrence, if numerous private enforcers are attracted by the prospect of high rewards.

The risk is that private enforcement will be employed for purely strategic reasons that conflict with the public goals of the laws sought to be enforced. As was concluded in a cogent recent study of this issue in a specifically Canadian context, the various advantages and disadvantages of public and private enforcement suggest the need for an appropriate mix of the two, 'with careful attention being paid to design features of a private enforcement regime such as sanctions for strategic behaviour and allowing public officials to intervene in, or in some cases even to terminate, private enforcement which may disrupt prosecutorial policies' (Roach and Trebilcock 1996, 19).

Unlike in the United States, where the prominent role for private enforcement under antitrust laws has largely been justified as a means of promoting optimal deterrence, Roach and Trebilcock conclude that a corrective justice rationale makes more sense in Canada (26–36). Should greater deterrence be considered desirable, it is suggested that a more straightforward response would be to provide for a regime of optimally structured and public enforced fines. Overall, the study concludes that there is a compelling case for private enforcement of the reviewable practices provisions of the Competition Act, primarily on corrective justice grounds, but secondarily in terms of enhancing the accountability of the public enforcement regime.

While thus favouring a greater role for private enforcement, the study is also very concerned to preserve the role of the director's enforcement policies and to combat strategic behaviour. Plaintiffs would have to notify the director before commencing a private action and the director would have discretion to commence her own action, intervene in the private proceeding, or simply allow the private action to proceed. If the proposed private proceeding has important policy implications, it is envisaged that the director could commence her own action or intervene in the private proceeding. Limitation periods would be crafted to discourage private actions that follow up on the director's enforcement efforts. However, where the director has pre-empted a private action, private parties could be allowed to intervene to seek compensation should the director establish liability.

It was envisaged that actions undertaken for strategic reasons would be deterred by allowing the tribunal to order the plaintiff to pay the respondent's costs for cases that do not survive summary judgment. A mandatory summary judgment rule would require plaintiffs to present affidavit evidence at the outset to support their claim and to ensure that litigation is not delayed for strategic reasons. The discovery process would be supervised closely to protect against abuse and to ensure that it is used only for legitimate purposes under the Competition Act. As well, the tribunal would be required to approve (or not) all settlements, to ensure that private parties have not reached a collusive agreement inconsistent with the purposes of competition law (Roach and Trebilcock 1996, 92–3).

As with any shift in accessibility to the tribunal from a procedural perspective, greater reliance on private initiative (which will undermine the director's monopoly on enforcement) will further shift the balance struck in the 1986 compromise. However, in the particular context of this volume's stocktaking of Canadian regulatory institutions, of even greater significance is the law and policy governing the interface of competition policy and regulation. It is to that we must now turn.

An Overdrawn Regulated Conduct Defence?

It would be difficult to question the basis for a regulated conduct defence. Its essence is that where an activity is authorized or compelled by validly enacted legislation, or by regulations made and enforced thereunder, persons engaged in such specific activity should be afforded immunity from criminal (and possibly civil) liability under the Competition Act, as that activity must be presumed to be in the public interest. The jurisprudence relating to the regulated conduct defence has remained essentially unchanged since *Jabour* (1982) and arguably, given the narrow focus of that case, since *Canadian Breweries* (1960), notwithstanding cases that have periodically touched upon this matter in the intervening years (Romaniuk 1995, 23–4).

In order for the defence to apply, four conditions, all of which can be derived from *Canadian Breweries*, must obtain:

- the industry or activity must be subject to validly enacted legislation;
- the defence must be limited to those activities or types of conduct specifically required or authorized by the legislation or regulation;
- the authority to control the activity or conduct in question must actually be exercised by the regulator;
- the activity in question most not have hindered or prevented the regulatory authority from protecting the public interest through the exercise of its statutory powers.

Regrettably, this understanding was to be substantially undermined by the Supreme Court of Canada in *Jabour*, when it did not require specific authorization to render the defence available. As well, while *Canadian Breweries* did require that the authority must actually be exercised by the regulator, not merely possessed by it, it remains far from clear just what this now means (Romaniuk and Janisch 1986, 634–47).

The director has taken the position that the 1986 partial shift away from reliance on the criminal law means that the regulated conduct defence has been greatly narrowed in that it is not available with respect to the *Competition Act*'s civil provisions (Mercer 1995). This has yet to be established by the courts, however. Indeed, it is possible to identify enough by way of potentially difficult issues to discourage any confident procompetition policy generalization.

Three 'for instances' should suffice. First, where conduct is compelled by the state under penalty of criminal sanction from a party, it would appear incongruous for another agency of the state to seek to impose civil liability upon the same party for the very act of complying with its governing legislation and validly enacted regulations thereunder. Second, even if the civilly impugned conduct under the Competition Act is merely authorized, and not compelled, by an agency of the state pursuant to validly enacted legislation, there would be something unsavoury about subjecting to damages or other civil liability a party acting in good faith pursuant to the approval of such conduct granted by a higher authority itself acting in the public interest. Third, it is a rare circumstance when the carrying out of some activity in the public interest does not adversely affect some private interest. The very process of the state having validly determined something to be in the public interest should arguably carry with it immunity from liability for the adverse impact caused to private interests lest conduct in the public interest be stifled from fear of upsetting private interests (Romaniuk 1995, 26).

Opportunities have been missed to clarify the respective roles to be played by competition policy and regulation. For example, in the late 1970s, at the time of the debate leading up to the Competition Act, Gordon Kaiser, a leading competition lawyer, called in vain for legislative clarification of the regulated conduct defence (Kaiser 1979). More recently, when the new Telecommunications Act (1993) was introduced, there was a proposal from the Senate Standing Committee on Transportation and Communications, which had undertaken a detailed prestudy of the bill, that the defence be significantly curtailed. In particular, this proposal sought to address the difficulties that would inevitably arise in the event of regulatory forbearance (Janisch 1993, 696).

Short of outright deregulation, regulatory forbearance is the best way by which a regulator can allow for a transition toward competition. It has been defined as 'any act, pursuant to legislative authority vested in the regulator, tending to lessen the regulatory burden an economic entity or activity is, or may be subject to and which follows a positive determination by the regulator that the purposes of the relevant legislation are best served by such action or inaction' (Janisch and Romaniuk 1985, 466). Because forbearance falls short of actual deregulation, it is by its nature conditional, i.e., should market forces not prove to be strong enough, the activity may be brought back under regulation. Does this leave enough room for competition policy to apply? The difficulty here is compounded by the propensity of regulators such as the CRTC to forbear from exercising only some of their regulatory powers (Yale and Blackwell 1997, 14–18).

While the director has asserted in a submission to the CRTC that he did intend to play a significant role in the evolution of telecommunications competition (Director 1993), lack of clear legal authority with respect to the regulated conduct defence continues to minimize the role of competition policy in the face of aggressive re-regulation in the transition toward a greater role for 'competition,' but not for competition policy. Indeed, the CRTC provides us with a striking example of the extent to which a regulator, if prepared to adapt to changing times, may be able to block competition policy institutions from any significant role. And this impasse will be compounded if amendments to the Telecommunications Act, which provide for a broad new licensing regime ostensibly to implement the WTO agreement on basic telecommunications (the Fourth Protocol to the GATS), are adopted (Janisch 1997).

The Triumph of Re-regulation?

As Richard Schultz has pointed out elsewhere in this volume, the CRTC has ultimately been successful in retaining its predominant policy role in the face of challenges from other branches of government. It has been equally successful in allowing in competition in all aspects of telecommunications, while at the same time minimizing the role of competition policy.

With a flurry of major decisions on 1 May 1997 (CRTC 1997), the regulator brought to a conclusion a long, drawn out series of major policy decisions favouring competition, initially with respect to equipment, then private lines and data, then wireless, then long-distance, and finally local service. This type of deliberate, incremental approach to change did not, of course, involve any elimination of regulation or any 'flash cut' to competition and competition policy. The 'regulated competition' (an oxymoron to economists) this approach introduced required a massive shift in regulatory resources from traditional concerns of monopoly regulation to new concerns about 'fair' competition on an 'even playing field.' The entrenched nature of the former monopoly and its continued control over crucial 'bottleneck' access points to the established networks was seen as justifying a whole new form of regulation designed to ensure 'sustainable' competition.

With the conclusion of the large-scale regulatory hearings, the focus will no longer be on setting rules but on mediating disputes between participants in the telecommunications market. As the chair of the CRTC, Françoise Bertrand, put it, 'I see a need, for some time, for an expert referee to ensure that the competition is sustainable and to see that the interests of consumers and citizens are protected. Clearly, in an increasingly deregulated environment, the role of the commission as a referee is not likely to end in the near future' (Bertrand 1997). There is little recognition that it is the 'invisible hand' of competition, not a regulatory referee, that should be protecting citizens and consumers. There is no recognition of the irony involved in speaking of a 'deregulated environment' while at the same time establishing a whole new regulatory regime for the 'expert referee' to enforce. Nor is there any recognition of the 'creative destruction' of true competition that does not guarantee that it will be 'sustainable.' Indeed, shortly before Françoise Bertrand spoke, Giles Menard of the bureau had observed, 'Regulators have a tendency not only to want to set the rules of the game, but to referee it in a fashion that all participants come out as winners' (Menard, 1997).

As it wound down its policy rule-making hearings, the CRTC has become increasingly preoccupied with process issues. Not only has this involved a massive shift away from traditional rate base/rate of return type of regulation to price cap regulation, but it has included outsourcing of regulatory decision making to industry committees with varying degrees of staff involvement, along with experiments with a variety of alternative dispute resolution (ADR) schemes. It also seems likely that there will be, as well, an element of privatization, with regulation being provided under contract with private parties (Yale and Blackwell 1997, 19–26). While these process innovations are interesting in and of themselves, for our purposes, their importance is that they provide new means by which the regulator can continue to respond to concerns that arise in any shift toward competition. In effect, the regulator is finding means to occupy the field at the expense of competition policy.

For many new entrants into telecommunications, the former monopolists loom as threatening giants. They find little comfort in the director's austere approach to competition law, in which 'predatory pricing' is considered highly unlikely. By contrast, the regulator at least expresses some sympathy for their much broader concerns about 'anticompetitive pricing.'

Nor were new entrants reassured by the manner in which the director dismissed their concerns with respect to the Stentor Alliance, which is made up of the former telephone company monopolists. While this 'cartel' facilitates a fully interconnected national telecommunications network, it also constrains the telephone companies from entering into competition with one another. The director concluded that concerns about vertical integration and agreements not to compete were tempered by evidence of competitive entry into long-distance markets and significantly declining rates for long-distance services since the CRTC opened the door to facilities-based competition in 1992 (Director 1997, 12–13). While it is true that the Stentor companies have lost up to 30 per cent of the long-distance market, when viewed from the perspective of a new entrant competitor, the telephone companies still enjoyed considerable structural advantage. They considered that this should be of great concern to the competition authorities, at least to the extent that their inherent advantages were reinforced through membership in the Stentor Alliance.

What is particularly significant in this situation is the lack of confidence (and resultant unwillingness to invest in expensive forms of participation) of new entrants in the ability of the competition authorities to act effectively. In the end, competition officials blamed the new entrants for failing to provide them with concrete evidence that could have been taken to the tribunal, while new entrants treated the discontinuance of the proceedings as further evidence of the disinclination of the director to protect them from unfair competition.

This new entrant scepticism is reinforced by concerns about the relatively low level of telecommunications expertise at the bureau and the intrinsically *ex post* nature of competition law. As a generalist competition authority, the bureau has not developed a level of expertise comparable to that of a specialist CRTC, although, as we will see in the next section, the bureau is by no means bereft of relevant sectoral experience. However, the regulator holds out the prospect of immediate access to an 'expert referee' in a manner that is very attractive to regulatory experts who have played such an important role in getting the new competitors into the business. By constantly emphasizing the importance of expertise (with its particular resonance for their 'opposite numbers' at the new entrants) regulators undermine the credibility of generalist competition policy as an alternative to regulation.

To this must be added the new entrants' fear that if *ex ante* regulation is replaced by *ex post* competition law, it would amount only to too little, too late. Indeed, they look at applications made to the tribunal in April 1994 with respect to Yellow Page Directories with a decision all of three years later (Tele-Direct 1997) as clear evidence of the ineffectiveness of the competition law process. *Ex post* adjudication is seen as inherently inadequate when compared to *ex ante* protective regulation: who wants justice long after having been put out of business?

Interventions before the Regulation: A Valuable Less Direct Approach?

Thus far the relationship between competition policy and regulation has been approached on an either or basis: either the director finesses the regulated conduct defence and applies unalloyed competition law principles, or the regulator applies its policy of 'regulated competition' exclusively. As we have seen, on this basis the competition authorities have largely been marginalized. However, Canadian competition law does provide for an alternative avenue of influence for the competition policy institutions. Under section 125 of the Competition Act, the director is authorized to intervene before regulatory agencies to stimulate and encourage competition. This opportunity has been taken up quite liberally by various directors, who undertook almost two hundred regulatory interventions between 1976 and 1995 (Monteiro 1995). Of these, over seventy were in the communications sector, primarily with respect to telecommunications. Given their prominence, an assessment of that group of interventions might usefully be undertaken for the purposes of this chapter.

Six specific impressions emerge from an analysis of these interventions, which may serve as a backdrop against which a number of somewhat broader points can be developed. First, where interventions focused on the anti-competitive effects of specific policies and provisions, they were usually influential, often decisive. Second, at an early stage of devising rules for interconnection, an essential prerequisite to competition, the director played a key role in the development of effective procedures and standards for nondiscriminatory access. The director had little specific impact with respect to cost accounting procedures, perhaps because his heart was never in costing as a means of limiting cross-subsidization. (But see item six below.) Fourth, where broad-based procompetition arguments were made, it is very difficult to determine a causal relationship, even where the CRTC decisions ended up being congruent with the overall position advocated by the director. Fifth, where the director ventured into political policy choices, such as foreign ownership limits or Canadian content requirements, he was smartly rebuffed. Sixth, and somewhat similarly, where structural arguments (preferred over costing) were put forward favouring, for example, separate subsidies where a monopoly in one segment of the industry provided competitive services in another, the director was again routinely rebuffed.

Significantly, the greatest success for the director came when he drew directly on the core of his specialized expertise in competition law. Thus in response to his forceful intervention with respect to regulatory forbearance and the criteria that needed to be developed in that regard, the CRTC was to draw extensively on competition policy literature and jurisprudence in its decision (CRTC 1994).

It is also interesting to note that the director's influence fluctuated over time and this may well illustrate that people should, indeed, be taken into account in any comprehensive assessment of the regulatory process (Doern 1995). From 1976 to 1982, interventions met with considerable success. This was when Lawson Hunter was director, and perhaps out of frustration with his lack of success in major cases, Hunter concentrated to some considerable extent on regulatory interventions. During this period interventions were very well received, as the CRTC and other regulators began to feel their way toward competition. By the mid-1980s, the director was to have less success. This was particularly so during Cal Goldman's tenure as director, when he concentrated on mergers and compliance. It was also a period during which the CRTC gained greater confidence in its own ability to manage the transition to competition, only looking to the director for guidance in the most specifically competition-law-related issues.

It is also possible that arguments of the director that were initially rejected (such as those favouring long-distance competition and price caps) acted as 'sleepers.' These interventions, although not accepted at the time, helped lay the basis for longer-term policy developments.

Any assessment of interventions by the competition authorities before the regulators needs to take into account the modesty of original aims. Indeed, interventions were initially seen only as an aid to regulators to ensure that they had information regarding the impact of particular regulatory decisions on competition. The goal was not to extend but simply to preserve competition. Thus the director's role as an advocate was not stressed, emphasis being on the conveyance of information, not advocacy.

Finally, the inherent limits of the intervention process itself have to be carefully kept in mind. The process allowed little room for policy initiative in that it constituted a response to the regulator's agenda. Most importantly, the director was forced to play on the regulator's field, according to its rules and policies. This meant that from time to time sound competition policy arguments would have to be abandoned (or at least substantially cut back) if the director was to maintain his credibility in the regulatory forum. Nevertheless, despite the limitations inherent in the nature of interventions, they have served as an important means of seeking to do indirectly what could not be done directly.

Conclusions

Two principal causes for the marginalization of competition law and policy have been identified: first, the disinclination of businesses or the director to resort to the tribunal, due to excessive judicialization; second, the inapplicability of competition law due to an overbroad regulated conduct defence and the continued ability of regulators to occupy the field. Both call for brief final comment, along with an equally cryptic assessment of the prospects for change.

It might have been thought that as the particular values diminished by having decisions brokered by the director and not decided by the tribunal, there would have been support for a proposal to revitalize the tribunal. Such values as transparency, accountability, and reasoned public decision making are said to be those cherished by the legal profession. Yet at the Annual Meeting of the Canadian Bar Association, Competition Law Section, in Ottawa in September 1996, when this was proposed (Campbell, Janisch, and Trebilcock 1996), the response was overwhelmingly negative. Proponents of reform were castigated for espousing an essentially European approach inimical to common law process values. It was not acknowledged that the closed door process employed by the director was itself in conflict with values such as openness and predicability, which lie at the heart of common law procedural fairness. How can this hostility be accounted for, and what does it tell us about prospects for reform?

A good portion of the answer may well be found by considering the influential role played by former directors and officials at the bureau in the practice of competition law. Those who have a confident feel for the inside track are unlikely to support any shift to a more open decision-making process. And as long as these circumstances prevail and the tribunal is not required to be more informal and approachable, competition law and policy will not (ironically) expand to play a more significant role in the transition from regulation to competition.

As we have seen, competition policy institutions have not been able to grasp the initiative and have had to be content to play, at best, an essentially second-fiddle role as interveners in the regulatory process. However, experience in other countries with similar legal traditions to our own is suggestive of innovative ways by which the two solitudes of regulation and competition policy may be brought together in a manner that belies the need for either or choices. It may be possible, eventually, to envisage the unalloyed application of competition law principles; to get there may require the sort of blended approach recently adopted to deal with the highly dynamic telecommunications industry.

In Australia multiple agencies are involved, with the cross-appointment of both commissioners and staff between the competition authorities and the regulator. The Australian Competition and Consumers Commission (ACCC), a generalist competition tribunal, administers competition policy under the Trade Practices Act. Telecommunications-specific provisions of this Act govern access arrangements and there are supplementary anticompetitive-conduct provisions. The Australian Communications Authority (ACA), a specialized regulatory agency, issues licences, decides on technical matters such as spectrum allocation, and monitors performance. Great reliance is placed on Codes of Practice, developed and enforced through industry self-regulation, and governing matters such as privacy and customer credit.

In Britain, a new regime has been designed/established not only to integrate the roles of the competition and regulatory authorities, but to accommodate, the European dimension as well. Thus the Office of Telecommunications (OFTEL) undertakes both regulatory and competition functions and has concurrent powers with the competition authority, the Office of Fair Trading (OFT). Telecommunications companies are subject to licences that contain a number of formal 'conditions,' which deal with anticompetitive behaviour. For example, British Telecom (BT) is subject to Condition 17, which prohibits it from unduly discriminating or showing undue preference to particular customers. At the end of 1996, BT's licence was amended to include a more general Fair Trading Condition (Condition 18A), which mirrors Articles 85 and 86 of the Treaty of Rome. This incorporates European competition law indirectly by prohibiting the abuse of dominant position and the making of anticompetitive agreements. OFTEL is incorporating identical conditions into the other telecommunications licences. More recently, the government has announced its intention to incorporate Articles 85 and 86 directly into domestic law. Once this is done, OFTEL will act under the new Competition Act rather than under the Fair Trading Condition, although it may still use other licence conditions where appropriate.

It is unlikely (and undesirable) that these models could be transposed to Canada, but they should encourage us to think of ways to break out of our present impasse and allow competition policy to move to centre stage as the shift from regulation toward competition proceeds.

REFERENCES

Bertrand, Françoise. 1997. Choice, Competition and Convergence for Canada. Unpublished paper presented at the Canadian Telecommunications Superconference, Toronto, 9 May.

Campbell, A.N. 1993. The Review of Anti-Competitive Mergers. SJD dissertation, Faculty of Law, University of Toronto.

– 1994. Proposals for Reforming the Merger Review System. Unpublished paper presented at the Symposium on Competition Law, University of Toronto, February.

Campbell, A.N., H.N. Janisch, and M.J. Trebilcock. 1996. Rethinking the Role of the Competition Tribunal. Unpublished paper presented at the Annual Meeting of the Canadian Bar Association, Competition Section, Ottawa, 27 September (forthcoming in the *Canadian Bar Review*).

Campbell, A.N., and J.W. Rowley. 1992. Refusal to Deal (with Economics). Unpublished paper presented at the Symposium on Competition Law, University of Toronto, December.

Canadian Breweries. R. v. Canadian Breweries [1960] *O.R.* 601.

CRTC. 1994. *Review of Regulatory Framework – Targeted Pricing, Anti-Competitive Pricing and Imputation Test.* Telecom Decision CRTC 94–13, 13 July.

– 1997. *Local Competition.* CRTC Telecom Decision 97–8; *Price Cap Regulation and Related Issues.* Telecom Decision CRTC 97–9, 1 May.

Competition Act, 1986. *Revised Statutes of Canada, 1985* (2nd Supp.), c. 19.

Crampton, P.S. 1993. The Efficiency Exception for Mergers: An Assessment of Early Signals from the Competition Tribunal. *Canadian Business Law Journal* 21:371.

Director. 1993. Director of Investigation and Research, *Submission re Telecom Public Notice CRTC 92–78*, 13 April.

– 1997. Director of Investigation and Research, Competition Act, *Annual Report for the Year Ending March 31, 1996.*

Doern, G. Bruce. 1995. *Fairer Play: Canadian Competition Policy Institutions in a Global Market.* Toronto: C.D. Howe Institute.

– 1996. Canadian Competition Policy Institutions and Decision Processes. In G. Bruce Doern and Stephen Wilks, eds., *Comparative Competition Policy: National Institutions in a Global Market*, 68–102. Oxford: Clarendon Press.

Evans, J.M., H.N. Janisch, David J. Mullan, and R.C.B. Risk. 1995. *Administrative Law: Cases, Text and Materials.* 4th ed. Toronto: Emond Montgomery.

Grover, Warren, and Jack Quinn. 1991. Recent Developments in Canadian Merger Law. In Khemani and Stanbury, eds., *Canadian Competition Law and Policy at the Centenary.* Halifax: Institute for Research on Public Policy.

Hay, Donald. 1993. The Assessment: Competition Policy. *Oxford Review of Economic Policy* 9, no. 2 (Summer): 12.

Hillsdown. 1992. *Director of Investigation and Research v. Hillsdown Holdings Ltd.*, 41 *C.P.R.* (3d) 289.

Jabour. 1982. *Attorney General of Canada v. Law Society of British Columbia,* [1982] 2 *S.C.R.* 455.

Janisch, H.N. 1993. At Last! A New Canadian Telecommunications Act. *Telecommunications Policy* 691.

–   1997. Submission to the House of Commons Standing Committee on Industry on Bill C-17, 3 December.

Janisch, H.N., and Bohdan S. Romaniuk. 1985. The Quest for Regulatory Forbearance in Telecommunications. *Ottawa Law Review* 17:455.

Kaiser, G.S. 1979. Competition Law and the Regulated Sector. In *Canadian Competition Policy: Essays in Law and Economics*, 347 at 350–7. Toronto: Butterworths.

Menard, Giles. 1997. The Role of Competition Law and Policy. Unpublished paper presented at Angus Telecommunications Conference, 29 April.

Mercer, Don. 1995. The Regulated Conduct Defence and the Telecommunications Industry. Competition Bureau, September.

Monteiro, Joseph. 1995. *Interventions by the Bureau of Competition Policy.* Economics and International Affairs Directorate, Bureau of Competition Policy, Industry Canada, July.

Roach, Kent, and Michael J. Trebilcock. 1996. *Private Party Access to the Competition Tribunal.* A study prepared for the Amendments Unit, Competition Bureau, Industry Canada, May.

Romaniuk, Bohdan S. 1995. Regulation, Forbearance and Antitrust: The Fine Art of Knowing When to Hang On, When to Let Go and When to Jump. Unpublished paper presented at the Telecommunications Antitrust Symposium, Bureau of Competition Policy, November.

Romaniuk, Bohdan, and Hudson N. Janisch. 1986. Competition in Telecommunications: Who Polices the Transition? *Ottawa Law Review* 18:561.

Schwartz, L.P. 1992. The 'Price Standard' or the 'Efficiency Standard'? – Comments on the Hillsdown Decision. *Canadian Competition Policy Record* 13, no. 2, 42.

Stanbury, W.T. 1992. An Assessment of the Merger Review Process under the Competition Act. *Canadian Business Law Journal* 20:442 at 451–4.

–   1997. Expanding Responsibilities and Declining Resources: The Strategic Responses of the Competition Bureau, 1986–1996. Forthcoming in special issue of *Review of Industrial Organization*, Thomas W. Ross, ed.

Tele-Direct. 1997. *Director of Investigation and Research v. Tele-Direct (Publications) Inc.*, 73 *C.P.R.* 1.

Wetston, H.I. 1992. Decisions and Developments in Competition Law and Policy. Unpublished paper presented at the Canadian Institute Conference, 8 June.

Yale, Janet, and Suzanne Blackwell. 1997. The Evolution of Telecommunications Regulation in Canada. Unpublished paper presented at the International Institute of Communications Annual Conference.

6

Retreat from Regulation: The Evolution of the Canadian Environmental Regulatory Regime

KATHRYN HARRISON

The Canadian environmental regulatory regime has undergone significant change in recent decades. When public attention to the environment re-emerged in the late 1980s, the regulatory process was transformed from closed, bilateral business–government negotiations to a process involving a broader range of interests via consensus-based 'multistakeholder consultations' and litigation (Hoberg 1993). At roughly the same time, the federal government signalled renewed willingness to employ its regulatory instrument after years of allowing it to wither in deference to the provinces. Yet, despite the greater involvement of environmental groups in the policy process and an apparently stronger commitment to regulation, the popular image of an exploding federal environmental regulatory mandate is largely a myth. While there has been an explosion of regulatory potential in the form of new framework statutes, those statutes have yielded surprisingly few regulations to date. Moreover, there are signs that even those few sparks are about to be extinguished. The federal government is retreating from the strong regulatory stance it adopted a decade ago in response to a combination of declining public attention to environmental issues, budgetary restraints, concern for economic competitiveness, and pressure for devolution in response to the national unity agenda.

This chapter examines the evolution of the federal environmental regulatory regime over the last thirty years, with particular emphasis on the last decade. The sections following will consider in turn the evolution of each component of the regime – organizational capacity, statutory mandates, intergovernmental context, process and players, and ideas – before concluding with a discussion of the implications of regime change for policy outcomes.

Organizational Capacity

The federal government created Environment Canada in 1970 in response to the first wave of public attention to the environment (Doern and Conway 1994; Harrison 1996). The new department was hailed as one of a growing number of horizontal portfolios that had the potential to influence a broad range of economic sectors. However, relatively few federal regulations have been promulgated and thus in practice Environment Canada has interacted with only a handful of sectors. It might therefore be better characterized as a department pursuing sectoral regulation in a handful of sectors, each with its own array of actors and political economy (Doern 1995).

Environmental regulation is also horizontal in the sense that it has the potential to influence the activities of other governmental departments. Again, however, that potential has been largely unrealized. An early program created to promote sound environmental practices at federal facilities had little impact and was dissolved in 1975 (Brown 1992, 29). More recently, the introduction of the $3 billion Green Plan in 1990 occasioned renewed interdepartmental conflict as departments other than Environment Canada fought – successfully – for their share of the new moneys and to ensure that Environment Canada did not become a central agency for the environment (Hoberg and Harrison 1994; Toner 1994). The potentially coercive role of Environment Canada within the federal government has also been mitigated by a particular construction of the concept of sustainable development (discussed below), which advocates that environmental concerns be integrated in economic decision making *by the traditional decision makers*. Thus, while line departments have been given new mandates to assess environmental impacts of their decisions and activities and to generate sustainable development plans, they retain considerable discretion in doing so.[1]

Since its creation, Environment Canada has experienced a 'roller coaster ride,' with its budget and staff resources rising and falling in response to public attention to the environment (Toner 1996). Unfortunately for the department, peaks in the issue attention cycle have been fleeting. Even as Environment Canada was being created in response to the first green wave in public opinion, public attention to the environment was already declining precipitously. Thereafter the department was marginalized for a decade and a half by a series of weak and short-term ministers, internal divisions, interdepartmental and provincial resistance, and dwindling resources.

Environment Canada's fortunes turned around in the late 1980s, with the renewed salience of environmental issues. The heavy emphasis on expenditures in the federal government's 1990 Green Plan was particularly beneficial to the department (Hoberg and Harrison 1994). However, with the Green Plan reaching the end of its five-year life, public attention to the environment fading, and deficit reduction high on the government's agenda, budgetary restraint returned in the mid-1990s (Toner 1996). Although the department's resources

FIGURE 6.1

Comparison of Trends in Public Attention to the Environment and Environment Canada's
Budget

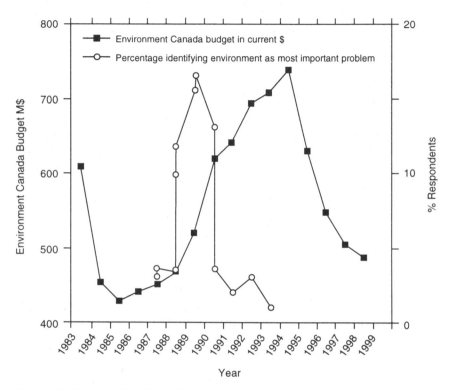

Source: Environment Canada; Gallup Canada

Note: Budget figures are from the Main Estimates for 1993/4 and later, and are mid-year
forecasts for earlier years. In 1993/4 the Parks Service was moved from the Environment
Department to the new Canadian Heritage Department. For comparative purposes, the
Parks budget has been subtracted from budget figures for 1992/3 and earlier. Prior to
February 1987, Gallup Canada did not report percentages of respondents identifying the
environment as the most important problem.

remain above levels immediately before the Green Plan, they are below those
of the early 1980s, before the Conservative government's first round of budget
cuts. Figure 6.1 compares the public's issue attention cycle with the rise and
fall of Environment Canada's fortunes. The lag between the latter and the
former is consistent with Peters and Hogwood's (1985) finding that there is
often a delay between a decline in public attention to an issue and the corresponding decline in administrative activity.

Although the costs of regulation to government tend to be small in comparison to those imposed on the private sector, regulators with insufficient resources to develop and implement regulations are in a weak position to coerce anyone. Although Environment Canada shielded its enforcement and compliance branch from the most recent round of budget cuts, its capacity was already strained (Toner 1996). In any case, compliance officers cannot enforce regulations that have not been developed. From that perspective, the timing of the periods of budgetary restraint could not have been worse. In both the 1970s and 1990s, Environment Canada had to contend with declining budgets just when it needed an injection of new resources to meet the challenge of implementing new legislation. Given the framework nature of Canadian environmental statutes, which tend to authorize regulations but leave their resource-intensive development and implementation to the discretion of the executive, the result was few regulations, weakly enforced.

Legislative Mandates and Policy Instruments

Environment Canada is not a regulatory agency per se – indeed, the majority of its budget is spent on nonregulatory programs, such as weather monitoring and research. However, its core legislative mandates are regulatory statutes. Like the department's budget, legislative, regulatory, and enforcement activity has fluctuated with the salience of environmental issues.

The heightened environmental awareness of the early 1970s led to the enactment of the Fisheries Act amendments, the Canada Water Act, the Clean Air Act, the Ocean Dumping Control Act, and the Environmental Contaminants Act. With the exception of occasional amendments to existing statutes, no new legislation was introduced thereafter until the late 1980s, when public attention to the environment re-emerged. The Canadian Environmental Protection Act (CEPA) was passed in 1988 and the Canadian Environmental Assessment Act (CEAA) in 1992 (though the latter was not proclaimed until 1995).

The federal government's willingness to issue and enforce regulations under the authority of those statutes has also vacillated. Federal politicians on both sides of the aisle have been more inclined to express support for a strong and unilateral federal role in adopting uniform national standards during periods of peak public attention (Harrison 1996), although even then they exhibit a preference for spending programs over coercive regulation (Hoberg and Harrison 1994). When public attention has subsided, however, the federal government's follow-through on its regulatory promises has been weak.

In the 1970s few regulations were promulgated – six discharge regulations under the Fisheries Act, four under the Clean Air Act, five under the Environmental Contaminants Act, and none under the Canada Water Act – and those were weakly enforced at best (Harrison 1996, 102–8). In the mid-1970s, the federal government delegated enforcement of its own regulations to the provinces through a series of federal-provincial accords, and it only rarely intervened when the provinces failed to enforce national standards (Huestis 1984; Giroux 1987). By the late 1970s, the federal government had also conceded its role in developing national standards. In 1983/4, Environment Canada's annual report noted that 'regulatory powers are used sparingly as a last resort' (Environment Canada 1984). The image of the federal government as tough regulator did not return until the late 1980s, with the introduction of the CEPA.

Like the first generation of environmental statutes, however, the CEPA has had a very limited impact (Leiss 1996, 131–5). It was designed to identify and control toxic substances from 'cradle to grave.' However, although twenty-five of the first forty-four priority substances to be evaluated were found to be toxic, only five had been regulated seven years after the Act was proclaimed (Environment Canada 1995). Of those, dioxins and furans were regulated only from one source (pulp mills); 1,1,1-trichloroethane was regulated along with other ozone-depleting substances, in keeping with Canada's international agreement in the Montreal Accord; and the other two substances are not in Canadian production, use, or commerce in any case. This track record can be placed in perspective against the backdrop of some 60,000 existing industrial chemicals with a thousand new ones being introduced each year (Leiss 1996). In any case, this already limited will to regulate appears to be withering. Although the federal government promised in its Green Plan to regulate all substances found to be toxic under the CEPA, it is now promising only to develop 'action plans,' which may rely on nonregulatory approaches.

The regulatory philosophy underlying these various statutes and regulations has evolved over time. The early regulatory philosophy was most apparent in the 1970 Fisheries Act amendments. Consistent with the prevalent approach during the same period in the United States, effluent standards were developed for different industrial sectors, based on the availability of affordable control technology. Technology-based standards were preferred, among other reasons, because they would ensure that comparable facilities in different locations had to meet the same standard. The first federal environment minister, Jack Davis, felt strongly that uniform national standards were needed to preclude the emergence of 'pollution havens.'[2]

Although this traditional approach, which has since been labelled 'command and control,' suggests abundant coercion and little flexibility, in practice there have been few commands and limited control. With the exception of chlor-alkali plants, existing facilities were covered only by guidelines under the

Fisheries Act, rather than by the enforceable regulations to which new facilities were subject. This was done to allow more flexible and gradual implementation. While in theory immediate compliance was demanded of facilities constructed after the issuance of new federal regulations,[3] compliance schedules for existing plants were negotiated on a case-by-case basis, taking into account the economic circumstances of individual polluters. In practice these flexible compliance schedules, which were negotiated and renegotiated, resulted in dismal rates of compliance (Huestis 1984; Harrison 1996).

The 1988 Canadian Environmental Protection Act modified the Fisheries Act approach in several respects, but at its core remains command-and-control legislation. The first departure concerns the basis for regulations. Although the authority to issue regulation is discretionary under CEPA, just as it was under earlier environmental statutes, the Act's emphasis on hazards to human health and the environment implies that risk, rather than availability of technology, will play a greater role in determining the stringency of standards. Second, rather than focusing exclusively on controlling discharges to specific media, as did the Fisheries Act amendments and Clean Air Act, the CEPA adopts a 'cradle-to-grave' approach, which could in theory yield regulations of product composition, exports, or disposal, in addition to discharges to any medium. Third, and perhaps most significant, is the formal CEPA Enforcement and Compliance Policy, which was released at the same time as the draft legislation (Environment Canada 1987). The policy's promise that compliance with the CEPA would be mandatory was nothing short of a 'radical shift in philosophy' from the traditional approach of gradual, negotiated compliance (Duncan 1990).

The introduction of environmental impact assessment in the federal environmental policy framework in 1974 represented a potentially important shift in regulatory philosophy.[4] While the traditional regulatory approach tends to address environmental problems after they emerge, environmental assessment seeks to anticipate and prevent problems by subjecting projects to thorough reviews before construction begins. Before 1987, however, the impact of this philosophical shift toward prevention was modest at the federal level, since Environment Canada tended to defer to the provinces' own environmental assessment processes (Kennett 1993). However, in the landmark 1987 Rafferty-Alameda case, environmentalists successfully sued the federal government to force it to comply with its own environmental assessment regulation. As a result, the federal government was compelled to enter a field it had previously left to the provinces. This new benchmark of federal activism was subsequently enshrined in the Canadian Environmental Assessment Act, which significantly departs from other federal environmental statutes in establishing nondiscretionary duties for the federal government to conduct assessments, and thus provides an opportunity for citizens to sue the government to compel it to perform those duties.

Although the federal government has made a strong commitment to perform environmental assessments in enacting the CEAA, it is difficult to assess the regulatory implications of this policy instrument. The immediate requirements of environmental assessment processes tend to be quite general: requirements for regulators to review certain projects and, in some cases, hold hearings, and requirements for project proponents to participate in the process as a condition of project approval. These requirements can entail significant direct costs. More importantly, however, environmental assessment processes may yield significant indirect costs if their recommendations for additional control measures are adopted by decision makers. However, there are no guarantees that decision makers will be any more inclined to adopt regulatory requirements following from environmental assessments than from other regulatory statutes.

Although the CEPA and the CEAA represented a departure from the regulatory philosophy underlying the Fisheries Act, the current trend away from regulation promises much greater changes. Regulatory reform efforts are proceeding toward more flexible implementation of regulations, greater reliance on market-based instruments, experimentation with less coercive regulations requiring information disclosure, and voluntary, nonregulatory approaches.[5]

A decade after the CEPA enforcement and compliance policy's seeming rejection of negotiated enforcement, there is renewed interest in more flexible approaches to compliance. Proposed revisions to the CEPA introduced in 1996 would authorize negotiated 'Environmental Protection Alternative Measures.' Although this approach is being characterized in some quarters as an innovative co-operative alternative to legalistic enforcement, in many respects it merely reinstates the traditional Canadian approach pre-CEPA, albeit with greater contractual formality.

Market-based instruments include discharge or user fees and tradeable permits. The greater economic efficiency and incentives for innovation offered by these instruments make them an attractive alternative to command-and-control regulation. They remain, however, inherently regulatory. With few exceptions, discharge fees create incentives to reduce pollution because they impose costs previously not incurred by polluters.[6] Similarly, marketable permits work because the total discharges allocated by permit are less than current or future discharges. Thus market-based alternatives are still coercive, though the distribution of losses will be different than under a command-and-control scenario (and there may even be some winners). While there has been much talk about and many positive studies of market-based instruments, Leiss (1996) observes that 'Canada cannot seem to be able to take even the most tentative steps in the direction of implementing market-based instruments for environmental regulation.'

The third reform is experimentation with less coercive regulations that require dissemination of information or planning, rather than direct actions to reduce the creation or discharge of hazardous substances. An example of the latter is the National Pollutant Release Inventory, created under the authority of the CEPA, which requires facilities to report all releases or transfers of some 178 substances. The intent is that public availability of the resulting inventory will induce firms to voluntarily reduce their discharges. Indeed, Environment Canada reports a 16 per cent reduction in total discharges from 1994 to 1995 (Environment Canada 1996). Proposed amendments to the CEPA, which died on the order paper in 1996, also included authority to require firms to prepare pollution prevention plans.[7] Again, the approach is regulatory in that plans are required, but any actions that follow from them remain voluntary.

Finally, as discussed in greater detail below, there is growing interest in voluntary alternatives to regulation. Some voluntary programs involve government acting in a persuasive or educational capacity. Examples include the Accelerated Elimination/Reduction of Toxics program (Leiss et al. 1996), the national Voluntary Challenge and Registry Program to reduce discharge of greenhouse gases, and voluntary pollution prevention agreements between government and private sector actors (Clark 1995). The new CEPA bill also seeks to promote voluntary pollution prevention through creation of a national clearing house on pollution prevention and public recognition of industry leaders. Other educational initiatives, such as the federal government's Environmental Choice eco-labelling program (Harrison, forthcoming), are directed at individuals rather than firms. Finally, there is also growing interest in initiatives independent of government, such as the Canadian Chemical Producers' Association's Responsible Care Program (Bregha and Moffet 1996) and International Standards Organization certification of corporate environmental management systems.

Environment Canada's recent regulatory reforms are consistent with the larger governmental agenda, which stresses, among other things, reducing overlap with the provinces, alternative approaches to securing compliance, consideration of nonregulatory alternatives, mandatory cost-benefit analysis, and 'consensus building with industry' (Treasury Board 1993, 1995). However, this broader regulatory reform agenda sits uneasily with Environment Canada's continuing legislative mandates. Indeed, proposals for new wildlife protection legislation and amendments to the CEPA would increase the department's regulatory authority. Yet, as past experience has amply demonstrated, the mere fact of statutory authority to issue and enforce regulations does not mean that it will be exercised.

The Federal–Provincial Context

The environment is an area of shared constitutional jurisdiction and, as a result, intergovernmental arrangements are an important institutional feature of the regulatory regime. Federal-provincial relations have also fluctuated in response to public opinion, with the federal government asserting a stronger role during peak periods of public concern and leadership shifting back to the provinces when public attention wanes (Harrison 1996).

Intergovernmental tensions first emerged when the federal government asserted an independent role in the environmental field in the early 1970s (Dwivedi and Woodrow 1989). However, the potential for overlapping federal and provincial regulatory activity was largely avoided through reliance on the bilateral federal-provincial administrative accords discussed above. In practice, the provinces once again became the lead players in the environmental field, with the federal government playing a supporting role, providing research and ambient monitoring (Thompson 1980).

Tensions re-emerged in the late 1980s, when the federal government reasserted a unilateral role in setting and enforcing uniform national standards with the passage of the CEPA. Disagreements over that Act paled in comparison to those that soon emerged concerning environmental assessment, when environmentalists' legal victories forced the federal government to reclaim an enterprise it had historically delegated to the provinces.

Efforts to restore harmony proceeded in two stages (Harrison 1994). In the first stage, the Canadian Council of Ministers of the Environment (CCME) sought to promote cooperative joint approaches as an alternative to unilateralism. In the second stage, the CCME launched a harmonization initiative in 1993, with a primary goal of eliminating overlap and duplication. This ambitious effort to redefine federal and provincial roles in the environmental field was driven by four factors. First, with the decline in salience of environmental issues, the federal government was no longer as eager to assert a strong and independent role. Second, both federal and provincial departments had suffered deep budget cuts, and thus hoped that rationalization would yield cost savings. Third, regulated interests were fearful that overlapping regulatory authority would lead to delays and duplication. Finally, harmonization of the environment portfolio was consistent with the federal government's desire to demonstrate to Quebeckers that federalism can work.

The outcome of this initiative was a new Canada-wide Accord on Environmental Harmonization, which was approved in principle by all environment ministers in November 1996. The intent is to ratify the fairly general accord and three more detailed subagreements – concerning standards, compliance inspections, and environmental assessment – at the November 1997 CCME meeting. Seven additional subagreements are planned over a three-year period.[8] In many respects, the new accord echoes the bilateral accords of the 1970s. It is foreseen that the provinces will take the lead in implementing national standards, with the federal government taking responsibility only for federal lands and matters concerning international boundaries and agreements. However, there is recognition that different approaches may be required for different environmental problems and in different provinces.

In other respects, the accord envisions a radical departure from either the status quo or past practice. The standards subagreement proffers 'Canada-wide' standards developed jointly by the federal government and the provinces as an alternative to 'federal' standards. The federal government's role is thus redefined from primary responsibility for setting national standards to mere participation as one of eleven governments seeking consensus on national standards.

Another significant departure from past practice lies in the narrower definition of standards. The primary focus is on developing uniform Canada-wide standards for ambient environmental quality, rather than discharge or product quality standards. This distinction is not merely semantic. Consistent environmental quality standards will typically lead to inconsistent discharge standards in different regions, given different dispersion conditions and different concentrations of sources. Indeed, there is no expectation that a lead government will develop enforceable discharge standards at all, since the subagreement guarantees each jurisdiction complete flexibility to adopt any approach it considers most appropriate to achieve the environmental quality goal, including voluntary measures. This focus on uniform environmental quality standards, to the exclusion of uniform discharge standards, represents a significant departure from federal and provincial governments' historical emphasis on uniform discharge standards as a means to avoid forum shopping and 'races to the bottom.'

The new Canada-wide accord thus seems likely to significantly limit federal government involvement in setting and enforcing national standards. The narrower federal role implicit in the accord and its subagreements is inconsistent with the strong federal legislation currently on the books. However, the signatories commit to amending their legislation as appropriate and, in any case, typically have discretion to decline to exercise their statutory powers.

The fact that Canadian environmental regulation occurs within an institutional setting of federalism has had significant implications for the emergence of national standards. The federal government has asserted a strong regulatory role during periods of peak public attention. However, it has been able to take advantage of provincial jurisdictional sensitivities to evade the political challenge of imposing costs on regulated interests when public attention has subsided (Harrison 1996).

The International Context

Globalization is an increasingly important force shaping the Canadian environmental regulatory regime, although this factor should not be over-emphasized, given the dominance of domestic influences on environmental policy (Hoberg 1998). The regime is influenced by three factors: international environmental commitments, internationalization of the environmental community, and free trade agreements.

The growing number of international environmental agreements to which Canada is a signatory, including the Montreal protocol on ozone-depleting substances and the conventions on climate change and biodiversity, tends to reinforce the federal regulatory regime relative to the provinces, contrary to the current devolutionary trend. The extent to which international commitments will lead to enhanced federal regulations in practice is open to question, however. Environment Canada faces pressure from other federal departments to commit internationally only to nonregulatory approaches (Toner and Conway 1996, 138). Moreover, in the past, the federal government's strong role on the international stage has not been matched by strong domestic follow through at home (Doern and Conway 1994, 125).

Taking advantage of advances in telecommunications and computerization, the environmental community is quickly catching up to business in its internationalization (Toner and Conway 1996). This development promotes transfer of ideas and coordinated cross-border lobbying campaigns. Environmentalists are in a stronger position than ever before to hold the federal government accountable to its international commitments.

The directional influence of globalization of trade is less obvious (Hoberg 1998). Free trade exacerbates deregulatory pressures to the extent that companies fear being undercut by competitors in other jurisdictions. There is also concern that environmental regulations will be vulnerable to challenge as barriers to trade. However, at the same time, with increasingly free exports, there is potential for upward pressure from international markets. Green demand from consumers in other countries, particularly Germany, has already had the effect of strengthening Canadian trapping and forestry practices and reducing pulp mill discharges (Toner and Conway 1996). Moreover, the international community is increasingly pursuing harmonization of product and process standards, both to counteract a potential 'race to the bottom' and to ensure that environmental standards are not merely barriers to trade in disguise.

Regulatory Process and Players

The transformation of the Canadian environmental policy process and expansion of the policy network that occurred in the late 1980s has been well documented elsewhere. The regulations of the 1970s were developed in closed consultations between business and government (Thompson 1980; Schrecker 1984). This 'bipartite bargaining' model (Hoberg 1993) assumed that regulated industries had essential knowledge otherwise unavailable to regulators, that they would be more willing to comply with standards that they helped to devise, and that regulators could effectively represent the public interest in negotiations. While dissatisfied, environmentalists 'lacked the organizational sophistication and political clout to induce officials to invite them into the process, and the legal or procedural rights to pry the doors open' (Hoberg 1998). By the late 1980s, this model had been discredited both by persistently low levels of compliance with environmental regulations and a more generalized public distrust of closed processes.

Reforms have proceeded in two quite distinct directions. The first reform was a move by Environment Canada to multipartite bargaining. The most obvious difference from the earlier model is that environmentalists and other interested parties are now invited to the table. Less obvious was a shift in the role of government, from representative of the public interest to referee among competing interests or 'stakeholders' (Hoberg 1993). A unique feature of such consultations was the pressure for participants to reach consensus. Although there was no formal concession of decision-making authority by government, there was typically an implicit promise that if consensus emerged, it would be incorporated in policy.

The regulatory process moved in a very different direction after the Rafferty-Alameda decision in 1987, which granted environmentalists (among others) a right to sue the federal government to compel it to perform environmental assessments. In contrast to multipartite bargaining, this 'legalism' model is not directed toward setting standards. However, the success or failure of efforts to force environmental assessment can have implications for regulatory requirements that emerge from those assessments. The Canadian Environmental Assessment Act subsequently institutionalized this approach in the environmental assessment field. Legalism, however, still sits at the margins of the Canadian regulatory regime (Hoberg 1998). This adversarial process fits uneasily with the substantial discretion typically afforded the executive in parliamentary government, and this has limited federal and provincial governments' willingness to extend opportunities for citizen suits.

These procedural changes will tend to deter both deregulation and devolution. The new actors at the table, environmentalists, tend to be wary both of voluntary alternatives to regulation and devolution to the provinces. Thus, in the multipartite 'Strategic Options Process' committees established to advise Environment Canada on options to control various substances listed as toxic under the CEPA, environmentalists have tended to offer a countervailing voice to industry's preference for nonregulatory approaches. Environmentalists may also be able to use litigation to advance environmental assessment and enforcement of existing regulations. However, in the current deregulatory climate, industry may have few incentives to compromise, and may prefer to present competing views to government. Environmentalists' influence will then depend on their ability to inform and mobilize a diffusely affected and increasingly inattentive public.[9]

Ideas

The ideas underlying the regulatory regime were transformed with the federal government's embrace of the concept of sustainable development in the late 1980s. The concept of sustainable development was popularized by the Brundtland Commission, which defined it as development that meets the needs of the current generation without sacrificing the ability of future generations to meet their own needs. The popularity of the concept owes much to the fact that it means different things to different people (Jacobs 1991, 59).

On the one hand, the Brundtland Commission stressed that economic development can only be sustained if the resources upon which it is based are sustained. Given our responsibility to future generations, it follows that economic activity that is not environmentally sustainable should not be allowed to continue. This interpretation of the concept, which emphasizes the incompatibility of much of our current economic activity and environmental sustainability, has profoundly redistributive implications, both between developed and developing countries and between sustainable and unsustainable enterprises within those countries.

On the other hand, an alternative reading of the sustainable development concept, which stresses the potential compatibility of economic growth and environmental conservation, has been adopted by the federal government (Leiss

1996). Federal politicians 'have displayed little stomach for condemning un-sustainable economic activity, preferring instead to highlight "win-win" oppor-tunities, in which environmentally sound practices are profitable. This concep-tion has implications for instrument choice since, if profit-seeking and environ-mental protection are indeed compatible, one need only educate people and they will voluntarily change their behaviour, without need for coercive mea-sures' (Hoberg and Harrison 1994, 125). While the former construction of the concept grants environmental sustainability a veto over economic decisions, in this alternative universe one need not choose.

Environment Canada's construction of sustainable development is very dif-ferent from its original regulatory philosophy, which assumed a tension be-tween environmental protection and profit that could lead to movement of capital and thus a race to the bottom among individual jurisdictions. Indeed, Environment Canada now stresses Michael Porter's arguments that environ-mental protection measures are good for business (Porter and van der Linde 1995).

This construction of sustainable development also has implications for the environmental policy process. If one believes that the goals of business and environmental groups are potentially compatible, consensual decision-making processes are a viable option. And finally, sustainable development has impli-cations for who is targeted by environmental policy. Reliance on the free market highlights the role of individual consumers, which has prompted the federal government to pursue such policies as 'eco-labelling' and 'environmen-tal citizenship.' If consumers and producers have sufficient incentives to inte-grate economic and environmental concerns, then there is no need for environ-mental policy makers to restrict the autonomy of traditional decision makers, be they in business or other government departments.

One particular manifestation of this conception of sustainable development, 'pollution prevention,' has been hailed as the guiding philosophy for CEPA reforms and the principle underlying Environment Canada's recent reorganiza-tion. The federal government announced a federal pollution prevention strategy in June 1995 (Environment Canada 1995). The new policy promises to shift policy making 'from treating symptoms to eliminating causes.'

The idea of pollution prevention is not as novel as proponents imply. Even command-and-control regulations can provide powerful financial incentives to avoid creating pollutants in the first place, though more powerful signals can be sent by market-based regulatory approaches. Similarly, environmental as-sessment is inherently preventative in seeking to identify adverse environmen-tal impacts before they occur. What is new about pollution prevention, as it is now characterized, is the emphasis on planning by both existing facilities and new ones (only the latter are covered by environmental assessment) and the emphasis on process or product change as opposed to end-of-pipe controls.

In keeping with the dominant sustainable development paradigm, Environment Canada assumes that 'pollution prevention is not only a sound environmental strategy, it's good for business' (Environment Canada 1996, 1), and that '[i]t does not hamper competitiveness – it increases it' (Environment Canada nd, 6). This explains the almost exclusively nonregulatory focus. Government's role is not to coerce but to provide 'leadership and direction' and to work with business and industry to 'achiev[e] a climate in which pollution prevention becomes a major consideration in private sector activities.' The language of the various policy documents could not be less coercive, emphasizing 'partnerships,' 'invitations to change behaviour,' and 'providing access to information and tools.' Similarly, the highlighted programs, such as codes of practice, a national pollution clearing house, and public education, are nonregulatory.

The policy prescriptions following from sustainable development are not consistent with all current regulatory reform initiatives. For instance, cost-benefit analysis continues to weigh the costs of regulation against benefits to the environment, even though those costs may be needed to ensure long-term economic viability.[10] The framing of such costs in terms of impacts on international competitiveness flies in the face of Environment Canada's reassurances that environmental protection is 'good for business.' (The business community's continuing resistance to regulatory measures suggests that it too is sceptical.) However, the fact that the policy prescriptions that have flowed from the federal government's philosophy of sustainable development are almost entirely nonregulatory has averted a potential conflict between environmentalism and neo-conservative forces of deregulation (Hoberg and Harrison 1994, 124).

Conclusions

The federal environmental regulatory regime has evolved in response to several factors. First and foremost, the salience of environmental issues has been cyclical, exhibiting two quite dramatic peaks in the late 1960s and late 1980s, which, not surprisingly, prompted corresponding governmental attention to environmental regulation. At other times, the environment has fallen from the 'top of mind' of both voters and politicians, only to be replaced by economic concerns such as unemployment and the deficit, which tend to oppose a strong federal regulatory role. The environmental regime has also been influenced by spillovers from other policy spheres. Federal-provincial tensions and Quebec separatism, efforts to reduce the deficit, and renewed emphasis on economic competitiveness in increasingly global markets have all influenced the federal government's willingness to pursue environmental regulation. The influence of partisan politics via changes of government has been important at the provincial level, though less significant at the federal level.[11] Finally, international forces are increasingly shaping domestic regulation.

The influence of public opinion on the institutional components of the regulatory regime is readily apparent. The federal government's budgetary resources, will to exercise regulatory authority, and role relative to the provinces have all fluctuated in response to public attention to the environment. Tough talk about the need for national regulations and uniform enforcement during brief periods of heightened salience of environmental issues has given way to uneven implementation, weak enforcement, devolution to the provinces, and greater reliance on less coercive approaches when public attention has subsided. The speed with which heightened public attention to the environment has subsided has meant that there has been little time for follow through on regulatory commitments before politicians' enthusiasm has faded.

Several regime components are evolving in a direction consistent with deregulation. Budgetary restraint will undoubtedly limit Environment Canada's capacity to develop and enforce regulations, despite an expanding statutory mandate. The broader regulatory reform and international competitiveness agendas also present a deregulatory influence. The devolutionary trend within the Canadian federation will constrain regulation, at least at the federal level. And finally, the sustainable development and pollution prevention paradigms, which stress the profitability of environmental conservation, tend to reinforce nonregulatory approaches.

There is concurrent regulatory pressure from other elements of the regime, however. The fact remains that Environment Canada already has strong regulatory mandates, with significant new mandates, in the form of amendments to the CEPA and wildlife protection legislation, waiting in the wings. Sustained international attention to environmental issues and the harmonization activities resulting from trade liberalization both tend to reinforce federal regulatory mandates. And there is no question that environmentalists exercise greater influence than ever before in the policy process. They routinely have a place at the table, and arguably exercise even greater influence via litigation in the field of environmental assessment. However, that does not mean that the table is now leaning toward environmentalists, particularly in a climate of limited public attention to the environment and governmental priority on jobs and competitiveness.

The current tension between these various regime elements, with some pointing toward expanded regulation and others toward deregulation, suggests instability in the environmental regulatory regime. In a climate of deregulation in other policy spheres, the expansion of federal regulatory mandates in the last decade is indeed noteworthy. How aggressively those mandates will be acted upon remains to be seen. The fuse to a regulatory explosion has been lit, but international forces and domestic pressures from environmentalists may provide scant shelter from the winds of deregulation.

Appendix

CHRONOLOGY OF EVENTS

September 1987	Montreal Protocol on ozone-depleting substances signed
June 1988	Proclamation of Canadian Environmental Protection Act
April 1989	Federal Court decision in Rafferty-Alameda case allows citizens to sue the federal government to perform environmental assessments
July 1989	Public attention to environmental issues peaks according to Gallup
December 1990	$3 billion federal Green Plan released
January 1992	Supreme Court's Oldman Dam decision upholds citizen suits to force environmental assessments in some circumstances
June 1992	Canadian Environmental Assessment Act receives Royal Assent
June 1992	Canada signs conventions on climate change and biodiversity at the United Nations Conference on Environment and Development in Rio
November 1993	Canadian Council of Ministers of the Environment announces harmonization initiative
January 1994	Canada, U.S., and Mexico create the Commission for Environmental Cooperation via parallel agreement to NAFTA
January 1995	Canadian Environmental Assessment Act proclaimed
Spring 1996	Green Plan quietly terminated
November 1996	Federal, provincial, and territorial environment ministers approve in principle Canadawide Accord on Environmental Harmonization
December 1996	Minister of Environment releases proposed CEPA amendments
February 1997	Supreme Court hears challenge to constitutionality of Canadian Environmental Protection Act in Hydro Quebec case

NOTES

Research for this chapter was funded by a grant from the Social Sciences and Humanities Research Council. Thanks are due to Sophie Champeau-Pelletier and Paola Baca for research assistance.

1 However, the minister of the environment can overrule decisions by responsible departments pursuant to environmental assessments under some circumstances. Another limited exception lies in the role of the new commissioner for the environment, who oversees departmental preparation of sustainable development plans.

2 See Jack Davis in House of Commons, *Debates*, 20 April 1970, 6052; Jack Davis, 'The fish and the law that guards against pollution,' *Globe and Mail*, 7 August 1969, 7.

3 In practice, levels of compliance for pulp mills built after the 1971 regulations took effect were no higher than for old mills. See Harrison (1995).

4 Federal environmental assessment policy was not codified in regulations until 1984, when the Environmental Impact Assessment and Review Process Guidelines Order was issued under the authority of the Department of the Environment Act.

5 Hoberg (1998) discusses the last three of these.

6 In theory, regulators should set a discharge fee at the point where average marginal control cost equals marginal social cost. The fee would then apply to all discharges, not just those above a regulated level. (The alternative of charging a fee only on emissions above a certain level offers a flexible alternative for enforcing command-and-control regulation but fails to capture the most important advantages of the discharge fee approach.) The polluter thus ends up incurring the costs of controls, *and* continuing to pay a fee on all remaining discharges. Although the desired result is achieved at less cost to society as a whole, there is at the same time a net transfer from polluters to government. Exceptions occur when discharge or user fees replace charges that are already incurred via other means, as in moving toward user fees for garbage collection as an alternative to payment via property taxes.

7 Bill C-72, ss. 58–63.

8 Additional subagreements are planned for enforcement, ambient monitoring, emergency response, research and development, policy and legislation, international agreements, and state of environment reporting.

9 On the vulnerability of groups seeking collective benefits to the public's issue attention cycle, see Joppke (1991).

10 Michael Jacobs (1991) has proposed salvaging cost-benefit analysis by incorporating a sustainability constraint. However, this approach has not been adopted by Environment Canada or other federal departments.

11 Significant changes in regulatory regimes have accompanied the transition from Social Credit to New Democratic government in British Columbia and from New Democratic to Conservative government in Ontario.

REFERENCES

Bregha, F., and J. Moffet. 1996. Canadian Chemical Producers' Association Responsible Care Program. Paper prepared for Exploring Voluntary Codes in the Marketplace, a symposium sponsored by the Office of Consumer Affairs, Industry Canada, and Regulatory Affairs, Treasury Board, September.

Brown, M.P. 1992. Organizational Design as Policy Instrument: Environment Canada in the Canadian Bureaucracy. In Robert Boardman, ed., *Canadian Environmental Policy: Ecosystems, Politics, and Process*. Toronto: Oxford University Press.

Clark, K.L. 1995. The Use of Voluntary Pollution Prevention Agreements in Canada: An Analysis and Commentary. Canadian Institute for Environmental Law and Policy.

Doern, G.B. 1995. Sectoral Green Politics: Environmental Regulation and the Canadian Pulp and Paper Industry. *Environmental Politics* 4:219–43.

Doern, G.B., and T. Conway. 1994. *The Greening of Canada: Federal Institutions and Decisions*. Toronto: University of Toronto Press.

Duncan, L.F. 1990. Trends in Enforcement: Is Environment Canada Serious about Enforcing its Laws? In Donna Tingley, ed., *Into the Future: Environmental Law and Policy for the 1990s*. Edmonton: Environmental Law Centre (Alberta) Society.

Dwivedi, O.P., and R.B. Woodrow. 1989. Environmental Policy-Making and Administration in Federal States: The Impact of Overlapping Jurisdiction in Canada. In W.M. Chandler and C.W. Zollner, eds., *Challenges to Federalism: Policy-making in Canada and the Federal Republic of Germany*. Kingston: Institute of Intergovernmental Relations, Queen's University.

Environment Canada. 1984. *Annual Report*. Ottawa: Environment Canada.

– 1987. *Canadian Environmental Protection Act: Enforcement and Compliance Policy*. Ottawa: Environment Canada.

– 1995. *Canadian Environmental Protection Act: Report for the Period April 1994 to March 1995*. Ottawa: Environment Canada.

– 1996. News Release: Federal Report Documents Reduced Pollutant Release to the Environment. Ottawa, 21 October.

– nd. *Strengthening Environmental Protection in Canada: A Guide to the New Legislation*. Ottawa: Government of Canada.

Giroux, L. 1987. Delegation of Administration. In Donna Tingley, ed., *Environmental Protection and the Canadian Constitution*. Edmonton: Environmental Law Centre (Alberta) Society.

Harrison, K. 1994. Prospects for Harmonization in Environmental Policy. In D. Brown and J. Hiebert, eds., *Canada: The State of the Federation 1994*. Kingston: Institute for Intergovernmental Relations.

– 1996. *Passing the Buck: Federalism and Canadian Environmental Policy*. Vancouver: UBC Press.

– (forthcoming). Promoting Environmental Protection through Eco-Labelling: An Evaluation of the Environmental Choice Program. In D. Cohen and K. Webb, eds., *Exploring Voluntary Codes in the Marketplace*. Ottawa: Government of Canada.

Hoberg, G. 1993. Environmental Policy: Alternative Styles. In M.M. Atkinson, ed., *Governing Canada: Institutions and Public Policy*. Toronto: Harcourt Brace Jovanovich.

– 1998. North American Environmental Regulation. In G.B. Doern and S. Wilks, eds., *Changing Regulatory Institutions in Britain and North America*. Toronto: University of Toronto Press.

Hoberg, G., and K. Harrison. 1994. It's Not Easy Being Green: The Politics of Canada's Green Plan. *Canadian Public Policy* 20, no. 2: 119–37.

Huestis, L.B. 1984. Policing Pollution: The Prosecution of Environmental Offenses. Law Reform Commission of Canada, Working Paper, September.

Jacobs, M. 1991. *The Green Economy: Environment, Sustainable Development and the Politics of the Future*. London: Pluto Press.

Joppke, C. 1991. Social Movements During Cycles of Issue Attention: the Decline of the Anti-nuclear Movements in West Germany and the USA. *British Journal of Sociology* 42:43–60.

Kennett, S.A. 1993. Hard Law, Soft Law and Diplomacy: The Emerging Paradigm for Intergovernmental Cooperation in Environmental Assessment. *Alberta Law Review* 31:644–61.

Leiss, W. 1996. Governance and the Environment. In T.J. Courchene, ed., *Policy Frameworks for a Knowledge Economy*. Kingston, Ont.: John Deutsch Institute for the Study of Economic Policy.

Leiss, W., D. Van Nijnatten, and É. Darier. 1996. Lessons Learned from ARET: A Qualitative Survey of Perceptions of Stakeholders. Working Paper 96–4, Environmental Policy Unit, School of Policy Studies, Queen's University, Ontario.

Peters, B.G., and B.W. Hogwood. 1985. In Search of the Issue-Attention Cycle. *Journal of Public Policy* 47:238–53.

Porter, M.E., and C. van der Linde. 1995. Toward a New Conception of the Environment-Competitiveness Relationship. *Journal of Economic Perspectives* 9:97–118.

Shrecker, T. 1984. *The Political Economy of Environmental Hazards*. Ottawa: Law Reform Commission of Canada.

Thompson, A.R. 1980. *Environmental Regulation in Canada: An Assessment of the Regulatory Process*. Vancouver: Westwater Research Centre.

Toner, G. 1994. The Green Plan: From Great Expectations to Eco-Backtracking to
    Revitalization? In S. Phillips, ed., *How Ottawa Spends 1994–95: Making Change.*
    Ottawa: Carleton University Press.
− 1996. Environment Canada's Continuing Roller Coaster Ride. In G. Swimmer, ed.,
    How Ottawa Spends 1996–97: Life Under the Knife. Ottawa: Carleton University
    Press.
Toner, G., and T. Conway. 1996. Environment. In G.B. Doern, L.A. Pal, and B.W.
    Tomlin, eds., *Border Crossings: The Internationalization of Canadian Public
    Policy.* Toronto: Oxford University Press.
Treasury Board of Canada. 1993. Enlightened Practices in Regulatory Programs.
    Vol. 1. Ottawa, May.
− 1995. Regulatory Policy 1995. Ottawa, November.

7

Deregulation, Pressures for Re-regulation, and Regulatory Shifts: The Case of Telecommunications and Transportation

W.G. WATERS II and W.T. STANBURY

This chapter seeks to identify problems and concerns arising from the deregulation or liberalization of transportation and telecommunication services markets in North America, which have given rise to pressures for re-regulating parts of these sectors or regulating them in new ways. 'Re-regulation' is a widely used phrase, but we think 'regulatory shift' is a more accurate description of what is going on. While there are a few specific pressures for the return of traditional economic regulation (i.e., price and entry controls), an ongoing shift of emphasis on various types of social regulation, dealing with health, safety, environment, and 'fairness' is more significant (Nemetz et al. 1986). There are also pressures for new types of regulation, which may arise in their own right or as subterfuges for protectionism by groups adversely affected by the removal or liberalization of price and entry controls.

We include both transport and communications in the analysis because there are important links between these two sectors; there are also parallels in their historical regulation and the rise of deregulation in response to changes in technology, market structure, and public attitudes. The deregulation movement has generally gone further in transportation than in telecommunications in North America, but changes in telecommunications are coming rapidly (CRTC 1997a, 1997b).

The chapter begins with a discussion of the historical and contemporary links between transport and communications. The second section provides a summary of the transportation deregulation movements in Canada and the United States and similar trends in communications (particularly telecommunications). Our discussion is very brief, as these topics have been well documented in many studies. In the third section we identify some problems and issues arising from the deregulation (or liberalization) experience that may give rise to 'regulatory shift' or other form of government action. These may arise from either normative or positive reasons, e.g., failures of deregulated markets to achieve efficient economic outcomes, or situations where adversely affected groups may seek government intervention to increase (or prevent the decrease) in rents accruing to these groups. Brief conclusions follow.

Communications and Transportation

Transport and communications industries share some economic attributes: they are multiproduct industries with shared (joint, common, and overhead) costs and both deal in infrastructure-based services provided over a network. Historically, scale economies were said to be an important characteristic, leading to monopoly or oligopoly market structures and justifying government regulation of pricing, output, and, sometimes, investment decisions. Both sectors have undergone significant technological changes, which have lowered costs and eliminated natural monopoly conditions, thus permitting more competitive market structures to replace government regulation. The technological changes and market adjustments came first in transportation, hence deregulation in the transport sector is generally some years ahead of the process in communications. Moreover, as Table 7.1 shows, changes in both sectors occurred in the U.S. some years before they occurred in Canada.

Although often discussed as substitutes, transportation and communications also complement each other (Mokhtarian 1990; Salomon 1986). As the geographic scope of markets and business operations expand, either in terms of coordinating production and/or sales at different locations, there will be greater need for business travel. The globalization of economic activity has probably also resulted in increased demand for transport services, first to bring together the components of products and then to distribute them across many markets and countries. And the lower real costs of personal travel and communications have stimulated contact, travel, and communications among friends and relatives at distant locations. The conquest of distance stimulates both travel *and* communications; solving old problems gives rise to new ones (Salomon 1985).

A well-recognized characteristic of modern, developed economies is the shift from goods to services and now to a so-called information-based economy. The decline of manufacturing's share of the economy and the expansion of the service sector are well documented. The relative shift from tangible goods and traditional services to information-based services has direct implications for transport and communications. Communications can be thought of as a transport mode for moving information (Mokhtarian 1990), i.e., the transport of digitalized goods/services at 186,000 miles per second over fibre optic cables,

TABLE 7.1
Transport Deregulation in North America

Mode	U.S. Date	Canada Date
Air		
passenger	1978++	1987 ('south')++
		1996 ('north')++
freight	1977++	early 1980s++
Railways		
Freight	1980++	1967 pricing
		1987+, 1996++
passenger, e.g.,		
Amtrak; VIA Rail	not applicable	not applicable
Trucking		
intrastate/provincial	mixed	late 1980s; still underway
interstate/provincial	1980++[1]	1987++
Freight forwarders & couriers		
air freight	1979	air, early 1980s
other forwarders	1980s	land, 1987
Intercity buses	1982+	planned 1998[2]
Urban transport		
taxi cabs	regulated locally	regulated locally
buses and transit	govt. owned and	govt. owned and
	regulated	regulated
Marine shipping		
coastal	unregulated, but no	unregulated, but no
	cabotage[3]	cabotage
international		
bulk	not applicable	not applicable
liner and NVOCC	1984+	essentially unregulated
inland water	regulated (much is	1987 (north)
	exempt)	

++ extensive deregulation
 + moderate deregulation

1 Household movers continue to be regulated.
2 Effective 1 July 1996 federal regulation of interprovincial and transborder buses
  ended.
3 Flag protected.

traditional copper wires, or through the air. The explosion of courier businesses in the transport sector per se, and the growth of communications markets are indicative of the long-term substitution of communications for transportation. Note that it is not necessarily direct substitution of an act of communication for a trip, although that may be a part of what happens. Rather, the growth in market share of communications relative to transport is the real indicator of this underlying phenomena. This should come as no surprise; historically, the substitution of one type of economic activity for another generally arises through the expansion of new sectors compared to the slower growth or decline of older sectors, rather than the outright substitution of one industry for another. Transport's share of GDP has declined noticeably over the last two decades, despite steady growth in absolute terms.

A way to illustrate the relationship is to plot market shares of modes of transport *and* communications. This can be done by expenditure shares or physical measures of output over time. Mode market shares often use tonne-kms, which have a known weight-distance bias, hence a more useful illustration is to show trends in market shares on a total revenue basis. Expenditure share comparisons are useful because they reflect the willingness to spend on a sector. However, note that productivity advances mean that revenue growth will tend to under-represent the real growth in that sector. Figures 7.1 and 7.2 plot the share of GDP in communications and transport from 1970 to the early 1980s for Canada and the U.S., respectively. Both show a relative shift from transport to communications; this shift is particularly striking for Canada. The share of transportation in GDP has fallen about 20 per cent over the twenty-five-year period, whereas the share of communications has increased more than two and a half times! The same shift between transport and communications can be seen in the American data, although it is much less pronounced than for Canada (a 6.5 per cent decline in transport share and a 28 per cent increase in the share of communications). We note that the share of communications in Canadian GDP started from a lower point than similar figures for the United States.

The Deregulation Movement

'Deregulation' refers to the reduction or elimination of government controls on prices, entry-exit, and/or rate of return. Economic regulation emerged during a monopoly era of railroads, telegraph, telephones, and other public utilities (Economic Council of Canada 1979; DeMuth 1983). These industries were characterized by scale economies (if not natural monopoly) and local

FIGURE 7.1
Canadian Communications and Transportation Share of GDP

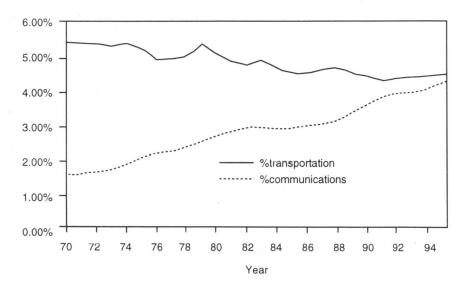

FIGURE 7.2
U.S. Communications and Transportation Share of GDP

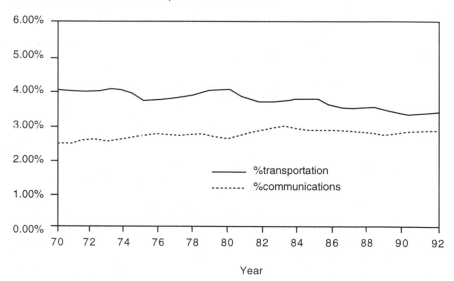

monopoly power. Any competition tended to be associated with price wars to drive rivals out of business (possibly supplemented by non-price competition, such as sabotaging the rival's equipment).

It is important to note that regulation was imposed both for reasons of economic efficiency (allocative and technical) and as the result of concerns about fairness. As is well known, the latter received as much emphasis and were in conflict with efficiency criteria (Stanbury and Lermer 1983). Regulation persisted in the face of new technologies (e.g., trucking and air transport), which did not necessarily exhibit notable scale economies. In fact, where competition arose, the opposite of monopoly, i.e., fear of 'destructive competition,' became a motivating rationale for regulation, particularly in trucking.

Transport Deregulation

The transport deregulation movement emerged in the U.S. in the mid-1970s, following at least two decades of growing criticism of poor economic performance of transport regulation, including evidence from isolated instances where transport had somehow eluded regulation (Meyer 1959; Nelson 1959; Jordan 1970). Growing recognition of unsatisfactory performance of regulation coincided with a broader disenchantment with government performance generally. The deregulation movement has been accompanied or followed by privatization of some government activities (Stanbury 1994) and, more recently, by growing emphasis on cost recovery for many services provided by government, often by means of user fees (MacAvoy 1989).

The timing and extent of deregulation has differed among modes and countries, and it often came about gradually, rather than in a single legislative Act. Hence it is simplistic to reduce deregulation to a series of specific dates. It is also important to recognize that deregulation has *not* occurred in all transport markets in North America, and that there are residual regulations in some otherwise deregulated industries. For instance, regulations still limit prices in market-dominant U.S. rail markets, and inland barge operations are still regulated (although a substantial amount of traffic is exempt). There is a danger that casual observers will overgeneralize from the highly visible experience with the airline industry (led by the U.S. and followed by Canada).

The intercity bus industry in Canada is only now undergoing deregulation (in Ontario). In both the U.S. and Canada, in selected markets, the bus industry has faced competition from government-owned and subsidized rail passenger services. The latter have certainly not been 'deregulated,' but their market share is small and they are not a major component of transport markets.

Urban transport, by and large, has not undergone fundamental restructuring in North America, compared to the U.K., Australia, and New Zealand. In North America, urban bus service and other forms of local transit are generally supplied by government-owned, unionized, monopoly services.[1] Taxi supply continues to be regulated by local governments, with few exceptions.

With respect to international shipping, Canada has long relied on international carriage and accepts shipping conferences (the federal Shipping Conferences Exemption Act has been renewed every five years). The U.S. has made procompetitive steps for liner shipping (1984) but also retains some flag discrimination. Coastal shipping – not a major part of the transport sector – is flag-protected both in Canada and the U.S., but competition can work subject to this constraint. Inland water transport is not important in Canada, except for the Great Lakes (and the St Lawrence seaway system) and northern river transportation. The latter services have been privatized and regulation has been reduced.

The majority of transport modes and markets in North America have now been deregulated (or at least liberalized) and this process has been the subject of much analysis.[2] While a few controversies remain, the majority accept that transport deregulation brought about substantial efficiency improvements and increased service at lower prices for most customers. In general, competition eliminates rents accruing to owners, employees, or managers; it eliminates X-inefficiency; and it creates pressures for innovation and the rapid adoption of innovations. Economists had predicted these outcomes for at least a couple of decades. More has been written about the experience of the airline industry (particularly in the U.S.), but most of the developments in air deregulation have parallels in other modes.

In addition to efficiency gains, there have been income transfers among various groups. For example, wages have tended to fall and labour inputs have been reduced, but in the air markets, the latter was offset by market expansion stimulated by competition and lower rates. Shareholders of unprofitable and bankrupt firms have suffered – but inefficiency should hardly be rewarded. More than rents have been eliminated by the 'gales of creative destruction' unleashed by deregulation. Business air travellers object to substantial increases in fares but benefit from more frequent service and better connections.

Deregulation brought some surprises, too. Generally, a more complex price structure has arisen in connection with diverse services supplied to different customers and, in some cases, price discrimination. Greater reliance on hub-and-spoke operations, which reflect a higher utilization of capital equipment by pooling freight/travellers for part of their journey, is also discernible. Substantial merger activity has taken place, despite apparent limited cost advantages of size (the advantages of size reflect demand-side advantages of the attractiveness to consumers of full network coverage by a carrier and/or any market power advantages that come with size). There have been persistent low (even inadequate) rates of return to investors, especially in air transport, but the problem has affected many railroads and trucking lines as well.[3]

Communications and Deregulation

The deregulation of telecommunications in North America is still in progress, even in the U.S., which is the acknowledged world leader in this movement (Crandall and Waverman 1996). The origins of communications regulation were very similar to those in transportation. There was a presumption (probably correct at the time) that telephony was a natural monopoly and it had to be regulated, for the usual efficiency and equity reasons. A major additional influence was a desire for universal access to the network. There were similar pressures in transport, *viz.* the common carrier obligation and regulatory cross-subsidy to favour small shippers and smaller communities. But the public policy goal of 'universal affordable telephone service' influences communications policy to this day in both countries.[4] Indeed, it can be found in their basic legislation (albeit in more detail in the new U.S. legislation) and is recognized in the principles in the WTO reference paper on basic telecommunications services in 1997.

As with transportation, a technological revolution has eliminated or greatly reduced the problem of scale economies and, combined with general population and market growth, makes competition feasible, at least in several markets. The traditional distinction of voice and data transmission has become increasingly meaningless, as is that between local and long distance (Cairncross 1995). By the early 1970s in the U.S., there were growing pressures for companies to enter profitable long-distance communications markets and government policy makers were sympathetic. But there was (and still is) political support for 'taxing' long-distance calls in order to cross-subsidize local service.[5] Unfettered competition could not be permitted; it would have to be managed to some extent and allow 'rate rebalancing' to take place over time. Scale economies are important for local network services and there is the problem of specifying the terms of interconnection regulating the price of access by competitive long-distance suppliers (Globerman, Janisch, and Stanbury 1996a). An even more complicated problem concerns the terms of interconnection among rival suppliers of local service.

Effective 1 January 1984, the well-known break-up of AT&T in the United States took place, leaving seven local/regional monopolies (Regional Bell Operating Companies, RBOCs, or 'Baby Bells'), and freeing up the 'long lines' part of the company (AT&T) both to compete in existing services and to explore new technologies (Crandall and Waverman 1996). This followed a series of FCC decisions that opened up a number of telecommunications markets, notably terminal equipment and long-distance service. The convergence of telecommunications, broadcasting, and computer technologies all but eliminated the technological boundaries between these (and related) industries. The RBOCs continually pushed against the constraints imposed on the scope of their activities in the Modification of Final Judgment, which came into effect in 1984. Most notably, it blocked their entry into long-distance markets – until new rules were established under the Telecommunications Act of 1996. A wide and growing range of issues were the subject of that Act: deregulation of cable TV rates, ownership of broadcasting outlets, competition in local telecom markets, and regulation of pornography on the Internet.[6]

In Canada, the telecommunications story is similar (Globerman, Oum, and Stanbury 1993), although there was even greater government involvement in Canadian telecommunications than in the U.S. Three provincial governments owned telephone companies (two have been privatized), primarily because the goal of providing universal service in large, sparsely settled regions could be achieved more easily under direct government control than it could be via a regulated private monopolist.[7] Hence the underlying cross-subsidy between local and long-distance rates was greater in Canada (Crandall and Waverman 1996).

The same march of technology and growth and change in market demand has been taking place in Canada as the U.S. Competition has been or will soon be introduced in all telephone services markets. The first notable steps were taken in 1979, when CNCP was permitted by the CRTC to interconnect its private lines (voice and data) to the local networks in BC Tel and Bell Canada territories, generating some limited competition with the dominant companies.[8] In the early 1980s, the CRTC permitted terminal attachment, which opened up competition in the supply of telephones and related equipment. Duopoly competition emerged in (local) cellular telephones via the Department of Communications' decision in 1984. In 1985, the CRTC denied CNCP entry into public voice long-distance service, but some resale and sharing was permitted. The commission permitted resale of service in the public voice long-distance market (MTS/WATS) in 1990; this was the start of real competition in that market (Globerman, Oum, and Stanbury 1993, 1994). Telecom Decision 92–12 opened public voice long distance to facilities-based competition, and in 1994 the

CRTC opened local/access markets to competition in principle (Globerman, Janisch, and Stanbury 1996b). Finally, on 1 May 1997, the CRTC formally opened local exchange markets to competition, effective 1 January 1998, at which time price caps will replace the traditional rate-base/rate-of-return system in place for a century (CRTC 1997a, 1997b).

The CRTC and the federal government have sought to control the deregulation process (Stanbury 1995a), with the inevitable clashes of economics and technological forces versus political priorities and entrenched interests. Perhaps because of Canada's geography and population, the growth of the communications sector in the Canadian economy has been much faster than that in the U.S. At this point, Canada might even be moving ahead in deregulating telecommunications. In Canada, local telephony has been declared open for competition in practice on 1 January 1998. While the U.S. opened its local markets in the Telecommunications Act of 1996, actual entry depends on several factors: (1) changes by the RBOCs to facilitate entry into local/access markets; (2) the willingness of state regulators to permit such competition (which varies a great deal); and (3) judicial interpretations of FCC policy initiatives under the Act. Canada has an advantage here because, since 1989, the provincial governments no longer regulate intraprovincial telecommunications, as the states do in the U.S.

Regulatory Shift and Concerns Arising from Deregulation

The deregulation story is not exclusively a positive experience. Pareto efficiency improvements in public policy are a theoretical ideal, but non-existent in practice. In any policy action there are always 'losers' who are not compensated, hence certain individuals and groups will be dissatisfied with at least some deregulatory outcomes and might advocate some manner of re-regulation.

The Concept of Regulatory Shift

Regulatory shift encompasses several distinct phenomena, which we now describe briefly.

Re-regulation
Deregulation may fail or may create a sufficiently strong backlash that traditional price and entry controls are reimposed on an industry. This re-regulation is not likely to occur often, since most social processes are not easily reversible (e.g., National Commission for a Healthy Competitive Air Industry 1993).

Partial Re-regulation
This term refers to the reimposition of some aspects of a regime of economic regulation, following an adverse political reaction to outright deregulation.

More Economic Regulation
While deregulation was occurring, new regimes of economic regulation were created. An example may be found in the Patented Medicines Prices Review Board.[9]

New Regulatory Techniques
Here a regulatory regime is changed by the substitution of new techniques of regulation, such as using price caps to replace rate-base/rate-of-return regulation (Stanbury 1997).

More Social Regulation
This phenomenon involves substantial growth in social regulation while the amount of economic regulation declines. This form of regulatory shift takes two forms. It might result from the creation of new regulatory regimes in areas not previously regulated (e.g., 'victim protection' regulation for the handicapped,[10] visible minorities, Natives, and women and regulation of new reproduction technologies).[11] Or it may arise from modification, often extension, of an existing regulatory regime. For example, various intellectual property laws in Canada have strengthened and established new rights for the creators of intellectual property (Nankivell 1997). In a related change, the new Copyright Act imposes a tax on blank audio cassette tapes. The money goes into a fund for Canadian performers and producers to compensate them for home copying of their recordings.

User Fees
Here the objective is to have the first-line beneficiaries of regulation pay part of the government's costs in administering a regulation regime. For instance, in 1998, user fees are expected to generate revenues equal to one-quarter of the Competition Bureau's budget. Generally, user fees imposed on telephone companies now cover all the CRTC's costs of regulating those companies.

Changes in the Regulation-Making Process
In 1986, the federal government made extensive changes in the process by which new regulations are created by a committee of the cabinet. These included requirements for consultation prior to drafting, 'pre-publication' of pro-

posed regulations, a notice and comment period, and the preparation of a regulatory impact analysis statement, which includes a cost-benefit analysis of 'major' new regulations (Stanbury 1992). The implementation has been problematic, however (Mihlar 1997).

Cost Reduction
Fiscal constraints/cutbacks have resulted in a variety of moves to reduce government's cost of regulation. These include (a) shifting from government regulation to 'self-regulation' (a term applied to a variety of phenomena; see Priest (1997); (b) substitution of voluntary codes for traditional command-and-control regulation; (c) reduced frequency of inspection, perhaps focusing on 'critical points'; (d) getting regulatees to adopt programs of compliance, which result in less effort by government to achieve its goals; (e) getting regulatees to adopt ISO standards of 'good practice' facilitating compliance with government regulation; and (f) shifting the regulatory burden to another (usually lower) level of government. (This is likely to be a negative-sum game.)

Protecting Regulatees
This version of the 'regulatory shift' occurs when a particular department takes on the role of championing the interests of regulatees within a government. Industry Canada seems to have adopted this role with the objective of 'filtering out' costly, inefficient new regulations.

Transitional Regulations
Regulatory shift includes the creation of new regulations (rules) to facilitate the transition from regulated monopoly to full competition in industries long subject to economic regulation. The best example is that of the telecommunications sector in Canada (Stanbury 1995a, 1996a, 1996b; CRTC 1997a, 1997b). While competition has been or is about to be introduced in virtually all telecom markets, the CRTC has never been busier creating new rules under which competition occurs.

Incumbent Protection
Regulatory shift includes new forms of incumbent protection created by regulators while competition is being introduced in what were formerly monopoly markets. Perhaps the best example is the CRTC's protection of conventional broadcasters (e.g., over-the-air TV) or broadcast distribution undertakings (notably cable TV). The new policy is couched in the rhetoric of 'fair competition.' While the term has not been defined, its meaning can be inferred from the actions of the CRTC. In practice, 'fair competition' has meant:

1 Delaying the telephone companies' entry into cable TV until it will be possible for the cable companies to enter the local telephone market (1 January 1998).
2 Allowing (and in at least one case actively encouraging) incumbents to acquire or to create firms that will supply a near substitute for the incumbent's services; e.g., the CRTC sought to have all the major cable companies acquire (joint) control of a single DTH satellite broadcasting company. This effort failed, but it came close to accomplishing its objective.
3 Imposing new, more burdensome Canadian content requirements on all direct and indirect rival broadcasters and distribution undertakings.
4 Suggesting strongly that the Internet should be regulated, in the name of protecting Canadian content, but perhaps also to avoid an unregulated substitute. The Internet has the potential to radically change the distribution of broadband services like video, although a number of other changes must occur before this potential will be realized.

Obviously, 'regulatory shift' can include a wide range of regulation-related activities. We are particularly interested in forces that may result in increased regulation, whether economic or social. Increased regulation could arise from within the transport or communications sectors or it could reflect broader social trends in public policy generally. In telecommunications, the proliferation of new regulations appears to be attributable to several factors:

1 Regulators (and politicians) have been unwilling simply to deregulate, in large part because of the position of dominance of the incumbents. The worry is that they will continue to have market power for a long time, particularly if 'safeguards' are not put in place.
2 Technology and economic efficiency (at this point) require that almost all the telecom carriers be interconnected and interoperable. Spontaneous coordination may not occur smoothly (e.g., the local exchange may be a 'bottleneck' or 'essential facilities' for long-distance carriers) and the benefits of effective competition will be delayed. The downside is that the transition period of 'regulated competition' will be drawn out unnecessarily.
3 It is no easy task to 'unravel' a complex, vertically integrated, horizontally coordinated set of regional telephone monopolies. The problem is far more than a technical one. Rather, regulation was used largely to achieve social policy goals (notably universal service and affordable local rates), and so prices were not used as efficiency-promoting signals, but as regulatory decision variables to achieve other goals. This 'freedom from market forces' could continue only so long as entry was blockaded by the regulator.

4 Canadian regulators have been at least as much concerned about 'fairness'
   vis-à-vis incumbents and potential entrants as about efficiency and a
   speedy transition to almost total reliance on competitive forces rather than
   direct regulation. This has meant more regulation to 'manage' the transition
   and, usually, a less rapid transition.

There are new concerns about the burden of regulation generally. Financially constrained governments are increasingly turning to regulation as a way
to exert influence without spending directly on new programs or using so-
called tax expenditures. In effect, they are shifting the costs onto the private
sector. Thus, a group of the BCNI's member CEOs identified simplifying
regulations as a top public policy priority. And they argued that while regulations can help protect consumers and the environment, too often governments
add them as if they cost nothing. Yet just like excessive taxation, regulations
cause major business expenses.

Broadly speaking there are two types of rationales for more regulation. The
first reflects economic efficiency concerns, i.e., situations where the performance of deregulated markets has not conformed to theoretical ideals and
where it is believed that re-regulation or some other form of government intervention might improve performance. In practice, however, the real choice is
between imperfectly functioning markets and imperfect government regulation. The second rationale we lump together as 'non-efficiency' motives: pressures on government to use regulatory restrictions as a means of conferring
economic benefits to certain groups ('rent-seeking'), and/or to pursue social
goals advocated by these groups (Stanbury 1993b; Tollison 1991).

Some Adverse Economic Outcomes under Deregulation

For the most part, economists have been satisfied with economic performance
under deregulation (Morrison and Winston 1989). But some outcomes have
caused rumblings of discontent and, in some cases, demands for regulatory
protection. The first concern is that of market power arising from mergers and
consolidations in the industry. The second is an echo of the old concern about
'destructive' competition: the possibility that competitive markets are not sustainable, that is, not capable of generating adequate rates of return.

Mergers and Consolidations
Mergers and consolidations raise concerns about market power. Such concerns
have arisen in at least some markets and relate to: (1) foreclosures of routing in
rail mergers; (2) hub dominance in air travel; and (3) predatory actions by large
carriers whose market power was increased by mergers.

Merged rail companies will favour routing traffic over their own system rather than using 'foreign' lines, thus depriving shippers of alternate routes and adversely affecting the economic prospects of these alternate rail lines. There is considerable debate about the motives and underlying economics of rail-routings and markets (Grimm and Harris 1983; Meyer and Tye 1988; Kleit 1990, 1993; Tye 1993a, 1993b). Some residual regulatory protection for 'captive shippers' exists in the U.S. and under the Canada Transportation Act, 1996. But it is safe to say that shippers would prefer real competition to regulatory protection. Also at issue is whether this is truly an economic efficiency question of railroads with market power not minimizing total social costs or an equity issue, whereby shippers receive benefits from regulation relative to the rates they pay in a competitive, unrestricted market.

The attention paid to possible monopoly power under transport deregulation has focused on the airlines. The switch to hub-and-spoke operations by large network carriers was one of the surprises of deregulation (Levine 1987). In some cases, this has resulted in hub dominance, i.e., a single carrier offers the majority of flights to and from its hub and there are no closely substitutable hubs. Hub dominance is associated with higher average fares for flights originating in the hub, although it has also been noted that the higher fare levels are associated with more frequent and non-stop service.[12]

Some people blame lax antitrust enforcement for permitting anticompetitive mergers, as does Alfred Kahn. But all the blame cannot be placed on the antitrust authorities.[13] The merger/consolidation movement in all modes took place contrary to econometric evidence that scale economies were small or non-existent.[14] We did not expect significant advantages of large size, hence mergers were not to be feared. Transportation markets (other than railroads) were thought to be contestable. Gradually it became apparent that airline and other markets are not perfectly contestable (Morrison and Winston 1987). Further, there are significant market advantages of large carriers: they offer comprehensive market coverage, simplified dealings, and service, all of which are valuable to freight and passenger customers (Oum, Stanbury, and Tretheway 1991a, 1991b). A simple but particularly revealing outcome in American airline competition is that the surviving and dominating large carriers are not low-cost carriers but relatively high-cost ones (with the exception of the fast-growing Southwest Airlines). Moreover, they are forming global alliances with their counterparts in Europe and Asia (Oum and Taylor 1995).

We can watch for signs of anticompetitive behaviour and try to minimize firm- or government-created barriers to entry. (This is a key source of market power.) But whether antitrust regulation can play much of a role once large carriers are established is questionable. Antitrust regulation is a far more general tool than direct regulation by a specialized agency (Anderson et al., forthcoming; Stanbury 1996c); its limitations might be demonstrated by looking at predatory behaviour. Airlines (and most other modes) now have immensely complicated pricing policies and are largely unable to measure the exact costs of any specific service, hence proving predation can be extremely difficult.[15] Predation may also involve flooding specific markets with additional capacity to undermine competitors (Levine 1987). While in principle it might be possible to use an airline's own computer reservation system analysis to uncover deliberately unprofitable pricing strategies, as a matter of practice this task is beyond what can be expected from a regulatory agency (Competition Tribunal 1989, 1993).

One procompetitive policy has not been invoked in North America, although it has been discussed at times, namely, allowing entry to foreign airlines. Thus far both Canada and the U.S. retain foreign ownership restrictions on airlines[16] and do not grant cabotage or 'fifth freedom' rights to foreign airlines. (Cabotage is not even permitted between Canada and the U.S. under NAFTA, although this situation is expected to change eventually.) Foreign airlines are a potential source of additional competition, although it may be limited, given the possibility of global alliances formed among large international carriers (Oum and Taylor 1995).

Inadequate Returns for Carriers

The generally low rates of return in most transport industries has revived the 'destructive competition' argument. Subnormal profits cannot persist indefinitely. While there were many entrants to the American airline industry, losses forced a large fraction of them out. One low-cost carrier, Southwest, thrived and expanded; originally a 'niche' carrier, it gradually encroached on larger markets. In recent years there have been additional low-cost entrants, such as Reno Air and ValuJet. In Canada, two new discount scheduled carriers (WestJet and Greyhound), entered the market in 1996, and one exited in 1997. It is too early to assess the long-term prospects of newer, low-cost carriers.[17] If they survive, however, they will place additional competitive pressure on the large, established carriers, whose rates of return have been disappointing (even dismal) since deregulation, although they have improved since the mid-1990s. The low returns in early years could be explained as a combination of initial shock and recession, compounded by the American air traffic controller strike and their mass firing by President Reagan. But the persistence of low rates of return in airlines (and in many carriers in other modes) has raised questions about the sustainability of competitive markets in transportation, the so-called empty core problem.[18]

A high bankruptcy rate in trucking also raises concerns. Periodic bankruptcies accompany a healthy market (the 'revenge of the capital market' phenomenon), but the number and size of bankruptcies after deregulation were probably larger than expected. Bankruptcies are not costless; they are a disruption not only to failed owners, but also to employees and customers.

How can below-normal rates of return persist for long periods of time? Economists generally dismiss the prospect of sustained, irrational losses (a 'lemming model' or 'greater fool' theory according to which there is a highly elastic supply of overly optimistic investors prepared to enter and effectively subsidize an industry until their capital is exhausted). But there may be market circumstances in which there might not be a sustainable set of prices under competition. That is, given a high proportion of fixed or unallocatable costs, could competition drive prices below what would be sustainable in the long run? A major influence is the problem of long-lived assets: bankruptcy merely leads to recapitalization so excess capacity 'haunts' the market and could keep prices below long-run costs for years at a time.

Analysts have suggested that the American bankruptcy laws have aggravated the problem: effectively bankrupt carriers continue to operate, driving down returns to other carriers.[19] But note that even if the company shuts down, the aircraft will be sold, possibly at a large discount, and may stay in the market with a lower capitalized value. There will be downward pressure on prices until the excess capacity is extinguished. If supply expands during 'boom' periods, this will inject another increase in capacity, which will persist for many years whether or not the companies owning the assets can survive. Such arguments have been used to justify the existence of collusive arrangements in shipping.

Externalities

An efficiency concern that has received only limited attention is externalities in transport, such as congestion, pollution, and other unpriced environmental impacts. Safety can involve externalities or other market failure such as inadequate or asymmetric information. By and large, economic deregulation has been accompanied by increased safety regulation, often explicitly emphasized as a means of reassuring the public (this is clearly the case in the Canadian transport deregulation legislation effective 1 July 1996).[20]

Environmental concerns have received increasing attention, although regulatory policies may not be the best means of dealing with them. Examples of regulatory intervention include installation of 'hush kits' on older, noisy aircraft, emission controls on vehicles, and local restrictions on airport operations due to noise.

Arguably the most important transport modes/markets in which externalities are a factor are those in urban transportation rather than intercity freight and passenger travel. Local air pollution and global warming are more affected by urban transport than by other modes. Congestion and related externalities can arise in all modes, notably in hub-and-spoke airport operations, but in the latter case at least some of the costs of congestion delays are internalized by the airline (but not the delay costs to passengers, except as they influence quality of service and ultimately influence the choice of airline or routing). The most serious examples of congestion occur in urban areas. Here there are economic efficiency grounds for substantial government intervention, but little has taken place, other than expenditures on subsidized transit and higher taxes on gasoline and diesel fuel.[21] Urban automobile use is largely unregulated and undertaxed during periods of congestion. Inconsistent links between land use planning, auto use, and transit pricing are the norm rather than the exception. Urban transportation problems might be better dealt with by taxation policies[22] than by regulation, although there is probably a role for both. It is ironic and perhaps misguided to focus the regulation/deregulation debate continually on nonurban transport. Apart from subsidies on intercity rail travel in North America, probably no mode or market in transport incorporates as much economic inefficiency as that present in urban transportation. This is where policy innovation and harnessing of market forces are most needed.

Equity and Rent-Seeking Concerns in Deregulated Transport and Communications Markets

Turning from economic efficiency rationales and concerns about regulation, at the risk of oversimplification we address a number of non-efficiency concerns under one heading. Deregulation adversely affects, or threatens to adversely affect, groups that were explicitly favoured under regulation. We identify two broad groups of users: small and remote communities and 'captive' shippers or travellers. There are many other groups in society who seek to use regulation (or other government policies) as a means to enhance their economic well-being or to push their choice of social-political goals (which, in turn, favour the well-being of certain groups). These are discussed under 'rent-seeking.'

'Captive' Customers
Monopoly pricing generates both efficiency and equity concerns. The efficiency concern is the dead-weight loss of pricing above economic costs, along with possible X-efficiency effects, which arise under situations of market power.

Regulation generally sought to protect customers at the mercy of sole suppliers of transport or communications services. Deregulation removes such protection and allows market forces to work, whether perfectly or imperfectly. Even where deregulation has occurred, however, some residual regulatory protection was retained; rail regulation in North America has already been cited as an example.

It is difficult to sort out efficiency versus equity concerns regarding 'captive' shippers/travellers. Given the substantial amount of unallocatable costs in all transport modes, especially the more capital intensive they are, an optimal pricing strategy (Ramsey pricing) is to allow differential mark-ups above directly identifiable costs, where the mark-ups reflect the value of service (i.e., ability/willingness to pay). For a multiproduct firm, the test of monopoly power is whether or not total revenues more than cover total economic costs. If a carrier is efficient and not earning economic profits, then economic or Ramsey pricing principles would accept even high mark-ups on carriers with less elastic demands. Given the typically low rates of return in the rail industry, despite apparent monopoly power in many markets, this can be an efficiency rationale for not regulating railroads (Heaver and Waters 1982).

But even here, an equity issue remains. Because some shippers or travellers have transport alternatives, their derived demand will appear less elastic to a carrier despite a potentially high willingness to pay. That is, those fortunate to face intramodal or intermodal competition pay lower mark-ups than those without competitive alternatives, i.e., Ramsey pricing does not necessarily impose markups according to willingness to pay, but combine it with the presence or absence of competitive substitutes. In principle, Ramsey pricing should be applied more widely than to a single firm, but this is impractical or would require elaborate regulatory controls (Damus 1984; Taplin and Waters 1985).

Another quasi-captive group consists of business air travellers. They are 'must fly' passengers, although their plight attracts little sympathy from the general public. While air fares have decreased on average, primarily via discounts, the short-notice business or full-fare traveller has seen an increase in fares. It is true that the premium is for a service, *viz.*, the availability of last-minute flight decisions, but it is still a source of some discontent. Business travellers also benefit from increased flight frequency, due to greater amounts of travel, but unless they pay the premium for 'business class' fares, they generally have had less elbow room. During the era of regulation, the load factors were lower, hence there was a higher probability of an empty seat next to you. Under deregulation, airlines use aircraft more efficiently and it is likely that the otherwise empty seat has been sold at a discount. Large companies can negotiate discounts from airlines but smaller companies cannot do as well. On balance, although business travellers constitute a group with some complaints about deregulation, we do not see them as a force for re-regulation.

Service to Small or Remote Communities and Small Customers

Service to small communities was a concern prior to transport deregulation, but for the most part it has not been a major issue. Air transport generally has seen expansion of service and increased frequency to small communities, albeit by turbo-prop planes, which offer less comfort but more frequent service. Prices of service to small communities have tended to rise more quickly after deregulation, when any cross-subsidies ended and prices more closely reflected the full costs of service.

The proponents of deregulation were aware of and took steps to ease the effects on small communities. In the U.S., a subsidy program was put in place but it was not used much, since loss of service was rare. In Canada, the National Transportation Act, 1987 contained the possibility of subsidies for remote communities served only by air, but the provision was never used. Also, Canada continued to regulate air carriers serving the North – albeit with a far less restrictive regime. The North was only deregulated effective 1 July 1996.

In both transport and telecommunications,[23] the feared loss of service to small communities has not been much of an issue. While regulatory regimes eventually brought substantial inefficiencies, arguably they did achieve social goals of extending service to unremunerative areas. Roads and wires are now nearly ubiquitous in North American communities, and new and lower-cost technologies are enabling even remote communities to 'plug into' the communications network. We see this equity issue as having lost much of its momentum in the last few decades.[24]

Another issue in transportation is the freight rate or ticket price for small customers. Under regulation, there were restrictions on offering better prices for large customers, even if there were cost or demand reasons for doing so. Under deregulation, this type of 'discrimination' is, for the most part, no longer regulated. Although there are those who advocate regulatory protection for small shippers, they are not a powerful force for re-regulation.

Rents and Rent-Seeking

Rent-seeking is one of the four most basic drives of human beings (the others being water, food, and sex) (Tollison 1987). While much regulation (in practice if not in rhetoric) stemmed from rent-seeking by the various actors, deregulation does not lessen the urge. It merely tends to frustrate and redirect it.

Rents may be sought in other forms of government assistance (e.g., subsidies or other types of government-created barriers to entry) or from the creation of positions of market power (e.g., mergers to create a dominant position). The way in which the presence of regulation stifled innovation and competition is well known. The most important managerial skills became those related to dealing with regulators and the regulatory process, rather than entrepreneurial abilities and sales. Not surprisingly, there were few in the transport or communications industry who advocated deregulation. Most advocates of deregulation were those wanting to get in and frustrated by the regulators' protection of incumbents. Yet there was no organized 'League of Potential Entrants,' and so the incumbents held sway for a longer time.[25]

Companies will still seek to advance their position by exploiting whatever public policies are available. With deregulation well-established, the best opportunities now appear to lie in finding subtle linkages between transport activities and other government objectives that might be embraced to advance entrenched positions, e.g., protecting the environment, social policy issues with respect to minorities or gender issues, etc., or obtaining restrictions on foreign competitors

Two groups suffered the most in terms of the loss of rents following deregulation: the owners of profitable firms under regulation who were unable to compete in a more competitive environment and organized labour. The owners have taken their losses and moved to other fields. Employees (and their unions) are still feeling the effects of deregulation. Under regulation companies faced less pressure to minimize costs and governments felt answerable if prolonged strikes took place, so labour captured part of the rents from protective economic legislation. Since cost increases can be passed on via a regulatory process, wages and benefits tend to do well under regulation. Wage rates and employment levels have been under strain in all the transport modes since deregulation. Employment levels in air transport actually rose rather than fell because of the overall market stimulation, but average real wages fell as labour's share of industry rents was eliminated (Andriulaitis et al. 1986). But the story is similar in other modes: where competition has increased (due, for example, to globalization), there is downsizing of work forces and stagnation or declines in wage levels. The burgeoning market in telecommunications has offset part of the impacts of deregulation,[26] but the drive to cut costs will persist.

In telecommunications, local phone users are also resisting the impact of deregulation. As is well known, large margins on long-distance service were used to cross-subsidize local phone service (and low local rates were compounded by unmeasured usage, in contrast to long-distance service). Until recently, the telephone companies supported these regulatory-induced cross-subsidies. Regulators in both Canada and the United States have tried to 'phase in' deregulation to allow time for beneficiaries to adjust (Crandall and Waverman 1996). The pressures come from both sides: those anxious to enter and share in the rents available in profitable (usually long-distance) services, and those resisting, who realize that their cross-subsidy will be undermined by competition. Pressure from antipoverty groups has been effective in preventing regulators from eliminating large cross-subsidies in the telephone system in Canada. There has been some rationalization of the price structure, however. Although the latter groups are politically effective, we believe that 'the genie is out of the bottle' and there is no turning back this particular deregulatory tide.

However, we see the 'tax' and 'transfer' scheme controlled by the CRTC as a continued source of wrangles among various players in telecommunications. Worse, the continuation of cross-subsidies provides a justification for the continued existence of the CRTC. In fact, the system is a scandal in terms of the huge dead-weight costs incurred relative to the amounts redistributed. Further, most of the cross-subsidies do not go to low-income households. 'Contribution' is not only a misnomer, it is also a middle-class scam conducted in the name of the poor.

More generally, the number of groups and organizations in society advocating increased government activity are proliferating and larger sums are being spent on efforts to influence governments (Rauch 1995, Stanbury 1993a). These groups are not necessarily adversely affected by deregulation, but they oppose it in favour of increased government intervention to redress various perceived social ills and injustices. Some groups may genuinely be pursuing a social agenda, others may be cloaking personal interests under a 'social' umbrella.

Conclusions

Where does all this lead? In North America, the transportation industries have gone through a sustained period of deregulation, a movement consistent with dissatisfaction with government economic performance (and the analysis by many academics). This movement has spread both to other sectors, including telecommunications, and to many other countries. But the memory of inefficient and ineffective economic regulation of transport is beginning to fade; fear of monopoly power and its paradoxical opposite, 'destructive competition,' is being expressed once again. New economic efficiency concerns have become more prominent, particularly concerns about environmental externalities and safety in transportation. Social equity concerns also persist, and, more importantly, growing numbers of people and groups are acquiring the knowledge and skill to lobby government, whether for personal/group interests or to forward a particular social agenda. Government fiscal constraints are real and limit the ability of governments to respond to social pressures via tax and expenditure policies. This makes regulation an attractive alternative to pursue social goals.

While the once-vast domain of economic regulation has been shrinking quite dramatically over the past two decades, notably in transportation and telecommunications, that of social regulation has expanded. This expansion has taken two broad forms: the widening and deepening of health, safety, and environmental regulation and the creation of new types of social regulation (e.g., the Canada Transportation Act of 1996 contains new rules aimed at making all modes of transportation accessible to persons with disabilities). This is the largest of the various components of what we have called regulatory shift. Others include new regulatory techniques, user fees, changes in the process for creating regulations, and the expansion of economic regulation during the transition period to full competition.

Our analysis suggests that every substantial change in public policy (like deregulation in the transport or telecommunications sector) not only results in important unanticipated consequences but also generates new demands for government intervention to cope with the 'fall out' from those changes in policy. Re-regulation is unlikely, but the reaction to deregulation may inhibit similar moves elsewhere, although international agreements to deregulate or liberalize (like the one on basic telecommunications services) may offset such tendencies in some cases.

As usual, the way ahead is unclear. The economic deregulation movement still has momentum, but it might be weakening. At the same time, interest groups clamour for environmental improvements and want to reduce risks and correct perceived social inequities. These desires place pressures on government to act, and regulatory policies are increasingly the most feasible policy mechanism in the face of fiscal constraints. The desire for reductions in government activity is now being contested by those whose ideas were pushed aside by supporters of deregulation and fiscal responsibility. This clash is likely to be a major focus of public policy debate as we approach the millennium.

NOTES

1 Urban transport in North America is primarily a state/provincial or even local responsibility. Deregulation is more of a national or even international movement, pushed by federal governments. Deregulation has moved much more slowly or been resisted by most states and provinces in North America.
2 There are numerous articles and books on the deregulation experience. At the risk of offending many deserving authors, here we list only a few. More has been

written about air deregulation than any other mode. Borenstein (1992), Levine
(1987), and Morrison and Winston (1989, 1995) are particularly insightful and
comprehensive reviews of the American air deregulation experience. For Canadian
air deregulation, see Oum, Stanbury, and Tretheway (1991a, 1991b). A review of
motor carrier deregulation and its effects in both Canada and the U.S. is provided
by Chow (1995). American surface freight deregulation is reviewed in Winston et
al. (1990), U.S. passenger transport (and other modes) are discussed in Meyer and
Oster (1987). An overview of Canadian surface transportation, primarily rail, is
found in Heaver (1990, 1997), while Canadian shipping regulations are reviewed in
Heaver (1992).
3 Of the twenty largest LTL (less-than-truckload) motor carriers existing in 1979, ten
had gone bankrupt by 1988 and four more merged with other large carriers. The
three largest carriers remained on top and expanded considerably (Lambert and
Stock 1993, 195).
4 Traditionally, this has been taken to mean low (even below-cost) local rates.
However, in 1995 the CRTC made it clear that affordability referred to both local
and long-distance rates.
5 Sadly, while the CRTC has now permitted competition in the local/access market,
effective 1 January 1998, it did not move to phase out the 'contribution' payments
from long-distance to local service. It did, however, make them portable in the
sense that new entrants to the local exchange market can receive contribution. See
CRTC (1997b).
6 The last two matters were quickly challenged in the courts. The result is likely to
be that the introduction of competition in local exchange services will be slowed
down.
7 The Canadian federal government has had direct involvement in telecommunications apart from its regulatory role. Originally, it owned 50 per cent of CNCP
Telecommunications (now AT&T Canada, previously Unitel); 100 per cent of
Teleglobe, which provided international telephone service; and 53.7 per cent of
Telesat, Canada's satellite carrier. All were privatized in the 1980s or 1990s, see
Stanbury (1994). The federal government continues to be very active in regulating
broadcasting for cultural reasons. See Globerman, Janisch, and Stanbury (1996).
8 BC Tel is over 50 per cent owned by GTE of the U.S. Bell Canada, affiliated with
AT&T early in its history, has long been an independent, Canadian-owned
company which serves Ontario and Quebec (and, through its parent, has effective
control over several telephone companies in eastern Canada).
9 The chair of the Patented Medicines Prices Review Board set up in 1987 claims
that price regulation by the board has saved consumers between $2.9 billion and
$4.2 billion. Patented drug prices rose 1.6 per cent per year since 1988 versus 3.1
per cent for the CPI (*Financial Post*, 28 February 1997, 8). The board became

more important in 1993 when patent protection was extended to twenty years for new drugs and licensing by generic drug makers was made more difficult and expensive.

10 See Vedder (1996). The Canada Transportation Act of 1996 contains extensive provisions dealing with transportation of persons with disabilities. 'Undue obstacles' in the transportation network must be eliminated, but the term is not defined and is to be determined according to the nature of each case. Codes of practice for each mode have been or will be developed.

11 In general, while economic or direct regulation has been eliminated or made less restrictive, there has been a substantial growth in social regulation, particularly to achieve health and safety, and environmental protection objectives. The Forest Practices Code of B.C. Act (1995) is an outstanding example. The legislation, regulations, standards, and guidebooks amount to over five feet of paper. There are over three hundred provisions that can result in a civil monetary penalty (i.e., a fine) and possibly other sanctions. Stanbury has described the volume of new environmental regulations as a 'green tsunami.'

12 See for example, Borenstein (1989, 1991), Huston and Butler (1989), and Dresner and Windle (1992).

13 Indeed, in Canada the Competition Bureau played an important role in preventing Air Canada from acquiring Canadian Airlines by helping the latter to get out of the onerous contract with Gemini computerized reservation system so Canadian could form an alliance with American Airlines, which wanted Canadian to use its Sabre reservation system. See Competition Tribunal, Reasons and Order re Director of Investigation and Research and Air Canada et al., CT–88/1, 22 April 1993.

14 The number of empirical studies into scale economies in various transport modes are too numerous to cite individually. For a summary see Winston (1985), Jara-Diaz (1982), or Oum and Waters (1996).

15 Part of the problem is that the definition of predatory pricing in the antitrust laws is based on theory developed for goods-producing markets rather than services with heterogeneity of output and difficulty of assigning costs.

16 In Canada, foreign shareholders are limited to 25 per cent of the direct voting shares and no more than one-third held indirectly. Further, Canadians must have control in fact of carriers serving the domestic market. The U.S. is slightly less restrictive.

17 All the new low-cost carriers have been shaken by the public's response to the crash in Florida of a ValuJet DC-9. See *Wall Street Journal*, 17 May 1996, p. B2; 22 May 1996, pp. B1, B2. Later ValuJet agreed to a temporary suspension of all service after FAA inspectors found 'serious deficiencies' in its operations (*Globe and Mail*, 18 June 1996, p. B11) and subsequently statistics were released showing that the low cost airlines (except for Southwest) had poorer safety records than the

established carriers (*Vancouver Sun*, 19 June 1996). (These carriers are still far safer than driving your car.)

18 See Button (1996) on airlines; Sjostrom (1989), (1993) on shipping; and an overview of the issue in Button and Nijkamp (1997).

19 Perhaps the best example is Continental Airlines. It went through Chapter 11 twice and continues to operate today.

20 It has been suggested the American savings and loan débâcle is an example of economic deregulation unaccompanied by better safety regulation to protect depositors.

21 In a couple of cases in Canada and the U.S., road capacity is being expanded by private sector firms authorized to charge tolls.

22 New computer and communication technologies permit the pricing of roads by time of day by photographing licence plates or recording passage of an owner identity strip attached to vehicles.

23 In telecommunications, higher local rates and lower long-distance rates resulted in an increase in the penetration rate (the percentage of households with a phone) in the U.S. In Canada, the 98.5 per cent penetration rate is unlikely to fall as rate rebalancing and local rate restructuring occurs because the price elasticity of demand for local service is about –0.1 per cent (Globerman, Janisch, and Stanbury 1996a).

24 We note that the CRTC held extensive hearings on how to maintain 'universal affordable telephone rates' (i.e., low local rates) in the face of the need for eliminating the cross-subsidy from toll to local services and restructuring rates within the local category. See CRTC Public Notice 95–49.

25 An excellent example of the never-say-die spirit of incumbents is the American RBOCs' (largely successful) efforts to persuade state-level regulatory bodies to resist entry into local telephony. Some state regulators are preventing the implementation of the federal Telecommunications Act of 1996.

26 Both AT&T and the RBOCs have reduced total employment substantially. The entrant long-distance carriers (e.g., MCI, Sprint) have taken up part of the slack.

REFERENCES

Anderson, Robert D., Abraham Hollander, Joseph Monteiro, and W.T. Stanbury. Regulatory Reform and the Expanding Role of Competition Policy in the Canadian Economy, 1986–1996. *Review of Industrial Organization* (forthcoming).

Andriulaitis, Robert J., David L. Frank, Tae H. Oum, and Michael W. Tretheway. 1986. *Deregulation and Airline Employment: Myth Versus Fact.* Vancouver: Centre for Transportation Studies, University of British Columbia.

Borenstein, Severin. 1989. Hubs and High Fares: Airport Dominance and Market Power in the U.S. Airline Industry. *Rand Journal of Economics* 20 (Autumn): 344–65.

–   1991. The Dominant-Firm Advantage in Multi-Product Industries: Evidence from the U.S. Airlines. *Quarterly Journal of Economics* 106:1237–66.

–   1992. The Evolution of U.S. Airline Competition. *Journal of Economic Perspectives* 6, no. 2 (Spring): 45–73.

Button, K.J. 1996. Liberalizing European Aviation: Is there an Empty Core Problem? *Journal of Transport Economics and Policy* 30:275–91.

Button, K.J., and P. Nijkamp. 1997. Network Industries, Economic Stability and Spatial Integration. Discussion Paper, Institute of Public Policy, George Mason University, Fairfax, Va.

Cairncross, Frances. 1995. The Death of Distance, A Survey of Telecommunications. *The Economist* 30 September, 1–28.

Chow, Garland. 1995. North American Trucking Policy. In T.H. Oum et al., *Transport Economics: Selected Readings*. Korean: Seoul Press.

Competition Tribunal. 1989. *DIR v. Air Canada and Canadian Airlines International (Gemini I)*. Consent Order, 7 July.

–   1993. *Canada (Director of Investigation and Research) v. Air Canada et al. (Gemini II)*. Modification of July 1989 Consent Order, 23 April 1993.

Crandall, Robert W., and Leonard Waverman. 1996. *Talk is Cheap: The Promise of Regulatory North American Communications*. Washington, D.C.: Brookings Institution.

CRTC. 1997a. *Price Cap Regulation and Related Issues*. Telecom Decision CRTC 97–9, 1 May.

–   1997b. *Local Competition*. Telecom Decision CRTC 97–8, 1 May.

Damus, Sylvester. 1984. Ramsey Pricing in U.S. Railroads: Can it Exist? *Journal of Transport Economics and Policy* (January): 51–63.

DeMuth, Christopher. 1983. What is Regulation? In R.J. Zeckhauser and D. Leebaert, eds., *What Role for Government? Lessons From Policy Research*, 262–78. Durham, N.C.: Duke University Press.

Dresner, Martin, and R. Windle. 1992. Airport Dominance and Yields in the U.S. Airline Industry. *Logistics and Transportation Review* 28, no. 4: 319–40.

Economic Council of Canada. 1979. *Responsible Regulation: An Interim Report*. Ottawa: Minister of Supply and Services.

Globerman, Steven, Hudson N. Janisch, and W.T. Stanbury. 1996a. Moving Toward Local Distribution Network Competition in Canada. *Telecommunications Policy* 20, no. 2: 141–57.

–   1996b. Convergence, Competition and Canadian Content. In W.T. Stanbury, ed., *Perspectives on the New Economics of Telecommunications*, ch. 12. Montreal: Institute for Research on Public Policy.

Globerman, Steven, Tae H. Oum, and W.T. Stanbury. 1993. Competition in Public
    Long Distance Telephone Markets in Canada. *Telecommunications Policy* 17 (May/
    June): 297–310.
– 1994. The Nature and Evolution of Telecommunications Policy in Canada. In
    Hajime Oniki, Tae H. Oum, and Rodney Stevenson, eds., *International Perspec-
    tives on Telecommunications Policy* 5:163–202. Greenwich, Conn.: JAI Press Inc.
Grimm, Curt, and Robert G. Harris. 1983. Vertical Foreclosure in the Rail Freight
    Industry. *ICC Practitioner's Journal* 50 (July/August): 508–31.
Heaver, Trevor D. 1990. Transport Regulation and Privatization in Canada. In
    J.J. Richardson, ed., *Privatization and Deregulation in Canada and Britain*,
    109–37. Aldershot, U.K.: Dartmouth Publishing.
– 1992. Canada and the Evolving System of International Shipping Conferences. In
    A. Claire Cutler and Mark W. Zacher, eds., *Canadian Foreign Policy and Interna-
    tional Economic Regimes*, 215–36. Vancouver: UBC Press.
– 1997. Restructuring of Inter-City Railway Freight Services in Canada. *IATSS
    Research* 21, no. 1: 24–32.
Heaver, Trevor D., and W.G. Waters II. 1982. Public Enterprise under Competition:
    A Comment on Canadian Railways. In W.T. Stanbury and Fred Thompson, eds.,
    Managing Public Enterprises. New York: Praeger.
Huston, John H., and Richard V. Butler. 1988. The Effects of Fortress Hubs on Airline
    Fares and Service: The Early Returns. *Logistics and Transportation Review* 24:
    203–15.
Jara-Diaz, Sergio R. 1982. The Estimation of Transport Cost Functions: A Method-
    ological Review. *Transport Review* 2, no. 3: 257–78.
Jordan, William A. 1970. *Airline Regulation in America: Effects and Imperfections*.
    Baltimore: Johns Hopkins University Press.
Kleit, Andrew N. 1990. The Unclogged Bottleneck: Why Competitive Access Should
    not be an Antitrust Concern. *Logistics and Transportation Review* 26, no. 3:
    229–47.
– 1993. Problems Come Before Solutions: Comment on Pricing Market Access for
    Regulated Firms. *Logistics and Transportation Review* 29, no. 1: 69–74.
Lambert, Douglas M., and James R. Stock. 1993. *Strategic Logistics Management*.
    3rd ed. Boston: Irwin.
Levine, Michael E. 1987. Airline Competition in Deregulated Markets: Theory, Firm
    Strategy, and Public Policy. *Yale Journal on Regulation* 4 (Spring): 393–494.
MacAvoy, Paul W., et al. 1989. *Privatization and State-Owned Enterprises: Lessons
    from the United States, Great Britain, and Canada*. Boston: Kluwer Academic
    Publishers.
Meyer, J.R. 1959. *The Economics of Competition in the Transportation Industries*.
    Cambridge: Harvard University Press.

Meyer, J.R., and C.V. Oster, Jr. 1987. *Deregulation and the Future of Intercity Passenger Travel.* Cambridge, Mass.: MIT Press.

Meyer, J.R., and William B. Tye. 1988. Toward Achieving Workable Competition in Industries Undergoing a Transition to Deregulation: a Contractual Equilibrium Approach. *Yale Journal on Regulation* 5:222–55.

Mihlar, Fazil. 1997. Federal Deregulation, Regulatory Reform and Regulatory Management: Rhetoric and Reality? *Public Policy Sources* No. 6. Vancouver: Fraser Institute.

Mokhtarian, Patricia L. 1990. A Typology of Relationships between Telecommunications and Transportation. *Transportation Research A* 24, no. 3: 231–42.

Morrison, Steven A., and Clifford Winston. 1987. Empirical Implications and Tests of the Contestability Hypothesis. *Journal of Law and Economics* 30:53–66.

– 1989. Airline Deregulation and Public Policy. *Science* 245, no. 18 (August): 707–11.

– 1995. *The Evolution of the Airline Industry.* Washington, D.C.: Brookings Institution.

Nankivell, Neville. 1997. Drug patent protection hearings set off a frenzy of lobbying activity, *Financial Post*, 1 February, 25.

Nelson, James C. 1959, *Railroad Competition and Public Policy.* Washington: Brookings Institution.

Nemetz, Peter N., W.T. Stanbury, and Fred Thompson. 1986. Social Regulation in Canada: An Overview and Comparison with the American Model. *Policy Studies Journal* 14, no. 4: 580–603.

Oum, Tae Hoon, W.T. Stanbury, and Michael W. Tretheway. 1991a. Airline Deregulation in Canada and Its Economic Effects. *Transportation Journal*, 30, no. 4 (Summer): 4–22.

– 1991b. Airline Deregulation in Canada. In Kenneth Button, ed., *Airline Deregulation: International Experiences*, 124–87. New York: New York University Press.

Oum, Tae Hoon, and A.J. Taylor. 1995. Emerging Patterns in Intercontinental Air Linkages and Implications for International Route Allocation Policy. *Transportation Journal* 34, no. 4 (Summer): 5–27.

Oum, Tae Hoon, and W.G. Waters II. 1996. Recent Developments in Cost Function Research in Transportation. *Logistics and Transportation Review* 32, no. 4: 423–63.

Rauch, Jonathan. 1995. *Demosclerosis: The Silent Killer of American Government.* New York: Random House.

Salomon, Ilan. 1985. Telecommunications and Travel: Substitution or Modified Mobility? *Journal of Transport Economics and Policy* (September): 219–35.

– 1986. Telecommunications and Travel Relationships: A Review. *Transportation Research A* 20A, no. 3: 223–38.

Sjostrom, W. 1989. Collusion in Ocean Shipping: A Test of Monopoly and Empty Core Models. *Journal of Political Economy* 97:1160–79.

– 1993. Antitrust Immunity for Shipping Conferences: An Empty Core Approach. *Antitrust Bulletin* 38:419–23.

Stanbury, W.T. 1992. *Reforming the Federal Regulatory Process in Canada, 1971– 1992 (Minutes of Proceedings and Evidence of the Subcommittee on Regulations and Competitiveness of the House of Commons Standing Committee on Finance)*, Issue 23, 17 Nov.–10 Dec., A1–A293.

– 1993a. *Business-Government Relations in Canada: Influencing Public Policy.* Toronto: Nelson Canada.

– 1993b. A Skeptic's Guide to the Claims of So-called 'Public Interest Groups.' *Canadian Public Administration* 36, no. 4 (Winter): 580–605.

– 1994. Privatization by Federal and Provincial Governments in Canada: An Empirical Study. In Robert Bernier and J.I. Gow, eds., *Un Etat Reduit? A Down-Sized State?*, 165–219. St Foy: Presses de l'Université du Québec.

– 1995. Redeeming the Promise of Confluence: Analysis of Issues Facing the CRTC. In Steven Globerman et al., eds., *The Future of Telecommunications Policy in Canada*, ch. 30. Vancouver: Bureau of Applied Research, Faculty of Commerce and Business Administration, University of British Columbia; Toronto: Institute for Policy Analysis, University of Toronto.

– 1996a. Chronology of Canadian Telecommunications: January 1992 to January 1996. In W.T. Stanbury, ed., *Perspectives on the New Economics of Telecommunications*, ch. 15. Montreal: Institute for Research on Public Policy.

– ed. 1996b. *Perspectives on the New Economics of Telecommunications.* Montreal: Institute for Research on Public Policy.

– 1996c. The Routine Pathologies of Regulations Designed to Reduce Risks to Human Health and Safety. Paper presented at the National Workshop on Canadian Maritime Safety sponsored by Transport Canada, Vancouver, 13–14 November.

– 1997. New Thinking, New Developments and Emerging Issues Related to Government Regulation: A Quick and Possibly Idiosyncratic Tour. Vancouver: Faculty of Commerce and Business Administration, University of British Columbia, September, mimeo.

Stanbury, W.T., and George Lermer. 1983. Regulation and the Redistribution of Income and Wealth. *Canadian Public Administration* 26, no. 3: 378–401.

Taplin, John H.E., and W.G. Waters II. 1985. Boiteux-Ramsey Pricing of Road and Rail Transport under a Single Budget Constraint. *Australian Economic Papers* (December): 337–49.

Tollison, Robert D. 1987. Is the Theory of Rent Seeking Here to Stay? In C.K. Rowley, ed., *Democracy and Public Choice*, 143–57. Oxford: Blackwell.

Tye, William B. 1993a. Pricing Market Access for Regulated Firms. *Logistics and Transportation Review* 29, no. 1: 39–68.

– 1993b. Pricing Market Access for Regulated Firms: Reply. *Logistics and Transportation Review* 29, no. 1: 75–80.

Vedder, Richard. 1996. America the Disabled. *Wall Street Journal*, 4 September, A14.

Winston, Clifford. 1985. Conceptual Developments in the Economics of Transportation: An Interpretive Survey. *Journal of Economic Literature* (March): 124–5.

Winston, Clifford, Thomas M. Corsi, Curtis M. Grimm, and Carol A. Evans. 1990. *The Economic Effects of Surface Freight Deregulation*. Washington, D.C.: Brookings Institution.

8

Winning and Losing: The Consumers' Association of Canada and the Telecommunications Regulatory System, 1973–1993

RICHARD J. SCHULTZ

More than twenty years ago, consumer activist and legal scholar Michael Trebilcock (1975) poignantly asked, 'must the consumer always lose' in the modern regulatory system? His answer, like that of most interest group analysts, was not particularly positive. Consumer groups, as a subset of what became conventionally grouped together as 'public interest groups,' were said to suffer from a number of congenital defects that consigned them to a secondary, if not peripheral, role in the political process, whatever the arena. They lacked sufficient financial and staff resources, had limited memberships with fragmented interests, and were denied, by other actors, societal and state, that most crucial necessity, legitimacy, a prerequisite to effective, sustained participation and influence (Trebilcock 1975; Goldstein 1979; Berry 1977; Presthus 1973; Kwavnick 1972; Engelhart and Trebilcock 1981). Consequently, Trebilcock (1975, 626) appeared to share Stigler and Cohen's negative assessment that 'we can't construct ... a viable continuing broad-based consumer political lobby' (Stigler and Cohen 1971, 49).

Ironically, almost simultaneously with the publication of Trebilcock's bleak assessment, the Consumers' Association of Canada (CAC) was emerging as a respected and effective participant, at least in the regulatory arena (Goldstein 1979; Dawson 1963). Not only did it gain official standing before the regulators but it acquired sufficient financial resources to employ the necessary legal and complementary expertise to influence regulatory decisions. Although it faced opposition, its views and contributions ultimately became both welcomed and solicited by regulatory agencies and other political actors addressing regulatory issues. It is of course difficult to link CAC advocacy precisely to specific regulatory and other outcomes, but most observers in the 1980s assigned considerable weight to CAC interventions. Indeed, one senior federal telecommunications regulator interviewed for this chapter maintains that in the first five years of the 1980s the CAC was the only effective regulatory intervener and certainly more effective than any group representing business telecommunications subscribers.

Its influence and effective role were relatively short-lived, however, for by the end of the 1980s the CAC's regulatory arm had largely disappeared. Even its hard-won legitimacy was undermined, as other participants, including the Canadian Radio-television and Telecommunications Commission (CRTC), questioned the value of CAC regulatory contributions. No clearer sign of the CAC's fall from regulatory grace could be found than the CRTC's decision in 1992 to deny the association most of its request for the costs of its participation in the most important telecommunications regulatory proceeding to date, namely, that to open the public long-distance voice market to competition.

My objective in this chapter is to analyse the period from 1973, the year of the creation of what became known as the CAC Regulated Industries Program (RIP) to 1993, the year in which the CAC lost its eligibility for core governmental funding. I will first explain how the Consumers' Association of Canada overcame considerable obstacles to emerge as an effective, influential participant in the federal telecommunications regulatory system. In the second section I attempt to account for how it lost that effectiveness.

The CAC and Organizational Struggles in the Regulatory Arena

Students of interest groups have stressed that 'public interest groups' such as the Consumers' Association are typically disadvantaged from the beginning in their struggle to become effective.[1] In particular, they are viewed as lacking three essential organizational attributes: status or, more generally, legitimacy as political participants; resources, financial and otherwise; and autonomy. How the CAC was able to overcome these obstacles, at least in the regulatory arena, during the latter half of the 1970s can tell us much about the CAC, the regulatory process, and the larger interest group universe in Canada at this time.

Organizational Legitimacy

The first major obstacle that any public interest group must confront is its lack of standing or status in the specific political process or policy network in which it seeks membership. Such interest groups are presumed to lack the most basic legitimacy that is accorded, almost automatically, to other participants, particularly corporations and their associations. This lack of acceptable status would seem to be especially pronounced in highly specialized political processes, such as those involving regulatory agencies, where the norm was the closed policy network or community. Although one variant of such a network is that of the 'captured' agency (Bernstein 1955), one need not subscribe to the presumption that all regulatory agencies fall under the control of the regulated companies to recognize that, until the 1970s, most regulatory agencies and processes had both a limited number of participants and close relationships based on continuity and a 'clublike' atmosphere.

Consequently, the appearance of new groups in Canada and their demands for inclusion and voice caused by the growth of consumerism and environmentalism beginning in the early 1970s, a decade after their appearance in the United States (Vogel 1989; Berry 1977; Pross 1986) challenged the consensus of 'elite accommodation' (Presthus 1973) that was perhaps nowhere more pronounced than in the regulatory arena. Prior to the 1970s, as Kane (1980, 13) argues, 'the range of interest articulation before the [regulatory] tribunals has indeed been limited.' In the case of telephone regulation, for example, there were few participants other than the federally regulated telephone companies themselves. Traditionally, as Kane points out, other than two provincial governments, starting in the 1960s, and, before that, municipalities, 'there is little record of activity or interest on the part of other individuals or groups' (Kane 1980, 13).

The 1970s witnessed several fundamental challenges to the traditional Canadian telecommunications regulatory system, as a result of a convergence of technological, economic, international, political, and judicial issues (Schultz 1982; Stanbury 1986; Janisch and Romaniuk 1995; Globerman et al. 1995; Schultz and Brawley 1996). One of the first signs of the impending shift was the phenomenal growth in regulatory proceedings. Whereas there had only been ten in the previous six decades since Bell Canada and the British Columbia Telephone Company came under federal regulation, the 1970s were characterized by almost constant regulatory activity as a result, in the first instance, of the growth of inflation and the concomitant demand by the companies for rate relief. If the regulatory turbulence of the 1970s were not a sufficient cause for concern on the part of the regulated companies and, indeed, their regulators, who were accustomed to a much quieter regulatory life, away from public scrutiny, the arrival of new interests and groups such as the Consumers' Association reflected the larger threat to the traditional regulatory consensus.

Both regulated firms and regulators were reluctant to welcome the new participants. For the firms, groups such as the CAC could only threaten their dominance, complicate the process, and delay and possibly undermine favourable regulatory decisions. For the telecommunications regulator, then the Canadian Transport Commission, the CAC and similar groups constituted a double threat.

In the first place, they further politicized an increasingly political process and forum. Secondly, they challenged the deeply entrenched, self-defined role perceptions of the regulator. Regulators, in the words of one of them, saw themselves 'as custodians of the public interest' (quoted in Kane (1980), 15). Consumer groups contended that not only was that not the role of regulators, but that no group, including the CAC, represented the 'public interest.' As Greg Kane, the CAC's second general counsel, argued, 'the public's interest is an amalgam of a variety of sub-interests which are affected by any public issue' (Kane 1980, 19). Given the challenge that views such as these posed to the status quo, it is not surprising that they were greeted with ' a certain degree of scepticism if not outright hostility from both commissioners and the staff of tribunals' (Kane 1980, 15).

Such reactions were reinforced when the CAC, among others, challenged not only the comfortable regulatory 'modus operandi' but even, on occasion, the impartiality of the regulators. They emphasized the adversarial, as opposed to the conventional nonconfrontational, almost consensual, nature of the regulatory process. Furthermore, the willingness of the new interveners to use not simply the regulatory proceedings but also the media; the larger political process, such as appeals to cabinet and presentations to Parliament; and the courts to insist both on being recognized as legitimate participants and accorded weight only further alienated regulators. The successful challenge by three public advocacy groups, including the Consumers' Association, to the right of the chair of the National Energy Board to preside over the Mackenzie Valley Pipeline hearing only underscored the demand for status and reinforced the hostility of at least some incumbent regulators and their staff (Kane 1980, 33–5).

It is likely, notwithstanding the initial reaction, that such opposition, at least from the regulators, would eventually have been diluted. First the reluctant regulators and then regulated firms were forced to recognize that the CAC and similar groups not only would not disappear but they had to be treated as legitimate participants. There were two specific causes for the change that did occur, both of which reflect the role that the Canadian state, especially since the 1960s, has played in fostering interest group activity in a wide range of areas (Dawson 1963, 1975; Pal 1993). The first was the decision by the Government of Canada, through its Department of Consumer and Corporate Affairs, in 1973 to announce an 'interim experiment' to fund the CAC, particularly its regulatory advocacy program. Less than a year later the 'experiment' was extended and the funding level increased.

Undoubtedly, the single most important factor in the CAC's attainment of regulatory legitimacy followed the 1976 legislation to transfer jurisdiction for telecommunications regulation from the Canadian Transport Commission (CTC) to the renamed Canadian Radio-television and Telecommunications Commission (CRTC). Although there were several reasons for this transfer, it was widely perceived to be a vote of non-confidence not only in the CTC as regulator but in the telecommunications regulatory status quo. Underscoring this judgment was the immediate release by the new CRTC of a position paper on procedures and practices (CRTC 1976, 2), which declared that two of its central objectives were 'to facilitate the involvement of the public in the regulatory process through greater informality and public access' and 'to increase the capacity of intervenors to participate in an informed way.' In a complementary paper (CRTC 1978b, 3) on broadcasting, the CRTC emphasized its view, which corresponded to that of consumer advocates, that 'no single person or group embodies the public interest and that the assistance and active participation of significant numbers of the general public are indispensable to the decision-making process.' The commission went on to argue that 'the Commission should build upon its past experience so as to enhance the public's participation in the regulatory process ... This paper ... examines a number of particular practices and procedures with a view not only to facilitating public involvement but also to facilitating a more intense and efficient exploration of issues at hearings' (CRTC 1978b, 4).

In short, the CRTC's emphasis on broad public participation and the government funding of the CAC's regulatory intervention program (see below) constituted an official granting of standing and legitimacy for public interest groups in general and the CAC in particular. Henceforth, at least in the telecommunications arena, neither regulators nor regulated firms could or would challenge the right of the CAC to intervene.

Although the CAC fought a hard battle for regulatory legitimacy, as Kane and other participants at this time can attest, the successful outcome was only partially due to their efforts. Rather, the outcome says much about the role of the state and state actors in encouraging and facilitating interest groups and their demands on state agencies. Courting the CAC began shortly after the Department of Consumer and Corporate Affairs was created in 1968, as the new department sought to build up its various constituencies, especially in light of the suspicion of the business community that ensued. One of the first steps was the creation of an advisory Consumer Council, which commissioned a number of studies on regulatory agencies (Stanbury 1976). Second, according to Goldstein (1979, 146) the department immediately encouraged the CAC to create a consumer advocacy program.

Partisan as well as departmental politics were also influential: the initial advocacy grant came at a time when the minority Liberal government was threatened by the New Democratic Party with a withdrawal of its support if the government did not overturn a CTC-approved rate increase for Bell Canada. Nor was it a coincidence that the renewal and increase in the grant came prior to the 1974 election. As we shall note below, after the Liberals regained their majority in 1974, they were less committed to the Regulated Industries Program (RIP) grant and only vigorous lobbying efforts both from within and without the government protected the funding. Even the CRTC's embrace of 'facilitating public involvement' must be understood in terms of bureaucratic needs as well as genuine sympathy for such involvement. The CRTC had been forced by the CAC through a court action to accept more liberal information disclosure practices in the broadcasting sector and was caught up in battles both with the increasingly powerful cable sector and its departmental allies. Having proclaimed a new era in telecommunications regulation in contradistinction to that of the 'ancien regime' under the CTC, the CRTC needed its own allies in its efforts to bring this about. Public interest groups such as the CAC provided perhaps one of the few available possibilities that could aid the CRTC objective, especially given the formidable resources at the disposal of the regulated telephone companies.

Organizational Funding

Overcoming the hurdle of legitimacy was only one of the organizational disabilities confronting the CAC. There was little to be gained by the association from a mere right to participate in regulatory proceedings. Absent sufficient resources, including financing and an ability to call upon both in-house and external expert advice, it was hardly in a position to make an effective contribution to the regulatory process. Access to such funding and other resources has long been an endemic problem for groups such as the CAC, owing to the limited opportunity to provide collective goods for members and the significant 'free rider' problems confronting such groups (Olson 1965).

The CAC was able to avoid such problems because of the manner in which it acquired the necessary resources. They came from the government, both directly and indirectly, with the result that the association did not have to seek membership support for its regulatory work. The CAC's entrance into the regulatory arena was facilitated by the $100,000 grant it received in 1973 from the Department of Consumer and Corporate Affairs as part of its 'experiment.' It is instructive to note that the initiative for this grant came from the department and not in response to a CAC request. From the initial grant, the association allocated $35,000 for formal regulatory interventions (Trebilcock 1975,

TABLE 8.1
Consumer and Corporate Affairs Grants to CAC Regulatory Industries Program,
1973–1992

Year	Amount $
1973–4	35,000
1974–5	116,000
1975–6	215,000
1976–7	183,837
1977–8	170,000
1978–9	175,000
1979–80	150,000
1980–1	225,000
1981–2	315,000
1982–3	300,000
1983–4	315,000
1984–5	300,000
1985–6	327,500
1986–7	325,000
1987–8	335,000
1988–9	336,000
1989–90	185,000
1990–1	185,000
1991–2	175,000
1992–3	175,000

Sources: Trebilcock (1975); Annual Reports, Regulated Industries Program; Office of
Consumer Affairs, Industry Canada – author's calculations for the last three years.

631). Table 8.1 provides information on the amount of the money that the CAC
received from the Department of Consumer and Corporate Affairs from 1973
to 1993.[2]

Total amounts relative to the funds available to regulated firms and to the
range of interventions and activities of the CAC program suggest that the
program could not be described as overly endowed. The substantial increase in
the post-1982 period represented a decision by the department to continue to
provide an operational grant for ongoing expenses and a contribution grant for
regulatory 'research,' such as the manual, 'Costs Awards in Regulatory Proceedings' (RIP 1979), developed by the CAC to aid other public participants.
One of the problems the CAC faced in the early years was that the grant was
made on an annual basis, with no assurance of continuity. The reductions after
the initial grants reflected the lessened commitment of the government to supporting the program. In fact, in the late 1970s there was a concentrated effort

by Bell Canada to have the government eliminate the grant as part of the 'war on inflation' (Engelhart and Trebilcock 1981, 149). Only effective lobbying by some of the · rogram's advisers, combined with support from senior regulators and departmental officials, in itself a measure of legitimacy acquired by the program, managed not only to fend off such a threat but to gain a five-year funding commitment, albeit one that permitted reductions and provided no protection against inflation.

The second major step in the development of the CAC's resources came in 1978, with the CRTC's decision to award costs to public participants in its regulatory proceedings. A major irony of this decision was that the CRTC used the same section of the relevant statute, the National Transportation Act, that the CTC had used three years earlier, invoking a 1911 precedent, to deny costs to public interveners such as consumer groups (Trebilcock 1978; Kane 1980, 106–7). While the CRTC acknowledged that awarding costs to be paid by regulated firms was not its first preference (CRTC 1978a, 39), it had no alternative if its objective of increased intervener capacity was to be attained (CRTC 1978a, 37–8):

The commission has concluded that if the objective of informed participation in public hearings is to be met, some form of financial assistance must be made to responsible interveners, both active and potential, who do not have sufficient funds to properly prosecute their cases, particularly where such interveners represent the interests of a substantial number or class of subscribers. The complexity and importance of the issues which come before the Commission often demand that expert resources be available for their adequate treatment. Such resources are employed by the regulated companies. In the Commission's view, it is critical to, and part of the regulatory process that such resources also be available to responsible representative interveners.

Consequently, the CRTC established the rules governing the awarding of costs to public interveners. Costs would be covered for interveners who had either a substantial interest in the proceeding or represented a substantial number of subscribers but lacked the resources necessary to participate. Awards were conditional, however, on the commission's judgment that such participation had been responsible and contributed to a better understanding of the issues by the commission.

The CRTC costs decision, while the most significant advance in the development of consumer representation before the telecommunications regulator, was neither open-ended nor an automatic guarantee that the CAC or any applicant would be awarded costs. Costs were initially to be limited to telephone rate cases, but the CRTC soon extended them to other telecommunications regulatory proceedings. More crucially, costs were dependent on 'responsible' interventions that 'contributed to a better understanding ... by the Commission' of the issues before it. In short, the CRTC reserved to itself considerable discretion in awarding costs.

CAC dependency on the commission's discretion was quickly evident when, within two years, the CRTC in one instance denied half of the costs requested and then immediately denied the total request for another proceeding. In the latter case, the problems for the CAC were compounded by the fact that interim costs had been awarded, which would have to be reimbursed. The CAC was particularly unsettled by these decisions (RIP 1980–1, 79–81) because no reasons were provided for either the original decision or the appeals. At this early stage of costs awards the CAC feared that the CRTC policy was a double-edged sword, with considerable potential for arbitrariness, which could inhibit CAC interventions. Notwithstanding these early setbacks at the hands of the commission, subsequently, at least until 1992, the CAC had few complaints or criticisms of CRTC cost decisions.

The same could not be said about the telephone companies. The telephone companies still denied that the CAC and similar groups were legitimate participants. Having failed to persuade the government to cease annual funding, they were opposed to having to pay the costs of individual regulatory interventions. In the case of Bell Canada this opposition led to a series of court challenges including one to the Supreme Court over the right of the CRTC to award costs. Bell had argued that the CRTC should not award any costs if the intervener had some funds, as the CAC did, to participate. When the CRTC rejected that argument on the grounds that it would weaken and possibly destroy the commission's policy on public participation, Bell Canada argued that the commission should adopt a very narrow definition of costs, namely one based on civil litigation jurisprudence, which limits costs to the indemnification of litigation costs actually incurred. If this definition had been accepted, the CAC would not have been able to claim the costs of its counsel, who received a regular retainer from the Association regardless of the CAC's intervention in a hearing. When the CRTC rejected this line of reasoning, Bell decided to appeal the decision to the Federal Court of Appeal. When it lost that appeal, it further appealed to the Supreme Court, which ruled in 1986 in favour of the CRTC.

While the appeals were working their way through the courts, Bell Canada and, to a lesser extent, BC Tel, waged what can only be described as a petty guerrilla war in an attempt to wear down the CAC and possibly the CRTC itself. Company lawyers at times contended that CAC participation had been 'irresponsible and not constructive' and therefore not worthy of costs. They would routinely challenge the rates for the fees of the CAC's expert witnesses, the hourly rates of legal counsel, and specific items included in the costs. Perhaps the most absurd was BC Tel's claim that the CAC should not be reimbursed approximately $1,200 to cover the costs of its lawyer's hotel and air fare expenses for a hearing in Vancouver, 'considering that an abundance of counsel are [*sic*] available in Vancouver' (CRTC 1981, 4). Company tactics that led to considerable delays in CRTC costs decisions caused the CAC to complain to the commission that the association's inability to pay the fees of its expert witnesses 'has seriously undermined the confidence of expert consultants in the association' (RIP 1980–1, 81).

Despite the legal challenges, harassing tactics, and consequent delays the CAC activists nevertheless considered the CRTC cost awards decision, which remained unique among federal agencies, to be of fundamental importance in enabling the association to mount a rigorous intervention program. Table 8.2 provides details of the actual amounts awarded to the CAC by the CRTC during the 1980s. The major setback in CAC cost awards came in 1992, in the decision referred to above, which will be discussed at greater length in the second section of the paper.

Organizational Autonomy

A third organizational attribute crucial to group effectiveness is autonomy. A number of dimensions of autonomy appear to be central: the ability to establish the basic principles or goals of the organization; the issues on which it will intervene; the strategies, tactics, and specific positions it will advance; and how

TABLE 8.2
CAC Cost Awards

Year	Amount $
1980	2,242
1981	71,300
1982	101,734
1983	58,754
1984	9,265
1985	78,809
1986	143,821
1987	39,273
1988	167,189
1989	87,176

Sources: CRTC Taxation Orders for individual proceedings (totals rounded).

and what resources it will deploy, including which expert witnesses to use. For a group such as the CAC and its Regulated Industries Program, organizational autonomy, both with respect to external organizations and within itself, can be highly problematic and divisive. The failure to establish and entrench organizational autonomy ultimately led to the decline in the CAC's effectiveness in the telecommunications regulatory system.

From the outset, the CAC regulatory program faced two potential threats to its autonomy. The first was external, namely, the government generally and in particular the Department of Consumer and Corporate Affairs and the CRTC, because of the conditional funding. The second was the parent organization of the Consumers' Association of Canada vis-à-vis the unit created to manage its regulatory advocacy activities. Consumer activists involved in obtaining and managing the governmental grants that enabled the CAC to establish what became officially designated as the Regulated Industries Program were aware of the potential dangers to the organization posed by such grants. As Michael Trebilcock (1975, 638) noted: 'It is important from the point of view of political legitimacy that any consumer advocacy programme, even though state subsidized, be under citizen control so that broad policies and positions reflect the views of those on whose behalf they are presented.' He went on to suggest that one of the problems facing the CAC in the long run was that 'being funded by the party in power by executive grant, CAC's advocacy program faces the danger of compromising its independence through concern over funding continuity' (Trebilcock 1975, 638).

The fear of external, particularly governmental, control was not unjustified, at least in the early days of the regulatory advocacy program. As noted earlier, the initiative for such a program came from the newly created Department of Consumer and Corporate Affairs in the early 1970s. When the department renewed its original grant in 1974, it expressed concern that the CAC had only allocated $35,000 of the original $100,000 to regulatory advocacy. While the original grant was supposed to be 'unconditional,' conditions were soon imposed. The department wanted a greater concentration on regulatory advocacy at the expense of general consumer advocacy. Consequently, the 1974 grant stipulated that all of the money was to be used for regulatory interventions. The department also insisted on the CAC creating a specific 'Regulated Industries Program' within the overall organization of the association, which would manage and control the governmental grant. As we shall see, this stipulation was to cause recurring problems for relations between the CAC and its Regulated Industries Program, problems that would eventually lead to a fundamental schism.

Aside from this initial demand on the part of the department, there is no evidence that governmental authorities, either within the department or more generally, sought to use the annual grant to influence the Regulated Industries Program in any manner. Even in the 1980s, when tension developed between the CAC program and the Bureau of Competition Policy in the Department of Consumer and Corporate Affairs over the issue of telecommunications competition, there was no suggestion that the department tried to influence the program. In part, this reflected the fact that it was the Consumer Affairs Branch and not the bureau that was responsible for recommending the grant. In any event there is no evidence that, even if it wished to do so, the bureau would have attempted to undermine the program's independence. Nor has there been any suggestion from anyone connected with the program that the CRTC ever exploited its power to determine cost awards to infringe on the program's autonomy. A case can be made, however, that the CRTC cost awards did influence the program indirectly. The fact that the CRTC, alone among federal agencies, awarded costs meant that the program overemphasized communications cases at the expense of other regulatory areas.

If there were no threat to the regulatory advocacy program of the CAC from governmental actors, there certainly was from the larger organization of the Consumers' Association. As discussed earlier, the idea of the regulatory advocacy program was more a departmental than CAC initiative. The fact that the CAC assigned only one-third of the original grant for formal regulatory interventions suggests the association was not particularly committed, initially at least, to the purpose of the grant. The decision in 1974 by the Department of Consumer and Corporate Affairs to insist that all of the grant be used for such interventions or test cases in the courts on regulatory issues caused considerable consternation within the organization. What was even more unsettling was the requirement imposed on the association that it establish an advocacy committee that would control the use of the grant under the umbrella of the CAC.

The creation of the program, with its own staff and an active advisory body that included corporate lawyers, academics, and other professionals committed to the ideals of consumer advocacy caused considerable tension within the CAC and between the CAC and its ostensible sub-unit. Such tensions and conflicts in public interest groups are not uncommon, according to students of public advocacy groups (Berry 1977; Rothenberg 1992). In the case of the CAC, however, they quickly became very intense and threatened the viability of the program. In 1975 the Advocacy Committee was reconstituted as the Regulated Industries Policy Board, and this board, and especially its general counsel, Andrew Roman, with the tacit support at least of the Department of

Consumer and Corporate Affairs, insisted on full control of the advocacy decisions of the program. The CAC directors, for their part, deemed this to be unacceptable if the program were to be part of the CAC. The conflict that ensued reflected almost as much hostility as that which the program had initially encountered from regulators and their staffs. Trebilcock (1978, 112) effectively described both the problems and some of the causes:

... the strong grassroots, almost consciously amateurist ideology of the association, with the heavy emphasis on volunteer participation and control, has made for tensions with the professional staff in the Advocacy program. In the fast-moving regulatory arena, the slow-moving, cumbersome, and often ritualistically participatory decision-making procedures of the association have been seen by the staff as an impediment to effective action. On the other hand, the elected volunteer organs of the association have rightly emphasized that if professional advocates are to invoke the association's name, the association as client must be consulted in some meaningful fashion and decide whether the positions proposed are congruent with their perception of the association's policies.[3]

The intraorganizational conflicts and rivalries came to a head in 1975. Roman chafed under the restrictions and constraints that the CAC wished to impose on him. His perspective was that the program should have full autonomy to act in effect as a private law firm within the overall organizational framework of the CAC. As this was unacceptable to the association, Roman resigned and his assistant general counsel, Greg Kane, was appointed general counsel and program director in February 1976.

The departure of Andrew Roman – who went on to establish an advocacy centre along his preferred lines, the Public Interest Advocacy Centre (1987) – only resolved some of the personality conflicts. It did little to address the intraorganizational tensions. Using the occasion of Roman's resignation and the Department of Consumer and Corporate Affairs' insistence on a separate regulatory advocacy unit, the Regulated Industries Policy Board, chaired by James Robb, a Montreal corporate lawyer with close contacts with both the department and the government generally, imposed a new and explicitly defined structural relationship on the association. Although the program, in its 1976–7 annual report (RIP 1977, 7), spoke of the board and the association 'operating in a spirit of mutual dependence and respect,' the dependence that existed was far from mutual. The CAC was faced with the prospect of insisting on control and losing the governmental grant or accepting an explicit and extensive degree of autonomy for the program, which would have only a reporting relationship with the association. It grudgingly accepted the latter.

As a result the program was placed under the authority of its own Policy Board (RIP 1976–7, Appendix B, 94–6). The association was to be regularly informed of the program's activities and consulted where the chair of the board deemed it appropriate. The association was prohibited from taking any 'action with respect to any aspect of the program without full consultation with the RIP Board.' The program could consult with any other party and make public statements on any matter relevant to its activities. The program was also given full control of its own staffing and budget decisions.

The restructuring in 1976 of the program-association relationship gave the former the full autonomy to which it aspired. It did little to end the rivalries, tensions, and jealousies between the two organizations, however. If anything these were somewhat exacerbated by the program attaining governmental multiyear funding in the first instance and then cost awards from the CRTC. The fact that the program was both reasonably endowed and fully independent of the association, according to participants, never ceased to grate on the CAC. For their part, members of the program, especially the chairs of the Policy Board and successive program directors, devoted considerable attention over the first decade of operations to what one called 'the political care and feeding' of the association and its executive. Annual meetings of the CAC, for example, were regularly attended and full reports of the program's activities were made. Notwithstanding any such efforts, CAC personnel appeared to resent the attention the program received from both politicians and the media. In the early 1980s the program rejected demands from the CAC that its personnel move into the CAC's new offices outside the centre of Ottawa. Whatever the logic of the program's decision to remain downtown, the refusal reopened old and continuing wounds in the relationship between the two organizations. The re-emergence of this particular issue would eventually lead to the end of the Regulated Industries Program at the close of the decade.

The Rise and Fall of the CAC Regulated Industries Program

Within only a few short years of entering the regulatory arena, the CAC Regulated Industries Program was reasonably well financed, had demanded and acquired legitimacy as a participant, and had established itself as a relatively autonomous organization. In short, the program had met the crucial threshold tests in its quest to become an effective, influential regulatory and political actor. By the early 1980s almost all the other key actors in the telecommunications regulatory sector – regulators, staff, telephone companies, and other interveners – judged that the CAC-RIP had more than passed the test. Few would have disputed the assessment of a senior regulator, cited earlier, that the CAC was the only effective intervener and far more effective than those representing business telecommunications subscribers, who presumably would have more resources at their disposal than did the CAC. Yet by the middle of the eighties the reputation of the CAC was diminished and by the end of the decade the Regulated Industries Program had disappeared as an active participant. Within a few years governmental funding of CAC regulatory interventions had been reduced to case-specific grants rather than annual commitments. The task of this section is to explain these developments.

The decreased regulatory effectiveness and termination of the Regulated Industries Program and the subsequent reduction in governmental funding for CAC regulatory interventions can largely be accounted for by two factors. The first is the difficulties the CAC encountered in articulating its mission in the face of changing regulatory issues. While the CAC was reasonably effective in defending consumer interests on issues of telecommunications companies' regulated conduct or behaviour, such as price setting or service quality, it was less so on structural issues, such as monopoly versus competitive markets. In some respects the CAC, a relatively new actor in the regulatory arena and effective critic of the telephone company behaviour, quickly became the staunchest defender of the telecommunications status quo and a primary ally of the incumbent telephone companies in their battles against the introduction and spread of competition.

When it began, the mission of the Regulated Industries Program was, in the words of its second director, relatively straightforward: 'to ensure that the public's voice is more effectively heard' in regulatory proceedings (Kane 1980, 2). Fulfilling that mission was also relatively easy, once the obstacles discussed above were overcome. Consumer advocacy, at least in Canada, began at a time when the assumptions and principles of existing regulatory systems were not yet in question. Natural monopolies were presumed to be just that – natural. Where competition was limited by public policy, as in the airline industry, for example, the soundness of the premises of such policies was taken for granted. The only real concern was the limited attention given to voices and interests other than the regulated firms, particularly at a time when inflation was becoming a serious concern and regulated firms were routinely turning to their regulators for relief. Consequently, the CAC's advocacy mission statement, was defined at the time by Michael Trebilcock in an internal CAC memo as follows: 'the importance of a strong consumer voice being heard, especially before regulatory agencies, is crucial in a period of high inflation. More than ever, it is important that every rate increase be meticulously scrutinized and exactingly proved' (RIP 1976–7, 4).

In its telecommunications activities the Regulated Industries Program focused almost exclusively during its first five years of operation on the need to ensure that 'the manner in which the [telecommunications] services are provided ... be responsive to the public's needs and desires' (RIP 1977–8, 17). This meant that rate increase applications as well as quality of service issues received rigorous scrutiny. CAC lawyers began routinely to employ financial and other experts to challenge Bell's claims about its cost of capital as well as its productivity. In addition the CAC sought to impose regulatory controls on Bell Canada's intracorporate relations in order to protect subscribers from undue gains made by shareholders at their expense. Perhaps nowhere was this emphasis more pronounced than in the CAC's demand that all the revenues, not simply a minor portion, of the Bell Canada–Saudi Arabia contract be included for rate-setting purposes. The CAC first won the right, over Bell's objections, to examine the confidential provisions of this contract and then undoubtedly influenced the CRTC's decision, which followed the CAC proposal. This successful intervention by the CAC clearly shaped Bell's opposition both to the governmental funding of the CAC program and especially to CRTC costs awards that they had to pay. More importantly, the CRTC precedent on the integrated nature of corporate relations for regulatory purposes ultimately drove Bell Canada into its corporate reorganization, which created BCE.

While the CAC and most other participants were concentrating on regulated behaviour the basic premises of governmental regulation began to change, as structural alternatives to 'natural monopolies' were imagined. In this regard, it is worth noting that, as early as 1975, Michael Trebilcock, perhaps then the intellectual driving force of the Canadian consumer movement, acknowledged that American critics of regulation, including Ralph Nader 'are now urging massive de-regulation of the economy and an attempt to restore vigorously competitive markets, wherever possible' (Trebilcock 1975, 642). Trebilcock went on to suggest that in Canada 'prime sectors for substantial de-regulation and enforced competition might include transportation, communications, banking, agriculture and the professions.'

In terms of the position that would be adopted by the CAC on major structural change in telecommunications, the CAC was in the forefront in advancing structural solutions to protect consumer interests in the air transportation sector. The Regulated Industries Program was, in fact, the first champion of competition as the instrument to advance consumer issues in the airline sector. After seeking effective regulatory relief, much as it was doing in telecommunications, the CAC concluded that competition was needed to reduce airfares and offer consumers choice. The CAC became the primary advocate for domestic charters, both before the regulator and cabinet on appeal, as an alternative to scheduled services and it opposed Air Canada's acquisition of Nordair on grounds that it would be anticompetitive. The program defended its position by arguing 'that maintenance of a diversified aviation structure within which various airlines would compete to at least some degree was just as important in protecting airline passengers as regulatory scrutiny of rates and services' (RIP 1978–9, 7).

Although the CAC maintained in its 1980–1 RIP Annual Report (p. 4) that 'the program has been a longstanding proponent of increased competition in telecommunications as a means of keeping rates down and improving consumer choice,' its record on this issue to that point was much more ambiguous. It did urge the Clyne Committee (Clyne 1979) to consider 'proposals on restructuring the telecommunications industry in a manner which would promote competition and its attendant benefits to consumers such as service innovation, price competition and efficiency.' Beyond that, however, its 'voice' on telecommunications competition was not only inconsistent but its support for other decisions helped reinforce obstacles to the introduction of competition.

In the late 1970s the CRTC conducted two proceedings with structural implications for the telecommunications industry. The first was the application, filed in June 1976, by CNCP to interconnect with the facilities of Bell Canada in order to offer private line long-distance competitive services with Bell. The decision approving the application was issued three years later (CRTC 1979). For our purposes the notable aspect of this application was the fact that the CAC did not intervene in the hearing, which was held in March and April 1978, either to support or to oppose the application. This was the most important structural hearing in the history of Canadian telecommunications to that date and, if the American experience with private competition was any guide, would be a precursor to an application for public voice long-distance competition. The CAC's silence then, especially in view of its claim to the Clyne Committee quoted above, is surprising. There is in fact no mention of the issue in the relevant annual reports of the RIP.[4]

The second structurally significant decision in this period involved the liberalization of customer premises telecommunications equipment. Such liberalization had begun in 1968 in the United States, with the precedent-setting Carterphone decision by the Federal Communications Commission, and in the 1970s pressure was developing for Canada to follow the American example. In this case, the CAC was at the forefront of the battle against the telephone companies' maintenance of their monopoly provision of equipment. In fact, the CAC was one of the first to purchase its own office switching equipment or PBX and, in effect, challenged Bell to disconnect the association, as it had done in previous cases where a customer attempted to use non-Bell equipment.

The CAC's position before the CRTC was that 'competition in the terminal equipment market will result in increased innovation and efficiency and ultimately lower prices and better quality products for consumer products' (RIP 1979–80, 24). When Bell replied that such competition would threaten telephone revenues and result in local rate increases, the CAC was not persuaded and contended that American evidence did not support such an argument (RIP 1981–2, 11). Notwithstanding its support in principle for competition, the CAC was sufficiently influenced by the Bell argument that it 'qualified' its support and wanted conditions that would prevent higher local rates for residential subscribers. This case provides a good indication of the tensions that were to develop in the CAC's position on structural changes in the telecommunications sector.

Additional examples of tensions within the CAC's position with respect to telecommunications competition are to be found in the association's support for specific aspects of CRTC decisions on Bell Canada rate increase applications in this period. In both the 1978 and 1980 decisions (CRTC 1978a; 1980) the regulator approved reduced amounts but placed greater rate increases on long-distance users than residential subscribers. The CAC, which endorsed the CRTC decisions, did not appear to recognize or, alternatively, to consider significant that such decisions reinforced the cross-subsidization in the pricing system and as such constituted a structural barrier to the CAC's presumed objective of telecommunications competition. Similarly, the CAC opposed Bell Canada's applications in 1980 and 1981 to increase competitive service rates less than monopoly services on the grounds that this might place an undue burden on monopoly service subscribers. The Regulated Industries Program stated that it was 'sceptical' of Bell's justification and that it would 'make every effort to protect basic telephone subscribers from being gouged through Bell's efforts to continue to dominate the telecommunications industry' (RIP 1980–1, 28).

With the terminal attachment and private line competition decisions the prime exceptions, until the early 1980s conduct issues dominated the regulatory agenda and the CAC had the luxury of ambiguity in its positions on structural issues. In the 1980s, and particularly after CNCP applied in 1983 to compete in the public voice long-distance market distance, that ambiguity would no longer be possible. The CAC would be required to take a stand on how and whether to maintain the extensive system of cross-subsidies that was central to the existing telecommunications market structure.

Cross-subsidies, largely from long-distance service, have traditionally been used to maintain relatively low local residential service charges. The system of cross-subsidization developed primarily in the 1940s and 1950s as a result of significant cost decreases in the provision of long-distance service and was used by Canadian and American telephone companies to extend service to more and more residences. As a result, by the early 1980s almost 98 per cent of Canadians had telephone service, a penetration rate that was the second highest in the world. The cross-subsidy system was originally a telephone company initiative but, when putatively threatened, quickly acquired the aura of a public policy under the social welfare rubric of 'universal service at affordable rates' (Schultz 1995). Such subsidies were hidden and telephone subscribers were largely unaware of receiving them. Moreover, the telephone companies could not provide a full costing of the actual amount of such subsidies or identify which class of subscribers provided what proportion of them. All of these circumstances contributed to the nature and intensity of the public debate that ensued when telecommunications restructuring through the introduction of competitive provisioning became a possibility. Similarly, the extent to which service demand was dependent on their maintenance at contemporary levels was also both unknown and a contributing factor in the conflicts.

The potential problems for a group such as the CAC that were posed by an extensive system of cross-subsidization as found in telecommunications pricing were identified by W.T. Stanbury just as the CAC was beginning its regulatory interventions: 'The consumer advocate is faced with a difficult problem in the issue of internal subsidization by utilities and common carriers. Price discrimination implies that some consumers will benefit from lower prices or additional services while other consumers will be taxed to finance the regulated firms' largesse. There are clearly conflicts of interest among classes of consumers' (1976, 137).

In 1980, Hudson Janisch, then chair of the Regulated Industries Policy Board of the CAC, acknowledged such problems. In particular, he asked 'does the consumer interest require that local rates be kept as low as possible if this means that long distance rates are considerably higher than they have to be?' He also asked pointedly whether 'in this day and age long distance [is] a luxury to be taxed to support a necessity, local service?' (Janisch 1980, 13–17).

In the early skirmishes over structural solutions, such as equipment competition to protect consumers' interests, the CAC was cognizant of the potential conflicts of interest it was both facing and raising. Hence the conflicted voice it raised in the relevant regulatory proceedings. These internal tensions were resolved after 1983, following CNCP's application for full public long-distance voice competition: the CAC opted to become an unqualified opponent of telephone competition and defender of the structural status quo. Henceforth, the CAC would not acknowledge, in Stanbury's phrase, that there were 'conflicts of interest among classes of consumers.' As far as the CAC was concerned, there was only one consumer interest when it came to competition and that was served by its denial.

In the proceeding on CNCP's application and subsequent battles over the liberalization of resale and sharing, the CAC became one of the staunchest defenders of monopoly provision of long-distance telecommunications services and a central ally of the incumbent telephone companies. In the CNCP case, the CAC's arguments echoed those of Bell Canada and the other monopoly telephone companies that competition would threaten universal service and that the demand for long-distance service was inelastic. It insisted that CNCP had not established either the market demand or public need for its service. It only parted company with the telephone companies when they applied for rate balancing in 1987, to argue that 'rebalancing was neither necessary nor desirable at this time.' The association rejoined the informal alliance with the telephone companies in a series of conflicts involving a reseller in the late 1980s. So opposed was the CAC to any spread of competition during this period that it acted almost as an agent for Bell Canada when it routinely filed letters with the cabinet supporting Bell's appeals, after Bell informed the association of its original filings.

The CAC's adamant opposition to telecommunications competition had two consequences. First, it alienated previous supporters within the CRTC and the Department of Consumer and Corporate Affairs. Those in the CRTC, for example, who sympathized with the CAC's position, thought that the single-minded opposition of the association was not particularly helpful to the cause and failed to offer any particularly distinctive arguments to help them shape their decisions against competition. CRTC commissioners thought that the CAC was undermining its effectiveness and its reputation as a participant in the regulatory arena through this period. And officials in the Department of Consumer and Corporate Affairs began to question the appropriateness of continued funding of such strident, uncompromising opposition to telecommunications competition.

Second, it caused problems within the CAC. Although it is possible that the Regulated Industries Program could have continued both in its organizational form and in its opposition to structural change in telecommunications, developments within the larger organization of the CAC made this impossible. The first of these developments was the significant deterioration in the financial situation of the Consumers' Association. In 1988, after a failed and very expensive attempt by the CAC to expand its membership through its publication activities, the Department of Consumer and Corporate Affairs had to bail the association out of its financial crisis by means of a special grant of almost $2 million. The department made the grant conditional on the association separating its advocacy activities from its other work, especially its publishing activities. Although the department did not make its bail-out grant conditional on the CAC changing its position on telecommunications competition, officials indicated that they would favour such a development.

Simultaneously, the CAC went through an internal reorganization that culminated in 1988 with the hiring of a full-time executive director, who was mandated to enhance the public profile of the CAC as a whole and improve its financial situation. The new executive director found himself in conflict with the staff members running the Regulatory Industries Program on two grounds. He wanted the RIP to make a greater contribution to the CAC's overhead costs by relocating to the CAC offices. This proposal had been raised and rejected in the early 1980s. Secondly, he did not share the program's opposition to long-distance competition, believing it to be short-sighted and not in the long-term best interests of the association. On both issues, however, the executive director confronted the 1976 'management structure' agreement, which precluded CAC control over either the RIP budget or its substantive regulatory interventions.

The CAC executive opted to deal with the budget question first and did so by unilaterally abrogating its agreement with RIP at the 1989 annual meeting of the association. RIP's staff members were instructed to terminate the downtown office lease and move to the CAC general offices as soon as possible. Shortly thereafter the staff members of the Regulated Industries Program and its Policy Board resigned. This ended the Regulated Industries Program as it had existed as a separate unit of the CAC for the previous thirteen years.

Indicative of the support that the Department of Consumer and Corporate Affairs gave to the new CAC executive for its actions was the fact that, notwithstanding the requirement imposed by the department in 1976 that its grant was conditional on a separate regulatory advocacy unit within the CAC, the departmental funding of the CAC's regulatory activities continued until 1993, when both its continuing regulatory grant and its core funding were terminated.

Once the program had been dismantled, the CAC directed its attention to the association's policy on telecommunications competition. Within a year, the CAC's executive director was supporting a consultant's recommendation to the CAC that the association not oppose long-distance competition on the grounds that 'the benefits of maintaining a monopoly in long-distance for social policy purposes are outweighed by its disadvantages. These disadvantages include reduced competitiveness of the Canadian economy, higher than necessary long-distance rates for the Canadian residential consumer and a greater reliance on expensive regulatory proceedings than necessary' (T.M. Denton Consultants

1990, 5). Particularly significant was that the revised CAC position was based on extensive consultations with members of the association's executive council and provincial boards, many of whom, according to the consultants' report 'were unequivocally in favor of competition in long-distance' (7). This suggests that the previous RIP position reflected the views of the program's personnel and not those of the larger association.

In the 1991 CRTC hearing on the Unitel application, the CAC, reflecting the policy recommended by its new executive director, in effect repudiated previous Regulated Industries Program positions on long-distance competition. The association criticized its own traditional fixation with local rates to argue that 'exclusive interest in the basic monthly charge is disguising certain important developments in the pattern of consumption of residential telephone service, and is distorting policy making accordingly' (CAC 1991, 1). The CAC rejected its own 1987 claim that universality had been undermined in the United States and contended that the issue in the hearing was not really competition but rather 'rapidly increasing productivity in telecommunications, wrought by technological advances.' Consequently, it identified as its priority concern whether or not the benefits of such increases 'will be made available to very large users exclusively, rather than to all classes of users.' Unlike previous proceedings, such as the 1985 CNCP application or the 1987 Bell Canada application for rate rebalancing, the CAC opted in 1991 to support neither monopoly nor competition but simply to look for 'the best possible deal for consumers.' Such a deal would include stable increases, if these were deemed to be necessary, for both basic and optional services and an equitable distribution of the benefits of productivity increases for all classes of consumers and not solely large business subscribers.

However traumatic the reversal on the issue of competition was for the CAC itself, in the end it appears that neither the new position in particular nor the participation in the regulatory hearing generally had a significant effect on the deliberations of the CRTC. In fact, it appears to have harmed the CAC inasmuch as the traditional telephone companies, who had until recently counted on the CAC in their battle against competition, turned on it to urge the commission to deny the association its request for costs. They complained to the CRTC that CAC evidence had contained errors and that the CAC had not contributed to a better understanding of the issues. Bell Canada contended that the 'CAC's evidence and argument demonstrated a misunderstanding of certain fundamental concepts,' while BC Tel was particularly dismissive in suggesting that CAC participation 'largely constituted a learning process for its representative (CRTC 1992, 2).' Although the CAC attempted to defend itself, the CRTC was not persuaded. In its decision the commission criticized parts of the CAC evidence as 'simplistic and based on flawed assumptions.' In addition, the CRTC concluded that the focus on the overall consumer bill, which was the core of the CAC's position, 'was not of assistance' in considering the applications. Finally, it concluded that 'some of the CAC's cross-examination time was spent exploring issues which were not of direct relevance to CAC's position, and indeed, which were of only marginal relevance to the proceeding as a whole (5).' As a result, the commission granted the CAC only 35 per cent of its requested costs.

It is difficult to explain either the tone or the severity of the CRTC's decision on the CAC's costs request. The CAC regulatory intervention program and its position on competition in telecommunications, in particular, had been embroiled in extensive internal controversy at the end of the 1980s. The mass resignations from the Regulated Industries Program and the subsequent effort by the CAC to revise its position and prepare its specific intervention on the Unitel application caused considerable strain both for the organization and for the CRTC commissioners and staff who had developed a familiarity, if not approval, with the RIP personnel and the positions they advanced. Jettisoning long-held policy positions and depending on new representatives who advocated radically different arguments, which addressed generic rather than case-specific issues, clearly did not win the association any converts within the commission. It was the clearest possible measure of the extent to which the CAC had declined in effectiveness as a public interest group in the regulatory process that the one agency that had been so central to the CAC's acquisition of both the legitimacy and the resources necessary for it to participate effectively in the regulatory process concluded that it no longer merited either.

Conclusions

For more than a decade the activities of the Consumers' Association, in the form of the Regulated Industries Program, offered a compelling negative answer to Trebilcock's question: 'Must the consumer always lose?' The program was an early winner, as it very quickly established itself as an effective, indeed influential, voice for consumers in the regulatory system in general and particularly in telecommunications regulation. There can be no doubt that within short years of its entry into the regulatory system it helped shape not only public debates but regulatory outcomes and indeed public policies on major issues and questions that confronted regulators from the mid-1970s on.

Although consumer activism, in the form of the Regulated Industries Program, initially encountered serious obstacles in asserting its right to play a role, those obstacles were quickly overcome. In large part RIP's claim to be a legitimate participant and demand for the necessary resources to participate effectively were contingent on state actors, departmental and regulatory, bestowing both legitimacy and resources, a not unusual result. Once granted, however, skilful and effective advocacy by RIP advocates, particularly when such advocacy resonated with regulators' ideals and ambitions, as they did in the telecommunications regulatory system after the CRTC acquired jurisdiction, assured the RIP of its place in the regulatory process. Even its foremost adversaries, the telephone companies, who did not welcome the disruption to the quiet regulatory life the program represented and fought efforts of state officials to ensure it had adequate resources, eventually both conceded the RIP's right to participate and accorded its personnel respect for how they performed.

The decline and eventual disappearance of the formal Regulated Industries Program, as opposed to subsequent episodic CAC interventions, reflected both internal and external factors. What links both is the apparent inability of the program to come to an effective accommodation with the emerging telecommunications structural issues as opposed to the conduct concerns on which the program earned its reputation. The RIP did not appear to recognize, let alone concede, the difficult issue facing the consumer advocate in cross-subsidization. Nor was the program in the 1980s willing to attempt to answer the question posed by one of its former chairs, 'does the consumer interest require that local rates be kept as low as possible if this means that long distance rates are considerably higher than they have to be?' (Janisch 1980, x).

By the late 1980s, the Regulated Industries Program had few allies. Its reputation as a valuable participant in the regulatory process had been undermined and its former admirers found diminished value in its contributions. Its most recent allies, the telephone companies, proved fickle indeed and turned against the successor to the program when it refused to continue to oppose competition. Even its sponsoring organization, the Consumers' Association of Canada, turned against it for both substantive and financial reasons. The fact that the CAC was able, almost overnight, to reverse its policy on telecommunications competition suggests that the program in the latter half of the 1980s had become isolated even from its own constituency. Such a development was paradoxically perhaps the consequence of government funding, which permitted it the luxury of not depending on membership support. The demise of the program was proof of Stigler's proposition concerning the difficulties of constructing 'a viable continuing broad-based consumer political lobby.' On the other hand, if telecommunications is on the way to becoming a 'normal sector' of the economy (Noam 1989), the idea of a 'consumer lobby' in the regulatory process is perhaps outdated: the lobby will be the marketplace.

NOTES

Thanks are due to Hudson Janisch, Michael Prince, William T. Stanbury, and Ian Scott for helpful comments on the original version of this chapter. The chapter draws on material from a larger paper prepared for the Donner Foundation Project 'Analysing Interest Group Behaviour in the Information Age.' Professor W.T. Stanbury is director of that project. For this project, twenty-five interviews were conducted, on a not-for-attribution basis, with individuals involved in, or knowledgeable about, the CAC's regulatory activities.

1 There is, and has been, considerable debate over the use and meaning of the phrase 'public interest groups,' with some arguing that it not only has no analytical or conceptual significance but that it confuses discussions about interest group activities and their consequences for the political process. See Stanbury (1993) for a recent instance of such debate. For earlier discussions see, for example, Berry (1977) and Pross (1986). For purposes of this paper, I will not attempt to resolve the debate, although I believe in part that the debate is somewhat overheated because of the confluence of the words 'public interest' in connection with groups that might more properly be identified as 'public' interest groups. The latter makes no claim that such groups represent the 'public interest' but rather perceives them as being motivated less by private or self-interest than what are traditionally designated 'private' interest groups. This does not deny that an element of self-interest exists in their advocacy activities, but suggests that in the mix of collective and individual goods, 'public' interest groups place more weight on the former than do 'private' interest groups.

2 Although the CAC's eligibility for core funding from the Department of Consumer and Corporate Affairs ended in 1993, the association continued to receive funds for its advocacy activities after 1993. The total amount for the years 1993–6 was $210,000. Its advocacy grant was terminated in fiscal year 1996–7.

3 See also Goldstein (1979), 147.

4 In an interview, a former senior CAC staffer indicated, however, that the CAC advocated, by letter, that the government reject the Bell appeal against the decision.

REFERENCES

Bernstein, M. 1955. *Regulating Business by Independent Commission*. Princeton: Princeton University Press.
Berry, J.M. 1977. *Lobbying for the People*. Princeton: Princeton University Press.
Consultative Committee on the Implications of Telecommunications for Canadian Sovereignty (Clyne Committee). 1979. *Telecommunications and Canadian Sovereignty*. Ottawa: Minister of Supply and Services.

Consumers' Association of Canada. 1991. *Residential Telephony: Evidence of the Consumers' Association of Canada.*

CRTC. 1976. *Telecommunications Regulation – Procedures and Practices.* Ottawa: CRTC, 20 July. CRTC Notice of Public Hearing, CRTC 1976–2.

– 1978a. Telecom Decision CRTC 78–4, Ottawa: 23 May.

– 1978b. *Proposed CRTC Procedures and Practices Relating to Broadcasting Matters.* CRTC Public Announcement, 25 July.

– 1979. *CNCP Telecommunications, Interconnection with Bell Canada.* Telecom Decision CRTC 79–11, 17 May.

– 1980. *Bell Canada Rate Increase Application.* Telecom Decision CRTC 80–10.

– 1981. Taxation Order. Ottawa, 22 May.

– 1992. Telecom Costs Order CRTC 92–7. Ottawa, 30 June.

Dawson, H.J. 1963. The Consumers' Association of Canada. *Canadian Public Administration* 6, no. 1: 92–118.

– 1975. National Pressure Groups and the Federal Government. In A.P. Pross, ed., *Pressure Group Behavior in Canadian Politics.* Toronto: McGraw-Hill Ryerson.

Engelhart, K.G., and M.J. Trebilcock. 1981. *Public Participation in the Regulatory Process: The Issue of Funding.* Regulation Reference Working Papers, vol. 17. Ottawa: Economic Council of Canada.

Globerman, S., W.T. Stanbury, and T.A. Wilson, eds. 1995. *The Future of Telecommunications Policy in Canada.* Toronto: Institute for Policy Analysis, University of Toronto.

Goldstein, J. 1979. Public Interest Groups and Public Policy: The Case of the Consumers' Association of Canada. *Canadian Journal of Political Science* 12, no. 1: 137–55.

Janisch, H.N. 1980. Regulation and the Consumer Interest: In Search of the Holy Grail. 33rd Annual Meeting of the Consumers' Association of Canada, Hamilton, Ontario.

– 1981. Administrative Tribunals in the 80's: Rights of Access by Groups and Individuals. *Windsor Yearbook of Access to Justice* 1:303–26.

Janisch, H.N., and B.S. Romaniuk. 1995. Canada. In E. Noam, S. Komatsukzai, and D.A. Conn, eds., *Telecommunications in the Pacific Basin.* New York: Oxford University Press.

Kane, T.G. 1980. *Consumers and the Regulators.* Montreal: Institute for Research on Public Policy.

Kwavnick, D. 1972. *Organized Labour and Pressure Politics.* Montreal: McGill-Queen's University Press.

Noam, E. 1989. International Telecommunications in Transition. In R. Crandall and K. Flamm, eds., *Changing the Rules: Technological Change, International Competition and Regulation in Telecommunications.* Washington, D.C.: Brookings Institution.

Olson, Mancur. 1965. *The Logic of Collective Action.* Cambridge: Harvard University Press.

Pal, Leslie V. 1993. *Interests of State*. Montreal: McGill-Queen's University Press.

Presthus, R. 1973. *Elite Accommodation in Canadian Politics*. London: Cambridge University Press.

Pross, A.P. 1986. *Group Politics and Public Policy*. Toronto: Methuen.

Public Interest Advocacy Centre (PIAC). 1987. *PIAC – The First Ten Years, 1977–87*. Ottawa: PIAC.

Regulated Industries Program (RIP). *Annual Report* (various years). Ottawa: Consumers' Association of Canada.

Rothenberg, L.S. 1992. *Linking Citizen to Government: Interest Group Politics at Common Cause*. Cambridge: Cambridge University Press.

Schultz, R.J. 1982. Partners in a Game without Masters: Reconstructing the Telecommunications Regulatory System. In R.J. Buchan et al., eds., *Telecommunications, Regulation and the Constitution*. Montreal: Institute for Research on Public Policy.

– 1995. Old Whine in New Bottle: The Politics of Cross-Subsidization in Canadian Telecommunications. In S. Globerman, W.T. Stanbury, and T.A. Wilson, eds., *The Future of Telecommunications Policy in Canada*. Toronto: Institute for Policy Analysis, University of Toronto.

Schultz, R.J., and M.R. Brawley. 1996. Telecommunications. In G.B. Doern, L.A. Pal, and B.W. Tomlin, eds., *Border Crossings: The Internationalization of Canadian Public Policy*, 82–107. Toronto: Oxford University Press.

Stanbury, W.T. 1976. The Consumer Interest and the Regulated Industries. In K. Ruppenthal and W. Stanbury, eds., *Transportation Policy: Regulation, Competition and the Public Interest*. Vancouver: UBC Press.

– ed. 1986. *Telecommunications Policy and Regulation*. Montreal: Institute for Research on Public Policy.

Stigler, G., and M. Cohen. 1971. *Can Regulatory Agencies Protect Consumers?* Washington: American Enterprise Institute.

T.M. Denton Consultants Inc. 1990. *Telecommunications Services in Canada: Draft Issue Paper and Discussion Document*. Ottawa: Consumers' Association of Canada.

Trebilcock, M.J. 1975. Winners and Losers in the Modern Regulatory State: Must the Consumer Always Lose? *Osgoode Hall Law Journal* 13, no. 3: 619–47.

– 1978. The Consumer Interest and Regulatory Reform. In G.B. Doern, ed., *The Regulatory Process in Canada*, 94–127. Toronto: Macmillan of Canada.

Vogel, D. 1989. *Fluctuating Fortunes: The Political Power of Business in America*. New York: Basic Books.

9

Civic Regulation: Regulating Citizenship, Morality, Social Order, and the Welfare State

MICHAEL J. PRINCE

Over twenty years ago, Bruce Doern (1974) noted that the budgetary process of spending, taxation, and borrowing dealt with only half of the reality of government and that 'the other half,' regulation and regulatory structures, was being rediscovered through the renewed interest of academics and practitioners. Since then a great deal of work has examined and theorized about regulatory agencies, their rationales and impacts. A central argument of this paper, however, is that this considerable body of conventional literature itself addresses, at most, only half of this 'other half' of governance in modern democratic societies. The customary approach looks at government regulation of private sector activities and economic actors and identifies direct regulation and social regulation as the two types of this governing instrument. My purpose in this chapter is to identify and explore the nature of largely forgotten regulatory realms of the Canadian state. A new category, civic regulation, is presented, along with an expanded notion of the horizontal dimensions of regulating society. Within this new perspective, core regulatory institutions and relationships include Canada's welfare state, charities and the voluntary sector, federalism and the social union, families, marriage and divorce, the courts and the police, human rights bodies and codes, and the Canadian Charter of Rights and Freedoms.

The first section of the chapter comments on the limitations of the mainstream regulatory literature, including the circumscribed meaning of social regulation. It then argues for a new conceptualization of regulatory realms, one which encompasses regulating citizenship, morality, social order, and the welfare state. The second section considers why the mainstream political science, economics, and social policy literature has generally excluded civic regulation when discussing the regulatory state. In the third section, some defining characteristics of civic regulation are presented and the core institutions, processes, and values involved are examined. In this realm the rules and sanctions of the state are extremely intrusive and often bear most heavily on those least able to defend themselves. In the final section, the various interests and forces influencing the realm of civic regulation are identified, together with the emerging trends and issues in regulating the social union and civil society in Canada. Finally, some questions for future research on civic regulation and economic regulation are presented.

Studying Regulation: Bringing the Community Back In

The numerous definitions of government regulation can be placed along a spectrum ranging from relatively narrow ones to extremely wide notions. A common thread running through most of the narrow definitions is the idea of government intervening in the affairs of private sector organizations, market relations, and processes (Reagan 1987). This conventional definition of regulation not only differentiates regulation from other instruments of public policy, it also detaches economic regulation from other kinds of governmental regulation. At the other end of the spectrum, the domain of Canadian regulation has been defined by Hartle (1979) to encompass government rules of all kinds, including rules governing electoral and parliamentary procedures as well as 'collective rights regulations' – rules protecting the shared rights of individuals to public goods and common resources. Hartle views regulation as the most general policy instrument of government, indeed as *the* essential function of the state. In this perspective, essentially everything government does is regulatory, and taxation and expenditure are special cases of regulation. The definition of regulation presented in this chapter falls somewhere between these two extremes. I believe it is useful analytically to distinguish regulation from other policy instruments and to consider civic society as well as market activities in our work, but I do not equate the concept of regulation with governing itself.[1]

The mainstream regulation literature, whether written from the discipline of economics, law, or political science, concentrates upon private market organizations and transactions. Regulation is usually described as a political economy concept of state commands and controls, underpinned by the legal system in reference to market systems and state interventions in mixed economies. In this dominant approach or paradigm to studying regulation, economic concepts and models are central to the analysis. Regulation is about controlling the market activities of industry, technology, trade, competition, production, supply, price, and product quality. People are considered in their roles as employees, employers, producers, consumers, investors, managers or professionals, suppliers, distributors, or third parties. Government regulations are primarily justified, or not, in this approach, on the basis of correcting or compensating for one or other kind of market failure. In short, regulation is about the role of the state in relation to the economy (Ogus 1994).

Even the concept of 'social regulation' almost always refers solely to commercial, industrial, and occupational activities and their effects, again related to market deficiencies. Thus, social regulation comprises rules regarding workplace health and safety, consumer protection, environmental stewardship, and, perhaps, cultural content in popular media. These kinds of regulations might be called the caring and sharing aspects of market-based activities, endeavouring to inject certain public or social values into private economic domains. Often in the literature, they are mistakenly termed 'new regulation,' reflecting the wave of social regulation enacted in recent decades, following the introduction of many economic rules, but ignoring the fact that social regulations and other types of social policy rules were introduced in nineteenth-century Canada (Moscovitch 1983; Ursel 1992).

Though we sometimes refer to the topic of government involvement in economy and society, we then allow the existence of a highly developed discussion of market issues to displace discussion of government influence on society more generally. Government regulation of the market economy is, of course, extremely important in understanding public policy and political economy. However, it captures only part of the regulatory state and the range of laws and rules used by governments. For a more complete picture, it is essential to bring the community into the analysis and to look at a wider range of policy and program areas, such as child support, gun control, human rights, social assistance, and workfare. Legislation and related regulations certainly exist to influence decisions taken in social institutions outside the economy as well as inside. Besides intervention in the economy, we cannot overlook regulations in relation to individuals, households, agency clientele, communities, or provincial and federal societies.

Under this broader conception, regulation is as much a moral and social phenomenon as an economic and political one. It involves both state and private forms of commands and controls, roles and relationships. It is based on the legal system, which connects and at times collides with societal norms and customs. In addition to legitimate coercive powers, regulating is based on the exercise of material power – benefits, goods, and services – and normative power – symbols and statuses (Etzioni 1964). This notion of regulation is also embedded in systems of public service provision and cash benefits, which assign and withdraw statuses from clientele. I propose the term 'civic regulation' for designating this wider perspective on the regulatory affairs of a political community. Civic regulation refers to rule making by the state, or by agencies on its behalf, with respect to numerous social aspects of human behaviour and needs, moral conduct and standards, intergovernmental relations, and human rights and civil liberties. It pertains to the ordinary life and experiences of people and the extraordinary world of executive federalism. To a large extent, this intervention is made necessary by the fact that the economic institutions do not have prices for many of the unpriced social or environmental impacts of decisions taken within the economic sphere that have broader effects. Furthermore, civic regulation helps define and shape the meaning of citizenship in contemporary Canadian society.

Why Has Civic Regulation Been Neglected?

Several reasons can be given why mainstream social science literatures have basically disregarded the realm of civic regulation in their examination of the regulatory state. Both economics and political science, arguably the main disciplines in the regulation field, have tended to emphasize government-industry relations, to focus on the impact of regulations on economic activity or governmental processes, and to examine particular organizational forms, namely, nondepartmental or independent agencies, boards, and commissions. The economics literature tends to focus on the effect of regulation on pricing or rate setting, the related investment behaviour of regulated companies and industries, such as utilities and monopolies, and deregulation initiatives in particular sectors. The political science literature has been inclined to concentrate on the degree to which regulatory units have become captives of the industries they were intended to regulate (Bernstein 1955; Sabatier 1975; Wilson 1980), and the degree to which delegated regulatory activity has been removed from substantial parliamentary supervision or cabinet control.

In the Canadian literature on public policy, it has recently been noted that there is less emphasis given than in other countries to the 'high-level ethical issues' of abortion, biomedical choices, crime, human rights, and law and order (Dobuzinskis, Howlett, and Laycock 1996, 2). In the public administration field, the principal regulatory arena of government is equated with agencies, boards, and commissions, while departments, which in reality possess and exercise significant regulatory powers, are generally described as structures for developing policy and giving advice or operating programs, delivering services, and providing grants to their constituencies (Kernaghan and Siegel 1996; Sutherland 1993). Students of Canadian public administration recognize that government departments are charged with regulatory roles, but the field, along with political science, has traditionally been far more interested in the policy autonomy and accountability of regulatory agencies, and their consequences for ministerial responsibility (Hodgetts 1973; Thomas and Zajcew 1993). A significant amount of civic regulation lies inside regular departments and ministries at both the federal and provincial levels of government.

When regulation is conceived of as laws and rules 'aimed primarily at altering the *economic* behaviour of individuals in the private sector' and the 'substitution of administrative decision making for the forces of competition' (Economic Council of Canada 1979, 11 and 13), we can begin to understand why rules regarding citizenship, morality, social order and welfare state programs are overlooked. The reason for this particular conception of regulation, in the case of contemporary policy analysis in Canada, can in large part be found in the Economic Council's work over the years.

In 1978, the first ministers, in their discussion on the business environment, spoke of the burden of government regulation on the private sector and the need to reduce its negative impact on jobs and costs. Later that year, Prime Minister Trudeau wrote to the chair of the Economic Council requesting that the council undertake a series of studies evaluating areas of government regulation that appear to have a substantial bearing on the Canadian economy. The prime minister's letter noted that 'there has developed in Canada a strong concern that increasing government regulation might be having adverse effects on the efficiency of Canadian firms and industries and on the allocation of resources and the distribution of income' (reproduced in Economic Council of Canada (1979), 119). The council was specifically asked to assess the regulation of price, supply, entry, product standards, and environmental and safety standards and, among other items, to focus on the nature and magnitude of the economic impact of government regulation. The research staff assembled to undertake this regulation reference were quite aware of other sorts of regulation besides the economic kind, such as the government's regulation of other governments and government's regulation of itself through public service laws. The purpose and economic focus of their task, however, was clear. Moreover, there was the research need to set some conceptual boundaries around the vast field of government regulation and to meet fairly tight deadlines for reporting. What resulted over the late 1970s and early 1980s was a series of studies and publications that focused on economic regulation overall, by industry, and at the level of the firm.

In 1991, Prime Minister Mulroney requested the Economic Council to undertake a major project on the structure of government in Canada and how governments could achieve their objectives while effectively controlling costs to the private sector. The research program of what came to be called the Government and Competitiveness Project looked at several dimensions of government: efficient size and jurisdiction, regulation, efficient program delivery, efficient pricing, efficient purchasing, and policy-making processes. While the council was eliminated by the federal government in 1992, the project continued and a publication on competitiveness and regulation was published the next year (Hirshorn and Gautin 1993). Again, the focus was on government regulation as the regulation of business, industrial activities, and labour markets and on concerns over the scale of rules and the costs that result from regulations discouraging investment and innovation.

Even the mainstream social policy literature has tended to forget that the welfare state is, and has always been, a regulatory state as well. From liberal and social democratic viewpoints, social programs are about improving human well-being; distributing resources in accordance with concepts of compassion, justice, and fairness; relieving distress; and tackling inequalities (McGilly 1998; Rice 1995). This orientation can be traced back to Max Weber, who, as Room (1979) notes, emphasized, 'the positive role of the state: as an agent of life chance distribution, as an instigator of societal change and as a promoter of social integration. He saw social policies as central to this role' (35). Social integration has in turn been largely interpreted as creating a sense of community and enhancing unity, rather than as forming and maintaining a particular set of social arrangements.

Until fairly recently, the welfare state has comprised relatively large public bureaucracies delivering services such as education, health care, and social work as well as a range of universal and selective income security programs and tax benefits. Social policy texts and discourse have centred on redistribution, not regulation; care and co-operation, rather than control and coercion.[2] This is reflected in the language Canadians use to describe the welfare state: social policy as safety net, as a transcontinental railway or societal glue, as the social union, as a sacred trust, or as Robin Hood. Where the mainstream social policy literature has addressed the regulatory side of the welfare state, it is often in relation to promoting the ideas of minimum standards, social rights and entitlements, and paying some attention to the administrative and professional rules under which social services operate (McGilly 1998).

Alternatively, less mainstream and more critical perspectives on social policy do stress the regulatory and control functions of the welfare state.[3] Writers from a political economy or Marxist outlook, for example, have argued that in addition to providing benefits the welfare state has always regulated the working and living conditions of people, to quell any unrest and to ensure that the needs of the capitalist economy are met (Gough 1979). A radical stream within the social work and welfare literature agrees that the state's social welfare role involves the exercise of sanctions and controls on people's choices and actions.

A classic American study, *Regulating the Poor*, contends that public assistance measures chiefly function to regulate labour and civil order, by making some provision for the destitute but offering it in a degrading and punitive way so as to extol even the lowest of paid work (Piven and Cloward 1971). Contemporary debates and developments in Canada on 'workfare' – mandatory participation in public works or training programs in order to receive income assistance – as well as on curtailing welfare benefits and cracking down on welfare abuse, underscore the case that social programs can be instruments of compulsion and control (Sayeed 1995; Richards and Vining 1995; McFarland and Mullaly 1996).

Feminist writers, in considering welfare policy, emphasize the social construction and control of the private/domestic sphere by the public sphere of government (Pascall 1986). Feminists suggest that a central purpose of social policy has been to foster and preserve a specific form of the family, with particular roles for men, women, and children. The welfare state is not only an assortment of cash benefits and services, but also a set of ideas about the family, women, femininity, and so forth, plus a series of social controls and state repression to enact those ideas. Indeed, as Elizabeth Wilson, a feminist scholar, has expressed it, 'social welfare policies amount to no less than the *State organization of domestic life*' (Wilson 1977, 9).

Canadian literature on aboriginal peoples also argues forcefully that there is a dark side to social policy and the welfare state, with devastating consequences for the physical, mental, emotional, and spiritual aspects of aboriginal life. The relation between aboriginal people and social programs and human service organizations has frequently been called a process of 'colonialism' (Adams 1975; McKenzie and Hudson 1985). Through the Indian Act and other state policies and practices, such as child welfare and residential schools, aboriginal people have endured exclusion, paternalism, and extreme dependency (Armitage 1995). Despite some administrative and policy reforms (Prince 1994), policies and laws pertaining to aboriginal people still constrain and dominate them. Policies of domination and assimilation, however well-meaning, removed aboriginal people from their homelands, abducted their children, and suppressed their identities. Colonization persists and the Indian Act perpetuates a power imbalance between aboriginal communities and Canadian governments. In the words of the Royal Commission on Aboriginal Peoples (1996, 18–19), 'governments continue to block Aboriginal nations from assuming the broad powers of governance that would permit them to fashion their own institutions and work out their own solution to social, economic and political problems.'

Civic Regulation: An Overview

Canadians realize that when governments regulate they do more than intervene in the economy. They know that federal, provincial, territorial, and municipal governments use legal instruments to influence interpersonal and family relations, guide moral conduct, maintain communal peace and order, shape the nature of social programs, and define citizenship within the Canadian political community. The study of regulation needs to catch up to the everyday experiences and public awareness about the modern regulatory state. We have used the label 'regulation' too narrowly, to refer only to government intervention to correct market failure, or more generally, to influence behaviour within the economic system, rather than the more general structure of social and household institutions and decision-making processes. My aim in this section, therefore, is to offer an expanded taxonomy of government regulation and an initial understanding of a new category, civic regulation.

A distinction between regulation and regulations is usually made in the literature. Government regulation refers to a statute enacted by the federal Parliament or provincial legislature or a by-law passed by a municipal council. Regulations include orders, directives, standards, and other formal norms exercising powers conferred by and pursuant to statutory laws (regulation). The concept of civic regulation includes both of these dimensions. Both regulation and regulations seek to constrain or change the economic, moral, or social behaviour of individuals, families, and other organizations and institutions. Economic regulation, as we have discussed earlier, is the conventional category and is commonly presented as capturing the entire universe of regulating by the state. Within this category are two types, direct regulation and social regulation, both well known in the literature.[4] Civic regulation is the 'other half' of the regulatory activities of government, the realm not usually covered in the literature. Both categories share certain characteristics. Economic and civic regulation are instruments that governments use to pursue public policy goals and seek compliance; each has the force of law with coercive elements; and, among other targets, they both address conditions of entry or eligibility, methods of provision, and the attributes of a benefit or service.

By way of contrast, economic regulation is directed at the private sector and market transactions, where civic regulation is focused on civil society and political transactions. In simple terms, the former addresses commodities, the factors of production, and processes of distribution, and the latter addresses communities, the fabric of society, and processes of social organization. Economic and civic regulation also have different tests of performance, different evaluative criteria.[5] In the sphere of economic regulation, the criteria are largely consequential and aggregative, with ethical and procedural concerns being peripheral. For civic regulation, the primary concerns are duty- and rights-based, focusing on individuals and groups within society. In other terms, the main concern of economic regulation is wealth maximization, subject to some overriding standards for workplace conditions and lawful conduct, while in civic regulation the principal concerns are institutional and social capital and the values of justice and fairness.

With these points of difference, civic regulation adds a number of features to our understanding of government regulation. Civic regulation includes other regulators, the courts and police for example, and other groups to consider who are regulated in Canadian society. Additional rationales for government intervention are involved, as well as a different perspective on the effects of regulation. Economic regulatory analysis concentrates on the effects of state rules for resource allocation efficiency in the market. A civic regulatory analysis would emphasize distributional effects for income and wealth and positional effects for the allotment and definition of roles and statuses in society. Civic regulation differs also from economic regulation in that regulation may not simply constrain economic activities, it may create and support opportunities and choices for people; regulation may not just be a burden on the economy but a buttress to civil society. The converse may also be true, where a rule is beneficial for the private sector but costly to the community.

As a tool for ordering society, civic regulation is closely linked to the processes of societal evaluation and status differentiation. As Tumin (1967, 27) explains: 'There is, first, the need in every society to determine whether a given status and role are above a line of minimum acceptability, defined primarily in terms of legitimacy and morality. The status of the thief or criminal, for instance, typically falls below the line of minimal acceptability. All statuses are subject to this level of evaluation, since judgments of moral acceptability must be made if society is to endure.' This assigning of worthiness is quite apparent in current policy debates, such as responsible versus 'deadbeat' fathers, with respect to their child support obligations, or 'truly needy' versus less deserving claimants for social assistance. A related process is status differentiation, 'by which social positions such as father, mother, teacher and employer, are defined and distinguished from one another by assigning to each a distinctive role – a set of rights and responsibilities' (Tumin 1967, 19). Both of these processes are intrinsic to regulating access to benefits and services in the public domain, and thus determining the nature of civic identities within society (Hasenfeld 1983; Shragge 1997). Federal and provincial/territorial governments are actively engaged in modifying the status order of roles and identities within Canada. Whether in regard to gender, age, race, ethnicity, religion, abilities,

income, or sexual orientation, governments are closely involved in 'the ubiquitous process of constant renegotiation of the status of members of society'
(Cairns 1986, 73).

Civic regulation entails public and personal matters, local and national communities, and issues of civility and morality. This kind of regulation is directed
at citizens, clients, public service providers, families, and governments. The
term 'civic' refers to government and other state institutions along with social
organizations within civil society. In many respects, civic regulation is the
oldest regulatory realm. Public health laws pre-date Confederation, for example, and statutes dealing with compulsory school attendance, children's protection, juvenile offenders, immigration, and Indians were all passed in the late
1800s.

An overview of the types of civic regulation is presented in Table 9.1. The
taxonomy is a policy content approach, with each type rooted in a different
functional area of government. The four types involve laws and rules regarding
citizenship and human rights; justice and public order; moral and sexual
behaviour; and welfare state programs and the social union. In the first three
types, both regulation and regulations are common, while in the fourth, regulations are the main form of civic regulation. Framework laws and statutes are
prominent in the first three, and in the fourth rules are attached as procedural
and enforcement means to the primary instruments of social services and cash
transfers. Each of these various means of regulating society contains a relatively distinctive set of core institutions, dominant ideas, political issues, and
policies and programs. They are set out here separately for analytical purposes
and conceptual clarity, although in practice they are interconnected in a number of ways.

Citizenship and Human Rights

Citizenship and human rights are about membership in a society. Here civic
regulation concerns rules dealing with the terms and conditions under which
members of a community have agreed to live with one another and in relation
to the state (Cairns and Williams 1985). The institutions operating in this
regulatory arena are primarily located within the state, while their effects are
felt on individuals and groups inside (and also outside) the community. The
federal government and Supreme Court of Canada are key political and constitutional actors in this field, as are the provinces, and provincial legislation and
agencies charged with advancing human rights have played an important pioneering role since the 1940s. As a statutory concept, Canadian citizenship was
established in federal legislation in 1947. In 1960 the Canadian Bill of Rights,
a federal statute, was passed, and in 1977 the Canada Human Rights Act was

TABLE 9.1
Four Types of Civic Regulation

Type	Institutions	Ideas	Issues	Policies
Citizenship and human rights	Federal and provincial governments	Membership	Race relations	Citizenship Act
		Rights and duties	Immigration	Charter of Rights and Freedoms
	Human rights tribunals	Equality, equity, and diversity	Gender equity	Federal and provincial human rights codes
	Courts			
Justice and public order	Legal system:	Rule of law	Victims rights	Criminal Code
	Courts Police Prisons and parole boards	Safety and security	Access to courts Gun control Domestic violence	Common Law
Moral and sexual regulation	Families	Family values	Abortion	Criminal Code
	Marriage/divorce	Community standards	Sexual orientation	Family Law
	Police and courts			
	Churches		Reproductive technologies	
Welfare programs and the social union	Welfare states	Social security	National standards	Canada health and social transfer
	Federalism	Work ethic	Employability	
	Voluntary sector	Family responsibilities	Child support	Employment insurance
		Non-partisan charity	Advocacy by voluntary sector	Social housing
				Canada Health Act

Note: The above ideas, issues, and policies are illustrative and not intended to be exhaustive.

enacted, creating the Canadian Human Rights Commission, by which time all ten provinces and both territories had established human rights laws with a commission to administer and enforce the legislation.

With the Charter of Rights and Freedoms entrenched in the constitution in 1982, citizenship now has constitutional status. The term 'citizen' appears in sections 3, 6, and 23 of the Charter, dealing respectively with voting rights, mobility rights, and minority language educational rights. The Charter has other implications for citizenship in Canada, since it constitutionally recognizes and protects nonterritorial identities of citizens like race, ethnicity, gender, and age, among others.

Cynthia Williams (1985, 124–7) has traced the changing nature of human rights in Canada since 1945 and identified five key developments. In brief, these are:

1 Rights demands on the state have come to focus less on the negative civil liberties that predominated in the 1950s and more on demands that place expectations and obligations on governments to intervene through public policies, particularly in the areas of cultural policy, including language policy.
2 There has been a shift of concern at the popular level from political and democratic rights to egalitarian and cultural rights.
3 Group rights claims by cultural groups have been especially prominent and successful in the postwar period.
4 The constitutional recognition of human rights in Canada has always been hotly contested in the federal-provincial arena.
5 At the less formal level of rights recognition, recent developments in rights thinking also suggest changes in informal constitutionalism and the way in which politics is conducted in Canada.

Since Williams' account in the mid-1980s, rights claims by groups representing aboriginal peoples, women, gays and lesbians, and people with disabilities, have been manifest in Canadian politics, though often met with mixed responses by governments. Groups making citizenship claims is one part of civic regulation; governments making policy and resource commitments on human rights and sticking to them is quite another part. The constitutional recognition of certain social policy rights in the form of a Social Charter was hotly debated in the early 1990s, around the time of the Charlottetown Accord, the last failed effort at amending the Canadian constitution. Under federal and provincial human rights laws, newer prohibited grounds for discrimination include economic and income status, family status, and sexual orientation. Over twenty grounds now exist in federal and provincial/territorial laws. And from being virtually unknown in Canadian jurisprudence twenty years ago, sexual harassment in the workplace is now considered to be a form of sex discrimination in employment under human rights laws and has generated a new body of case law and tribunal decisions (Aggarwal 1992). This widening scope of prohibited grounds for discrimination has been extended into areas beyond the traditional ones of employment and accommodation to include the provision of goods, services, and income assistance. Other trends in human rights regulation are the strengthening of sanctions (awards and fines), the growing role of commissions into race relations and affirmative action program areas, and the increasing caseloads handled by these commissions (Howe and Johnson 1995).

The Indian Act is very much a regulatory regime concerned with, among other matters, citizenship and band membership. Traditionally under the Act, a woman's identity as a First Nations person was determined by the status of her husband; if he was a non-Indian, she lost her Indian status as did any children she might have. By contrast, First Nations men who married non-Indians did not lose their status and associated rights. In 1985, Bill C-31 allowed for the reinstatement of those women who had lost their Indian status and granted status to their children. But, as the Royal Commission on Aboriginal Peoples (1996, 101) reports, 'the process and criteria for first-time registration are confusing – and still offensive, because authority to determine who can be recognized as a status Indian lies with the federal government, not with Aboriginal people. As well, the children of women reinstated under Bill C-31 are still treated less favourably than those of men who married non-Indians before 1985. And children born of such unions after 1985 generally cannot pass their status on to their children.' As an attempt at inclusion, the law has generated new boundaries and misgivings, and the question of status and citizenship in aboriginal communities remains. In relation to treaty negotiations and land claims, the citizenship issue increasingly becomes for aboriginal people and other Canadians a question of eligibility for entitlement to property and other resources. As these processes unfold, citizenship will increasingly come to mean authorized access to and control over a chunk of ecological space, and hence further merge economic and social rights.

Continuing debate on the meaning of aboriginal governance and on the future of Quebec, within or without Canada, illustrate that matters of citizenship and dual citizenship are as much matters of domestic politics as of foreign policy.

Justice and Public Order

This form of civic regulation involves intervention in society through the formulation, arbitration and interpretation, and enforcement of a general framework of laws and rules. These are essential functions of government: law maker, umpire, and enforcer. They remind us that the democratic state is fundamentally based on the management and manipulation of legitimate coercion. This regulatory role of governments is a pre-welfare state aspect of governing; it even pre-dates Confederation. Early policing and corrections were provided by municipalities, colonial administrators, and the Hudson's Bay Company (Griffiths and Verdun-Jones 1989). If it is true that the welfare state is in its twilight years, then perhaps we will witness the re-emergence of 'the night watchman' state of an earlier age, when the main endeavour of government was regulating society through the legal and police powers of the state.

The primary institutions involved are within the state; such agencies as the courts, the police, law officers, prisons, and parole boards are all engaged in the allocation of public sanctions. This distinguishes regulating public order and justice from economic regulation. Ronald Manzer (1985, 100) expresses this difference in terms of the political ideas shaping these regulatory endeavours: 'The principles guiding economic progress assign great importance to individual efforts and private organizations, thereby forcing governments to depend mainly on selective material inducements to manipulate individual economic behaviour; but the accepted principles that guide policies for public order all assign the leading role in conflict resolution to the state, clearly relegating individual efforts and private organizations to subordinate, supportive activities.'

In Canada, regulating public order and justice is a federalized policy field. The federal parliament has exclusive authority to make criminal laws and the federal government serves a number of legal and correctional functions. The RCMP has responsibility for law enforcement in relation to about forty-five major federal statutes. The provinces have jurisdiction for the administration of justice and provincial courts. Most urban municipalities have their own police services and play a regulatory role in this field. There are also First Nations and Inuit policing services, as well as police services for aboriginal people off-reserve. Outside the Canadian state, private policing and security agencies are extensive and have grown in recent decades.

By adding some new rights and duties that bear on criminal justice, the Charter of Rights and Freedoms has perhaps had its greatest impact to date on this type of civic regulation. Section 8 of the Charter guarantees the right to be secure against unreasonable search or seizure. Section 10(b) added a new duty to those already in common law: anyone arrested or detained has the right to retain and instruct counsel without delay and to be informed of that right. And section 11(b) guarantees the right of an accused person to be tried within a reasonable time, a right formerly not acknowledged in Canadian jurisprudence.

In a number of criminal cases, these and other sections of the Charter have been used successfully to challenge certain police powers and procedures. When the courts use the Charter to dismiss a case, exclude evidence, or stay a prosecution, they are remaking our understanding of justice and the limits of the regulatory state. Overall, the Charter has modestly shifted the balance between police powers and individual rights in favour of the citizen (Griffiths and Verdun-Jones 1989; Macleod and Schneiderman 1994).

More generally, Michael Mandel (1992, 71) has argued that the Charter contributes to the 'legalization of politics' in Canada by its substitution of judicial forums for legislative ones and abstract judicial reasoning for concrete policy reasoning in resolving political and social concerns. There is no doubt that both the judiciary and the legal profession play crucial roles in the regulatory processes. Current issues in this area of regulation, however, reflect the role of political action by provinces, interest groups, and social movements in pressing for government action on street gangs across the country, motorcycle gang wars in Quebec, domestic violence against women and children, and greater recognition of victims' rights within the legal process. Reaction to a recent federal initiative respecting the control of firearms and other weapons by a number of provinces and the Yukon demonstrates the intergovernmental and regional dimensions of efforts to legislate safety and security.[6]

Moral and Sexual Regulation

Despite its Victorian-era label, this type of civic regulation is far from passé at the end of the twentieth century. Legal scholars in the 1960s sharply debated the relation of law, morality, and liberty (Hart 1963; Devlin 1968; Fuller 1969), and, more recently, the enforcement of morals by the state has been examined by feminists, sociologists, and political scientists (Ross 1988; Valverde 1994; Campbell and Pal 1989). In *Women and Canadian Public Policy*, Janine Brodie (1996, 359) and her contributors use the term to describe 'relationships between state and non-state actors involved in developing and reproducing codes of morality. Moral regulation is the privileging of certain forms of expression that results in the subordination of other forms of self-identification and social recognition. Sexual regulation forms a crucial part of the larger project of the production of moral subjects. The legal regulation of sexual representation through obscenity law and pornography policy are key examples of moral regulation.'

If society is viewed as a moral entity, as classical social theorists held, then law and regulation represent a normative order concerned with different kinds of moral transactions and social relations. 'Custom once provided for a social

order based upon a particular moral order. Custom also entailed shared under-
standings about how to behave in a wide variety of circumstances' (Jones,
Brown, and Bradshaw 1983, 121). In this context, moral and sexual regulation
is the authoritative determination and enforcement of customs. Certain actions
are deemed proper and lawful, others improper and unlawful. Thus, moral
regulation aims 'to bring about a change in people's "way of seeing" and "way
of thinking" about problems and issues' (Rodger 1995, 23). More than that,
regulating morality seeks to affect people's way of being and interrelating with
others.

Of the institutions involved in regulating morality and sexuality, several lie
outside the Canadian state, such as families, religious organizations, and gay
and lesbian communities. Within the state, all levels of government plus the
courts and the police are active in moral regulation, with the Criminal Code of
Canada effectively serving as the framework law. As Corrigan and Sayer (1985,
4) write, 'moral regulation is coextensive with state formation, and state forms
are always animated and legitimated by a particular moral ethos.' In public
policy terms, moral regulation deals with the areas of abortion, contraception,
divorce, drug use, euthanasia, family law, marriage, pornography, prostitution,
reproductive technologies, sexual orientation, and toplessness in public.[7] Sexual
regulation through criminal law deals with establishing the age of sexual consent and setting out illegal forms of sexual imagery and activity, including
child-sex tourism, obscenity, and different kinds of sexual assault. The impact
of moral and sexual regulation is often on specific groups rather than the
general public, generating specific interest structures and politics. As Lise
Gotell (1996, 281) has said of regulating morality and sexual norms, '[b]y
erecting legal prohibitions to some sexual materials, states have sought to
condition sexual behaviour, to maintain moral order, and, in this manner, to
shore up the "foundations" of society.'

Robert Campbell and Leslie Pal (1989, 150) suggest that governments in
Canada 'have not been anxious or able to legislate in moral areas in general
and with respect to sex and pornography in particular.' A number of factors
present challenges in regulating morality. First, the deeply felt and often contrary views and religious convictions held by Canadians on family, sexuality,
human life, and dignity make this a politically complex and socially charged
regulatory domain. There is an array of interests and claims within Canadian
political culture that inhibit the formation of a general consensus on many of
these issues. Second, experts are also divided or their research and advice on
these matters is inconclusive. Third, as a result of this social and expert dis-
cord, moral regulation does not lend itself to the tactics of incremental policy
making or stakeholder bargaining. Policy debates are infused with strongly

entrenched positions and often diverse principles of morality. Under such conditions, making trade-offs and cutting deals are viewed by many as ethically unacceptable. Fourth, there is the arduous challenge, in drafting legislation or rules in this realm, of 'translating philosophical or moral objectives into precise and operative legal terminology' (Campbell and Pal 1989, 112).

The difficulties Campbell and Pal identify, in my view, are more germane in some instances than in others. Indeed, the history of state intervention in Canada shows that governments are able, at times with some assurance, to legislate on matters of morality and sexuality (Little 1994; Ursel 1992; Valverde 1994). Governments may not regulate in this domain well or always with conviction, but many such laws do exist across the country and there are attempts to enforce them all the time. Moreover, moral regulation continues today; it is probably intensifying (Denis 1995) and changing in character. The intensification of moral regulation is connected to the rise, in recent decades, of the New Right, anxieties over the decline of community standards and institutions, the politics of antipornography feminism (Cole 1989; Lacombe 1994), and new developments in technology, such as the potential of cloning human embryos. In the current era of reducing deficits and restructuring the welfare state, the character of moral regulation is also undergoing change. For example, in the 1990s, a major element in the moral order is the glorification of the family. Janine Brodie (1996, 22–3) describes this theme and its policy implications as follows: 'The value accorded the private sphere of the family is particularly obtrusive in right-wing rhetoric, which blames the welfare state and feminism for the breakdown of the social fabric. More broadly, however, there is a growing consensus among policy-makers that families (whatever their form) should look after their own and that it is up to the neoliberal state to make sure that they do.'

Welfare Programs and the Social Union

Another area of civic regulation governs the distributional and redistributional practices of the welfare state. Macdonald (1985, 103–4) has noted the reach of regulatory delegation in this domain, remarking that 'almost every receipt of governmental largesse performs a semi-public regulatory function. That is, the allocation of direct subsidy or indirect rebate in the form of welfare, family allowances, old-age security, unemployment insurance, RRSP credits ... permits each beneficiary to disrupt any pre-existing distribution of resources.' Notice that Macdonald uses the traditional idea of regulation as government action to influence market distributions; hence, recipients are regulators. From a civic definition, however, what makes government social programs regulatory is the organization and delivery of the programs by staff. Rules control the entitlement, provision, and withdrawal of benefits, services, and transfer payments between governments and between government agencies and clients. Viewing social policies as forms of regulation emphasizes that programs entail relations of power and dependencies. Far more than recipients, service providers are service regulators. This regulation occurs through screening applicants by means of eligibility criteria, of course, but also through explicitly deterring claims, referring people to other agencies, delaying access, and charging user fees (Spicker 1995).

As well as a provider state, the welfare state is a disciplinary state with public power exercised through social services and agencies (Squires 1990). A general finding in the sociology of welfare literature is that 'welfare bureaucracies can be so obsessed with changing behaviour that their ostensible purpose of meeting need goes by the board' (Cranston 1985, 193). The National Council of Welfare (1987, 28–9), in a report entitled *Welfare in Canada: The Tangled Safety Net*, observed that 'the welfare system in every province in Canada is a complex operation governed by a vast array of rules which require interpretation and the exercise of administrative discretion. Personal judgments invariably give rise to inconsistencies in the treatment of recipients within and between jurisdictions. The fact that the rules are neither well known nor well understood by the public makes it difficult to verify whether they have been fairly and appropriately applied in any given situation.' Beyond welfare, social policy rules decree preferred behaviour on the part of clients such as social housing tenants, service providers such as nurses, public bureaucracies such as legal aid clinics, and community groups such as registered charities.

The primary regulatory actors in this field are the provinces, with the federal government playing a key role in certain social policy fields like health care, Indian affairs, and transfer payments. Regulating the provision of social benefits and programs has an impact at several levels, affecting the individual person or family, groups in need, voluntary agencies, and governments. With a mixture of institutions in the state and society involved, the power dynamics consist of intergovernmental politics, clientele-service provider relationships, government department–to–government watchdog processes, and relations between government departments and charitable organizations. The regulatory regime that Revenue Canada applies to charities, for example, is far-reaching and, in relation to the advocacy activities of groups with charitable status, the rules are restrictive (Pross and Stewart 1993). In response to calls for tightening the application process for new registrants and claims of some charities abusing their tax-preferred status, the 1997 federal budget papers announced that additional resources will be given to Revenue Canada to improve its ability to confirm that charities are in compliance with the Income Tax Act, so as to maintain donor confidence in charities.

There have been notable developments in this area of civic regulation in the 1990s. Existing social program rules have been strengthened and new ones introduced by governments, with the intent of making work more attractive relative to social insurance or income assistance by restricting access to benefits and lowering benefit amounts for certain groups, such as able-bodied youth. Across the country, most provincial governments and some municipalities have also taken action against welfare fraud and abuse, introducing welfare 'snitch lines,'[8] and hiring additional eligibility review officers, and many have embraced different versions of workfare measures (McFarland and Mullaly 1996; Shragge 1997). Workfare is an example of overtly using social policy to modify people's choices and behaviours. Controls are imposed on clients as a condition of their receiving a service or benefit. The reasons for this strategy are themselves expressed in regulative language: to advance community expectations of work, to channel the energy of clients toward enhancing their employability, to stress the obligations of recipients, to discourage the abuse of benefits, and to deter people from applying for benefits in the first instance, thus preventing dependency (Sayeed 1995).

The introduction of the Canada Health and Social Transfer (CHST) by the federal government in 1996 represents a momentous change in the way fiscal federalism and the social union are to be regulated. Margaret Biggs (1996, 1) defines the social union as 'the web of rights and obligations between Canadian citizens and governments that give effect and meaning to our shared sense of social purpose and citizenship.' While not encompassing a specific set of policies, the social union is often identified with social security programs, the benefits associated with those programs, and the intergovernmental financing arrangements, such as the new CHST. The CHST replaces federal transfers for social assistance and social services under the now-defunct Canada Assistance Plan (CAP) and health and post-secondary education under Established Programs Financing (EPF) with a single, significantly reduced block fund. Under the CHST, the federal government intends to uphold the five principles of medicare as before[9] but, with respect to social assistance and social services, Ottawa has said that just one principle of the five under CAP (no minimum residency requirement for social assistance) will be retained.

Tom Courchene (1995) believes the CHST will, if anything, enhance the federal government's role as a regulator of the Canadian social union, because it helps put Ottawa's finances in better order and allows the provinces greater flexibility to innovate in social policy. This reform, however, is about more than redistributing money, downloading costs, or creating room for program experimentation. The CHST is a framework law governing the social union, with likely fateful repercussions for the rights and duties of Canadians into the near future. From a civic regulation perspective, the CHST enacts a process of federal deregulation within social welfare programming by removing a number of national standards,[10] yet invites provinces to re-regulate welfare by cutting benefits and by introducing and expanding rules to enforce, for example, incentives to work or improve individual self-reliance (Rice 1995).

Conclusions

In taking stock of Canada's regulatory institutions we need to undertake a full inventory of the organizations, laws, issues, and interests concerned. Conventional theory and analysis miss a large part of the real world of regulatory politics. To bring the community and social union into the study of government regulation I have suggested a different theoretical perspective for understanding the nature of regulation and the relation between the state and society. The term civic regulation is used to cover all aspects of regulatory activity concerning the public, civil, and domestic spheres. At the macrolevel of the regulatory state, we have explored what regulating society means and considered some of the current policy issues and controversies. Civic regulation is a blend of vertical rules, affecting specific constituencies or particular activities and horizontal or framework rules designed to span a community or range of activities. The Indian Act and rules about benefits for seniors and veterans are examples of vertical civic regulation, while the CHST and the Criminal Code are framework rules for Canadian federalism and society. In this approach regulation is seen as an instrument of policy, not independent from spending, taxation, and service provision, but rather embedded in these instruments. These instruments also perform significant regulatory functions on behalf of the state. We also move beyond the notion of civil society as simply a bridge between the individual citizen or household and the state to focus on civil society in its own right, that is, to see civil society as set of institutions from which emerge decisions on human activity that government may seek to influence, not to improve economic performance, but to achieve greater social cohesion and justice.

The expanded taxonomy of regulation presented here generates a number of questions for future research. What is the interrelationship between economic regulation and civic regulation? How, for example, do particular civic rules affect the allocation of resources and the distribution of incomes? What are the connections between civil society and civic regulation? How do civic rules relate to and affect the fabric of community life and institutions? How do

Canadians view civic rule making, and do these views differ from opinions on economic regulating? Do calls for the kinds of rules labelled here as civic reflect public confidence in governments to do well and work well? In turn, what does civic regulation tell us about the sovereignty or policy capacity of the Canadian state? What factors contribute to the creation of civic rules? Is civic regulation shaped primarily by societal interests and trends or by state officials and agendas?

Civic regulation has a broad and probably expanding scope in contemporary Canada. In each of the four regulatory arenas, there are pressures for intervention and protection from citizens, interest groups, social movements, and governments. A trend toward the greater use of rules can be seen in the social services. In the adoption field, the regulation of private agencies through licensing is replacing expenditures through employed staff as the primary means of assuring quality control. The courts, too, are expanding their regulatory role by approving detailed supervision orders for persons considered to be neglecting or abusing children. In processes of privatization and contracting out, there is a heightened emphasis on control and accountability mechanisms, usually specified in contractual terms. When social service agency budgets and personnel are cut, a common management response is to further systematize and regulate the interactions between agency staff and citizens seeking benefits or services (Lipsky 1980).

The rise and growth in civic regulation is a significant development in modern public policy and governing. Depending on one's values and goals, this may or may not be regarded as a good thing for liberal democracy or the market economy. Radical analysts see the hidden hand of their concerns – patriarchy, capitalism, racism – within most regulation, while other analysts tend to see the regulation of social behaviour as the glue that holds society together in a civic order, by providing balance and protecting minority rights. Whatever one's perspective, the Canadian state is increasingly becoming a regulatory state. There is not one regulatory politics but the politics of many types of regulation.

NOTES

For comments and suggestions on earlier drafts, my thanks go to Andrew Armitage, Jim Cutt, Rod Dobell, Susan Phillips, Bill Stanbury, Kathy Teghtsoonian, and Brian Wharf.

1 The general thrust of this chapter is to expand our conception of regulation, although I do not wish to extend it so much as to make the concept meaningless.

The taxing and spending instruments of the state are not just special cases of regulation. Distinctions between taxing and regulating, for instance, have been made by the courts, with implications for constitutional law in Canada. While each level of government may levy taxes on institutions outside of its constitutional jurisdiction, such as provincial taxes on banks, one level cannot use taxes as a way of regulating industries or institutions that fall under the jurisdiction of the other level of government. Further, the courts have distinguished between indirect taxes (which are generally outside provincial authority) and regulatory charges, the latter of which the courts will uphold if the charges are imposed under one of the provincial legislative powers and are intended not to raise revenue for general purposes but rather to help finance the provision of the provincial service or activity to which the charge is attached (Hogg 1985, 613, 620). Other important political distinctions between these instruments have been advanced by the public policy literature (Doern 1974; Wilson 1980).

2 A notable exception is Armitage (1988) who gives fairly equal weight to the regulatory and redistributive functions of social welfare. Social services with deliberate control purposes include prisons, correctional centres, probation and parole, mental health programs, and many employment enhancement/workfare programs. Armitage notes that these services are often 'engaged in trying to change people against their wishes' (1988, 138). The police and the courts, however, are not usually seen as parts of social welfare.

3 I agree with Fiona Williams (1989), Peter Squires (1990), and Andrew Armitage (1996), that while the mainstream literature in social policy has come under challenge from a number of theoretical and ideological quarters in the past twenty years, much of this critique remains at the margins of the discipline and social policy making. One reviewer of a previous draft of this chapter noted that although Piven and Cloward (1971) may be outside the mainstream in economics, they are front and centre in other literatures, including political sociology and social welfare, that may be just as 'mainstream.' I accept this comment and would raise for further consideration, beyond this paper, the question of the relative profile and influence of different disciplinary mainstreams on public debates and policy developments.

4 Direct regulation aims to influence price, property, market structures, and outputs of specific industries. Social regulation seeks to influence the conditions, across many industries, under which goods and services are produced, advertised, and distributed.

5 I wish to thank Rod Dobell for suggesting this line of analysis.

6 Four provinces – Alberta, Ontario, Saskatchewan, and Manitoba – and the Yukon launched a court challenge to the federal government's legislation creating a national firearms licensing and registration system. The licensing procedure begins in 1997 and the gun registry is to start in 1999. These governments contend that the

federal law (i) does not address the concerns of rural and northern Canadians; (ii) will not be effective in reducing and fighting crime; and (iii) is unconstitutional because firearms are private property, which is a matter of provincial jurisdiction. Hence, this is not a Charter challenge but a traditional division of powers challenge. Most of these governments have also said that they will not administer the program for the federal government (Laghi 1996).

7 At the time of writing this paper, whether or not to regulate toplessness by women in public became a hot issue in Canada. In December 1996, the Ontario Court of Appeal ruled that women have the right to go topless in public, overturning an indecency conviction of a woman who had walked topless in public in July 1991. Across Canada, prior to the 1997 summer season, municipal councils debated the implications of this ruling, *primarily from a moral regulation perspective*. In May 1997, the Ottawa City Council, for instance, passed a by-law prohibiting women ten years of age and older from swimming topless at indoor city pools but made no rule for outdoor pools or public beaches. The by-law was seen by councillors as a compromise: protecting family use of indoor pools while allowing women the choice of where and how they want to swim (Canadian Press 1997).

8 Social assistance investigation lines or welfare 'snitch lines' are special phone numbers made known and available to the public to call authorities if they suspect someone has fraudulent access to welfare benefits. In early 1993, the then employment minister of the Conservative federal government floated the idea of a 1-800 snitch line for people to anonymously report suspected unemployment insurance 'cheats.' The idea was quickly dropped. In Ontario, the Harris government in 1997 launched a provincial line with a toll-free number with respect to social assistance. For an instructive analysis of the introduction and revocation of a snitch line in Sudbury, see Reitsma-Street and Keck (1996).

9 These are the principles of accessibility, comprehensiveness, portability, public administration, and universality. They are set out in the Canada Health Act of 1984, which the CHST relies on rather than replaces. For a discussion of the CHST, see Susan D. Phillips (1995).

10 These standards of welfare included the right to appeal decisions related to income assistance decisions, the non-profit provision of social services, and the provision of welfare solely on the basis that persons were in need.

REFERENCES

Adams, Howard. 1975. *Prison of Grass: Canada from a Native Point of View*. Saskatoon: Fifth House.
Aggarwal, A.P. 1992. *Sexual Harassment in the Workplace*. Toronto: Butterworths.
Armitage, Andrew. 1988. *Social Welfare in Canada: Ideals, Realities, and Future Paths*. 2nd ed. Toronto: McClelland and Stewart.

– 1995. *Comparing the Policy of Aboriginal Assimilation.* Vancouver: UBC Press.
– 1996. *Social Welfare in Canada Revisited: Facing Up to the Future.* 3rd ed.
   Toronto: Oxford University Press.
Bernstein, M.H. 1955. *Regulating Business by Independent Commission.* Princeton:
   Princeton University Press.
Biggs, Margaret. 1996. *Building Blocks for Canada's New Social Union.* Canadian
   Policy Research Networks, Working Paper No. F/02. Ottawa: Renouf.
Brodie, Janine. 1996. Canadian Women, Changing State Forms, and Public Policy. In
   J. Brodie, ed., *Women and Canadian Public Policy*, 1–28. Toronto: Harcourt Brace.
Cairns, Alan. 1986. The Embedded State: State-Society Relations in Canada. In
   K. Banting, ed., *State and Society in Comparative Perspective*, 53–86. Toronto:
   University Toronto Press.
Cairns, Alan, and Cynthia Williams. 1985. Constitutionalism, Citizenship and Society
   in Canada. In A. Cairns and C. Williams, eds., *Constitutionalism, Citizenship and
   Society in Canada*, 1–50. Toronto: University of Toronto Press.
Campbell, Robert M., and Leslie A. Pal. 1989. *The Real Worlds of Canadian Politics:
   Cases in Process and Policy.* Peterborough: Broadview Press.
Canadian Press. 1997. Ottawa rules on topless swimming. *Globe and Mail*, 22 May.
Cole, Susan G. 1989. *Pornography and the Sex Crisis.* Toronto: Amanita.
Corrigan, P., and D. Sayer. 1985. *The Great Arch: English State Formation as
   Cultural Revolution.* London: Blackwell.
Courchene, Thomas J. 1995. *Redistributing Money and Power: A Guide to the Canada
   Health and Social Transfer.* C.D. Howe Institute Observation 39. Toronto: C.D.
   Howe Institute.
Cranston, Ross. 1985. *Legal Foundations of the Welfare State.* London: Weidenfeld
   and Nicolson.
Denis, Claude. 1995. 'Government Can Do Whatever It Wants': Moral Regulation in
   Ralph Klein's Alberta. *Canadian Review of Sociology and Anthropology* 32, no. 3
   (August): 365–83.
Devlin, Patrick. 1968. *The Enforcement of Morals.* London: Oxford University Press.
Dobuzinskis, Laurent, Michael Howlett, and David Laycock. 1996. Introduction. In
   L. Dobuzinskis, M. Howlett, and D. Laycock, eds., *Policy Studies in Canada:
   The State of the Art*, 1–11. Toronto: University of Toronto Press.
Doern, G. Bruce. 1974. The Concept of Regulation and Regulatory Reform. In
   G. Bruce Doern and V.S. Wilson, eds., *Issues in Canadian Public Policy*, 8–35.
   Toronto: Macmillan of Canada.
Economic Council of Canada. 1979. *Responsible Regulation: An Interim Report.*
   Ottawa: Supply and Services Canada.
Etzioni, Amatai. 1964. *Modern Organizations.* Englewood Cliffs, N.J.: Prentice-Hall.
Fuller, Lon L. 1969. *The Morality of Law.* Rev. ed. New Haven: Yale University Press.

Gotell, Lise. 1996. Policing Desire: Obscenity Law, Pornography Politics, and
Feminism in Canada. In J. Brodie, ed., *Women and Canadian Public Policy*,
279–317. Toronto: Harcourt Brace.

Gough, Ian. 1979. *The Political Economy of the Welfare State*. London: Macmillan.

Griffiths, Curt T., and Simon N. Verdun-Jones. 1989. *Canadian Criminal Justice*.
Toronto: Butterworths.

Hart, H.L.A. 1963. *Law, Liberty, and Morality*. London: Oxford University Press.

Hartle, Douglas G. 1979. *Public Policy Decision Making and Regulation*. Montreal:
Institute for Research on Public Policy. Toronto: Butterworth.

Hasenfeld, Y. 1983. *Human Service Organizations*. Englewood Cliffs, N.J.: Prentice-
Hall.

Hirshorn, R., and J.-F. Gautrin, eds. 1993. *Competitiveness and Regulation*. Government and Competitiveness Seminar Series. Kingston, Ont.: School of Policy
Studies, Queen's University.

Hodgetts, J.E. 1973. *The Canadian Public Service: A Physiology of Government 1867–
1970*. Toronto: University of Toronto Press.

Hogg, Peter W. 1985. *Constitutional Law of Canada*. 2nd ed. Toronto: Carswell.

Howe, R.B., and D. Johnson. 1995. Variations in enforcing and funding equality: a
study of provincial human rights funding. *Canadian Public Administration* 38,
no. 2: 242–62.

Jones, Kathleen, John Brown, and Jonathan Bradshaw. 1983. *Issues in Social Policy*.
Rev. ed. London: Routledge and Kegan Paul.

Kernaghan, Kenneth, and David Siegel. 1996. *Public Administration in Canada: A
Text*. 3rd ed. Scarborough: Nelson Canada.

Lacombe, Dany. 1994. *Blue Politics: Pornography and the Law in the Age of Feminism*. Toronto: University of Toronto Press.

Laghi, Brian. 1996. Provinces fight gun registry. *Globe and Mail*, 27 September.

Little, Margaret. 1994. 'Manhunts and Bingo Blabs': The Moral Regulation of Ontario
Single Mothers. *Canadian Journal of Sociology* 19, no. 2: 233–47.

Lipsky, Michael. 1980. *Street-Level Bureaucracy: Dilemmas of the Individual in
Public Services*. New York: Russell Sage.

Macdonald, R.A. 1985. Understanding Regulation by Regulations. In I. Bernier and
A. Lajoie, eds., *Regulations, Crown Corporations and Administrative Tribunals*,
81–154. Toronto: University of Toronto Press.

Macleod, R.C., and D. Schneiderman. 1994. *Police Powers in Canada: The Evolution
and Practice of Authority*. Toronto: University of Toronto Press.

Mandel, Michael. 1992. *The Charter of Rights and the Legalization of Politics in
Canada*. Toronto: Thompson Educational Publishing.

Manzer, Ronald. 1985. *Public Policies and Political Development in Canada*. Toronto:
University of Toronto Press.

McFarland, Joan, and Robert Mullaly. 1996. NB Works: Image vs. Reality. In Jane Pulkingham and Gordon Ternowetsky, eds., *Remaking Canadian Social Policy: Social Security in the Late 1990s*, 202–19. Halifax: Fernwood.

McGilly, Frank. 1998. *An Introduction to Canada's Public Social Services: Understanding Income and Health Programs*. 2nd ed. Toronto: McClelland and Stewart.

McKenzie, Brad, and Pete Hudson. 1985. Native Children, Child Welfare, and the Colonization of Native People. In Kenneth L. Levitt and Brian Wharf, eds., *The Challenge of Child Welfare*, 125–41. Vancouver: UBC Press.

Moscovitch, Allan. 1983. *The Welfare State in Canada: A Selected Bibliography, 1840 to 1978*. Waterloo: Wilfrid Laurier University Press.

National Council of Welfare. 1987. *Welfare in Canada, The Tangled Safety Net*. Ottawa: Supply and Services Canada.

Ogus, Anthony I. 1994. *Regulation: Legal Form and Economic Theory*. Oxford: Oxford University Press.

Pascall, Gillian. 1986. *Social Policy: A Feminist Analysis*. London: Tavistock Publications.

Phillips, Susan D. 1995. The Canada Health and Social Transfer: Fiscal Federalism in Search of a Vision. In D. Brown and J. Rose, eds., *Canada: The State of the Federation*, 65–96. Kingston: Institute of Intergovernmental Relations.

Piven, Frances Fox, and Richard A. Cloward. 1971. *Regulating the Poor: The Functions of Public Welfare*. New York: Vintage Books.

Prince, Michael J. 1994. Federal Expenditures and First Nations Experiences. In S.D. Phillips, ed., *How Ottawa Spends 1994–95: Making Change*, 261–99. Ottawa: Carleton University Press.

Pross, A. Paul, and Iain S. Stewart. 1993. Lobbying, the Voluntary Sector and the Public Purse. In S.D. Phillips, ed., *How Ottawa Spends 1993–1994, A More Democratic Canada...?*, 109–42. Ottawa: Carleton University.

Reagan, Michael D. 1987. *Regulation: The Politics of Policy*. Toronto: Little, Brown.

Reitsma-Street, Marge, and Jennifer Keck. 1996. The Abolition of a Welfare Snitch Line. *The Social Worker* 64, no. 3 (Fall): 35–47.

Rice, James J. 1995. Redesigning Welfare: The Abandonment of a National Commitment. In Susan D. Phillips, ed., *How Ottawa Spends, 1995–96: Mid-Life Crises*, 185–207. Ottawa: Carleton University Press.

Richards, John, and Aidan Vining. 1995. *Helping the Poor: A Qualified Case for Workfare*. Toronto: C.D. Howe Institute.

Rodger, John. 1995. Family Policy or Moral Regulation? *Critical Social Policy* 43 (Summer): 5–25.

Room, Graham. 1979. *The Sociology of Welfare: Social Policy, Stratification and Political Order*. Oxford: Martin Robertson.

Ross, B. 1988. Heterosexuals Only Need Apply: The Secretary of State's Regulation of Lesbian Existence. *Resources for Feminist Research* 17, no. 3 (September): 35–8.

Royal Commission on Aboriginal Peoples. 1996. *People to People, Nation to Nation: Highlights from the Report of the Royal Commission on Aboriginal Peoples.* Ottawa: Minister of Supply and Services.

Sabatier, Paul. 1975. Social Movements and Regulatory Agencies: Towards a More Adequate – and Less Pessimistic – Theory of Clientele Capture. *Policy Sciences* 6: 301–42.

Sayeed, Adil. 1995. *Workfare: Does It Work? Is It Fair?* Montreal: Institute for Research on Public Policy.

Shragge, Eric, ed. 1997. *Workfare: Ideology for a New Under-Class.* Toronto: Garamond Press.

Spicker, P. 1995. *Social Policy: Themes and Approaches.* Toronto: Prentice-Hall, Harvester Wheatsheaf.

Squires, Peter. 1990. *Anti-Social Policy: Welfare, Ideology and the Disciplinary State.* London: Harvester Wheatsheaf.

Sutherland, Sharon L. 1993. The Public Service and Policy Development. In Michael M. Atkinson, ed., *Governing Canada: Institutions and Public Policy*, 81–113. Toronto: Harcourt Brace Jovanovich.

Thomas, Paul G., and Orest W. Zajcew. 1993. Structural Heretics: Crown Corporations and Regulatory Agencies. In Michael M. Atkinson, ed., *Governing Canada: Institutions and Public Policy*, 115–47. Toronto: Harcourt Brace Jovanovich.

Tumin, Melvin M. 1967. *Social Stratification: The Forms and Functions of Inequality.* Englewood Cliffs, N.J.: Prentice-Hall.

Ursel, Jane. 1992. *Private Lives, Public Policy: 100 Years of State Intervention in the Family.* Toronto: Women's Press.

Valverde, Mariana, ed. 1994. Special Issue on Moral Regulation. *Canadian Journal of Sociology* 19, no. 2: 24–41.

Williams, Cynthia. 1985. The Changing Nature of Citizen Rights. In A. Cairns and C. Williams, eds., *Constitutionalism, Citizenship and Society in Canada*, 99–131. Toronto: University of Toronto Press.

Williams, Fiona. 1989. *Social Policy: A Critical Introduction.* Oxford: Polity Press.

Wilson, Elizabeth. 1977. *Women and the Welfare State.* London: Tavistock Publications.

Wilson, James Q., ed. 1980. *The Politics of Regulation.* New York: Basic Books.

10

Aristotle's Benchmarks: Institutions and Accountabilities of the Canadian Regulatory State

MICHAEL J. PRINCE

'Without the essential minimum of offices there can be no state at all; without those concerned with good order and good conduct there can be no well-organized one.'

Aristotle, *Politics*, Book 6, chapter 8

The place and role of regulation within the Canadian state and in relation to the political community is the topic of this chapter. The analytic framework used is a political-institutional perspective, an example of the 'new institutionalism' in public policy studies (Atkinson 1993; Reagan 1987), which focuses renewed attention on questions of constitutional rules and organizational arrangements, social ideas and political interests, regulatory power and accountability, and the capacity to realize policy goals in a liberal-democratic polity. This approach contrasts with the prevailing view held by many governments and much of the recent literature, which considers regulation and regulatory reform largely in terms of fiscal responsibility, 'getting government right,' and concerns of market efficiency.[1]

The focus in this chapter is on the character of governmental and other political organizations and interrelationships comprising the regulatory state in Canada. These include the key institutions of cabinet, Parliament, federalism and intergovernmental relations, the judiciary and Charter of Rights and Freedoms, regulatory policy communities and interest groups. The central questions concern the structure and conduct of regulatory offices. How has the regulatory state in Canada changed over the last ten to twenty years, and what are the implications for regulatory accountability and democracy? How are regulation and the regulatory state viewed by leading ideologies? What is the effect of major political institutions on the regulatory process?

Regulatory Accountabilities and Democracy

In liberal-democratic states like Canada, the accountability and legitimacy of regulatory institutions and their activities are not simply the stuff of technique but vital ends in themselves. Regulatory reform, another phrase for choices and change in regulatory organizations, is about far more than 'getting government right.' It is about the full array of interactions and agencies in and around the state, not only government, and about choosing public purposes and seeking social acceptance and support, not only making the machinery of public administration function efficiently. Regulating is very much a normative exercise, involving a continual balancing act among values of executive control, political independence, policy expertise, stakeholder representativeness, public consultation, procedural justice, and timely regulation. Unlike the budgetary process, where contested values must eventually be converted into the common denominator of public money, regulatory measures, while they require public funding, are converted into the reality of governmental and non-governmental structures.

Accountability and democracy are both broad concepts of relationships and power involving politicians, public officials, and private actors and interests. In simple terms, accountability refers to the duty of an agency or official to answer for the exercise (use, abuse, non-use) of public responsibilities and resources given to them. In reality, the state in Canada is a complex system of institutions and agencies, making it difficult always to know with certainty who is accountable to whom, for what regulatory responsibilities and results, provided through what kinds and amount of information, and with what consequences.[2] In both the academic and governmental literature, the predominant meaning of the accountability of regulatory agencies is formal, ministerial control and responsibility to the legislature. However, as in other areas of government, there is not one accountability process, but numerous types and levels of regulatory accountabilities – societal, legislative, governmental, clientele, organizational, professional, managerial, financial, legal, and procedural. Even a common administrative culture between regulatory agency members and government officials has been cited as a potent element in the workings of accountability (Johnson 1991).

Regulators do more than simply make and enforce rules; they commonly carry out a number of administrative, judicial-like, policy analysis, and other functions. One step toward better understanding the nature of regulatory accountability is recognizing that three kinds of political power are generally in effect: the power to gain the initial adoption or enactment of a law, regulation, or guideline; the power to administer and implement that rule, that is, the capacity to produce desired patterns of behaviour over time; and the power to adjudicate and interpret regulatory decisions and disputes. When taking the pulse of power in a regulatory arena, one needs to touch on intragovernmental relations, such as between cabinet and a regulatory agency or between one regulating department and another, public sector–private sector relations, intergovernmental relations, and administrative-judicial relations.

Over the past twenty years, the accountability environments of regulatory institutions have become more complex and dynamic, with a large number of different factors at play, creating change and generating uncertainty for governments and policy communities. Likewise, in some important respects, Canada's regulatory system has become more democratically accountable in recent decades. Reform proposals and initiatives have been motivated, in large part, by a wish to place regulatory organizations and procedures under more regular control by political executives and more active and wider scrutiny by the courts, and to grant greater participation by other political interests, such as consumers, producers, and environmentalists. This democratization of the regulatory arm of the state is driven to a significant extent by the doctrines of the rule of law and natural justice. These constitutional and legal principles have been interpreted, tested, and elaborated in recent times through judicial review of administrative actions, legal aid programs, consultative mechanisms, plus the rulings of human rights tribunals and related public watchdog agencies. When the Charter of Rights and Freedoms was entrenched fifteen years ago, a new constitutional element was added to the Canadian political system, one further structuring public power as well strengthening and shaping the rights of individuals and various groups of citizens. The democratization of the regulatory state has also been prodded by the expectations and demands of social movements and interest groups for consultation or direct representation in regulatory structures and processes. Some notions of accountability, then, reflect existing authority relationships of hierarchical reporting upward to the ministry, while other views challenge and wish to alter conventional power arrangements.

The association between accountability and democracy may not always be complementary in government regulation. The connection may, in practice, contain contradictory elements. Whether, for example, the independent regulatory agency type is more accountable or democratically legitimate than regulatory departments depends at least in part on how one ranks the concept of ministerial responsibility of elected politicians as compared to forms of representation by collective boards or commissions appointed by elected politicians. If a set of regulatory powers is delegated to a single office holder, such as a superintendent of child welfare, accountability is in one sense clearer, but such concentrated power in an unelected official is also more likely to generate democratic concerns. Some regulatory agencies are increasingly relying on cost-recovery fees and user charges to finance their activities. On the one hand, this may enhance the regulator's responsiveness and accountability to its clients but, on the other, it could raise reasonable worries that a user-pay approach makes it harder for third parties to be involved in decisions or that the regulatory agency is losing sight of the greater public interest. Thus while regulatory accountability is taken to be a good thing for liberal democracy, there are many kinds of accountability, with potential for conflict between different interpretations and, furthermore, between one or another meaning of regulatory accountability and representative democracy. Both concepts today are politically constructed and contested.

Ideologies and Regulation

Ideologies and public values are an important component of the debate and policy thrust of regulatory decision making and reform. This section briefly examines some links between regulation and four ideologies in the current Canadian context: neo-conservatism, liberalism, social democracy, and feminism. Other ideologies in effect in Canadian politics, such as consumerism, environmentalism, and economic internationalism, are the subject of other chapters in this volume.

The four ideologies can be assessed in terms of their general depiction of the regulatory state and their preferences for regulating and deregulating various areas of community life through economic or civic regulation. Economic regulation is of two types, direct and social. Direct regulation seeks to influence price, market structures, and outputs of specific industries, while social regulation aims to influence the conditions, across many industries, under which goods and services are produced, advertised, and distributed. As Chapter 9 has shown, civic regulation is the other, usually forgotten half of the regulatory state, directed at citizens, clients, public service providers, families, and governments. There are four types of civic regulation, pertaining to citizenship and human rights; justice and public order; moral and sexual behaviour; welfare programs and the social union.

Neo-Conservatism

Right-wing views of recent years express the rhetoric of rolling back the state and reducing the burdens of 'red tape' on businesses and the economy. With an emphasis on private enterprise and liberty in the marketplace, neo-conservatism favours minimal direct regulation of economic actors and transactions and worries about existing and any new rules, be they direct or social regulations, adding costs to doing business and being competitive globally. In the area of human rights laws, conservatism supports most civil liberties and political rights, but believes there has been far too much talk by interest groups of social rights and entitlements and not enough about personal duties and responsibilities.

In the other areas of civic regulation, conservatives emphasize active rule making and enforcement by state agencies. On justice and law and order matters, they prefer stiffer sentencing of criminals, tighter parole policies, the criminalization of certain drugs, and the promotion of victims' rights. Conservatives are also not reluctant to regulate moral and sexual conduct to uphold community standards, protect children, or support the institution of the traditional family. The new right also wishes to regulate the welfare state, not simply reduce social expenditures. Except perhaps for medicare, few federal standards are seen as desirable in Canadian social policy. At provincial and local levels, there are calls for firm discipline in the school systems. And whether to uphold the work ethic, enforce parental duties to children, or break a 'culture of dependency,' neo-conservatives favour more directive and authoritarian social programs, such as in income assistance or child support, to enforce personal responsibility (Roche 1992).

Liberalism

Liberalism shares some of the basic beliefs of conservatism, like private property and a strong emphasis on individual liberty, and so is sympathetic to reducing or at least streamlining direct regulations on the private sector. Liberalism is generally supportive of social regulations for making the market a safer and fairer place for workers and customers, and of protecting the environment from adverse effects from industry. In this area, as in the areas of human rights, justice, and order, liberalism views regulation as contributing to the quality of life and opportunities of the population. The criminal justice system is recognized as central to providing a safe and secure society, but liberalism is concerned with balancing these concerns with individual liberty and freedom. Because of this commitment to personal liberty and privacy, liberalism is often ambivalent about moral and sexual regulation, regarding much of this area as personal and off-limits to the state while recognizing, at times, a need to protect vulnerable individuals and groups in society from harm.

With respect to the social union and welfare state, liberalism in Canada until recently accepted a role for federal standards in a number of social programs so that Ottawa could in effect police the provinces in their funding and delivery of welfare benefits and health and social services.[3] In many of these areas Ottawa is deregulating its role, while in other social programs, such as employment insurance, additional rules and duties have been imposed on clients. Pragmatism is sometimes used as another term for liberalism, suggesting that liberals are ready to try different approaches, be it regulation, deregulation, or re-regulation, to see if they satisfy some political or economic goal.

Socialism

Social democratic thought, the mild version of socialism today, supports an active legislative and regulatory role for the state in Canada. Economic rules of both the direct and social kind are regarded as essential for reducing inequalities in power, redistributing resources, and sharing information in the market. Social democrats favour improving and expanding the conditions of work subject to federal and provincial regulation. These areas include collective bargaining, minimum wages, employment standards, health and safety, pension standards, employment equity, obligations on employers to offer (re)training for all employees, rules to increase unionization, restrictions on the use of contract workers, and the participation of workers in the decision-making structures in industry (Moscovitch 1993, 4). Social democrats have long advocated an ever-growing range of positive rights of citizenship in the civil, political, and social spheres, for disadvantaged groups as well as individuals. Regulation is believed to enable or empower ordinary people to do things, as well as to place constraints on private sector activities.

Like some strands of conservatism, such as Red Toryism, social democratic thought has an organic rather than individualistic view of society and thus believes that the state has an important role in guiding community values and enacting moral standards (Manzer 1985). Social democrats differ strongly with the new right, however, on making social programs and services more restrictive and control-oriented. They reject workfare as a welfare and employment strategy (Shragge 1997). Social welfare programs are seen as creating rights, responsibilities, and commonalities in society. Social democrats call for a renewal of universality in a number of social program areas which, they contend, would reduce administrative controls and costs and eliminate the stigmatization and shaming of clients while promoting the preferred values of community and shared responsibility. They may accept selective, income-tested social assistance, but only as a genuine last resort within a full employment policy. On Canada's social union, social democrats tend to champion explicit federal standards and stable funding for public social services and child care (Moscovitch 1993).

234   Michael J. Prince

Feminism

Feminist thought recognizes that the law is critical to controlling the public and private worlds of women and has the potential, through removing disadvantages and creating rights, to enable women to gain fuller access to the public world of paid work and politics. Feminists of all kinds[4] view the Canadian state, including its regulatory activities, as gendered. Government rules and laws commonly and deliberately affect women differently than men, and often in adverse ways, by prescribing certain tasks and behaviours. Women are more frequently diagnosed with mental disorders and hospitalized in psychiatric institutions than men, for example (Ussher 1991). The regulatory state, like the welfare state, is laden with contradictions for women, serving as an arena for oppression and exclusion as well as for integration and equality (Pascall 1986). In relation to the labour market and economy, feminists see direct regulation and social regulation as absolutely essential for addressing issues of employment equity, harassment at work, maternity benefits, pay equity, workplace hazards, and other employment standards concerning, for instance, pensions, domestic workers, and part-time work.

In the realm of civic regulation, feminism gives strong emphasis to an expansive reach of human rights for eradicating women's subordination and promoting equality. The Canadian women's movement was very active in shaping key sections of the Charter of Rights in the early 1980s (Kome 1993). Ever since, feminist groups have been using the Charter, along with federal and provincial human rights laws, in litigation and complaints to further the equality rights claims of women, though with mixed results (Atcheson, Eberts, and Symes 1984; Brodsky and Day 1989; Mandel 1992). On matters of justice and public safety, feminists have transformed the previously private troubles of stalking, date rape, wife battering, and other forms of violence into public issues warranting legal action by state agencies. The feminist movement challenges governments to use their authority, coercively if necessary, on men who breach their moral and legal duties of civility not to violate and abuse others (Roche 1992, 51). With respect to the regulation of morals, the family, and sexuality, feminist organizations have advocated the decriminalization of abortion and prostitution and lobbied for tighter laws and regulations for child custody and support, reproductive and genetic technologies, and pornographic materials.[5]

None of these ideologies is an uncomplicated set of pro- or antiregulation beliefs. True, neo-conservatism tends to prefer less regulation rather than more, and social democratic thinking tends to favour more regulation, not dramatically less. Yet the key point is this: *these four ideologies and others cannot be easily placed along a single continuum running from minimal to maximum regulation.* Each ideology is a mixture of beliefs in and demands for strong intervention in certain activities and little or no regulatory intervention in other areas. This circumstance adds to the politics and complexity of policy communities and rule making by governments. It also points to the need to investigate the link between values and particular regulatory domains, like occupational safety, human rights, or workfare, in addition to the general ideologies.

Constitutional Dimensions of the Regulatory State

Five fundamental aspects of the Canadian constitution define and shape the regulatory state: the rule of law, the Charter of Rights and Freedoms, the distribution of powers between the federal and provincial orders of government, cabinet government, and the supremacy of Parliament. Each of these is a form of constitutional regulation. They embody laws (statutory and common law) and conventions (nonlegal customs and practices) that establish political and state institutions that regulate the exercise of public power by state agencies over individuals and groups in Canadian society.

Rule of Law

The doctrine of the rule of law has deep roots in political thought and Anglo-Saxon notions of administrative law and judicial review. It also reflects Canadian constitutional history and liberal conceptions of citizenship with an emphasis on peace, order, and good government and on individual autonomy. The preamble to the Charter of Rights and Freedoms states that 'Canada is founded upon principles that recognize the supremacy of God and the rule of law.' A relatively narrow definition describes the rule of law as '[t]he constitutional principle that citizens are governed by laws enacted by legislatures that they have elected, that public officials may do only what the law permits, and that the law must be applied equally to everyone unless the law itself permits unequal application' (Atkinson 1993, 375). Underpinning this definition are the ideas of political legitimacy from representative government; the principle of validity, that every official act must be justified by some legal authority; a commitment to the principle that no law may be applied retroactively; and the idea of equal treatment under the law, implying freedom from excessive and unfair state action. A wider understanding of the rule of law includes the following precepts:

- individuals are free in their relations with the state to do anything that is not unlawful, that is, not contrary to constitutional, statutory, or common laws;
- the burden lies on the state to establish a right, normally through specific powers from legislation to impede the liberties of individuals or groups;
- a separate and independent judiciary exists, from the government executive, to review the actions and inactions of public authorities;
- all agencies of the state are subject to and operate under the law in compliance with the procedural requirements of 'natural justice';[6]
- citizens have recourse to legal remedies through the courts and or tribunals for abuses and misuses of power by state authorities; and
- individuals have the equal right to protection under the law in their exercise of freedoms and civil liberties, such as freedom of speech or association, by the courts (Cranston 1985; Ogus 1994).

The rule of law, then, seeks to divide, constrain, and constitutionalize the exercise of public power and to give civil autonomy and legal protection to citizens against arbitrary uses of state authority. For regulatory institutions it means that their decision making must be grounded in a statutory foundation. In a sense, the rule of law is related to what is contemporarily referred to as empowerment, and traditionally called emancipation, of citizens.

Charter of Rights and Freedoms

The entrenchment of a Charter of Rights and Freedoms in 1982 was a transformational development in the Canadian state, what may properly be called a paradigm shift in our constitutional past and governmental system (Smiley 1986, 57). The Charter is now one of the overarching institutions of the political system and the regulatory state. Entrenched in the constitution, the Charter is part of the supreme law of the country and can only be changed by constitutional amendment. The basic purpose of the Charter is to authorize the courts to protect a set of fundamental civil liberties from the laws and actions of public sector agencies and officials by scrutinizing and limiting their actions. The courts are engaged in more rights-based and public policy–oriented judicial review of legislation and regulation by governments. The Charter applies to most public sector action – hospitals and universities are important exceptions – but not to private action. It regulates the actions of federal, territorial, and provincial levels of government, as well as community colleges, municipalities, school boards, police forces, childrens' aid societies, and administrative tribunals exercising statutory authority.[7]

The doctrine of parliamentary supremacy is not eliminated with the entrenchment of a Charter, but the principle is somewhat restricted. The federal Parliament or the legislature of a province or territory can override one or another of the rights or freedoms guaranteed in certain sections of the Charter, although not those in other sections, through explicit legislation that will have effect for a period of five years, at which time it will expire if not re-enacted by the legislative body.[8] The Charter also provides for the enforcement of rights and freedoms. Section 24 grants that anyone whose Charter rights have been infringed or denied may apply to court to obtain such remedy as the court considers appropriate and just in the circumstances. The range of remedies includes defensive remedies, 'where the court nullifies or stops some law or act, for example, by dismissing a charge, staying proceedings, quashing a conviction, enjoining an act, or declaring an apparently applicable law to be invalid' and affirmative remedies, 'where the court orders positive action to be taken by the defendant government or government official, for example, by awarding damages or a mandatory injunction' (Hogg 1985, 697).

The effects of the Charter on Canadian politics, governance, and regulation are intricate and multiple; some immediate impacts can be identified and its long-term effects have been the subject of considerable speculations by commentators. An overview of the influences of the Charter on several state institutions and processes is presented in Table 10.1. This political scan is drawn from the rich literature on the Charter (Cairns 1988, 1992; Cheffins and Johnson 1986; Greene 1993; Hogg 1996; Knopff and Morton 1992; Mandel 1992; Manfredi 1993; Russell 1994; Taylor 1992). From that literature it is not clear that the Charter is promoting a national style of regulation or law making in either procedural or substantive terms. The evidence suggests that Charter jurisprudence accepts both diversity and commonality in the formulation and administration of state laws and rules.

In the pre-Charter era, the courts were already influential in regulatory matters, such as deciding on whether specific laws were within the jurisdiction of one or other level of government, but the Charter has added a significant range of opportunities to pursue litigation and judicially review state actions. The success rate, however, of Charter challenges to federal and provincial laws is fairly low, about 15 per cent (Whittington and Van Loon 1996, 186). Laws dealing with moral and sexual regulation – hate literature, prostitution, pornography, and publication bans in sexual assault cases – have been upheld as reasonable limits on freedom of expression. Even when the courts interpret the Charter cautiously or narrowly, there can still be real regulatory and policy effects, in that governments may think twice about some measures out of

TABLE 10.1
Possible Effects of the Canadian Charter on Political Institutions and Policy Processes

Institution/Process	Effects of the Charter
Cabinet government	Marginal impact on executive and ministerial action.
Citizenship	Encourages a sense of citizenship. Constitutionalizes many rights and freedoms and increases opportunities for individuals and groups to pursue litigation and seek redress. Rights are limited and in a pecking order, with few justiciable social rights. Charter applies not only to Canadian citizens but to landed immigrants, visitors, and refugee claimants.
Constitutional and political culture	Directly links the citizenry to the constitutional order, making executive federalism reform processes less legitimate. Popular discourse includes more rights talk or 'Charter chatter,' a legalization and Americanization of politics.
Courts	Expanded workload and influence in policy review and modification, a politicization of the judiciary. Decisions have generally been moderate in giving meaning and application to the Charter.
Criminal justice system	Most Charter litigation is about the administration of criminal justice by police forces, Crown prosecutors, and courts, resulting in 'a low profile reform of the criminal justice system' (Russell 1994, 348).
Federalism	Promotes a pan-Canadian character by establishing rights that transcend territorial identities and apply to both orders of government. Yet the Charter can be divisive in national politics, and Supreme Court decisions have had both provincializing and nationalizing effects on policy and regulation.
Interests and interest groups	Increased access points to the political system. Considerable activity by groups using the Charter and rights talk to advance their claims and achieve policy goals. A judicialization of politics that produces winners and losers.
Policy formation	Enhanced role of lawyers in preparing and reviewing policy.

concern that they may run afoul of the Charter. Administrative law continues to be central to advancing procedural and substantive aspects of natural justice in administrative actions by the state.

Distribution of Powers: Regulatory Federalism and the Legal Union

In Canada's federal system, legislative powers are constitutionally divided between the federal and provincial governments. Each level has a series of responsibilities enumerated in the constitution, under which governments directly regulate the activities of citizens and organizations. The eleven regulatory states under Canadian federalism function with a mixture of separate and shared authority. The federal government has exclusive legislative powers to make laws in relation to such matters as the peace, order, and good government of Canada; the regulation of trade and commerce; navigation and shipping; sea coast and inland fisheries; banking, interest, and currency; weights and measures; bankruptcy; patents and copyrights; Indians and lands reserved for Indians; marriage and divorce; penitentiaries; the criminal law; and establishing courts for the administration of the laws of Canada. The federal government may also raise moneys by any mode or system of taxation. The provinces derive their authority to legislate and regulate from exclusive powers in relation to public and reformatory prisons; asylums; municipal institutions; 'shop, saloon, tavern, auctioneer, and other licences'; local works and undertakings; the incorporation of companies with provincial objects; the solemnization of marriage; property and civil rights; administration of justice in the province, including provincial courts of both civil and criminal jurisdiction; education; nonrenewable natural resources; forestry resources; electrical energy; and, generally, all matters of a merely local or private nature in the province. The constitution also grants to provincial legislatures powers of taxation and for the imposition of punishment by fine, penalty, or imprisonment for enforcing laws of the province.

The provinces and the federal Parliament have concurrent powers to make laws in relation to agriculture, immigration, and interprovincial trade in nonrenewable resources, with federal paramountcy, which means that where a federal law and provincial law coexist in these policy fields and are inconsistent, the federal law prevails. Concurrent jurisdiction is also found in relation to old age pensions and supplementary benefits, but with provincial paramountcy in this field.

In addition to this constitutional federalism, the judiciary has played a critical role throughout Canada's history, acting as the umpire of the rules of federalism, in determining the legitimacy of regulatory powers for both levels of government. In judicial federalism, the courts have rendered decisions with profound consequences for the scope and nature of regulatory jurisdiction for the federal Parliament and provincial legislature. Most of the leading decisions on federalism were made long ago by the Judicial Committee of the Privy Council, largely members of the British House of Lords (Russell, Knopff, and Morton 1989). Judicial interpretations, for example, narrowed the extent of the federal power to legislate for the 'peace, order and good government of Canada,' and the federal power to regulate trade and commerce to interprovincial and international business, giving the provinces control over intraprovincial trade and commerce. With some key exceptions, like banking, the regulation of business, industries, professions, and trades has generally been regarded by the courts as provincial jurisdiction under the property and civil rights power of the constitution.

Inevitably, when determining if a law is within the constitutional domain of a government, the courts are making discretionary judgments and political choices on questions of immense public policy importance. Policy making through judicial review raises concerns about the accountability by judges, within parliamentary democracy, for their decisions.[9] On this issue, Hogg (1985, 99) concludes 'that the lack of democratic accountability, coupled with the limitations inherent in the adversarial judicial process, dictates that the appropriate posture for the courts in constitutional cases is one of restraint: the legislative decision should always receive the benefit of a reasonable doubt, and should be overridden only where its invalidity is clear.' Fifteen years after the enactment of the constitutional Charter of Rights and Freedoms, the record of the Supreme Court of Canada appears overall to be one of judicial caution and moderation (Beatty 1997; Makin 1997; Whittington and Van Loon 1996).

Rather than the courts, the main shapers of the Canadian federal system today are intergovernmental fiscal relations and administrative federalism, that is, functional collaboration and delegation between Ottawa and the provinces/ territories. Administrative federalism marks a change in emphasis from the constitutional federalism of the 1980s and early 1990s, although it continues the elite-dominated nature of executive federalism.

Canada's system of modern federalism is usually described as highly decentralized and provincialized in relation to other federal states around the world. In particular, the Canadian welfare state reflects this pattern of decentralization, with the provinces being the primary level of government – constitutionally, legislatively, and financially – responsible for developing and implementing social policies (Prince 1996). The decentralized nature of the welfare state was further exemplified with the introduction in 1995–6 of the Canada Health and Social Transfer (CHST). Under the CHST, Ottawa substantially reduces cash transfers to the provinces and territories while seeking to maintain the five principles of medicare yet dropping the enforcement of all but one of the principles regarding social services and income assistance from the Canada Assistance Plan.

By contrast, the regulatory state in Canada has significant national features. Among these are the following:

1 *A basically unified judicial system.* The federal government appoints and provides the salaries of the judges of the superior, district and county courts

of each province. Provincial courts have 'jurisdiction over the full range of cases, whether the applicable law is federal or provincial or constitutional,' or private (Hogg 1985, 134). The Supreme Court of Canada is a general court of appeal for all kinds of cases from provincial and federal courts.

2   *Convergence in common law.* Because of the unified judicial system and the Supreme Court's preference for and promotion of consistency in the interpretation of similar statutes from province to province, the common law is fairly uniform across Canada (Hogg 1985, 173). Quebec's civil code law is, of course, an important exception.

3   *A national body of criminal law.* Unlike federal states like Australia and the United States, criminal law in Canada is the responsibility of the national government. Though the criminal law is enforced by both levels of government, embodied in the Criminal Code 'are some of the most important mutual claims of citizens and the Canadian community' (Smiley 1976, 218).

4   *National law enforcement institutions.* The Royal Canadian Mounted Police (RCMP) enforce the Criminal Code and other federal statutes. The RCMP provides policing services in the eight provinces without provincial police forces, all but Ontario and Quebec, as well as to the Yukon and Northwest Territories, and about two hundred municipalities over the country. In these jurisdictions, the RCMP is enforcing federal laws, provincial/territorial laws, and municipal by-laws. The Canadian Security Intelligence Services (CSIS), established in 1984 as an offshoot of the RCMP, investigates subversive activities and other threats to national security within and without Canada.

5   *National correctional and parole institutions.* The Correctional Service of Canada (CSC) operates a Canadawide system of penitentiaries for the imprisonment of persons sentenced for two years or more. The National Parole Board, another federal government agency, is responsible for making decisions on the release of prisoners sentenced for offences under the Criminal Code and other federal laws.

6   *National test case programs.* The federal government offers two test case programs that support nation building. 'One is the Court Challenges Program, whose purpose is to subsidize individuals and non-profit groups for test cases of national significance, mainly involving the Charter of Rights and Freedoms. This program was abolished in 1992 but has now been reactivated. The federal government also operates the Indian Test Case Funding Program, whose goal is to fund appeals of cases relating to important, unresolved legal questions relating to aboriginal peoples, such as interpretations of the Indian Act and Indian treaties' (National Council of Welfare 1995, 18).

7 *Human rights laws.* The territories, every province, and the federal government have human rights legislation and commissions for protecting and promoting equal rights. These commissions operate within a common legal environment of natural justice, judicial review, and the Charter of Rights and Freedoms.

As Canadian regulatory federalism has evolved, a number of arrangements between the federal government and other governments have been put in place. Some examples in the field of justice and legal affairs are: the twenty-year police service agreements for RCMP services under contract to eight provinces, fifty-two First Nations communities, and two hundred municipalities; the exchange of service agreements between CSC and most provinces and the territories regarding parole and corrections; a firearms control program; and federal-provincial/territorial agreements on cost sharing criminal legal aid services. Along with conflict, a good deal of regulatory cooperation exists between governments (Treasury Board of Canada 1994), as does the diffusion of regulatory reforms across jurisdictions, such as consumer protection laws or human rights commissions. The character of regulatory federalism also varies bilaterally and multilaterally, reflecting differences in regional cultures and economies, geography and resource endowments, social conditions, and political factors.

These national features of the regulatory state are essential elements of what may be called the Canadian legal union. They are claims, expectations, rights, and obligations Canadians share under the legal and justice system and in relation to the state. Regulatory regimes and institutions give meaning to common legal citizenship and to peace, order, and good government. Like the social union of welfare state programs, the legal union is pivotal to peoples' feeling of identity and security (Biggs 1996).

Cabinet-Parliamentary Government

The conventions and realities of cabinet parliamentary government at both levels of government confer most of the power to initiate laws and regulations on the executive – the prime minister or premier and their cabinets, with the senior bureaucracy as influential adviser. Of key importance in regulatory matters is the fact that while in theory bills, other than money bills, 'can be introduced in either House and by any member of parliament, ... the cabinet uses its majority in the House of Commons to ensure that the bulk of Parliament's time is devoted to consideration of the government's own legislative programme, and, ... it is only the measures which have been approved by the cabinet and introduced by a minister ("government bills") which stand any real chance of passage' (Hogg 1985, 203–4). The opposition parties and individual members of Parliament have the right to oppose, criticize, scrutinize and, in a general sense, prevent clandestine governing. In principle ministers are individually and collectively responsible to Parliament for their portfolios of laws, programs services, and decisions. Accountability in a legal and regulatory sense is aided by such requirements as the need to base all official acts on some legal authority.

The system of responsible government bestows a high degree of executive authority over policy making, budgeting, and intergovernmental relations. Cabinets largely determine a government's agenda and the legislature's timetable as the originator of new legislation and revised statutes. Cabinets are a major source of regulations, passing ministerial directives and orders-in-council. At the federal level, regulatory processes have been channelled through a central agency and to cabinet since the mid-1980s, a departure from previous practice. The political management role of cabinets in the regulatory state includes resolving disputes between, say, a regulatory department and regulatory agency, or a regulatory agency and Crown corporation, or a government agency and a clientele group. Thomas and Zajccw (1993, 144) cite the instance of 'when the CRTC ordered the CBC to drop commercials from all children's programming and the corporation complained to cabinet that it could not comply unless it was given a larger grant to make up for the revenue shortfall.' The decisions of some tribunals in Canada require the approval of cabinet or of the responsible minister in order to become effective. Though not a common occurrence, in some cases a cabinet has the power to hear appeals and vary or even override the policy decisions of a regulatory agency or administrative tribunal and issue a binding cabinet directive. More generally, cabinets and individual ministers give direction to regulatory agencies through policy statements and administrative orders, the appointing of individuals to agencies and tribunals, and determining funding levels and budgetary controls. Cabinets may also put reference questions to the judiciary, the Supreme Court of Canada by the federal cabinet and a province's court of appeal by the provincial cabinet, to obtain an advisory opinion on an important issue or piece of legislation, usually with constitutional implications.[10]

In understanding the regulatory decisions and behaviour of a cabinet, it is essential to remember that Canadian cabinets are quasi-representative structures. They are chosen with great sensitivity to regional considerations along with other criteria of representation. Ministers use their regional electoral base to influence regulatory decisions along with other types of decisions on programs or services. Bakvis and MacDonald (1993, 65–6) have written of the regional dimension of cabinet decisions involving regulations: 'When policies of a regulatory nature arise that bear on the interests of a province represented by a minister, that minister can expect to have, if not an actual veto, at least a special claim to being heard on the issue. Examples of such policies include fishery licence regulations on the east coast, the environmental review of a dam in Saskatchewan, and the proposed banning of cigarette smoking on international flights (which stood to affect in particular the economic welfare of Canadian Airlines International based in Calgary, Alberta).' Local and regional interests are highly relevant concerns to the making of regulatory decisions within a cabinet or cabinet committee. As with federal spending and taxation decisions, there is continuous pressure for regulatory policies to be, and to be seen to be, as regionally fair in some political sense.

Supremacy of Parliaments

The main functions of the federal Parliament and provincial legislatures in the regulatory process are debating, perhaps amending and delaying, usually ratifying, and ultimately passing laws, many of which delegate regulatory powers to other agencies of the state. Parliamentary government operates, of course, through the vehicle of political parties and intense partisan competition. Political parties represent important ideological clusters of opinion and belief about the role of government itself and the preferred legislative and regulatory measures, producing conflicting views of the 'public interest' in regulating. Legislatures also serve a surveillance role. Both federal and provincial legislative bodies have standing committees to review and debate government bills, and many provinces use the committee of the whole to debate bills and laws. Some provinces also have legislative committees to scrutinize all regulations proclaimed by the government. At the federal Parliament, a standing joint committee of the House of Commons and Senate for the scrutiny of regulations reviews all federal regulations. This committee 'can recommend changes to the government, report to Parliament on problems with regulations that members of the Committee have discovered, or propose to Parliament that a regulation be overturned' (Treasury Board 1992, 4).

Parliamentary watchdogs include auditors, human rights commissioners, privacy and information commissioners, and ombudpersons. These agencies are meaningful in focusing political and media attention on specific regulatory decisions by government departments or the effects of general regulatory processes on citizens, communities, or public and private budgets. More than that, these bodies are important avenues for receiving and investigating citizen complaints, conducting studies of the bureaucracy, auditing government organizations and, in some jurisdictions, issuing orders. Different watchdogs address different kinds of accountability; legislative auditors concentrate on financial accountability, human rights commissioners on substantive accountability, and ombudspersons on procedural accountability. These agencies are typically attached and accountable to the legislature, perhaps reflecting a mistrust of the mainstream executive-dominated accountability systems in Canada.

Using legislatures to hold regulators accountable has both benefits and limitations. The benefits of parliamentary accountability are that additional information on regulatory activities may be disclosed, public debate of regulatory agencies and their policies occurs, and a general overview of procedures and their fairness can take place. Limitations of parliamentary accountability are that legislators lack the time and expertise to digest the information on regulating (Ogus 1994, 113). There is often limited examination of regulatory agencies because of the independence they have been given and, in some cases, because of the quasi-judicial functions they serve.

Organizational Forms of Regulating

To regulate is to choose not only one instrument of governing over others, but also to choose among several possible structural arrangements. In some cases, groups are accorded virtually self-regulatory status, while other sectors are regulated by multimembered commissions, and still others by regular departments headed by cabinet ministers. These are not simply abstract organizational choices. 'Rather, they go to the root of *positional* policy in that they address those who will control the positions of authority in defined sectors of day-to-day decision-making' (Doern 1979, 161).

Along with program expenditure and any responsibilities for policy coordination, regulatory powers constitute a source of authority and influence for cabinet ministers and departmental officials. Some departments are therefore more regulatory than others. Rule making and enforcement are obviously primary characteristics of the Solicitor General and Justice departments, but also of the Agriculture and Agri-Food, Environment, Fisheries and Ocean, and Health departments. Most departmental regulations are governor-in-council (GIC) regulations, where the cabinet is named as the responsible authority, and these must be approved by the Special Committee of Council, a cabinet committee. Under some pieces of legislation an individual minister is authorized to make regulations, which are reviewed but need not be approved by the Special Committee of Council. For both types of regulation, departments are required to draft a Regulatory Impact Analysis Statement, which examines the objectives of a proposed regulation, any alternatives considered, the extent and outcome of consultation, likely social and economic effects, and enforcement mechanisms. In addition to GIC regulations and ministerial regulations, there are countless departmental directives and guidelines that can have the same effect as regulations.

Traditionally, government departments operated with few formal channels of notification and consultation with the public in the making of regulations. Over the past decade or so, the federal government and some provincial governments have reformed their regulatory processes and instituted requirements on departments to both notify the public about forthcoming regulations and to consult with client groups and other interested parties. The extent and nature of these consultations are normally at the discretion of each department (Treasury Board 1992).

Considerable regulation-making authority within the Canadian state is vested in independent agencies, boards, and commissions. A recent estimate is that there are approximately 1,500 of these agencies across the country (MacDonald 1993). At the federal level, they include the National Energy Board, the National Transportation Agency, and the Canadian Radio-television and Telecommunications Commission, among others. Typically, such agencies have multimembered boards to create an executive of its own at arm's length from the executive, perhaps to promote a more collegial and businesslike corporate culture, and to incorporate key outside interests and expert knowledge within the agency. While they are called regulatory agencies, these bodies usually have multifunctional mandates with a blend of administrative, advisory, legislative, and quasi-judicial powers. In order to be impartial in performing judicial functions such as adjudicating claims, and for other reasons, regulatory agencies are intended to be somewhat autonomous from the direct influence of politicians, in particular, a minister and cabinet.

The fact that regulatory agencies lie outside the conventional departmental system for Canadian public administration led Hodgetts (1973) to call them organizational nonconformists and 'structural heretics' deviating from the normal constitutional chain of command of reporting to a deputy minister and cabinet minister. In a major study on regulation, the former Economic Council of Canada (1979) also saw regulatory agencies as being unorthodox: 'Constitutionally, statutory regulatory agencies have been "structural heretics" for well over a century in that they are not politically accountable for their actions to a minister in the same way as is an executive department.'

The assumption that regulatory agencies are inherently less accountable than regular departments by virtue of their organizational form has been challenged in recent years. Schultz (1982, 104) has argued that regulatory agencies in the Canadian public sector are more responsive to a wider cross-section of affected interests than traditional departments. The publicness of regulatory agencies is due to statutory and judicially enforced reasons, Schultz suggests, in distinction to the bureaucratic norms of clientelism by departments. Likewise, Thomas and Zajcew (1993, 146) point out that 'the high visibility, openness, and public participation involved with most regulatory hearings stands in sharp contrast with the more closed and secretive deliberations of cabinet, central agencies, and line departments.' Furthermore, regulatory agencies are not contrary to our constitutional framework. At the end of the twentieth century, regulatory agencies are part of what is authoritatively approved and established in cabinet parliamentary government.[11] The extensive practice of creating, reorganizing, and continuing to rely on regulatory agencies has been followed for such a lengthy period in federal and provincial public sectors that they have acquired constitutional legitimacy as a customary way of exercising legal powers and are in harmony with contemporary ideas of alternative service delivery (Ford and Zussman, 1997).

Another series of organizational arrangements for regulating is the self-governance model for certain professions, producer groups, and occupations. As noted earlier, the regulation and licensing of companies, occupations, agricultural producer groups, and professions fall primarily within provincial jurisdiction. For self-regulating professions, such as nursing or architects, provincial laws recognize and empower an organization, comprised of members of the group, to establish a register of practitioners and create standards for practice. Professional regulatory organizations focus on ensuring some level of competence on the part of practitioners by setting entry standards, a code of ethics, peer review, and discipline. In varying degrees, professional regulatory organizations are political agencies, advising government officials, advocating for or against policies that affect them, and operating under delegated public authority.

Self-regulation by professional occupations is viewed critically by various disciplines. Administrative law has seen professional self-governance 'as an example of modern "corporatism," the acquisition of power by groups which are not accountable to the body politic through the conventional constitutional channels,' and economics stresses the potential of self-regulating professions 'to exploit their regulatory powers to establish anti-competitive conditions and thus generate rents (exorbitant profits) for existing practitioners' (Ogus 1994, 108). Feminism points out the gender division of professions and the hierarchical positioning of traditionally male-dominated professions, such as medicine, law, and engineering, over the traditionally female-dominated professions of nursing, teaching, and social work. Professions have been criticized for gender discrimination in their recruitment practices and in their treatment of women as clients. The field of public policy law, according to Ogus (1994, 108), is less critical of self-regulating regimes in principle. It acknowledges the validity of the above criticisms, but believes institutional reforms can meet these concerns while maintaining the benefits claimed for this organizational form of regulating.

Existing theories have problems explaining why some groups are allowed regulatory self-governance while others are not. Trebilcock (1989) suggests that self-governance is appropriate where there are highly developed training, service, and ethical norms within the occupation, such as engineering, law, and medicine. On the other hand, for industries, trades, or occupations lacking an established consensus on relevant training, quality service, and ethical standards direct regulation by government is preferred. The same applies, Trebilcock suggests, where the sector in question has a small number of players, like banking or insurance institutions, and self-governance could mean major risks of collusion or monopolistic behaviour. However, as Doern (1979, 175) has noted, 'these speculations break down when other group (professions and producers) are examined who have perhaps similar characteristics but have not succeeded in reaching the self-regulatory millennium.' To more fully understand whether or not self-regulation is appropriate and why a group obtains self-governance, the field needs to look beyond the internal attributes of an occupation and the interactions within a sector. Professional self-regulation and marketing boards are prized and contested resources. We need to look at interactions of a sector with other sectors aspiring for self-control, existing self-regulating groups, government organizations, the state of the economy, and societywide beliefs and myths. We should always recognize that calls for self-regulation can be challenges to the territory and status of existing professional organizations and their ways of doing things. By examining the interorganizational context in which professions and other occupations function, including cultural and political dimensions, we may find explanations for when and how this organizational form of regulating is chosen.

Regulatory Policy Communities

Whatever the type of state organizational form, each discrete regulatory arena creates categories of interest and relationships of power, in short, a policy community. Regulatory policy communities consist of clientele, interest groups, interests, mass media, and international institutions engaged in the exchange of ideas, claims, and positions. Interest groups abound, from producer to consumer public interest groups and from national umbrella bodies to local lobbies. Many are aligned with and keep a watchful eye on the central agencies, ministers and their departments, regulatory agencies, or self-governing occupations closest to their concerns. All want to be consulted in the regulatory process. Recent federal legislation on firearm registration and licensing – gun control – involved participation by the national Firearms Association, the Canadian Police Association, and the Canadian Association of Chiefs of Police, among many others.

Along with interest groups are interests. These are single entities, such as large corporations or other governments, which have the capacity to act by themselves rather than merely seek to influence others. Their own resources may dwarf those of the regulating authorities. Many larger companies have regulatory affairs units, which are responsible for designing regulatory policies for the company; liaising with federal and provincial regulators; managing the company's registration of products and applications for rates or tolls; possibly testifying at public hearings; and monitoring the relevant regulatory environment. Business interests tend to advocate less government regulating (and spending and taxing) in general, but often exert pressure for state action in particular situations. Throughout Canadian history, despite the anti-government rhetoric of individualism, businesses have sought and supported state regulation to minimize competition, stabilize infrastructure costs, and safeguard private investments (Bliss 1974; Finkel 1979; Economic Council of Canada 1979).

A free and vigilant press is a vital part of accountable government; thus, the media are a part of the regulatory process. News coverage of regulatory politics takes place within a context of legal rights and restraints for the media such as the revealing of sources, the right to a fair trial, and the Official Secrets Act (Siegel 1983). The news media perform political functions in terms of providing information to the public and raising issues and controversies that may, in turn, stimulate demands by groups within a policy community and affect what regulators do. Journalists have important though often unintentional impacts on the regulatory state and community. As Black (1982, 247–8) has observed: 'Few newsmen relish the idea of helping to enforce government rules and regulations. That is what they are doing, though, whenever they publicise new programs or policies, whether they deal with traffic fines, social welfare eligibility, water use restriction, or marijuana and narcotic control. News reports about the routine effects of existing programs – police checks, income tax refunds, convictions and sentences – all help to make known the official rewards and punishments. In the process, these reports are making substantial contributions to what have been called the rule enforcement and rule adjudication functions.' The degree and nature of media coverage can be an important influence on regulating in general and with respect to particular agencies. Human tragedy stories reported by the media of major accidents, industrial hazards, or crimes such as 'home invasions' can raise public anxieties, especially if there is no context given of the probability of risks and the costs of risk management. Such stories and the resulting public concern may encourage political leaders to make promises of further regulatory action on safety and security. Certain regulatory agencies, like the CRTC or Canadian Wheat Board, and certain regulatory policies, like provisions under the Criminal Code, are a regular source of political news. Other agencies and rules receive little regular media attention and thus less public exposure and political interest.

There is also an array of foreign and international institutions that influence domestic regulatory processes and decisions. These involve international agreements and bodies such as the General Agreement on Tariffs and Trade, the International Labour Organization, the World Trade Organization, and the North American Free Trade Agreement. Their influence can be direct and quasi-regulatory in some instances or they can be a more subtle source of pressure through the professional networks they foster. Foreign-state institutions can also exercise a direct influence over Canadian regulatory affairs. These include, for example in the United States, the Food and Drug Administration, the Federal Energy Regulatory Commission, and the Senate.

Conclusion

The regulatory state in Canada is not some unified Leviathan or omnipotent Big Brother, but an extremely diverse network of values, processes, and accountabilities. It is constitutionally based and organizationally complex. It is also a perpetually contested terrain within contemporary politics. Some notions of accountability reflect existing authority relationships of hierarchical reporting upward to the ministry, while other views seek to alter conventional power arrangements. Regulatory activities of the state are thoroughly embedded in the personal lives of Canadians and the larger social and economic structures. Regulation bureaucratizes but also politicizes us; excludes, but can also include; constrains activities, but can also create opportunities. Regulatory implementation involves public behaviour of government agencies and officials as well as considerable private behaviour, countless private actors and organizations calling for, responding to, and partly opposing the rules of the modern state. The regulatory state is always heading off in more than one direction.

Certain institutional elements of the regulatory state are relative constants, such as the constitutional division of legislative powers and the widespread application of nondepartmental forms for regulating. Given the long-standing use of regulatory boards and commissions, these kinds of administrative entities should no longer be viewed as structural heretics but rather be recognized as part of the organizational tradition in federal and provincial governments.

From a political-institutional perspective, the regulatory state has not been static. The most significant development, of course, has been the entrenchment of the Charter of Rights and Freedoms in the Canadian constitution. This has numerous consequences for the state and society, with notable effects for the role of the courts, the reform of the criminal justice system, and tactics of social movements and interests. In organizational terms, regulatory reform has meant the establishment of central agency functions and ministerial positions assigned responsibilities for managing regulatory processes. This has resulted in some reduction of regulations, but also in a formalization of consultation and impact analysis practices in government. The ability of legislatures to exact some accountability for regulatory activities has likely improved through the efforts and expanded mandates of the offices of auditors general and ombudspersons, and the more recent establishment of privacy and information commissions.

What of Aristotle's benchmarks? Do Canadian regulatory institutions constitute a well-organized state concerned with good order and conduct? Human history and political philosophy tell us there is no conclusive or single answer to this question. The accountability environments or regulatory institutions have become more complex and dynamic. Reform initiatives have been motivated, in large part, by a wish to place regulatory organizations and procedures under more regular control by political executives and more active and wider scrutiny by the courts and to allow greater participation by other political interests such as consumers, producers, and environmentalists. This democratization of the regulatory arm of the state is driven to a significant extent by the doctrines of the rule of law and natural justice. The democratization of the regulatory state has also been stimulated by Charter politics and the demands of social movements and interest groups for consultation or direct representation in regulatory structures and processes. Whatever attention is paid to efficiency and policy outcomes, regulating is about democratic process and social values.

NOTES

Special thanks are owed to several persons for comments on an earlier draft of this chapter: Ronald Cheffins, Robert Howse, Hudson Janisch, John McBride, Fazil Mihlar, and Richard Schultz.

1 In a speech, the president of the Treasury Board and Minister Responsible for Regulatory Affairs, Marcel Massé (1996, 1), spoke about federal regulatory reform in these terms, placing the reform process within the context of 'getting government right.' He said: ' "Getting government right" essentially means restoring the government's fiscal responsibility. For this to take place, the machinery of government must function as efficiently as possible and must concentrate on what it does best.' He added that, 'reforming our regulatory systems, together with reducing the deficit, are key to creating jobs.'

2 Perhaps exceptions to this general pattern of accountability ambiguity are the parliamentary 'watchdog' agencies, such as auditor generals, privacy and information commissioners, and ombudspersons. Various laws set out that these agencies are appointed by and directly accountable to federal and provincial legislatures.

3 The abolition of the Canada Assistance Plan and the introduction of the Canada Health and Social Transfer in 1996, along with the devolution of social housing and labour market policy to the provinces by the federal government, all suggest a significant shift in this aspect of liberalism as represented by the Liberal Party of Canada.

4 Like other belief systems, feminism has several branches, such as anti-racist, liberal, radical, and socialist perspectives. Each takes a particular approach to law and women's experiences of the law. The discussion here is of what may be called a mainstream approach, which other branches share to some extent (Sheehy and Boyd 1989).

5 Differences exist within feminism on whether and how these issues should be controlled through state regulation. For an excellent review of the contending positions in Canada, feminist and other, on pornography and obscenity, see Gottell (1996).

6 Peter Hogg (1985, 747)) points out that the reference to fundamental justice in the Canadian Charter really means natural justice, as the concept of due process is not included in the Charter. Natural justice is interpreted to include a set of procedural rules: that there be a public hearing for affected parties to be heard, that there be notice of such hearings, that the rules of procedure be published and known, that reasons be given for decisions, and that persons have the opportunity to appeal decisions to an independent and impartial body for adjudication. In a similar vein, Charles Taylor (1992) argues that the Charter promotes a procedural view of justice emphasizing individual rights over a communitarian view emphasizing substantive goals such as cultural diversity.

7 From a survey of Charter jurisprudence, Howse (1995, 148) concludes that 'where non-governmental actors exercise the coercive powers of the state, the Charter is likely to apply, at the very least to actions that involve the exercise of the coercive powers themselves.'

8 The override of certain rights is provided for in section 33 of the Charter, also called the notwithstanding section. Parliament or a legislature may expressly

declare in legislation that an Act or a part of it shall operate notwithstanding a right or freedom included in section 2 (the fundamental freedoms of association and peaceful assembly, conscience and religion, expression and the press) or sections 7 to 15 (the legal rights and equality rights) in the Charter. Other rights, on democratic rights, mobility, minority language, and sexual equality rights thus 'trump' parliamentary supremacy.

9 It can be suggested that judges are accountable to the doctrine of precedent or *stare decisis*, the procedures of the litigation process, and professional associations of federally and provincially appointed judges. Moreover, there exist federal, provincial, and territorial judicial councils concerned with the selection, education, and discipline of judges. In a major study on the Canadian judiciary, Russell (1987, 185) says, 'the establishment of judicial councils in Canada has probably succeeded in establishing a better reconciliation of security of tenure and accountability. One must say "probably" because the performance of these councils has not been systematically studied.' Russell adds: 'If the Canadian judiciary is to continue to exercise great power over Canadians and yet enjoy the security of tenure which is so vital to its independence, it must be accountable to Canadians for the way it governs itself.'

10 In 1996, after the dramatically close referendum result in Quebec the previous year, the federal government submitted three reference questions to the Supreme Court of Canada on the issue of Quebec's possible secession from the rest of the country. Essentially they ask: Can Quebec unilaterally secede under the Canadian constitution? Can Quebec unilaterally separate under international law? If there is a conflict between the constitution and international law, which takes precedence? A provincial cabinet may put federal laws for a reference to the province's court, and the federal government may do the same with provincial laws to the Supreme Court of Canada (Strayer 1983).

11 A recent example is the creation of the Canadian Food Inspection Agency in 1997 by the federal government. The agency consolidates all federally mandated inspection and quarantine services related to food safety, economic fraud, and animal and plant health programs formerly provided by four departments. The agency is responsible for about fifteen acts and forty regulations and orders, has 4,500 employees in over 200 offices across the country, and reports to Parliament through the minister of agriculture and agri-food Canada.

REFERENCES

Atcheson, M. Elizabeth, Mary Eberts, and Beth Symes. 1984. *Women and Legal Action: Precedents, Resources and Strategies for the Future.* Ottawa: Canadian Advisory Council on the Status of Women.
Atkinson, Michael M., ed. 1993. *Governing Canada: Institutions and Public Policy.* Toronto: Harcourt Brace Jovanovich.

Bakvis, Herman, and David MacDonald. 1993. The Canadian Cabinet: Organization, Decision-Rules, and Policy Impact. In M.M. Atkinson, ed., *Governing Canada: Institutions and Public Policy*, 47–80. Toronto: Harcourt Brace Jovanovich.

Beatty, David. 1997. Lament for a Charter. *Globe and Mail*, 15 April.

Biggs, Margaret. 1996. *Building Blocks for Canada's New Social Union*. Canadian Policy Research Networks, Working Paper No. F/02. Ottawa: Renouf.

Black, Edwin R. 1982. *Politics and the News: The Political Functions of the Mass Media*. Toronto: Butterworths.

Bliss, Michael. 1974. *A Living Profit: Studies in the Social History of Canadian Business, 1883–1911*. Toronto: McClelland and Stewart.

Brodsky, Gwen, and Shelagh Day. 1989. *Canadian Charter Equality Rights for Women: One Step Forward or Two Steps Back?* Ottawa: Canadian Advisory Council on the Status of Women.

Cairns, Alan. 1988. Citizens (Outsiders) and Government (Insiders) in Constitution-Making: The Case of Meech Lake. *Canadian Public Policy* 14, no. 5: 121–45.

– 1992. *The Charter versus Federalism: The Dilemmas of Constitutional Reform*. Montreal and Kingston: McGill-Queen's University Press.

Cameron, B. Jamie, ed. 1996. *Charter's Impact on the Criminal Justice System*. Toronto: Carswell.

Cheffins, R.I., and P.A. Johnson. 1986. *The Revised Canadian Constitution: Politics as Law*. Toronto: McGraw-Hill Ryerson.

Cranston, Ross. 1985. *Legal Foundations of the Welfare State*. London: Weidenfield and Nicolson.

Doern, G. Bruce. 1979. Regulatory Processes and Regulatory Agencies. In G. Bruce Doern and P. Aucoin, eds. *Public Policy in Canada*, 158–89. Toronto: Macmillan of Canada.

Economic Council of Canada. 1979. *Responsible Regulation: An Interim Report*. Ottawa: Minister of Supply and Services.

Finkel, Alvin. 1979. *Business and Social Reform in the Thirties*. Toronto: Lorimer.

Ford, Robin, and David Zussman, eds. 1997. *Alternative Service Delivery: Sharing Governance in Canada*. Toronto: KMPG Centre for Government Foundation and the Institute of Public Administration of Canada.

Gotell, Lise. 1996. Policing Desire: Obscenity Law, Pornography Politics, and Feminism in Canada. In Janine Brodie, ed., *Women and Canadian Public Policy*, 279–317. Toronto: Harcourt Brace.

Greene, Ian. 1993. The Courts and Public Policy. In M.M. Atkinson, ed., *Governing Canada: Institutions and Public Policy*, 179–205. Toronto: Harcourt Brace Jovanovich.

Hodgetts, J.E. 1973. *The Canadian Public Service: A Physiology of Government 1867–1970*. Toronto: University of Toronto Press.

Hogg, Peter W. 1985. *Constitutional Law of Canada*. 2nd ed. Toronto: Carswell.
– 1996. *Constitutional Law of Canada*. 4th ed. Toronto: Carswell.
Howse, Robert. 1995. Another Rights Revolution? The Charter and the Reform of Social Regulation in Canada. In P. Grady, R. Howse, and J. Maxwell, *Redefining Social Security*, 99–161. Kingston: School of Policy Studies, Queen's University.
Johnson, D. 1991. Regulatory agencies and accountability: an Ontario perspective. *Canadian Public Administration* 34, no. 3 (Autumn): 417–34.
Knopff, Rainer, and F.L. Morton. 1992. *Charter Politics*. Toronto: Nelson.
Kome, Penney. 1993. *The Taking of Twenty-Eight: Women Challenge the Constitution*. Toronto: Women's Press.
Law Reform Commission of Canada. 1986. *Policy Implementation, Compliance and Administrative Law*. Ottawa: Working Paper 51.
MacDonald, D.C. 1993. Ontario's agencies, boards, and commissions come of age. *Canadian Public Administration* 36, no. 3 (Autumn): 349–63.
Makin, Kirk. 1997. Top court's activism on wane. *Globe and Mail*, 17 April.
Mandel, Michael. 1992. *The Charter of Rights and the Legalization of Politics in Canada*. Toronto: Thomson Educational Publishing.
Manfredi, Christopher. 1993. *Judicial Power and the Charter: Canada and the Paradox of Liberalism Constitutionalism*. Toronto: McClelland and Stewart.
Manzer, Ronald. 1985. *Public Policies and Political Development in Canada*. Toronto: University of Toronto Press.
Massé, Marcel. 1996. Notes for a Statement on Regulatory Reform. Speech by the President of the Treasury Board and Minister Responsible for Regulatory Affairs. Ottawa, 28 November.
Moscovitch, Allan. 1993. From the Conservative Ill-Fare State to a Renewed Welfare State. *Canadian Review of Social Policy*, 32 (Winter): 1–12.
National Council of Welfare. 1995. *Legal Aid and the Poor*. A Report by the National Council of Welfare. Ottawa: Minister of Supply and Services.
Ogus, Anthony I. 1994. *Regulation: Legal Form and Economic Theory*. Oxford: Oxford University Press.
Pascall, Gillian. 1986. *Social Policy: A Feminist Analysis*. London: Tavistock Publications.
Prince, Michael J. 1996. At the Edge of Canada's Welfare State: Social Policy-Making in British Columbia. In R.K. Carty, ed., *Politics, Policy, and Government in British Columbia*, 236–71. Vancouver: UBC Press.
Reagan, Michael D. 1987. *Regulation: The Politics of Policy*. Toronto: Little, Brown.
Roche, Maurice. 1992. *Rethinking Citizenship: Welfare, Ideology and Change in Modern Society*. Cambridge: Polity Press.
Russell, Peter H. 1987. *The Judiciary in Canada: The Third Branch of Government*. Toronto: McGraw-Hill Ryerson.

– 1994. The Three Dimensions of Charter Politics. In James P. Bickerton and Alain-G. Gagnon, eds., *Canadian Politics*. 2nd ed., 344–65. Peterborough: Broadview Press.

Russell, Peter H., R. Knopff, and F.L. Morton, eds. 1989. *Federalism and the Charter: Leading Constitutional Decisions*. 5th ed. Ottawa: Carleton University Press.

Schultz, Richard J. 1982. Regulatory Agencies and the Dilemmas of Delegation. In O.P. Dwivedi, ed., *The Administrative State in Canada: Essays in Honour of J.E. Hodgetts*, 89–106. Toronto: University of Toronto Press.

Sheehy, Elizabeth A., and Susan B. Boyd, eds. 1989. *Canadian Feminist Perspectives on Law: An Annotated Bibliography of Interdisciplinary Writings*. Toronto: Resources for Feminist Research, Ontario Institute for Studies in Education.

Shragge, Eric, ed. 1997. *Workfare: Ideology for a New Under-Class*. Toronto: Garmond Press.

Siegel, Arthur. 1983. *Politics and the Media in Canada*. Toronto: McGraw-Hill Ryerson.

Smiley, Donald V. 1976. *Canada in Question: Federalism in the Seventies*. 2nd ed. Toronto: McGraw-Hill Ryerson.

– 1986. *The Federal Condition in Canada*. Toronto: McGraw-Hill Ryerson.

Strayer, Barry L. 1983. *The Canadian Constitution and the Courts: The Function and Scope of Judicial Review*. Toronto: Butterworths.

Taylor, Charles. 1992. *Reconciling the Solitudes: Essays on Canadian Federalism and Nationalism,* ed. Guy Laforest. Montreal and Kingston: McGill-Queen's University Press.

Thomas, Paul G., and Orest W. Zajcew. 1993. Structural Heretics: Crown Corporations and Regulatory Agencies. In M.M. Atkinson, ed., *Governing Canada: Institutions and Public Policy*, 115–47. Toronto: Harcourt Brace Jovanovich.

Treasury Board of Canada Secretariat. 1992. *How Regulators Regulate: A Guide to Regulatory Processes in Canada*. Ottawa: Minister of Supply and Services.

– 1994. *Regulatory Cooperation Between Governments*. Ottawa: Minister of Supply and Services.

Trebilcock, Michael J. 1989. Critical Issues in the Design of Governance Regimes for the Professions. *The Law Society Gazette* 23, no. 4: 351.

Ussher, J.M. 1991. *Women's Madness: Misogny or Mental Illness?* New York: Harvester Wheatsheaf.

Whittington, M.S., and R. Van Loon. 1996. *The Canadian Political System*. 5th ed. Toronto McGraw-Hill Ryerson.

Wilson, James Q., ed. 1980. *The Politics of Regulation*. New York: Basic Books.

PART III
MANAGING REGULATION WITHIN THE STATE

11

Managing the Regulatory State: From 'Up,' to 'In and Down,' to 'Out and Across'

MARGARET M. HILL

There is a tendency among students of regulation to focus attention on high-profile regulatory bodies, usually agencies such as the Canadian Radio-television and Telecommunications Commission and the Canadian Transportation Agency (formerly the National Transportation Agency). This chapter adopts a different perspective and looks at an often-forgotten aspect of government regulation. Taking us inside the Canadian regulatory state, the chapter examines how the regulatory function of government has been managed over the past twenty-five years and how it ought to be managed for the future.

The idea of managing regulation is distinct from the more familiar notions of deregulation and regulatory reform. The chapter begins by introducing the concept of 'regulatory management,' which is subsequently used as a touchstone for exploring some of the important developments in regulation in Canada from the 1970s through to the present. The chapter argues that we have moved from an original preoccupation in the 1970s and early 1980s with managing the regulatory state *'up'*, to a concern a decade later with managing it *'in and down'* and, in the mid-1990s, to a fixation on managing it *'out and across.'* Thus the past twenty-five years have been marked by key changes in how we understand and view regulation and its relationship to public administration. The final section in the chapter holds up the lens of regulatory management and discusses several emerging debates and issues related to the future of the Canadian regulatory state.

The chapter makes no pretence of providing an exhaustive history of regulatory developments in Canada.[1] It is hoped, however, that by using the approach adopted here, greater analytical rigour can be brought to bear on our understanding of changes in regulation at the federal level and, to a lesser extent, in the provinces. Moreover, looking at the ways in which the emphasis of regulatory management has changed over the course of the past twenty-five years places us in a better position to identify the requirements for managing the regulatory state effectively in the coming years. It also helps us to assess our capacity as students of regulation to meet the challenges of using regulation as a strategic instrument of government.

The Concept of Regulatory Management

The Concept Explored

The emergence of regulatory management in Canada and a handful of other Organization for Economic Cooperation and Development (OECD) countries in the mid-1990s both marked and guided a significant maturation in the debate about improving regulation. The focus had shifted from introducing ad hoc changes in processes and policies to considering how meaningful, effective regulatory change could best be accomplished and sustained. Regulatory management offered a new framework for viewing the regulatory state and for making decisions about how, why, and when governments regulate.

Regulatory management is distinct from deregulation and regulatory reform.[2] Deregulation, understood in its broadest sense, focuses principally on the quantity of regulation while the emphasis in regulatory reform is on the quality of regulation. Regulatory management, on the other hand, embraces a longer-term view of regulation and the regulatory state. It is concerned with issues such as the aggregate impacts of regulation, consistency and coordination among regulatory systems, setting regulatory priorities, alternatives to traditional command-and-control regulation, ensuring compliance and enforcement, and determining the optimal mix of regulatory and nonregulatory tools to achieve short- and long-term policy goals. The management perspective on regulation rests on a relatively sophisticated appreciation of the political economy of regulation.

Table 11.1 summarizes key differences in regulatory management, deregulation, and regulatory reform in terms of their characterization of the problem of regulation and the prescription they therefore suggest. The table also provides several examples of the three concepts in practice.

Regulatory management, as Table 11.1 shows, sees the problem of regulation in a holistic way. It is concerned with the aggregate effects of regulation for individuals, companies, society, and the economy, both now and in the future. Moreover, unlike deregulation and regulatory reform, regulatory management is concerned with more than getting the quantity or quality of regulation right. In the regulatory management paradigm, 'right' means determining the best mix of regulatory and nonregulatory instruments to address policy problems effectively and proactively. Regulatory management is therefore a problem-solving approach.

TABLE 11.1
Regulatory Management: The Concept Explored in a Comparative Context

Concept	The Problem of Regulation	Prescription	Examples
Deregulation	• The coercive power of regulation • The size of the regulatory burden imposed on individuals, companies, and the economy (e.g., red tape for small businesses and a major source of inefficiency for the economy)	• Eliminate or reduce existing stock of regulation to shrink the size of government • Introduce changes to simplify and streamline existing regulatory processes and administration	• Telecommunications, transportation, and financial services sectors in Canada and the U.S. in the 1980s
Regulatory reform	• Regulation per se is not the problem • Ensuring quality regulation (i.e., efficient, effective regulation) and quality regulatory processes (e.g., consultation and planning)	• Introduce greater analytical rigour and other changes to improve regulatory decision making and hence the quality of future regulation	• Federal Regulatory Policy, revised 1992 • Federal regulatory review process • Regulatory impact analysis
Regulatory management	• The aggregate effects (especially costs) of regulation for individuals, companies, society, and the economy, now and in the future • Using regulation and other tools of government to address policy problems in the most effective, proactive ways possible	• Introduce greater flexibility and responsiveness in regulatory systems • Use alternatives to regulation • Combine regulatory and nonregulatory tools • Structural reform within government	• Performance measures for regulation • Regulatory budgeting • Using environmental regulation as a lever for increasing competitiveness

The regulatory management prescription for what ails regulation is similarly different from that which follows from either the deregulation or regulatory reform perspective. Regulatory management proposes introducing means to ensure that regulatory regimes are sufficiently flexible, for instance, flexible enough to keep in step with technological advances that enable regulatees to meet regulatory standards in unanticipated ways or to build in incentives for greater compliance, and puts an emphasis on using performance measures for regulation. The concept also advocates a much broader scope for analysis. Rather than looking at regulation alone, as deregulation and regulatory reform do, regulatory management extends its consideration to governmentwide policy objectives and regulatory and nonregulatory instruments for achieving them, 'backstop' arrangements that combine regulatory and nonregulatory instruments, and the linking of domestic and international regulatory responses. Regulatory management recognizes that long-run success, with its system-level prescription, depends on structural and cultural reform within government as a whole.

It is worth underscoring that the concept of regulatory management rests on at least three important premises. The first is that regulation is a distinct instrument of government within a larger toolbox of policy instruments. This is the essential idea of the theory of instrument choice (see, e.g., Economic Council of Canada (1981); Hood (1994); Linder and Peters (1989); and Trebilcock et al. (1982)). The implication is that, as a tool, regulation can be used more or less effectively and, indeed, that its use can be managed, as is the case with spending and taxation. The design of regulatory responses – and responses that incorporate regulation – lies at the heart of the art and science of regulatory management.

Relatedly, the concept of regulatory management presumes that regulation can be (and is) used to achieve a variety of objectives. As Pildes and Sunstein (1995, 8) have argued, 'the key task for those interested in regulatory performance is to find ways of simultaneously promoting economic and democratic goals.' The goals range from efficient, effective, accountable government to jobs and growth, ensuring a voice for private interests, and reducing costs or risks.

The concept of regulatory management is also based on the idea that getting the regulatory state right is an ongoing, long-term process, in which the regulatory instrument is understood to be fundamentally relational. This is roughly analogous to what today's management theorists refer to as a process of 'continuous improvement.'

Finally, the concept of regulatory management helps us to make sense of the seemingly contradictory trends in government regulation in the first half of the 1990s. Commentators observed a continuing retreat by governments from direct regulation of economic activity and a new preference for defining the broad framework conditions for competition. At the same time, however, there was evidence of a renewed growth in regulation, mainly in the area of social regulation. The OECD (1993) and others concluded that the developments were contradictory. From another standpoint, the trends reflected the fact that the regulatory state was undergoing a process of redrawing (Schultz 1990) and that choices about government intervention were being made on the basis of a more complex set of ideas than simply more or less regulation (i.e., deregulation), or the quality of regulation (i.e., regulatory reform).

Regulatory Management and the Four-Regime Framework

Another way to understand regulatory management is to see it in relation to the approach developed in the book's introductory chapter. The four-regime framework contends that Canada's regulatory institutions involve an interplay among four regulatory regimes: Regime I is the immediate sectoral regime; Regime II is the horizontal-framework regime; Regime III is the government executive regime for managing regulation; and Regime IV is the international regime. Not surprisingly, Regime III is especially important for this chapter.

Regime III embraces the players and processes that exist in a broader, cross-governmental sense (Doern 1998). Its significance derives from the fact that it forces an understanding of how the regulatory function is managed within the executive or even within the state as a whole, including the courts (Doern 1998). Regime III, as the introductory chapter explains, is distinct from but intertwined with Regimes I, II, and IV.

Regulatory management and Regime III are closely connected. What Regime III captures, in short, is the structure of institutions within which regulatory management plays out. The regime framework reminds us that it is important to ensure that an analysis of the management of government regulation is anchored in a more general understanding of the regulatory state.

Approaches for Managing Regulation

There are many different models for managing regulation in the contemporary regulatory state. The models vary in terms of players and processes: who the central manager of regulation is, or whether there is a central manager at all; mechanisms for ensuring transparency and accountability in regulatory decisions; organizational complexity, for example, the relationship between central managers and departments and agencies; the degree to which regulatory analysis informs decision making and priority setting; and the range of policy instruments that is routinely considered. Another key variable is the degree to which the concept of regulatory management – and the supporting institutional arrangements and culture – has become a central feature of public administration.

Pildes and Sunstein (1995) adopt this kind of player-process perspective in their study of reinventing the American regulatory state. The authors characterize the American approach to managing regulation as one of presidential oversight where, since the birth of the administrative state, 'American presidents have struggled to assert more centralized control' over regulation (Pildes and Sunstein 1995, 11). After reviewing the reforms introduced under President Clinton, Pildes and Sunstein contend that 'From the recent evidence, it seems clear that presidential oversight of the regulatory process, though relatively new, has become a permanent part of the institutional design of American government' (Pildes and Sunstein 1995, 15). A similar kind of macrolevel, institutional analysis of managing regulation is found in the OECD's report on *Control and Management of Government Regulation* (OECD 1996).

It is equally instructive to differentiate approaches to regulatory management on the basis of 'managing up,' 'managing in and down,' and 'managing out and across.' The principal benefit of organizing a discussion around these terms is to highlight the multidimensionality of regulatory management and to introduce students of regulation to the inner workings of the regulatory state. The suggested approach also serves to draw attention, in a very concrete way, to the evolution from a classical interpretation of regulation to one reflective of a sophisticated understanding of the political economy of regulation. What is meant by 'managing up,' 'managing in and down,' and 'managing out and across' is explored and developed in the next section.

Managing the Regulatory State in Canada

The main contention in this chapter is that regulatory developments in Canada since the 1970s illustrate the gradual embrace of the idea of managing regulation inside the state or, in other words, the concept of regulatory management. Building on the conceptual discussion in the previous sections, the remainder of the chapter outlines three dimensions in the institutionalization of regulatory management in the Canadian regulatory state. The dimensions – managing up, managing in and down, and managing out and across – are admittedly somewhat arbitrary and are not intended to imply a natural progression. They are nonetheless useful for the purposes of analysis, since together they underscore the multifaceted nature of managing regulation.

A Proviso

It is important to keep in mind that regulatory management did not crystallize as a concept or tool to assist policy makers until the mid-1990s. Even now, the concept is unfamiliar to many outside the immediate regulatory community. This poses a challenge for historical analysis because it can be argued that it is inappropriate to examine past regulatory developments through the lens of a concept and tool that post-dates the developments themselves.

On the other hand, it is equally reasonable to defend the idea of viewing the past through a contemporary lens. The regulatory management concept provides coherence for analysis. Furthermore, the concept itself represents a cumulative development in thinking about how regulation can be used to achieve diverse economic and social policy goals. Management theorists would also add that, while we may have been late to recognize regulatory management officially, regulators and policy makers have been managing regulation in some way or another (and more or less effectively) since the advent of the regulatory state.

Managing Up

'Managing up' captures many of the classic issues of regulation. Foremost among these is delegation and the ensuing challenges of ensuring accountability and control, mainly through mechanisms linking the recipients of delegated authority in an upward direction with ministers, Parliament, and provincial legislatures. From the 'managing up' perspective, the central dilemma of the regulatory state is the wide scope for exercising discretion that resides in the hands of nonelected regulatory officials, especially with the creation of arm's-length regulatory agencies that are involved in promoting and planning regulation (Schultz and Alexandroff 1985). At the extreme, this discretion is said to be a gateway that allows appointed regulators to move beyond merely administering regulation to trespassing into the domain of policy making (Janisch 1979). The notion of managing up represents an attempt to resolve the tension between accountability and control on the one hand, and the independence of regulatory bodies and officials on the other.

Likewise, managing up responds to concerns about capture. Bernstein (1955), Stigler (1971), Posner (1974), Peltzman (1976), and others popularized the idea that regulators were susceptible to regulating in the private interest, not the public interest. While capture theory had distinct weaknesses (Andrew and Pelletier 1978; Makkai and Braithwaite 1992), it did, however, point to important issues related to participation, consultation, and representation (Fox 1979; Trebilcock 1978).

Managing up was the dominant approach to regulatory management in Canada in the 1970s and early 1980s. Reformers recognized the benefits of government by regulation (e.g., efficient, impartial decision making in highly technical areas and depoliticization of sensitive policy issues), but stressed the immediate need to rein in the burgeoning Leviathan via mechanisms that tightened accountability to elected officials (Schultz 1982; Thomas 1984; Vandervort 1979). Debate centred on policy directives, the appointment process for regulators, cabinet appeals, sunset clauses, approval of agency budgets, structured discretion, and other such direct and indirect methods. The 'managing up' theme ran through most recommendations for reform, such as those put forward by the Law Reform Commission of Canada (1980) and the Economic Council of Canada's Regulation Reference (1979, 1981). At the practical level, the leading changes in federal and provincial regulation during this period also reflected a strong commitment to managing regulation up. These included the new National Transportation Act, 1987,[3] which had several provisions regarding 'making regulators accountable,' and zero-based reviews of regulation in Saskatchewan and Manitoba in the mid-1980s, which were intended to improve accountability by eliminating unnecessary and outdated regulations.[4]

That said, 'managing up' continues to be an element in today's strategies for managing regulation (Eisner 1993). This is an inevitable consequence of the delegated nature of regulation and the continued persuasiveness of conventional principles of ministerial responsibility. In early 1997, the priority placed on ensuring regulation is managed upward effectively is seen in the debate over proposed changes to the federal Statutory Instruments Act (Bill C-25), which would, among other things, allow regulatory authorities to incorporate international and national standards by reference and give cabinet authority to exempt certain regulations from the normal regulatory review process (Weiler 1997). Similarly, the potential abuse of Parliament's powers as a result of the provision for compliance plans in the proposed Regulatory Efficiency Act was a key stumbling block in Bill C-62's aborted passage through the House of Commons.[5]

Managing In and Down

'Managing in and down' represents the middle phase in the institutionalization of regulatory management. 'In' refers to inside the regulatory state and 'managing in' to the establishment of governmentwide processes for regulatory review, planning, and priority setting. 'Down,' on the other hand, points to the disaggregated regulatory state. The focus of 'managing down' is on taking measures to improve regulation and regulatory decision making within individual departments and agencies.

At the federal level, 1986 was a watershed year for 'managing in.' The Nielsen Task Force on Program Review (Canada 1986c) showed that the federal government was responsible for 146 different regulatory programs employing 34,500 officials by the mid-1980s. The total cost of administering these programs was estimated at $2.7 billion per year. Not surprisingly, the task force made a number of recommendations for improving the management of federal regulatory programs and policies. These laid the foundation for the deputy prime minister's announcement, in February 1986, of a comprehensive regulatory reform strategy.

The strategy initially included the appointment of a minister responsible for regulatory affairs and a first-ever statement of a federal regulatory policy (Canada 1986a, and as amended, 1992 and 1995). It was soon extended to include a centralized review process for all new regulations and amendments to existing regulations, an annual regulatory planning cycle, and obligatory impact assessment by departments of the costs and benefits of proposed regulatory changes. Many of these measures responded to long-standing calls from the auditor general of Canada and others for regulation to be subject to the same kind of scrutiny as government's use of the spending and taxation instruments.

The review process was overseen by the Office of Privatization and Regulatory Affairs (OPRA). OPRA was responsible for the Federal Regulatory Policy and, using it as leverage, served a catalyst and challenge function in relation to departmental regulators. OPRA also acted as the gatekeeper to the Special Committee of Council (SCC), the cabinet committee responsible for approving governor-in-council regulations. The chair of the SCC was the minister responsible for regulatory affairs. While the OPRA-centred process was not perfect as implemented, it was applauded by the auditor general (1989) as a model framework for public sector accountability.

OPRA's regulatory review functions were transferred in 1992 to the Regulatory Affairs Division (RAD) of the Treasury Board Secretariat. This move was generally interpreted as signalling the government's wish to maintain a commitment to regulatory review, but to give the activity a lower profile. RAD has played a mainly transactional, coordinating role over the past five years. There are indications that, under new leadership, a more proactive, more strategic attitude will be seen at RAD as of mid-1997. What this might mean is explored in the concluding section of the chapter.

Life was also breathed into 'managing down' in the 1990s. An excellent example comes from the departmentwide regulatory reviews that were launched through the 1992 federal budget. The (then) Departments of Agriculture, Consumer and Corporate Affairs, and Transport were asked to identify regulations that were outdated or unnecessarily impeded competitiveness. Over the two-year process, several hundred regulatory changes were introduced in the three departments.[6] The interest in improving the downward management of regulation was also manifested in this period through the growing range of training and development activities departments offered to their regulatory officials (Canada 1992).

Managing regulation 'in and down' has become a priority at the provincial level as well. In Alberta, for instance, the Klein government's 1993 'Seizing Opportunity' initiative led to a series of measures to improve regulatory management inside the provincial regulatory state. Regulatory impact reports modelled on the federal Regulatory Impact Analysis Statement are now obligatory for all new and amended regulations and, under an order-in-council, must be submitted to the chair of the Regulatory Reform Task Force (a committee of public and private sector representatives). Regulatory work plans must accompany each department's three-year business plan. There is a managing-down element in the Alberta reforms as well, since all departmental regulations are scheduled to sunset by 1998 and sunsetting will trigger a thorough review.

Similar sorts of steps have been taken in other provinces. In New Brunswick, a joint government-industry reform project was launched in January 1994 to improve horizontal integration between departmental regulatory activities. Ontario's 1995–6 Red Tape Review Commission made recommendations to cabinet on, among other things, the design and implementation of a permanent impact test and governmentwide review process for new regulatory measures. In Saskatchewan, a Code of Regulatory Conduct was adopted in February 1994 and departments are responsible for applying its guiding principles in their regulatory activities. Compliance with the code is monitored by the Legislation Review and Regulatory Review Committee of the provincial legislature.

While the flurry of activity directed at managing in and down has perhaps slowed, it must be stressed that the theme has not been forgotten and, in fact, remains a vital element in managing the regulatory state in Canada. The provincial examples mentioned above show that the provinces are playing catch-up in this area, or that the provincial regulatory states are now large enough to merit careful, ongoing internal management. At the federal level, amendment of the Federal Regulatory Policy to incorporate management standards for the regulatory process confirms that managing in and down remains a part of the agenda for regulatory management (Canada 1996).

Managing Out and Across

With 'managing out and across,' regulation moves from being seen as a series of one-off events to something that is fully and fundamentally relational. Moreover, the notion of management becomes increasingly important and there is a clear emphasis on results and measuring performance. 'Managing out and across' is the final element in the development of full-blown regulatory management. It has come into ascendancy in Canada in the mid-1990s.

'Managing out' has several dimensions: the delivery of regulatory services to clients and the imposition of obligations on regulatees (Sparrow 1994); regulatory enforcement and compliance (Braithwaite, Walker, and Grabosky, 1987; Hutter 1989); increased resort to regulatory arrangements with other jurisdictions, for instance through harmonization and mutual recognition (Canada 1994); and the linking of regulation with other policy priorities in government (i.e., what is referred to as strategic regulation). 'Managing out' is reinforced by 'managing across.' The latter focuses on straddling the conventional boundaries between the public and private sectors (e.g., partnership arrangements, voluntary agreements, and covenants) and between areas of regulation and the associated regulatory bodies. Managing across also connotes the sense of there being a regulatory community, with a recognized body of knowledge, skills, practices, and experiences.

The outstanding example of managing out and across is the linking of regulation with the Liberal government's jobs and growth agenda. The House of Commons Standing Committee on Finance (Canada 1993), American Vice-President Gore's National Performance Review and the subsequent Common Sense Task Force, and a wide range of academic literature and research (Hart 1997; Jaffe et al. 1995; Stewart 1993; Thomas and Terepsky 1993; Yoon and Ouellette 1996) have established the impact of regulation on innovation, economic growth, and adaptation and competitiveness. While the evidence is sometimes anecdotal at best, there is consensus among all but the most determined ideologues that regulation's impact is both positive and negative. This has translated at the policy level to a recognition that regulation is potentially a very valuable instrument (especially when combined with other instruments in the larger governing toolkit) for meeting a governmentwide priority, such as competitiveness. This logic, in turn, has spurred on what in the past might have been considered 'unholy alliances' between certain federal departments. Environment Canada, Industry Canada, and the Department of Foreign Affairs and International Trade, for instance, are presently involved in pursuing opportunities to market Canadian environmental technologies in countries where the technological know-how is not available to meet prescribed regulatory standards.

Regulatory Management: Emerging Debates and Issues

One of the clear insights from the past two and a half decades is that regulation is not a policy instrument like all the others. In some respects, regulation parallels other instruments, for instance in the sense that any instrument of government can be used more or less effectively, or is more or less suited for achieving particular public policy goals. At bottom, however, the years since the 1970s have shown that regulation has its own distinctive political, social, economic, and administrative dynamics. It is therefore only natural that understanding the modern regulatory state calls for unique conceptual frameworks.

This chapter began with the observation that, despite the progress of the past two and half decades, a major part of the Canadian regulatory state still remains hidden. The hidden part is the inner workings of the regulatory state, or what has been cast in this book as Regime III. With a view to revealing the hidden, the chapter developed the idea of regulatory management and then used the concept as the basis for looking back on the Canadian regulatory state during the past twenty-five years. The analysis in the chapter suggested a long-term shift from simply managing the regulatory state 'up' to a situation today where regulation is also managed both 'in and down' and 'out and across.' The shift is perhaps most evident in the federal government, yet it is present at the provincial level as well.

The concept of regulatory management and the analysis in the chapter can also be used as a springboard for looking forward. Regulatory management is a central feature of public administration and government in Canada. It must be underlined again, however, that the institutionalization of regulatory management is a never-ending process. The regulatory agenda to the new century is rife with challenges related to managing 'up,' 'in and down,' and 'out and across.' Many of these challenges are closely connected with larger changes that are taking place in governance in the Canadian state.

Managing 'up' is concerned with the exercise of discretion by regulatory authorities and the balance that is struck between control and accountability on the one hand, and regulatory independence on the other. As perspectives on accountability have evolved alongside – and to take account of – the rise of new models of government organization and new ways of governing, it is only natural that regulatory reformers have had to pause to take stock of where regulation fits in with the larger accountability framework of government. At the same time, old notions of accountability have not been completely dismissed. Many proponents of reform, for instance, are in agreement on the need to ensure a more effective role for Parliament in the regulatory process. The final report of the House of Commons Standing Committee on Finance and Competitiveness (Canada 1993) recommended a more active role for House standing committees in studying proposed regulatory initiatives. In the highly fragmented Thirty-Sixth Parliament elected in June 1997, the political pressure to involve members of Parliament in monitoring regulatory performance may increase still further. Revamping the role and mandate of the Standing Joint Committee for the Scrutiny of Regulations is yet another option if being true to the principles of parliamentary sovereignty is the goal.[7]

Managing regulation 'in and down' relates to the mechanisms that have been put in place for departmental and governmentwide regulatory review, planning, and priority setting. One of the links that is still missing is a ministerial-level focal point for regulatory matters. Under the reforms introduced in 1986, the minister responsible for regulatory affairs served an important coordinating and challenge function. The minister chaired the Special Committee of Council and, in this capacity, performed an important oversight function for federal regulatory activities. The situation is very different at present, with no clear champion for regulatory matters in cabinet. Instead, the president of the Treasury Board, the president of the Privy Council Office, and the chair of the SCC must work together with other SCC members to get the regulatory side of government right and departments are sometimes required to manoeuvre proposed regulatory initiatives through both the SCC and the Treasury Board. There are clearly still ways, then, to bring further coherence to the horizontal machinery inside the Canadian regulatory state.

Finally, many of the challenges for managing 'out and across' in the coming years will arise from the ever-enlarging role that is being given to private actors in government regulation, both in Canada and in the international regulatory regimes of which Canada is part. This injection of more private stakeholders raises important questions about, among other things, political accountabilities and responsibilities and the effectiveness with which public interest goals can be achieved through private and voluntary action. These issues are plainly not unique to government regulation. Just the same, they should be expected to have growing significance for theorists and practitioners of regulation as the Canadian regulatory state continues to experiment with new ways of managing its business.

Perhaps the key challenge for the Canadian regulatory state in the new century is to raise regulation to what the secretary of the Treasury Board calls 'a more strategic level.' This idea tends to be translated in Ottawa as 'integrating agendas' or, put differently, finding ways to ensure decisions about regulation are integrated as closely as possible with the broader policy agenda of government. One vehicle for accomplishing the desired integration is through the annual business planning process for federal departments and agencies.

In the language of this chapter, a strategic perspective on regulation calls for managing regulation 'up,' 'in and down,' and 'out and across' at the same time and in mutually reinforcing ways. But the new interest in strategic regulation may also point to the limits of the concept of regulatory management. What is arguably missing is a sufficiently strong appreciation for how regulation is managed in relation to other governing instruments and the full range of public policy goals. The concept is also open to the criticism, as is managerialism (or public management), that it minimizes the essential political quality of public administration.

Raising regulation to a more strategic level – or integrating agendas – puts an emphasis on linkages. There is convincing evidence of links, both positive and negative, between regulation and innovation, between regulation and the ability of economies to adapt to change and remain competitive, and between regulation and environmental quality, health, and safety. Moreover, in the real world of policy making, awareness is growing of the supporting role that regulation can play in achieving public policy goals, especially when the economic and social well-being of citizens and countries are increasingly connected. The challenge of mixing regulation with other policy instruments is both practical and conceptual.

The drive to regulate strategically is taking place against the backdrop of a relatively mature regulatory state. Thus, to a large degree, the idea of managing regulation has seeped into the fabric of government and the mindsets of regulatory officials. The result is a more refined appreciation for the strengths and limitations of regulation and an ensuing confidence about when, where, and in what form regulation is appropriate. Given these developments, the stage may be set for a period of renewed experimentation inside the Canadian regulatory state.

The structures and administrative culture of the regulatory state may have changed, but regulatory management is a still-evolving concept. The present debate about strategic regulation owes much to the pioneering work that was undertaken during the past two and half decades to develop theories of regulation. Without a good grasp of the uniqueness and power of the regulatory instrument, it would simply be impossible to talk intelligently about regulation or about the regulatory capacity of the Canadian state, let alone about regulating strategically. That said, the debate about strategic regulation also hints that, from a conceptual standpoint at least, the appropriate next step may be for regulatory management to rediscover the broader tool kit of governing instruments. This may be one way to move beyond a transactional approach to the inner workings of the Canadian regulatory state and to ensure that our understanding of this once-hidden side of the regulatory state is firmly and explicitly connected with broader questions of public policy and administration.

NOTES

1 This has already been done, most ably, by W.T. Stanbury in his report 'Reforming the Federal Regulatory Process in Canada, 1971–1992,' which was prepared for the Standing Committee on Finance's Sub-Committee on Regulations and Competitiveness. See Stanbury (1992).

2 A similar argument is made in OECD (1996), a report by the OECD's Public Management Service (PUMA). PUMA contends that deregulation, regulatory reform, and regulatory management are three phases of regulatory change, with each phase representing a step in a long-term maturing process. No such sequence or logical progression is assumed in this chapter. The primary interest here is in the characteristics of regulatory management and how regulatory management has been manifested to different degrees at various points in the Canadian experience. The factors driving change in the approach to regulatory management (or, put another way, in the emphasis given to the different elements of regulatory management) are dealt with less directly.

3 On the 1987 National Transportation Act, see Chapter 4.

4 Saskatchewan's review resulted in revisions to or the elimination of 1,200 regulations (interview). In Manitoba, over 1,000 pages of regulations were repealed (interview). The best summary information on provincial regulatory initiatives is available through the Managing Regulation in Canada Web page, accessible through http://www.tbs-sct.gc.ca/tb/rad/index_e.html.

5 Bill C-62 was introduced into the House of Commons in December 1994. It received a very negative reception from the Standing Joint Committee for the Scrutiny of Regulation (see note 6) as well as from nongovernmental organizations. The bill died on the order paper the following summer.

6 Confidential interview, 5 January 1996.

7 The Standing Joint Committee for the Scrutiny of Regulations (SJC) was set up in the 1970s under Standing Order 90 of the House of Commons. The SJC scrutinizes all regulations under federal legislation and reports to the House and can make recommendations to departments. The SJC reviews about 800–1,000 statutory instruments every year.

REFERENCES

Andrew, Caroline, and Rejean Pelletier. 1978. The Regulators. In G. Bruce Doern, ed., *The Regulatory Process in Canada*, 147–64. Toronto: Macmillan.
Auditor General of Canada. 1989. *Report of the Auditor General of Canada to the House of Commons*, 31 March.

Bernstein, Marver. 1955. *Regulating Business by Independent Commission*. Princeton: Princeton University Press.

Braithwaite, J., J. Walker, and P. Grabosky. 1987. An Enforcement Taxonomy of Regulatory Agencies. *Law & Policy* 9:323–50.

Canada. 1986a. Treasury Board of Canada Secretariat. *Federal Regulatory Policy*. Ottawa: Treasury Board Secretariat.

Canada. 1986b. Task Force on Program Review. *Regulatory Agencies: A Study Team Report to the Task Force on Program Review*. Ottawa: Minister of Supply and Services Canada.

Canada. 1986c. Task Force on Program Review. *Regulatory Programs: A Study Team Report to the Task Force on Program Review*. Ottawa: Minister of Supply and Services Canada.

Canada. 1992. Public Service Commission of Canada. *Report on Needs Assessment and Training Needs of the Regulatory Community*. Ottawa: Training and Development Canada, August.

Canada. 1993. House of Commons Standing Committee on Finance. *Regulations and Competitiveness*. 1st Report of the Sub-Committee on Regulations and Competitiveness. Ottawa: Supply and Service Canada.

Canada. 1994. Treasury Board of Canada Secretariat. *Regulatory Cooperation Between Governments*. Ottawa: Treasury Board Secretariat.

Canada. 1996. Treasury Board of Canada Secretariat. *Federal Regulatory Process Management Standards: Compliance Guide*. Ottawa: Treasury Board Secretariat.

Doern, G. Bruce. 1998. The Interplay Among Regimes: Mapping Regulatory Institutions in the UK, US and Canada. In G. Bruce Doern and Stephen Wilks, eds., *Changing Regulatory Institutions in Britain and North America*, ch. 2. Toronto: University of Toronto Press.

Economic Council of Canada. 1979. *Responsible Regulation*. Ottawa: Minister of Supply and Services.

– 1981. *Reforming Regulation*. Ottawa: Minister of Supply and Services.

Eisner, M.A. 1993. Bureaucratic Professionalism and the Limits of the Political Control Thesis: The Case of the Federal Trade Commission. *Governance* 6: 127–53.

Fox, David. 1979. *Public Participation in the Administrative Process*. Ottawa: Law Reform Commission of Canada.

Hart, Stuart L. 1997. Beyond Green: Strategies for a Sustainable World. *Harvard Business Review* 75, no. 1 (January-February): 66–76.

Hood, Christopher. 1994. *Explaining Policy Reversals*. Buckingham: Open University Press.

Hutter, Bridget M. 1989. Variations in Regulatory Enforcement Styles. *Law and Policy* 11, no. 2 (April): 153–74.

Jaffe, Adam B., Steven R. Peterson, Paul R. Portney, and Robert N. Stavins. 1995.
    Environmental Regulation and the Competitiveness of U.S. Manufacturing: What
    Does the Evidence Tell Us? *Journal of Economic Literature* 33 (March): 132–63.
Janisch, H.N. 1979. Policy Making in Regulation: Towards a New Definition of the
    Status of Independent Agencies in Canada. *Osgoode Hall Law Journal* 17, no.1
    (April): 22–45.
Law Reform Commission of Canada. 1980. *Independent Administrative Agencies*.
    Ottawa: Minister of Supply and Services.
Linder, Stephen H., and B. Guy Peters. 1989. Instruments of Government: Perceptions
    and Contexts. *Journal of Public Policy* 9, no. 1 (Jan.-March): 35–58.
Makkai, Toni, and John Braithwaite. 1992. In and Out of the Revolving Door: Making
    Sense of Regulatory Capture. *Journal of Public Policy* 12, no. 1 (Jan.-March):
    61–78.
Organisation for Economic Cooperation and Development. 1993. *Public Management
    Developments: Survey 1993*. Paris.
– 1995. *Recommendation of the Council of the OECD on Improving the Quality of
    Government Regulation*, adopted on 9 March. Paris.
– 1996. *Control and Management of Government Regulation*. Paris.
Peltzman, Sam. 1976. Toward a More General Theory of Regulation. *Journal of Law
    and Economics* 19 (August): 211–40.
Pildes, Richard H., and Cass R. Sunstein. 1995. Reinventing the Regulatory State.
    University of Chicago Law Review 62, no. 1 (Winter): 1–129.
Posner, Richard. 1974. Theories of Economic Regulation. *Bell Journal of Economics
    and Management Science* 5 (Autumn): 335–58.
Schultz, Richard J. 1982. Regulatory Agencies and the Dilemmas of Delegation. In
    O.P. Dwivedi, ed., *The Administrative State in Canada*, 89–106. Toronto: Univer-
    sity of Toronto Press.
– 1990. Privatization, Deregulation and the Changing Role of the State. *Business in
    the Contemporary World* (Autumn): 25–32.
Schultz, Richard J., and Alan Alexandroff. 1985. *Economic Regulation and the
    Federal System*. Toronto: University of Toronto Press.
Sparrow, Malcolm. 1994. *Imposing Duties: Government's Changing Approach to
    Compliance*. Westport, Conn.: Praeger.
Stanbury, W.T. 1992. *Reforming the Federal Regulatory Process in Canada, 1971–
    1992*. Appendix SREC-2 to Canada. House of Commons. Standing Committee on
    Finance. *Minutes of Proceedings and Evidence*. Issue No. 23. December.
Stewart, Richard B. 1993. Environmental Regulation and International Competitive-
    ness. *Yale Law Journal* 102:2039–2106.
Stigler, George J. 1971. The Theory of Economic Regulation. *Bell Journal of Econom-
    ics and Management Science* 2 (Spring): 3–21.

Thomas, Christopher, and Greg A. Terepsky. 1993. The Evolving Relationship Between Trade and Environmental Regulation. *Journal of World Trade*, 27, no. 4 (August): 23–45.

Trebilcock, Michael J. 1978. The Consumer Interest and Regulatory Reform. In G. Bruce Doern, ed., *The Regulatory Process in Canada*, 94–127. Toronto: Macmillan.

Trebilcock, Michael J., Douglas G. Hartle, J. Robert S. Prichard, and Donald N. Dewees. 1982. *The Choice of Governing Instrument*. Ottawa: Economic Council of Canada.

Vandervort, Lucinda. 1979. *Political Control of Independent Administrative Agencies*. Ottawa: Law Reform Commission of Canada.

Weiler, Todd. 1997. Parliament Chooses to Delegate Power. *Ottawa Citizen*, 6 March.

Yoon, Dong-Sup, and André Ouellette. 1996. *Trade, Environmental Standards and Competitiveness: The Canadian Case*. Ottawa: Conference Board of Canada.

12

The Federal Government and the 'RIAS' Process: Origins, Need, and Non-compliance

FAZIL MIHLAR

As earlier chapters have demonstrated, the federal government has made several attempts to assess, control, and manage its regulatory decision-making process. Arguably, the most concerted of these is the requirement for the 'regulatory impact assessment statement' or the RIAS process. The RIAS process, introduced in 1986–7, requires each federal department to submit an impact statement for each new regulation and amendment. It provides guidelines for regulatory decision making, requiring basic cost-benefit analysis, but also containing other important features with respect to pertinent information and public transparency. The RIAS process was a central part of a larger federal regulatory policy that dealt with accountability to ministers, Parliament, and the public.

This chapter first traces the origin and need for such a process within the state and then provides an empirical assessment of the extent to which the federal government has followed its own guidelines for regulatory decisions. The central thesis in the chapter is that non-compliance is a persistent feature of the RIAS experience but that a strong RIAS process is needed if the federal government is not only to restrain its strong regulatory impulses but contribute to creating the conditions required for a more competitive economy. The process is all the more necessary if more systematic approaches to risk management are to be put in place in federal decision making.

Origins of Federal Regulatory Reform Policy and the RIAS Process

The origins of the RIAS process lie in three sources and types of criticism and pressure in the late 1970s and 1980s, which led to federal regulatory reform policy as a whole. The first was broadly political and ideological and relates to the views on regulation of the Mulroney Conservatives, who came to power in

1984 (Schultz 1988). The second source of criticism focused on the costs of regulation and whether the state had any way of actually dealing with those costs either in an aggregate way or in particular sectors (Stanbury 1992a). The third pressure arose from criticism of social regulation in particular, a criticism that was also initially rooted in costs (Doern and Phidd 1992). Such criticism has since extended further into the important issues of assessing and managing risk. This is an area that I emphasize as being especially crucial in the continuing need for a RIAS process.

The Mulroney government's regulatory reform agenda of the 1984–8 period was in many respects a milder version of American developments, which began with the deregulation of the airline industry in the late 1970s and extended into practices intended to create new internal processes for both further deregulation and regulatory reform (Peters 1998). Forged in a period of economic stagnation and high inflation, criticisms of government regulation were rampant and the Mulroney government took up this issue as its own. The regulatory state had to be restrained in a significant way, but with some sensitivity, given the greater support in Canada for regulation compared to the U.S. (Schultz 1988). The federal regulatory reform policies established by the Mulroney government also addressed broader regulatory accountability and transparency.

Emerging within this critical view was a generic argument that the federal government simply did not know what its regulatory decisions were costing. Unlike spending and taxing decisions, where scrutiny within the government is quite extensive and systematic, there was no parallel capacity for examining regulatory decisions, either at the centre of the government or at the department level (Stanbury 1992a). The government's annual volume of regulatory proclamations is not easily converted into a quantifiable measure. In other words, there is no regulatory budget, largely because most of the costs of regulation are borne by private sector firms and individual Canadians.

Social or health, safety, and environmental regulation became a particular focus for attention among those who sought regulatory reform and this was the first area in which a form of cost-benefit analysis was established. In 1978 the federal government began a process whereby regulations promulgated under a set of some twenty named statutes had to be subject to a form of rudimentary prior analysis. One of the concerns here was that while an earlier wave of social regulations in the late 1960s and early 1970s may have produced benefits at reasonable costs, a further tranche of regulation was unlikely to be so benign. Indeed, social regulations were now explicitly identified as a contributing cause of high inflation and slow growth (Doern and Phidd 1992).

There have accordingly been a number government initiatives to change the regulatory process in Canada. In 1977, a Treasury Board Circular required all federal departments and agencies to evaluate the effectiveness and efficiency of their programs in meeting their objectives and in the following year, the federal government set up the Office for the Reduction of Paper Burden to try to reduce the paperwork burden borne by businesses. The Treasury Board also announced a new program in 1978 called socio-economic impact analysis. As emphasized earlier, this program was meant to promote more systematic analysis of the socio-economic impact of new health, safety, and environmental protection legislation in order to improve the allocative efficiency of resources (Economic Council of Canada 1979). The 1980 Liberal government established the Office of the Coordinator, Regulatory Reform while the Progressive Conservative government of 1984 created the Nielsen Task Force, the main objective of which was to ensure better service to the public and improved management of government programs. The task force proposed that the federal government establish a 'regulatory budget' to set limits on the total economic costs of federal regulation; this proposal was not adopted, however. In 1986, the Conservative government announced yet another series of initiatives to reform the regulatory process, outlined in the Regulatory Process Action Plan. This document called for public consultations, regulatory reviews and evaluation, and regulatory impact analysis statements (Stanbury 1992a).

In addition, the movement toward the deregulation of the airline industry eventually led to the privatization of government-owned Air Canada. The trucking industry, historically a regulated industry, was deregulated. Specialized telecommunications services industries were deregulated and thrown open to competition (Block and Lermer 1991; Stanbury 1996b). In areas where the government considered continued regulation desirable and necessary, regulatory agencies were pressured to reform and improve the regulatory decision-making process to reduce inefficiencies, bureaucratic delays, and administrative red tape.

The RIAS Process: Key Features

Since the mid-1980s, the Regulatory Affairs Directorate (RAD) of the Treasury Board Secretariat (TBS) has, on paper at least, undertaken several reform initiatives. In 1986, for instance, it was prescribed that line departments submit a RIAS for all new regulations and amendments. The directorate even went so far as to specify what the RIAS should contain (Stanbury 1992a, 1992b). Line departments were expected to prepare a RIAS that could be used by ministers to approve or reject new regulations and amendments. The RIAS was to be published in the *Canada Gazette*, so as to inform the affected parties of what the government intends to do. For new regulations that have an estimated present value of over $50 million, line departments were also expected to prepare a cost-benefit analysis. The RIAS was supposed to

- describe the problem and explain why regulation is required;
- provide a clear and precise description of the regulatory proposal;
- outline the alternatives considered and the reasons for choosing to regulate;
- describe the major anticipated impacts;
- summarize the consultations undertaken; and explain the procedures and resources that will be used for compliance and enforcement (Regulatory Affairs Directorate, Treasury Board of Canada 1996).

Within the federal government, the process began with departments themselves undertaking an assessment process as a RIAS statement was developed. The RIAS was subject to challenge by the RAD, whose job was to review proposals to ensure that the RIAS policy and process was effectively being carried out. RAD, however, had only a small number of analysts and thus ultimately was forced to rely on a constructive relationship with the departments.

In 1992, a new Canada regulatory policy was initiated and certain policy requirements were set forth. Among the requirements were that before any regulation could be made, it had to be demonstrated 'that a problem or risk exists,' that the benefits of regulation outweigh the costs to Canadians, their governments and businesses,' and that '[a]dverse impacts on the capacity of economy to generate wealth and employment are minimized' (Regulatory Affairs Directorate 1995a).

The important issue of risk assessment is dealt with in the next section. At this point, it is simply noted that the RIAS process and federal regulatory policy were changed to recognize but not necessarily grapple with risk issues.

As Stanbury concludes, regulatory process reform in Canada is associated with an array of initiatives and proposals, some of which were actually implemented:

- the use of cost-benefit analysis in the evaluations of new regulations;
- the restriction of political appeals from regulatory agencies to the cabinet;
- the increased use of public participation (such as advance notice, regulatory agenda, pre-publication in the *Canada Gazette*, and more consultation with the parties directly affected by the regulations);
- the reduction of federal-provincial overlap and duplication; and
- central agency oversight of the regulation-making process so as to improve the effectiveness and reduce the burden of new regulations (Stanbury 1992a).

Indeed, in the evolution of the RIAS as a whole, it is important to stress that one of the purposes was to create a single tool. RIAS was to help establish a basis for engaging both the public (pre-publication and consultation) and ministers (e.g., on the Special Committee of the cabinet) and promote a more rational, informed decision making on regulatory issues. This single tool concept remains important but in the later 1990s, the RIAS rationale and requirements tilted toward the larger risk-benefit issues and hence, in theory at least, embraced regulatory management of a more subtle and complicated kind.

As Margaret Hill explains in Chapter 11, regulatory management is distinctly different from deregulation and regulatory reform. While deregulation concentrates on the quantity of regulation, regulatory reform emphasizes the quality of regulation. Regulatory management is said to take a long-term view of regulation as a policy tool within the state. Its primary concerns include the impact of regulation on Canadians, coordinating mechanisms between different regulatory systems, prioritizing regulation, and finding alternatives to command-and-control regulation so as to meet government policy goals.

Risk Management as a Broader Rationale for a RIAS Process

As the RIAS process has been put in place in the last decade, a broader rationale has emerged to include the needs of risk assessment and management. This goes beyond earlier concerns about the costs of health and safety regulation but adds to the case for a process like RIAS and raises questions both about further regulatory review and the limits of state intervention. Accordingly, before looking at how RIAS works, these ideas about risk need to be explored.

The modern Canadian state is somehow expected to ensure that transport is safe, that the conditions under which we work are safe and secure, that the homes in which we live are well built, that the air we breathe is clean, that the water we use is free from bacteria, that the food we consume is free of any health hazards, that the deposits we make at our banks and credit unions are secure, and so on. We have built a great Canadian 'safety net' to protect us from many of the perceived and real risks in society. The creation of this safety net has had important economic and social ramifications.

Economists have long known that state attempts to completely eliminate or reduce risks are enormously costly. In whatever activity individuals partake, there is a risk and eliminating that risk carries a cost (Hahn 1996b, Douglas and Wildavsky 1982). When the risk of an activity is reduced by government regulation and other means, the cost of being involved in such an activity falls

– the reduction of risk changes the set of incentives facing a particular individual. The state, by and large, for various reasons is unable to charge an optimal premium for the reduction of certain risks. In private insurance markets, however, charging the optimal premium is normal (Skidelsky 1997).

When the state provides risk reduction programs, it encourages individuals to indulge in activities that they would not have participated in otherwise. For example, many consumer advocacy groups argue that the state should try to protect drivers and their passengers by enacting strict car safety regulations. The argument is that with safer cars, there will be fewer traffic accidents and deaths. Some economists have argued that with safer cars, individuals will indulge in more reckless behaviour, since the risk of being seriously harmed in an serious accident is diminished. Peltzman's analysis of the effects of the U.S. National Traffic and Motor Vehicle Safety Act of 1966 provides empirical support for this position (Peltzman 1975).

A recent study completed by Professor Kip Viscusi on child-resistant medicine bottle caps indicate that 3,500 additional poisonings of children under the age of five have occurred annually from aspirin-related drugs since the introduction of the caps (cited in Lott (1997)). How and why did this new risk reduction strategy fail? Quite simply, parents are lulled into a false sense of security and are not as vigilant. In insurance parlance, this phenomenon is known as 'moral hazard.' By changing the set of incentives facing individuals, a well-intentioned policy of risk reduction can encourage individuals to make socially costly choices and also hinder productivity growth, and, consequently, the standard of living (Gray 1987; Hahn and Hird 1991; Mihlar 1996, 1998).

Politicians and policy makers often fail to consider the unintended consequences of their actions in their quest to build this larger notion of a risk safety net. There are two important considerations that merit attention in this overall failure. The first is that life is an inherently risky venture and it is impossible to eliminate all of the risks we face. Indeed, it is impossible to eradicate some of the more substantial risks. In our quest to reduce or in some cases obliterate risks, we expend huge sums of money. In 1995–6, the whole array of federal, provincial, and local regulations cost Canadians $83.4 billion in compliance costs. The cost of regulatory compliance due to federal regulations alone constituted roughly $48 billion. The three levels of government in Canada impose an annual burden of approximately $12,000 per family of four (Mihlar 1998). Not all of these estimated costs deal with risk regulation, but a large part does.

Spending these huge sums of money to comply with regulations has opportunity costs. For example, loss of life expectancy (LLE) is estimated to be 3,500 days for anyone living in poverty. LLE due to risks such as air pollution, where we spend substantial amounts of resources, is estimated to be about eighty days. In the case of airline crashes, LLE is one day (Sutherland 1997).[1] The relevant question is: should you expend scarce resources trying to control risks that have diminishing returns or should you attempt to reduce poverty? Lack of jobs is the primary reason for the lack of an adequate standard of living. More regulations can retard economic activity and growth, which leads to fewer jobs. Therefore, in order to increase life expectancy, should we not be ensuring that we reduce the regulatory burden so that enterprise can flourish? Choosing to spend additional resources on minor risks and ignoring the diminishing returns on risk-reducing investments that impede economic activity will result in job losses, which will in turn increase poverty. We also pay a heavy price for risk reduction with limits to our individual freedoms (Hayek 1973).

The second consideration that merits attention is that of zero risks versus relative risks (Boulding and Purohit 1996; Bernstein 1996). These again raise questions about the scarcity of resources, the question of trade-offs in decision making, the regressive (taxing) nature of regulation, and the diminishing returns on more spending on safety issues. Consider, for example, the choice about how much should be spent on breast cancer initiatives as opposed to a national AIDS program? As Professor Bill Stanbury notes, 'In 1992, Health Canada pledged $25 million over five years to the Breast Cancer Initiative. At the same time, it allocated $203.5 million for a five-year national AIDS strategy. And yet, since 1982, just over 9,500 Canadians have died of AIDS, while more than 60,000 died of breast cancer. In 1994, 1,628 people died of AIDS, or about one-third the number who died of breast cancer (Stanbury 1996a).'

While recognizing the sanctity of each individual life in a world with limited resources, it is important to raise these kinds of questions explicitly, because governments make trade-offs on a daily basis in terms of spending money on or regulating activity X or Y. Implicitly, governments place a dollar value on life by their policy actions or inactions.

These are undoubtedly difficult choices, but one has to take the larger picture into account so as to allocate scarce resources meaningfully among competing health and safety risks in order to maximize the number of statistical lives saved. For this kind of thinking to occur, the federal government has to state explicitly how much will be spent on averting each statistical death. In other words, how much are Canadians willing to pay to save a life? While many Canadians will understandably be repulsed at the thought of putting a dollar value to life, it is necessary in order to ensure that we save as many lives as possible. Drawing from several American studies, Viscusi estimates the value of a single life to be between U.S.$ 3 million and U.S.$ 7 million. Evidence from the U.S. also suggests that some regulations end up costing over U.S.$ 100 million per statistical life saved (Viscusi 1992; Hahn 1996b). While data of this nature is sparse in Canada, there is no evidence to indicate that the situation here is any better (Kasperson and Kasperson 1983). Setting an upper limit on resources to be spent per statistical life saved, therefore, is critical if we are to avoid wasting increasingly scarce resources.

In short, a process is needed that will ensure that all of the regulatory initiatives emanating out of the different federal departments and agencies are compared and ranked according to their relative risk magnitudes and costs. This type of 'big picture' analysis would require the federal government to prioritize its regulatory initiatives and in fact to go beyond its RIAS process (Stanbury 1996a).

For a democracy to work and bureaucratic and political accountability to be meaningful, the public needs to be informed about the 'realities' of risk man- agement. For example, for all occupations except fishing, hunting, forestry, and mining, people are safer at their places of work than in their homes. In other words, the average annual risk of death from accidents in Canada is lower at work than at home (see Table 12.1). Statistics on accidents suggest that, for instance, in 1993, about 50 per cent of all accidents in Canada oc- curred either at home or while playing sports. These activities are not subject to many safety regulations. At the same time, as American studies show that it is important to recognize that attempting to regulate activities at home or at the playground could potentially be expensive and end up hurting more individuals (O'Tengs et al. 1995).

TABLE 12.1
Average Annual Risk of Death in Canada from Accidents

Hazard	Annual Risk of Death
Fishing and hunting	1 in 500*
Forestry	1 in 900
Mining	1 in 1,100
Accidents on the road	1 in 5,000
Accidents at home	1 in 11,000**
Accidents at work	1 in 24,000**
Public risk from nuclear waste	<1 in 2,000,000,000,000
Public risk from nuclear waste disposal underground	<1 in 2,000,000,000,000

* For every 500 people employed in fishing and hunting, about one of them will lose his or her life at work each year.
** For all occupations in general (except for the top three) people are safer at work than they are at home!
Most figures from *Canada: Living With Radiation*, AECB, 1995.
Source: John K. Sutherland, 'Science and Risk,' *Fraser Forum*, April 1997, 8.

A final recent example illustrates the problems inherent in risk reduction strategies pursued by government. Even though the number of deaths in 1994 due to maritime accidents was only 135, there is much speculation about regulating jet skis, based in part on some tragic accidents. In Canada, the probability of dying in a water-transport-related accident is 1 in 214,800, while the risk of dying in an accident at home is 1 in 7,392 (Stanbury 1996a). Yet we continue to insist on regulating smaller risks. The risk assessment agenda is nominally a part of the RIAS process but, as we will see below, the RIAS process is flawed even without taking the more difficult risk assessment into account.

The RIAS Process in Practice: An Evaluation

On paper, it appears that the federal government is keen to ensure that regulations do not stifle Canadian entrepreneurship and economic growth. In the federal government there is an explicit and increasingly transparent process for proposing, analysing, reforming, and eliminating regulations. The processes can include comparative risk analysis and cost-benefit studies.

In terms of reducing the number of regulations that are passed each year, the federal government has had some success. As Table 12.2 indicates, since 1986 the number of new or amended regulations passed by the federal government has declined, especially in the 1987–96 period. Or, more accurately, the rate of growth of regulation has declined while regulation has continued to increase. The RIAS process is not the only cause of this slowing of the rate of growth but it is partially responsible. Table 12.2 also shows the number of pages it takes to record the regulations. This is a decidedly secondary indicator but may capture some sense of the potential paper burden and the complexity of rules. The page totals actually increase in the 1988–90 period (possibly due to the implementation of free trade agreements) and then decline somewhat and stabilize. These regulations in total, of course, pose a significant cost burden to Canadian businesses and consumers.

Consider now the larger features of the analytical and procedural aspects of the RIAS. The RAD at the TBS is responsible for ensuring that departments and agencies follow the government's regulatory policy, particularly regulatory reform and regulatory management (Treasury Board Secretariat 1996). In other words, RAD is expected to perform a gatekeeper function. This suggests two basic evaluative questions:

1 Are the line departments complying with the requirements set forth? and
2 What is the quality of the RIAS and cost-benefit studies being submitted by the line departments?

TABLE 12.2
Number of Regulations Enacted Each Year by the Federal Government, 1975–1996

Year	Number of Regulations	Number of Pages
1975	844	3,343
1976	1,028	3,393
1977	1,383	5,366
1978	1,136	4,496
1979	1,148	4,539
1980	1,166	4,254
1981	1,196	3,916
1982	1,348	4,196
1983	1,181	4,444
1984	1,223	4,450
1985	1,392	4,976
1986	1,369	5,368
1987	991	4,732
1988	901	5,626
1989	840	5,226
1990	1,035	6,799
1991	885	4,830
1992	981	5,363
1993	874	4,636
1994	818	4,278
1995	683	—
1996	624	3,415

Source: Registrar of Regulations, Privy Council Office, Ottawa, July 1995; *Canada Gazette Part II* (Ottawa: Ministry of Supply and Services, 1995 and 1996).

Tables 12.3 and 12.4 provide some answers to these questions. My survey of the *Canada Gazette Part II*, where regulations and their RIAS are recorded, indicates that all too frequently line departments are not complying with the policy guidelines set by RAD. Thus RAD does not appear to be effectively exercising its gatekeeper function. More importantly, the RIAS were of poor quality, as evidenced by the lack of detail and quantification of costs and benefits. It is certainly true that some aspects of costs and benefits are difficult to quantify, however, even in cases where costs and benefits could have been easily quantified it was often not done.

The survey summarized in Tables 12.3 and 12.4 are based on a questionnaire using elements of the policy guidelines delineated by RAD (Regulatory Affairs Directorate 1995a). The federal government passed 683 and 634 regulations in 1995 and 1996 respectively. The following snapshot reveals that line

TABLE 12.3
An Analysis of Regulations Passed by the Federal Government, 1995

Regulation type and quantity		No	Yes	N/A
Amendment:	346			
New Regulation:	86			
Sub-total:	432			
Others:	251			
Total:	683			
1. Does it identify the objectives of the regulation?		114	572	0
2. Is there a RIAS?		127	419	138
3. Does it identify the regulatory alternative considered?		109	166	144
4. Does it identify the nonregulatory alternative considered?		193	71	155
5. If there is no alternative, is this explained?		31	114	275
6. Does it identify who will receive the benefit(s)? ✓		91	328	0
7. Does it detail (quantify) the benefits of the regulations?		347	72	0
8. Does it identify who will bear the cost? ✓		285	136	0
9. Does it detail (quantify) the cost?		372	47	0
10. Does it include compliance cost to industry/public?		256	34	129
11. Does it include cost to government?		398	16	3

Note: N/A: not applicable.
Source: Compiled from *Canada Gazette, Part II* (Ottawa: Ministry of Supply and Services, 1995); The Fraser Institute, 1997.

departments and the RAD are not fully ensuring that the regulations and amend- ✓ ments that are passed have a RIAS and/or pass a cost-benefit test.

In 1995, as Table 12.3 indicates, 127 regulations (29 per cent) passed did not have a RIAS. In 91 cases (21 per cent) the RIAS did not identify the beneficiaries of the regulation. More importantly, in 347 instances (80 per cent) no details on the benefits of regulation were provided (i.e., there was no quantification). In 285 cases (65 per cent) the RIAS did not identify who will bear the cost. In addition, in 372 instances (86 per cent) there were no details of the cost of regulation (i.e., no quantification). The survey also revealed that in 256 cases (59 per cent) the RIAS did not include the compliance cost to industry or the public. Finally, in 398 of the cases (92 per cent) the RIAS did not include the cost to the government of administering regulation.

In 1996, as Table 12.4 indicates, similar results are evident. In 50 cases (12 per cent) regulations that were passed did not have a RIAS. In 37 cases (9 per cent) the RIAS did not identify the beneficiaries of the regulation. More importantly, in 241 instances (60 per cent) there were no details on the benefits of regulation (no quantification). In 116 cases (29 per cent) the RIAS did not

TABLE 12.4
An Analysis of Regulations Passed by the Federal Government, 1996

Regulation type and quantity		No	Yes	N/A
Amendment:	339			
New Regulation:	61			
Sub-total:	400			
Others:	224			
Total:	624			
1. Does it identify the objectives of the regulation?		67	549	8
2. Is there a RIAS?		50	405	169
3. Does it identify the regulatory alternative considered?		103	146	156
4. Does it identify the non-regulatory alternative considered?		192	56	157
5. If there is no alternative, is this explained?		33	172	200
6. Does it identify who will receive the benefit(s)?		37	332	36
7. Does it detail (quantify) the benefits of the regulations?		241	126	38
8. Does it identify who will bear the cost?		116	160	129
9. Does it detail (quantify) the cost?		189	109	107
10. Does it include compliance cost to industry/public?		191	65	144
11. Does it include cost to government?		188	60	157

Note: N/A: not applicable.
Source: Compiled from *Canada Gazette, Part II* (Ottawa: Ministry of Supply and
Services, 1996); The Fraser Institute, 1997.

identify who will bear the cost. In addition, in 189 instances (47 per cent) no
details of the cost of regulation were provided (no quantification). The survey
also revealed that in 191 cases (47 per cent) the RIAS did not include the
compliance cost to industry or the public. Finally, in 188 of the cases (47 per
cent) the RIAS did not include the cost to the government of administering
regulations.

It may be argued that RIAS was never intended to be fully complied with.
Indeed, further pressures to be flexible about regulation have also entered the
equation in recent years. However, even taking into account the fact that the
RIAS process is centred on guidelines, the tables show that non-compliance is
far too high and that the credibility of the policy is thus compromised. The
RAD and federal departments do not measure the costs and benefits of proposed new regulations in the majority of instances. Moreover, it appears that
the RAD does not count whether this policy requirement is met.

Other anecdotal evidence does not build confidence in the process. In April
1996, for example, the federal government announced that it would prohibit
the production and sale of raw cheese due to human health concerns. This ban
was suggested without any cost-benefit study and the RIAS process was seemingly evaded. The minimal risks to human health and the fact that this regula-

tion would have killed a fledgling industry appears to have been of little or no concern to the regulators. It was only due to the later recommendations of a scientific panel that, to the relief of many in the industry, this regulation was not enacted (Mihlar 1996, 38).

Clearly, while the RIAS process acknowledges risk assessment as a problem it is not particularly or centrally geared to risk management. Even in its more limited sphere of ensuring more rational regulation there is too much non-compliance. RIAS, or some amended version of it, is even more badly needed for risk management but the prospects of further elaboration and change are unlikely.

Conclusion

The RIAS process originated out of a mixture of rationales and pressures, each important and each contributing to the eventual requirements put in place in 1986–7. The broader issues of risk analysis and management constitute an even more vital basis for the need for a RIAS process or an amended version thereof but to date the federal government has not effectively or adequately complied with its own regulatory policies. The rhetoric of regulatory reform of successive governments at the federal level has not resulted in truly effective action.

The Chrétien government was twice elected on a job creation platform and has emphasized the need for creating an environment conducive to job creation. For example, in 1994, a report by the Small Business Working Committee established by Ottawa is reflective of the platitudes about the connection between regulatory reform and job creation. The report stated: 'Too many regulations are developed and administered with little consideration given to their impact on the competitiveness of small businesses. Governments must regulate less, simplify paperwork, limit information requirements and get out of the way so that small businesses can focus on creating wealth and jobs.' (Small Business Working Committee 1994, 3). Given that the objective of the federal government is to prevent entrepreneurs from being stifled by unnecessary and costly regulations, so that they can invest and create jobs, the regulatory bureaucracy should be ensuring that RAD guidelines are followed. Unfortunately, the aims of the regulatory reform process and outcomes have too often been circumvented by the incentives inherent in the safety-net state apparatus and its apparent quest to protect Canadians from all real and perceived risks. Line departments should also be held accountable for not adhering to RAD guidelines. In the final analysis, due to the lack of bureaucratic accountability to their political masters, political accountability to the public is diminished.

The federal government clearly recognizes that there is a cost of regulation to the economy and that regulation frequently has an adverse effect on economic activity and job creation. At the same time, successive federal governments have failed to recognize the unintended consequences of attempting to alleviate through regulation most, if not all, of the risks facing Canadians.

It is time for the federal government to improve the regulatory decision-making process by insisting that its departments and agencies, especially in a risk management age, rely on solid science, comparative risk assessment, and rigorous cost-benefit studies, and that they have a management structure that will ensure that these changes are carried out.

NOTES

Special thanks are owed to Danielle Smith and Liv Fredericksen for their superb research assistance.

1 In the case of air pollution and airline crashes, the estimated number of days lost is based on the average over the total population and in the case of poverty risk, it is based on those exposed to the particular risk. For details, see Sutherland (1997), 5–11.

REFERENCES

Bernstein, Peter L. 1996. *Against the Gods: The Remarkable Story of Risk.* New York: Wiley.

Block, Walter, and George Lermer, eds. 1991. *Breaking the Shackles: Deregulating Canadian Industry.* Vancouver: Fraser Institute.

Boulding, William, and Devaurat Purohit. 1996. The Price of Safety. *Journal of Consumer Research* 23 (June): 12–25.

Canada Gazette. 1995 and 1996. Various issues. Ottawa: Ministry of Supply and Services.

Douglas, M., and A. Wildavsky. 1982. *Risk and Culture.* Berkeley: University of California Press.

Doern, G. Bruce, and Richard Phidd. 1992. *Canadian Public Policy: Ideas, Structure, Process.* 2nd ed. Toronto: Nelson Canada.

Economic Council of Canada. 1979. *Responsible Regulation.* Ottawa: Canadian Government Publishing Centre.

Gray, Wayne B. 1987. The Cost of Regulation: OSHA, EPA, and the Productivity Slowdown. *American Economic Review* (December): 998–1006.

Hahn, Robert. 1996a. Regulatory Reform: What do Government Numbers Tell Us? Paper presented at the American Enterprise Institute Conference, Reviving Regulatory Reform, Washington, D.C.

– ed. 1996b. *Risks, Costs and Lives Saved: Getting Better Results from Regulation.* New York: Oxford University Press.

Hahn, Robert, and John Hird. 1991. The Costs and Benefits of Regulation: Review and Synthesis. *Yale Journal of Regulation* 8, no. 1: 233–78.

Hayek, F.A. 1973. *Law, Legislation and Liberty.* Chicago: University of Chicago Press.

Kasperson, Roger E., and Jeanne X. Kasperson. 1983. Determining the Acceptability of Risks: Ethical and Policy Issues. In J.T. Rogers and D.V. Bates, eds., *Risk: A Symposium on the Assessment and Perception of Risk to Human Health in Canada.* Ottawa: Royal Society of Canada.

Lott, John R. 1997. Gun Locks: Bound to Misfire. *Wall Street Journal*, 16 July.

Mihlar, Fazil. 1996. Regulatory Overkill: The Cost of Regulation in Canada. *Critical Issues Bulletin.* Vancouver: Fraser Institute.

– 1998. *The Cost of Regulation in Canada.* Vancouver: Fraser Institute.

O'Tengs, Tammy. 1997. Dying Too Soon: How Cost Effectiveness Analysis Can Save Lives. *NCPA Policy Report # 204.* Dallas, Texas: National Centre for Policy Alternatives.

O'Tengs, Tammy, Miriam E. Adams, Joseph S. Pliskin, Dana Gelb Safran, Joanna E. Siegel, Milton C. Weinstein, and John D. Graham. 1995. Five Hundred Life-Saving Interventions and their Cost Effectiveness. *Risk Analysis* 15, no 3: 369–90.

Peltzman, Sam. 1975. The Effects of Automobile Safety Legislation. *Journal of Political Economy* 83, no 4: 677–725.

Peters, Guy. 1998. Regulatory Institutions in American Government: Deinstitutionalization and Reinstitutionalization. In G. Bruce Doern and Stephen Wilks, eds., *Changing Regulatory Institutions in Britain and North America*, ch. 3. Toronto: University of Toronto Press.

Regulatory Affairs Directorate. 1995a. *Regulatory Policy.* November.

– 1995b. *Regulation Review – Checklist.* Ottawa: Treasury Board Secretariat.

Schultz, Richard J. 1988. Regulating Conservatively: The Mulroney Record, 1984–88. In Andrew Gollner and Daniel Salee, eds., *Canada Under Mulroney*, 186–205. Montreal: Véhicule Press.

Skidelsky, Robert. 1997. *Beyond the Welfare State.* London: Social Market Foundation. ✓

Small Business Working Group. 1994. *Report of Small Business Working Group.* Ottawa: Industry Canada.

Stanbury, W.T. 1992a. Assessment of Efforts to Reform the Federal Regulatory Process. In Canada. *House of Commons. Standing Committee on Finance, Regulations and Competitiveness.* Ottawa: Supply and Services Canada.

– 1992b. Efforts to Reform the Federal Regulatory Process in Canada in Thomas Hopkins, ed., *Regulatory Policy in Canada and the United States: Proceedings of a Conference.* Rochester: Rochester Institute of Technology.

– 1996a. *Routine Pathologies of Regulations Designed to Reduce Risks to Human Health and Safety.* Ottawa: Competition Bureau, Industry Canada.

– ed. 1996b. *Perspectives on the New Economics of Telecommunications*. Montreal: The Institute for Research on Public Policy.

Sutherland, John K. 1997. Science and Risk. *Fraser Forum* (April): 8.

Treasury Board of Canada Secretariat. 1996. *Managing Regulation in Canada: Regulatory Affairs Guide*. Ottawa: Treasury Board Secretariat.

Viscusi, Kip W. 1992. *Fatal Trade-offs: Public and Private Responsibilities for Risks*. New York: Oxford University Press.

13

Where the Regulated Are the Regulators: Privacy Protection within the Contemporary Canadian State

COLIN J. BENNETT

The policy-making literature contains a number of definitions of 'regulation' or 'regulatory policy' that display a 'confusing mix of intentions, consequences, objectives, tools, processes and targets' (Schultz and Alexandroff 1985, 3). The conceptual confusion reflects a common dilemma in political science, between balancing the 'connotation' and 'denotation' of a concept (Sartori 1970). Does one restrict the connotation (the properties that determine the things to which the word applies) to limit the denotation and assist the discovery of empirical referents and the building of parsimonious theory? Or does one adopt a more expansive approach, thus sacrificing precision but directing the spotlight on otherwise neglected aspects of the phenomenon?

In this chapter I adopt the latter strategy, recognizing that regulation is a 'multi-functional instrument' as well as an activity the target of which is not simply the economic behaviour of private sector firms and businesses (Schultz and Alexandroff 1985, 5). One recent and quite expansive definition sees regulation as a 'process or activity in which government requires or proscribes certain activities or behaviour on the part of individuals and institutions, mostly private *but sometimes public*, and does so through a continuing administrative process, generally through specially designated regulatory agencies' (Reagan 1987, 18 [my emphasis]). This formulation is useful for my purposes because it recognizes that the object of regulation (both at individual and collective levels) can be within the public sector. Most conceptions of regulation imply that the targets are actors external to the institutions of the state, a restriction of the concept that would exclude much of the policy sector analysed in this chapter, that of privacy protection.

The distinction between 'external' and 'internal' targets for the rules and instruments that comprise regulatory policy does, of course, raise theoretically and empirically questionable issues about the distinction between state and society. Most contemporary policy analysts are careful not to fall into the trap of assuming that there is a clear boundary between the public and the private, and recognize the existence of a complex range of 'mixed instruments' that span the state/society divide (e.g., Howlett and Ramesh (1995), 91). The literature on regulation has moved some way from the early American formulations that were based on Lowi's initial (1964) taxonomy of distributive, redistributive, and regulatory policy (e.g., Ripley and Franklin (1976), 21–6). Our categories are now far more sensitive to the spectrum of substantive and procedural instruments the locations of which within the state/society continuum are difficult to position, and whose degree of coercion varies in complicated and dynamic ways (Doern and Phidd 1992, 96–8; Howlett and Ramesh 1995, 82). We now have a more sophisticated and realistic appreciation of the 'tools of government' (Hood 1986).

However, this chapter argues (returning to Reagan's definition above) that most classifications and models still rely on the notion of a target for regulatory policy that is external to the institutions of the state. Both public and private actors and institutions might be involved in the delivery and implementation of public policy, and much of the theoretical effort has been devoted to developing frameworks that are sensitive to that variability in state involvement. Thus, most definitions of regulation and attempts to classify policy instruments rest on the assumption that there is an external target group whose behaviour needs to be changed if the programmatic goals of the policy are to be achieved.

This chapter shows that the 'target group,' admittedly an imprecise one, is principally located within the state. The impact of the policy is measured and evaluated in terms of changes in the behaviour of individuals and agencies that are internal, rather than external, to the state. Policy objectives do not exist independently of the structures and processes of the public bureaucracy. The regulated are the regulators.

However, only a few areas of public policy fall within this category and such phenomenon have not been completely ignored in the literature. One might argue that Lowi's later addition of a 'constituent' policy type to his initial threefold framework was intended to embrace this condition (Lowi 1972, 300). Schultz and Alexandroff (1985, 4) recognize also that many 'public' actors such as Air Canada, the CBC, and the Canadian National Railways are subject to regulation.

The four-regime typology that underpins this book (see Chapter 1) also provides some useful insights into 'how the regulatory function is managed within the executive or even within the state as a whole' (Doern 1996, 9). Doern specifies that these regimes should be seen as 'interlocking circles,' recognizing that the 'relative presence of the regimes varies across sectors' (Doern 1996, 5). Regime III in particular helps our understanding of this phenomenon, but I would contend that the phenomenon of 'internal' regulation is often overlooked in the theoretical work and definitely underresearched in the empirical literature. I would also insist that, if distinct types of policy are associated with distinct types of politics (an assumption that again flows from Lowi's early work), then we would expect such policy to be associated with some distinctive patterns of behaviour during policy formulation and implementation and, perhaps, some very different incentives for compliance.

This chapter examines these larger points with reference to the attempts within Canada to regulate the collection, storage, processing, and dissemination of personal data. These goals are expressed within 'privacy' legislation, although a more accurate label is used in European societies – 'data protection.' The chapter first outlines the general properties of data protection policy before describing how privacy is 'regulated' within Canada, and especially within the Canadian federal government through the 1982 Canadian Privacy Act. I then outline the powers and responsibilities of the central regulatory agency, the Office of the Privacy Commissioner of Canada (OPC) with appropriate comparisons with its provincial counterparts. The goals of this legislation – to regulate the conditions under which personal data are collected, processed, and disseminated by the agencies of the federal government – have produced some distinctive patterns of bureaucratic resistance. These patterns are described with reference to case studies from the history of data protection policy in Canada. The chapter concludes with a return to the wider policy literature and attempts to analyse data protection with reference to key classifications within this literature, that is, what policy type is exemplified here and what regulatory regime is associated with this particular set of 'organizations, statutes, ideas, interests and processes'(Doern 1996, 5).

The Properties of Data Protection Policy

Privacy is a complex, controversial, and multifaceted concept and there is an enormous body of philosophical, legal, and social scientific literature on the many dimensions of this subject (see Schoeman (1984)). The term overlaps with a number of interrelated values, including autonomy, solitude, intimacy, anonymity, reserve, and others (Flaherty 1989, 8). It can serve to justify a right to make private decisions, especially about intimate sexual and familial matters. It can be invoked to limit surveillance by law enforcement agencies. It also has a spatial dimension, referring to the claim for an exclusive physical space around individuals.

It is important, therefore, to stress that in this chapter I am concerned with information privacy or data protection, the aim of which is to grant individuals a higher level of control over the information that circulates about them (Westin 1967). The combination of two central characteristics of advanced industrial states, complex organizations and information technology, has produced a range of concerns about the erosion of information privacy. The problems associated with the increased capability of organizations to collect, store, manipulate, and disseminate vast quantities of personal data have been recognized since the 1960s. The principal policy response has been to enact data protection laws. These include the American Privacy Act of 1974, the Canadian Privacy Act of 1982, the UK Data Protection Act of 1984, and the German Data Protection Act of 1978, among others. Some twenty-two advanced industrial states have passed some version of data protection law to regulate the personal data held in public, and in many cases private, organizations (Bennett 1997b).

All such laws are founded upon a common set of 'fair information principles' for the treatment of personal data. These boil down to the following: the existence of personal record-keeping systems should be publicly known; individuals should have rights of access and correction to their own data; personal data should only be collected for legitimate and openly stated purposes; personal data should only be used (internally) in ways that are relevant to those purposes; personal data should only be disclosed (externally) in ways that are consistent with those purposes – unless the individual consents; and adequate and appropriate security safeguards should be established (Bennett 1992). At the level of the basic statutory principles, data protection policies have converged.

The laws differ on the extent of organizational coverage – those in North America mainly regulate the public sector, whereas those elsewhere (especially in Europe) encompass all organizations. They also differ in the extent to which they regulate noncomputerized files (i.e., the manila folder in the filing cabinet). Most notably, they differ with regard to the policy instruments established for oversight and regulation. Many countries (with the notable exception of the United States) have set up small privacy or data protection agencies with varying oversight, advisory, or regulatory powers (Flaherty 1989). The explanation for these patterns of convergence and divergence has been provided elsewhere (Bennett 1992).

Data protection is now institutionalized. In twenty-five years or so, it has acquired all the characteristics of a policy sector: a set of statutory instruments, regulatory bodies established to implement these laws, a circle of legal experts, a small group of journalists ready to publicize information abuses, a growing academic community with expertise in data protection and privacy, and a range of international fora in which the policy community can exchange ideas, collaborate, and negotiate a number of international agreements and conventions (e.g., OECD (1981); Council of Europe (1981); European Union (1995)). Data protection policy will be with us as long as we have complex organizations and high technology.

Regulating Privacy in Canada

The forces that brought the privacy issue to the agenda in Canada were generally the same as those in other countries: the computerization of personal information systems (especially in the public sector) and the development of a universal identifier (the Social Insurance Number) were the prominent concerns in the 1960s (Bennett 1990). There followed a quiet and wide-ranging debate about the issue over the next decade, focusing in particular on the recommendations of a task force report from the Department of Justice (Justice Canada 1972).

The first privacy legislation at the federal level was actually contained in Part IV of the 1977 Canadian Human Rights Act, which established the Office of the Privacy Commissioner, a member of the Canadian Human Rights Commission, whose main task was to receive complaints from the general public, conduct investigations, and make recommendations to Parliament. While Part IV succeeded in codifying the fair information principles in legislation for the first time, privacy sat very uneasily within a statute devoted to the question of discrimination, a related but obviously more controversial issue that tended to overshadow the importance of privacy protection (Bennett 1990, 559).

Parallel debates over a federal Access to Information Act in the early 1980s raised immediate questions about the compatibility between such legislation and the privacy standards within Part IV. The current 1982 Privacy Act, therefore, flows from a belief that data protection should be a corollary to freedom of information, and that the various exemptions in both pieces of legislation should be consistent. Bill C-43, incorporating an Access to Information Act and a revised Privacy Act, was passed by Parliament in 1982 and received Royal Assent in July 1983. The Canadian innovation of legislating access to information and privacy protection within the same statutory framework was later copied by many of the provinces: Quebec (1982), Ontario (1988), British Columbia (1993), and Alberta (1995). As of 1997, only Prince Edward Island currently lacks a legislated privacy protection policy for the personal information held by public agencies.

The passage in 1993 of Quebec's Bill 68, 'An Act Respecting the protection of personal information in the private sector,' gave effect to the information privacy rights incorporated in the new Civil Code and made Quebec the first jurisdiction in North America to produce comprehensive data protection rules for the private sector. Bill 68 applies to all pieces of personal information collected, held, used, or distributed by enterprises engaged in an 'organized economic activity.' Personal data shall be collected from and with the consent of the person concerned, and shall not be communicated, sold, leased, or traded without the consent of that person. The Commission d'Accès à l'Information du Québec, the body established under the 1982 public sector access and privacy law, oversees its implementation, hears complaints, and renders binding decisions.

After Quebec's action, Canada became the only country in which the scope of privacy protection in one of its member jurisdictions exceeds that of the federal government. In the rest of the country, we find only a few isolated statutes relating to specific sectors, such as the consumer credit industry (Bennett 1995). There may also be certain common law remedies and constitutional provisions of potential relevance (Lawson 1992). In general, however, legal remedies for the protection of personal data in the private sector are few and far between.

Canadian privacy protection policy has been described by the federal privacy commissioner as a 'patchwork' (Privacy Commission of Canada 1994, 5). Legislation embodying the standard set of 'fair information principles' applies to public agencies at the federal level and in most provinces. With the exception of Quebec, privacy protection in the private sector is largely dependent on the implementation of a set of voluntary and sectoral codes of practice developed according to the framework of the 1981 *OECD Guidelines* (Bennett 1995). A number of political, international, technological, and legislative developments have now convinced federal policy makers that this incoherent policy cannot be allowed to continue.

First, the recent passage of the European Union's *Data Protection Directive* (European Union 1995) will mean that no jurisdiction in Canada (save Quebec) can plausibly claim an 'adequate level of protection' and therefore safely process personal data transmitted from EU countries. Second, the passage of the Quebec legislation has created an 'unlevel playing field' within the Canadian federation, creating uncertainties and transaction costs for businesses that operate in different provinces (Bennett 1996). Third, the publication of a series of public opinion surveys has demonstrated that the general public regards privacy protection as a matter of major concern (Ekos Research Associates 1993; Harris and Westin 1995; Public Interest Advocacy Centre 1995). Fourth, the commercialization of some governmental functions has undermined the implementation of public sector data protection law and the ability of Canada's privacy commissioners to ensure the protection of personal data when it is transferred to a private contractor. Finally, the debates over the development and character of the Canadian 'information highway' have exposed the need for a common set of 'rules of the road' for the networked and distributed computing and communications environment of the twenty-first century (Information Highway Advisory Council 1995; Cavoukian and Tapscott 1995).

This current analysis, therefore, is conducted amidst a growing expectation that the patchwork will be replaced by a more coherent regulatory system for privacy protection, probably based upon the recently issued Canadian Standards Association's Model Code for the Protection of Personal Information (Canadian Standards Association 1996). In September 1995 the federal Advisory Council for the Information Highway, operating under the auspices of Industry Canada (Information Highway Advisory Council 1995), called on the federal government to: 'create a level playing field for the protection of personal information on the Information Highway by developing and implementing a flexible legislative framework for both public and private sectors. Legislation would require sectors or organizations to meet the standard of the *CSA Model Code*, while allowing the flexibility to determine how they will refine their own codes' (Information Highway Advisory Council 1995, 141).

On 23 May 1996 federal Industry Minister John Manley released the government's response to the IHAC report, in which it was concluded that 'the right to privacy must be recognized in law, especially in an electronic world of private databases where it is all too easy to collect and exploit information about individual citizens' (Industry Canada 1996, 25). In September 1996, Justice Minister Allan Rock addressed the Annual Conference of the International Privacy and Data Protection Commissioners in Ottawa and clarified this commitment: 'By the year 2000, we aim to have federal legislation on the books that will provide effective, enforceable protection of privacy rights in the private sector.' Thus the Government of Canada has reconsidered its two-tiered approach of legislation for the public sector and voluntary self-regulation for the private: 'The protection of personal information can no longer depend on whether the data is held by a public or a private institution' (Rock 1996). In an era of deregulation, privacy protection stands out as one of the few areas of public policy in which an extension of the scope of regulation is being seriously contemplated (Bennett 1997a). As I write, privacy legislation for the private sector (Bill C-54) has just been tabled in the House of Commons.

The Rules: The Privacy Act of 1982

In the absence of further reform, however, my analysis of privacy as a regulatory policy will focus on the implementation of the 1982 Federal Privacy Act and upon its implementation within the agencies of the federal government.

This legislation covers all federal government departments and a diverse range of other boards, agencies, and Crown corporations. A significant record of implementation can now be evaluated, in particular through the annual reports of the OPC.

The basic 'fair information principles' all find expression in the Privacy Act. Section 4 provides that 'no personal information shall be collected by a government institution unless it relates directly to an operating program or activity of the institution.' Section 5 stipulates that 'wherever possible personal information should be collected directly from the individual to whom it relates,' and that the individual shall be informed of the 'purpose for which the information is being collected.' Section 6 requires that personal information shall be retained and disposed of according to regulation, and that it should be as 'accurate, up-to-date and complete as possible.' Section 7 perhaps contains the central information privacy principle: 'personal information under the control of a government institution shall not, without the consent of the individual to whom it relates, be used by the institution except for the purpose for which the information was obtained or compiled by the institution or for a use consistent with that purpose.' Section 8 then lists thirteen separate uses and disclosures that might be permissible without individual consent.

Sections 10 and 11 express the principle of transparency, by requiring the proper indexing and publication of 'personal information banks.' Sections 12 to 17 grant a right of access and correction (subject to certain exemptions and procedures) for the individual to whom the data pertain. The rest of the statute defines those databanks and classes of information that are exempt from individual access. Various classes of information are defined for which the head of the government agency is required to refuse access (specifically personal information obtained in confidence from another government or international organization). Other classes are defined for which access is a matter of discretion on the part of the head of the institution concerned (including information that may prejudice federal-provincial relations, international affairs, defence, law enforcement, lawyer-client privilege, or an individual's physical or mental health). Many of these exemptions were modelled on the provisions of the American Privacy Act of 1974 (Bennett 1990, 564).

We have in the 1982 Privacy Act a set of rules that enjoin openness in some circumstances and confidentiality in others. The statute is designed to achieve the rational ideal of an optimum social balance between 'discretionary power and control by formal rules.' It aims to state explicitly all exceptions to the rule. It tries to be perfectly flexible and adaptable to all possible situations and tries to be neutral, affecting everybody similarly. It is written to be 'perfectly enforced' through automatic and unswerving application. The Privacy Act, like other data protection statutes, is a rule that attempts to approximate what Deborah Stone calls the 'rationality model' of rule making (Stone 1997, 300).

The Regulators

The principal, though by no means the only agency that is given oversight responsibility for the Privacy Act is the Office of the Privacy Commissioner of Canada. The privacy commissioner is appointed by the governor-in-council, after approval by resolution of both the Senate and the House of Commons, for a seven-year term, which may be renewed. Three individuals have so far occupied this office: Inger Hansen (1977–82), John Grace (1983–90), and the current occupant, Bruce Phillips. The office is separate from that which oversees the Access to Information Act, although they share a corporate management branch. Proposals to merge the two positions have occasionally been made.

The Office of the Privacy Commissioner currently has a staff of thirty-eight and a budget of nearly $3 million (OPC 1996, 63). It has the following responsibilities (see also the Appendix to this chapter). First and foremost, it receives and investigates complaints – the traditional 'ombudsman' role. The legislation specifies in considerable detail (sections 29–35) the procedures and powers for receiving, investigating, and reporting the results of complaints. Much of the work, then, is reactive. Second, the OPC can conduct investigations and audits of government departments; an audit program has been a constant, if underresourced, component of the OPC's work from the outset. Third, the commissioner can commission special studies of practices and technologies that have privacy implications. Reports on AIDS (OPC 1989), drug-testing (OPC 1990), and genetic testing (OPC 1992b) have been the most prominent. Other, shorter fact sheets are also released from time to time, even though no general educational mandate is included in the legislation. This contrasts with the more expansive list of powers granted to the commissioner's counterparts, and particularly the information and privacy commissioners of BC and Ontario, both of whom have order-making powers.

The OPC is the main, but not the only, agency responsible for oversight of the Privacy Act. Day-to-day advice on the implementation of the Act is the responsibility of Treasury Board, which also compiles and publishes the list of personal information banks. The Information and Privacy Branch of the Department of Justice gives day-to-day legal advice on the interpretation of both privacy and access to information statutes. To underscore the point about the lack of a distinction between the regulators and the regulated, the Privacy Act makes clear that primary responsibility for implementation rests with the 'designated minister' or 'head' of the government institution in question. The law then embodies a significant degree of 'self-regulation'; most of the implementation of the privacy rules takes place away from the gaze of the OPC.

The other actors within the community of regulators are, of course, individual citizens. The importance of the privacy commissioner would be undermined if citizens did not register complaints about the collection, storage, and dissemination of personal information. The operation of the entire regime also relies to some extent on individuals exercising their rights to access and correct personal information.

The implementation of data protection policy thus involves a considerable degree of learning and mutual adjustment and readjustment (Raab 1993). It is not characterized by a top-down process of command, control, and sanction. Consequently, 'data protection should not be seen as a system producing outputs and outcomes, but as a process that involves organizational change and learning and that involves a large implementation network of persons and organizations engaged in the co-production of data protection' (Raab and Bennett 1996, 553).

The Regulated: Patterns of Cooperation and Non-cooperation within the Canadian State

There is no defined 'interest' that opposes higher levels of privacy protection. No organization or actor fails to comply with the fair information principles because it does not believe that privacy is an important social value. For the most part, the regulation of privacy is not marked by highly public conflicts with resistant and non-compliant federal agencies. There are exceptions, when the practices of one or more federal departments are occasionally exposed to criticism in the privacy commissioner's annual reports. But this generally is not representative of the regulatory style. Any resistance to the implementation of privacy is more subtle, producing a very irregular, fluctuating, and somewhat informal policy dynamic. The privacy commissioner possesses a limited set of policy tools in terms of powers, resources, and personnel and he must use these resources carefully and sparingly. The limitations of the resources, together with the rapidly changing nature of the privacy issue, have produced certain characteristics of the regulatory process, which are described below.

The Marginalization of Privacy Protection within Federal Agencies

The absence of long pitched battles between the privacy regulators and opposing organizational interests is mainly attributable to certain features of Privacy Act enforcement. First, there are some key exemptions within the Act itself. In particular, the fact that large areas of information related to 'law enforcement' matters can be shared among government agencies with few restrictions and exempted from access by the individual to whom the record pertains places a number of controversial surveillance practices beyond the reach of the OPC. There are also a number of 'exempt data banks,' including those operated by the Canadian Security and Intelligence Service (CSIS) and the Communications Security Establishment (CSE).

A second feature that serves to distance privacy regulators from certain key areas is that the Privacy Act does not require agencies to consult with the OPC when developing new technologies or services. Consequently, the OPC has constantly to try to inject a privacy perspective at the earliest stages of the legislative process, technology development, or service delivery. High-profile legislative changes that involve radical implications for the processing of personal information are often the circumstances under which consultation is the most serious; examples would be the proposal for a DNA databank (OPC 1995, 19), or the new permanent voters register and the new firearms registry (OPC 1996, 47). Such developments are normally attended by significant media interest. The commissioner has commented that 'privacy staff are now more likely to be consulted early in program design and service delivery' (1996, 47).

On other occasions, however, the privacy commissioner has complained that privacy protection is a last-minute 'add-on' and that his staff are not consulted early enough in the policy development process. In some cases, the advice of the privacy commissioner is ignored completely. In 1989, the Treasury Board issued a regulation on the practice of 'computer matching' (the comparison of discrete databanks to identify those improperly receiving government benefits and services). This regulation requires government departments to provide a prior cost-benefit analysis, to notify the OPC sixty days prior to when the program is supposed to begin, to account publicly for all matching programs, and to verify the information generated by matching programs before using it. This policy is virtually ignored. The privacy commissioner complained in his 1990–1 annual report that 'some departments seem to view the Commissioner's role as something of a rubber stamp to be applied after a last minute phone call' (OPC 1991, 47). In 1991–2, the OPC reported the receipt of only three computer matches, all from Agriculture Canada (1992a, 38). If more pressing programmatic goals override privacy protection (and they often do), then agencies have a wide latitude to treat the issue in a perfunctory manner.

The perennial problem is that privacy can always be subordinated to other social and political goals and interests. Voters and their elected representatives tend to be more concerned about effective law enforcement, the efficient delivery of services, the responsible management of the government deficit, managed health care, and so on. Collective demands and interests still sustain the actors, policies, and institutions of the Canadian state. And it is exactly these more materialistic policies that require the effective management of personal information, and which then clash with the more postmaterialistic values that are embraced by the term 'privacy.' This tension will endure and subsume the implementation of data protection policy to a range of collective interests that provide more short-term benefits to elected and unelected public officials of all political persuasions (Bennett 1992, 253–4).

The Tension between Reactive and Anticipatory Roles

The privacy commissioner is mandated to receive and investigate complaints, a task that consumes an extensive proportion of the OPC's personnel and financial resources. Complaints must be logged, categorized, and, if necessary, investigated. From 1995–6, the office received 1,625 complaints, completed 1,681 (including of course many carried forward from the previous year), and had a further 1,630 complaints under investigation (OPC 1996, 43–5) This work is reactive, time-consuming, and often disconnected from larger policy solutions. The privacy commissioner extols the virtues of an 'ounce of prevention' (1996, 47) but has few resources to concentrate on functions that are more general and anticipatory in nature.

The office's audit program for several years concentrated on particular agencies, which had been identified through a pattern of complaints as warranting attention. The OPC now concentrates on practices and technologies that span institutions. This has resulted in more general guidelines (on practices such as the use of fax machines, on 'surfing' the Internet, and so on). However, much more could be achieved with further resources. The tension between the reactive and anticipatory functions is a perennial one, not only for the privacy commissioner of Canada, but also for his provincial and international counterparts.

The Erosion of Institutional and Technological Boundaries

Where the 'public' sector ends and the 'private' sector begins is increasingly difficult to determine. Questions raised about the application and meaning of the privacy provisions in the federal Privacy Act and related provincial statutes will have an evolving impact on the practices of the private sector. The federal privacy commissioner has been drawing attention to the privacy implications of commercializing government operations for several years. In his 1991–2 annual report (OPC 1992a, 76), he complained that 'personal files handed over to private firms get no formal privacy protection unless specific clauses are written into the contracts' – and they rarely are. In 1996, citing the new air navigation system (NAVCANADA) as an example, Bruce Phillips noted that privatization can effectively end the privacy rights of clients and employees (OPC 1996, 1–2).

The distinction between the public and the private is eroded whenever 'private' organizations perform traditional 'public' functions and require the use of 'public' data to fulfil those obligations. Other illustrations include the use of smart cards and ATM machines for the dispensing of government benefits; the matching of data on welfare recipients with bank or financial records to ascertain eligibility; the trading of government personal information to enhance revenue; and the use of credit reports for security checks.

The Privacy Act was written to respond to the problems inherent in a relatively manageable number of discrete 'databanks' or 'personal information systems,' each maintained for precisely defined purposes. Since 1982 the technological environment has become more distributed, networked, dynamic, and complicated. Personal data is not processed in distinct stages (collection, storage, disclosure, etc.) and it knows fewer organizational attachments. Responsibility for those data is now far more difficult to locate. The pervasiveness and adaptability of the new technologies will make it increasingly difficult to determine which organizations in which location 'hold' personal data, and therefore what rules (if any) apply.

The Complex, Dynamic, and Global Character of the Privacy Issue

The privacy commissioner and his colleagues must now attempt to comprehend the implications of a staggering range of new surveillance tools. Table 13.1 indicates that the range of 'privacy issues' mentioned within annual reports from 1983 to 1996. It also roughly outlines the variety of new technologies that the privacy commissioner and his staff must comprehend and attempt to regulate from a privacy point of view. The table indicates that the range of issues has been extended, that the technologies have become more complex, and that these practices may involve a variety of public and private organizations over which the federal privacy commissioner may not have jurisdiction. The OPC must therefore constantly educate itself about these practices and technologies. Increasingly, the office cannot respond unless the commissioner receives the cooperation of provincial and/or international counterparts.

As a result, the privacy commissioner has also become an international actor. If personal data can be instantaneously transmitted through transnational networks, then the commissioner needs to be in close contact with counterparts

TABLE 13.1
Mention of Privacy Issues in Annual Reports of the Federal Privacy Commissioner

Issue	83/4	84/5	85/6	86/7	87/8	88/9	89/90	90/1	91/2	92/3	93/4	94/5	95/6	96/7
Wiretapping	•			—				•						
Cell phone surveillance								•		•				
Call display									•					
E-mail surveillance/ encryption												•		
Cookies														
Anonymous remailers														
Clipper chip														
Telemarketing								•			•			
Direct mail						•		•			•			
Credit-reporting		•							•					
Interactive cable services														
Video rental														
Keystroke monitoring														
Video cameras in workplace			•											
Security cards														
Drug testing						•	•	•		•		•		
Active badges														
'Smart' cards								•	•	•	•		•	
Driver & vehicle reg. systems														
Personal identification numbers														
Pharmaceutical databases											•			
Patient & medical records	—	—		—		—				•	•			
Collection & use of census data								•	•			—	•	
Criminal record matching													•	
Computer profiling /matching	•	•	•	•		•		•	•		•			
Video-surveillance														
Electronic monitoring devices														
Genetic databanks													•	

TABLE 13.1 *(continued)*
Mention of Privacy Issues in Annual Reports of the Federal Privacy Commissioner

Issue	83/4	84/5	85/6	86/7	87/8	88/9	89/90	90/1	91/2	92/3	93/4	94/5	95/6	96/7
AIDS					•	•		•	•	—				
Transborder data flow		•	•					•						
Contracting out of processing					•	•			•	•	—	•	•	
S.I.N.		•	•	•	•		•	•	•	—		•	—	
Exempt banks		•	•	—			•		—					
Personal identity cards											•		•	
Internet/'Information Highway'											•	•	•	
DNA testing							•	•	•			•		

• Issue discussed/analysed at length at least once, occasionally mentioned again in brief.

– Issue simply cited as the basis for a complaint or mentioned in passing; no analysis of issue given.

in other jurisdictions and to remain aware of the emerging international standards for data protection. In 1996, Bruce Phillips hosted the annual meeting of the International Privacy and Data Protection Commissioners in Ottawa. The conference theme, 'Privacy Beyond Borders,' reflected the common presumption that privacy protection is now an international problem requiring a coherent and harmonized response (Raab and Bennett 1994).

The Evolving Privacy 'Regime'

The identification of a 'policy regime' requires the existence of 'an interacting set of organizations, statutes, ideas, interests and processes' (Doern 1996, 5). The preceding analysis suggests that while the statute and the policy instrument have remained relatively unchanged, the scope and object of the regulatory activity has been continually shifting. A limited arsenal of legal, financial, and personnel resources must be brought to bear upon a set of government agencies that always have higher priorities than privacy and within an institutional and technological environment that regularly brings new privacy issues to the fore. In this context, policy goals shift, strategies evolve in an ad hoc manner, and the impact of the Privacy Act is virtually impossible to measure (Raab and Bennett 1996). 'Impact' has to be evaluated according to complex changes in the treatment of an intangible, elusive, and ephemeral commodity – personal information – processed within a rapidly changing technological environment. What constitutes 'policy success' for the Privacy Act and its associated regulations and instruments can never be clearly defined.

I began with the argument that privacy protection does not fit neatly within traditional categorizations of policy or instrument types. Data protection policy (at least in relation to the public sector) does not 'convey tangible governmental benefits' and hence is not distributive. Nor does it 'manipulate the allocation of wealth, property rights, or some other value among social classes or racial groups in society' and thus redistribute resources from one group or class to another. It is neither competitive regulation, 'limiting the provision of specific goods and services to only one or a few designated deliverers,' nor protective regulation 'setting the conditions under which various private activities can be undertaken' (Ripley and Franklin 1976, 21–6).

Data protection policy (as expressed in the Privacy Act) sets the conditions under which public activity should be undertaken. Its purpose is to promote a normative value derived from a common set of liberal-democratic assumptions about the proper relationship between the individual and the state. No 'target group' is rewarded or deprived by the policy, and successful implementation is not dependent on such a group changing its behaviour over time in conformity with the programmatic goals. The 'protected' are all citizens. The 'target group' is the federal bureaucracy. Policy 'impact' takes place within, and not external to, the agencies of government. The behaviour to be regulated is that of the regulators.

I concluded in my earlier comparative study (Bennett 1992) that these properties produced a common pattern of bureaucratic resistance during the formulation of data protection law in different countries. This brief analysis of the implementation of the Canadian Privacy Act suggests that resistance also extends to the implementation process. Priscilla Regan has identified an inherent dilemma in formulating such policies: 'When implementation questions are left unresolved in policy design, bureaucratic concerns will dominate the implementation stage, but when implementation questions are resolved in policy design, bureaucratic concerns will dominate the formulation stage' (Regan 1984, 27).

These conclusions about the patterns of policy making and implementation for data protection policy were reached with reference to a now dated body of policy literature, according to the analysis of four countries besides Canada (Britain, the United States, Sweden, and Germany), and in relation to the privacy problems generated by an earlier generation of technology. The question in conclusion is whether the more contemporary conceptualization of 'policy regimes' helps us to understand a policy area like data protection more effectively than the literature of the 1970s and 1980s.

Privacy protection, as already stated, cuts across the traditional policy sectors. It therefore has few similarities with the regulatory institutions with their core policy communities defined by Regime I in Doern's (1996) typology. It has more in common with Regime II, being a policy that operates within a horizontal framework. If applied to the private sector, privacy regulation will no doubt take on many of the same features of these policy areas and will fit quite neatly within this category. We have also noted the increasing significance of policy communities that operate in the international arena (both international organizations and national authorities). Regime IV is increasingly salient, given the internationalization of the data protection problem.

The most interesting analysis, however, is still offered by the conceptualization of Regime III. Doern is correct in asserting that this is 'often the least appreciated regime in conventional regulatory literature because it is easy, at first glance, to think of regulation only in terms of well known regulatory bodies' (1996, 9). It seems that Regime III has two particular features: first, that the regulatory activity takes place within the agencies of the state, and second, the emphasis is on procedural (rather that substantive) rules. Regime III might be said to refer to the 'rules for rule making' and may include procedures such as cost-benefit analysis, legal and constitutional tests, examinations for regulatory flexibility and competitiveness, and so on. The implicit argument is that the regulations for the regulators are underresearched and yet increasingly significant in an era of deregulation.

Data protection in general fits this regime type more closely than it does the other three. The Privacy Act establishes a set of procedural requirements for the implementation of any policy that requires the collection, processing, or disclosure of personal information. It governs the treatment of information about individual citizens, as well as about government employees. It also offers a measure for the development of new legislative and program initiatives. Such initiatives must pass a range of financial and legal tests; privacy protection is one of those tests. I noted above that the 'ounce of prevention' ethos has translated into an attempt to inject a privacy argument into the earliest stages of policy development. Doern's typology is, I would conclude, more inclusive than some of the classifications of policy types and instruments offered heretofore. However, there are still some aspects of this issue that fit uneasily within the categories and discourse of regulatory policy making.

First, the definition of privacy protection policy in purely procedural or 'regulatory management' terms may not be entirely accurate (see Chapter 11). Distinctions are now made between 'substantive' and 'procedural' policy instruments (Howlett 1997). The federal Privacy Act certainly mandates a set of procedural norms for the collection, storage, processing, and dissemination of personal data. But these procedures are established in order to attain a quite substantive value, which is articulated in the legislation itself: 'to extend the present laws of Canada that protect the privacy of individuals with respect to personal information about themselves held by a government institution' (section 2). The Privacy Act is more, I would argue, than a procedural test like a cost-benefit analysis. It seeks to attain in its own right a substantive value and the privacy commissioner is a 'value auditor' (Sutherland and Doern 1986).

Second, to the extent that citizens are involved in the implementation of the legislation, the regime does involve actors outside of the contours of the state. Indeed, the implementation of the Privacy Act rests to a considerable extent on complaints and access requests from the 'data subjects.' In this respect, privacy regulation has more in common with Ombudsman and Freedom of Information Acts (Bennett 1997b). The privacy commissioner interacts with outside clientele to a greater extent than is envisioned under the current Regime III formulation.

A final reservation relates to the term 'regulation.' The OPC does, in the strictest sense, regulate. It tries to use the various tools at its disposal to apply the privacy rules in an even-handed and predictable manner. Yet, most data protectors would probably baulk at the suggestion that they were 'regulating.' The word connotes a more top-down and hierarchical posture than is the style in Canada and probably the case in most other countries with data protection agencies. Even in Britain, whose 1984 Data Protection Act is administered by a Data Protection Registrar with extensive registration and regulatory powers, the character of the data protector's job is little different from that of the privacy commissioner in Canada. The role must stress mutual learning and education over the application and enforcement of rules. It must stress an accommodating and advisory style rather than one that is overly high-handed. It must try to work with a flexible range of instruments (including the development of codes, the education of the general public, and the promotion of privacy-enhancing technologies), and cannot rely on the governing statute to specify what 'rules' should be applied to whom and at what time.

I argued above that the Privacy Act (like most other 'regulatory' policies) reads as if it were based on what Deborah Stone calls a 'rationality model' of rule making. The implementation of the Privacy Act, however, is more consistent with her depiction of a 'polis model.' This model stresses discretion in the balancing of competing values. It recognizes that policy problems are too complex to allow for perfectly detailed rules. It suggests that rules are often ambiguous and contain perverse incentives. It embraces an inevitable trade-off between flexibility and vagueness. It concedes that all rules benefit some people and harm others. And it recognizes that enforcement will be carried out by people who are subject to many influences and pressures besides their official responsibility (Stone 1996, 300). The realities of most rule making and enforcement must always be kept in mind when we are trying to construct meaningful constructs for regulatory policies, instruments, or regimes in Canadian and comparative perspective. The case of data protection policy in Canada, and probably elsewhere, underscores the indefinite and flexible character of contemporary regulation.

Appendix

POWERS AND RESPONSIBILITIES GRANTED TO FEDERAL PRIVACY COMMISSIONER UNDER THE 1982 PRIVACY ACT

Complaints Investigation and Resolution

The Privacy Commissioner has the power:

- to summon and enforce the appearance of persons before the Privacy Commissioner and compel them to give oral or written evidence on oath and to produce such documents and things as the Commissioner deems requisite to the full investigation and consideration of the complaint, in the same manner and to the same extent as a superior court of record;
- to administer oaths;
- to receive and accept such evidence and other information ... whether or not such evidence or information is or would be admissible in a court of law;
- to enter any premises occupied by any government institution on satisfying any security requirements of the institution relating to the premises;
- to converse in private with any person in any premises entered ... and carry out inquiries within the authority of the Privacy Commissioner;
- to examine or obtain copies or extracts from books or other records found in any premises entered ... containing any matter relevant to the investigation.

Enforcement Powers

The Privacy Commissioner may:

- apply to the Court ... for a review of any refusal to disclose personal information requested in respect of which an investigation has been carried out by the Privacy Commissioner, if the Commissioner has the consent of the individual who requested access to the information;

- appear before the Court on behalf of any individual who has applied for a review;
- with leave of the Court, appear as a party to any review applied for.
- The Court shall, if it determines that the head of the institution is not authorized under the Act to refuse to disclose the personal information, order the head of the institution to disclose the personal information, subject to such conditions as the Court deems appropriate, to the individual who requested access thereto, or shall make such other order as the Court deems appropriate.

Advisory Functions on Privacy Implications of Legislation and Technologies

- The Privacy Commissioner may, at any time, make a special report to Parliament referring to and commenting on any matter within the scope of the powers, duties, and functions of the Commissioner.

Public Education and Research Functions

- The Privacy Commissioner shall, within three months after the termination of each financial year, submit an annual report to Parliament on the activities of the office during that financial year.
- The Privacy Commissioner may, at any time, make a special report to Parliament referring to and commenting on any matter within the scope of the powers, duties, and functions of the Commissioner.

·NOTE

I am very grateful to Aaron Hokanson of the University of Victoria for research assistance.

REFERENCES

Bennett, Colin J. 1990. The Formation of a Canadian Privacy Policy: the Art and Craft of Lesson-drawing. *Canadian Public Administration* 33:551–70.
- 1992. *Regulating Privacy: Data Protection and Public Policy in Europe and the United States.* Ithaca, N.Y.: Cornell University Press.
- 1995. *Implementing Privacy Codes of Practice: A Report to the Canadian Standards Association.* Rexdale, Ont.: CSA, PLUS 8830.

Privacy Protection within the Contemporary Canadian State   313

- 1996. Rules of the Road and Level-Playing Fields: The Politics of Data Protection in Canada's Private Sector. *International Review of Administrative Sciences* 62:479–91.
- 1997a. Adequate Data Protection by the Year 2000: The Prospects for Privacy in Canada. *International Review of Law, Computers and Technology* 11:79–92.
- 1997b. Understanding Ripple Effects: The Cross-National Adoption of Policy Instruments for Bureaucratic Accountability. *Governance* 10:213–34.
Canada. An Act to enact the Access to Information Act and the Privacy Act, S.C. 1980-81-82-83, c. 111, Schedule II. The Privacy Act is at http//infoweb.magi.com/~privcan/
Canadian Standards Association (CSA). 1996. *Model Code for the Protection of Personal Information* (CAN/CSA-Q830-96) Rexdale, Ont.: CSA. The CSA Model Code is at www.csa.ca.
Cavoukian, Ann, and Don Tapscott. 1995. *Who Knows: Safeguarding your Privacy in a Networked World.* Toronto: Random House Canada.
Council of Europe. 1981. *Convention for the Protection of Individuals with Regard to Automatic Processing of Personal Data.* Strasbourg: Council of Europe.
Doern, G. Bruce. 1996. Regulatory Bodies, Regimes and Institutions: A Framework and Issues for Reform. Paper prepared for the Conference on UK–North American Regulatory Institutions, University of Exeter, 9–10 April.
Doern, G. Bruce, and Richard W. Phidd. 1992. *Canadian Public Policy: Ideas, Structure, Process.* 2nd ed. Toronto: Nelson Canada.
Ekos Research Associates. 1993. *Privacy Revealed: The Canadian Privacy Survey.* Ottawa: Ekos.
European Union. 1995. *Directive 95/46/EC of the European Parliament and of the Council on the Protection of Individuals with regard to the Processing of Personal Data and on the Free Movement of Such Data.* Brussels: OJ No. L281. 24 October.
Flaherty, David H. 1989. *Protecting Privacy in Surveillance Societies.* Chapel Hill: University of North Carolina Press.
Harris, Louis, and Alan F. Westin. 1995. *The Equifax Canada Report on Consumers and Privacy in the Information Age.* Ville d'Anjou: Equifax Canada.
Hood, Christopher. 1986. *The Tools of Government.* New Jersey: Chatham House.
Howlett, Michael. 1997. Legitimacy and Governance: A Preliminary Taxonomy and Analysis of Procedural Policy Instruments. Paper presented to the Annual Meeting of the British Columbia Political Science Association, Capilano College, 3 May.
Howlett, Michael, and M. Ramesh. 1995. *Studying Public Policy: Policy Cycles and Policy Subsystems.* Toronto: Oxford University Press.
Industry Canada. 1996. *Building the Information Society: Moving Canada into the 21st Century.* Ottawa: Industry Canada. [http://info.ic.gc.ca/info-highway/ih.html].

Information Highway Advisory Council (IHAC). 1995. *Connection, Community, Content: The Challenge of the Information Highway.* Ottawa: Minister of Supply and Services Canada.

Justice Canada. 1972. *Privacy and Computers.* Ottawa: Information Canada.

Lawson, Ian. 1992. *Privacy and Free Enterprise: The Legal Protection of Personal Information in the Private Sector.* Ottawa: Public Interest Advocacy Centre.

Lowi, Theodore. 1964. American Business, Public Policy, Case Studies and Political Theory. *World Politics* 16:677–715.

– 1972. Four Systems of Policy, Politics and Choice. *Public Administration Review* 32:298–310.

Organization for Economic Cooperation and Development (OECD). 1981. *Guidelines on the Protection of Privacy and Transborder Data Flows of Personal Data.* Paris: OECD.

Privacy Commissioner of Canada (OPC). 1989. *Aids and the Privacy Act.* Ottawa: Minister of Supply and Services.

– 1990. *Drug-Testing and Privacy.* Ottawa: Minister of Supply and Services.

– 1991. *Annual Report 1990–91.* Ottawa: Canada Communication Group.

– 1992a. *Annual Report 1991–92.* Ottawa: Canada Communications Group.

– 1992b. *Genetic Testing and Privacy.* Ottawa: Minister of Supply and Services.

– 1994. *Annual Report 1993–94.* Ottawa: Canada Communications Group.

– 1995. *Annual Report 1994–95.* Ottawa: Canada Communications Group.

– 1996. *Annual Report 1995–96.* Ottawa: Canada Communications Group.

Public Interest Advocacy Centre (PIAC). 1995. *Surveying Boundaries: Canadians and their Personal Information.* Ottawa: PIAC.

Raab, Charles D. 1993. Data Protection in Britain: Governance and Learning. *Governance* 6:43–66.

Raab, Charles D., and Colin J. Bennett. 1994. Protecting Privacy Across Borders: European Policies and Prospects. *Public Administration* 72:95–112.

– 1996. Taking the Measure of Privacy: Can Data Protection be Evaluated? *International Review of Administrative Sciences* 62:535–56.

Reagan, Michael D. 1987. *Regulation: The Politics of Policy.* Boston: Little Brown.

Regan, Priscilla M. 1984. Personal Information Policies in the United States and Britain: The Dilemma of Implementation Considerations. *Journal of Public Policy* 4:19–38.

Ripley, Randall B., and Grace A. Franklin. 1976. *Congress, the Bureaucracy and Public Policy,* Homewood, Ill.: Dorsey Press.

Rock, Allan. 1996. Address to the 18th International Conference on Privacy and Data Protection. Ottawa, 18 September.

Sartori, Giovanni. 1970. Concept Misformation in Comparative Politics. *American Political Science Review* 54:1033–53.

Schoeman, Ferdinand D., ed. 1984. *Philosophical Dimensions of Privacy: An Anthology*. Cambridge: Cambridge University Press.

Schultz, Richard J., and Alan Alexandroff. 1985. *Economic Regulation and the Federal System*. Toronto: University of Toronto Press.

Stone, Deborah. 1997. *Policy Paradox: The Art of Political Decision-Making*. New York: Norton.

Sutherland, Sharon, and G. Bruce Doern. 1986. *Bureaucracy in Canada: Control and Reform*. Toronto: University of Toronto Press.

Westin, Alan F. 1967. *Privacy And Freedom*. New York: Atheneum.

PART IV
INTERNATIONAL AND CROSS-JURISDICTIONAL
REGULATION

14

Rules about Rules?
The Canadian Internal Trade Agreement
and Cross-Jurisdictional Influences

G. BRUCE DOERN

The 1994 Agreement on Internal Trade (AIT) between the federal government and Canada's twelve provincial and territorial governments is essentially a regulatory agreement (Agreement on Internal Trade 1994). It is in many respects a set of rules about rules and warrants close analysis in a book on Canada's regulatory institutions, since its provisions extend into many features of Canada's set of regulatory regimes in the late 1990s (Doern 1998). The product of old-style executive federalism, in which Canada's political leaders struck a deal largely behind the scenes, the AIT sets out how, in future, federal and provincial governments will or should go about making regulatory choices in over fifteen policy-regulatory fields.

The AIT has been grouped in the book's discussion of Regime IV regulation in large part because it is a prime example of the growing penetration of international trade rules, values, and processes into realms of domestic regulation and policy. The agreement exhibits cross-jurisdictional influences in a dual way. It demonstrates international influences on Canada as a whole but it is also cross-jurisdictional in that relationships among provinces and between the federal and provincial governments are affected. Moreover, the AIT negotiation process in 1993–4 itself altered the arenas of decision making and the players involved compared to what they would have been had normal federal-provincial regulatory relations prevailed. Normal federal-provincial relations have certainly included aspects of negotiation but not simultaneously across such a wide set of policy and regulatory fields. Thus, the agreement altered regulatory institutions because it changed the politics of regulation in diverse ways (Trebilcock and Schwanen 1995; Doern and MacDonald 1999).

In this chapter four regulatory features are examined, each implying, in part at least, different cross-jurisdictional influences and effects. First, we look at the architecture of the AIT to see to what extent the agreement qualifies as a central trade-modelled agreement on regulation, where regulation is conceived broadly to include laws and policies as well as narrowly defined regulation (regs and standards). Second, we examine the issues and dynamics that accompanied the negotiations of standards. Standards can be seen as just another kind of rule or regulation but they also constitute a separate realm (Jacobs 1995; Michael 1996) and they raise issues of preferred framework regulatory principles, such as mutual recognition, harmonization, and performance-based regulations and standards, the origins of which are increasingly found in international trade and related agreements, but which play out differently in domestic politics.

Next, we look at two sectoral case studies within the broader AIT process: agriculture and food and labour mobility. Efforts in the AIT to promote performance as opposed to procedural regulation and related concerns about the harmonization or mutual recognition of standards can be seen in the two case study areas, where separate sectoral negotiating teams worked out deals. International and cross-jurisdictional effects also vary.

The chapter concludes with an examination of the extent to which the AIT can be seen to be a deal that promotes rules about rules, and hence seeks to become a fully functioning part of internationally pressured framework regulation in Canada as a whole and among the provinces in particular.

The Agreement: A Framework Agreement on Regulation?

Space does not allow a detailed presentation of the full agreement. However, the basic architecture of the agreement must be appreciated to allow us to examine the extent to which the AIT constitutes a new intergovernmental framework regime for Canadian regulation. Table 14.1 sets out the six parts and eighteen chapters of the deal. Each part is discussed briefly below.

The most basic point to be made about the agreement is that the bulk of it lies in Part IV, in the eleven chapters dealing with specific rules. These chapters were handled mainly by the sectoral negotiating teams or 'tables,' although the procurement provisions were also kept very close to the main table of negotiators. The main table of chief negotiators oversaw the entire package. It is also worth noting that the 'sector' chapters and tables were in fact not typically sectors in the sense of vertical industrial sectors, such as autos or steel. Some fit this category, such as the chapters on alcoholic beverages and agriculture and food goods, but many other so-called sectors were in fact aspects of internal trade (and regulation) that were horizontal: framework rules that cut across all or most sectors of the economy. This is certainly true of procurement, investment, labour mobility, consumer-related measures and stan-

TABLE 14.1
The Internal Trade Agreement at a Glance
(Six Parts and 18 Chapters)

Preamble

PART I – GENERAL
Chapter 1 – Operating Principles
Chapter 2 – General Definitions

PART II – CONSTITUTIONAL AUTHORITIES
Chapter 3 – Reaffirmation of Constitutional Powers and Responsibilities

PART III – GENERAL RULES
Chapter 4 – General Rules

PART IV – SPECIFIC RULES
Chapter 5 – Procurement
Chapter 6 – Investment
Chapter 7 – Labour Mobility
Chapter 8 – Consumer-Related Measures and Standards
Chapter 9 – Agricultural and Food Goods
Chapter 10 – Alcoholic Beverages
Chapter 11 – Natural Resources Processing
Chapter 12 – Energy
Chapter 13 – Communications
Chapter 14 – Transportation
Chapter 15 – Environmental Protection

PART V – INSTITUTIONAL PROVISIONS AND DISPUTE RESOLUTION PROCEDURES
Chapter 16 – Institutional Provisions
Chapter 17 – Dispute Resolution Procedures

PART VI – FINAL PROVISIONS
Chapter 18 – Final Provisions

Annexes

Source: *The Agreement on Internal Trade* (Ottawa: Government of Canada, 1994).

dards, and the environment. Other chapters, such as those on communications, transportation, natural resources processing, and energy, are more hybrid. They were certainly seen as industrial sectors but they are also horizontal and economywide in nature, in that they are clearly a crucial aspect of production in virtually every other sector of the economy.

The division between general versus specific rules is crucial. Ideally, in any international trade agreement the general rules ought to be paramount, with specific rules flowing from and not contradicting them. No agreement is perfect in this respect and the AIT certainly flouts this general rule in a number of ways. Indeed, much of the negotiations conducted in 1994 concerned which chapters would take precedence over others (Trebilcock and Schwanen 1995).

The preamble and the provisions in Parts I, II, and III set out the basic objectives, operating principles, and general rules. Essentially, the purpose of the agreement is to promote 'an open, efficient and stable domestic market for long-term job creation, economic growth and stability' and, accordingly, 'to reduce and eliminate to the extent possible, barriers to the free movement of persons, goods, services and investments within Canada.' The agreement was also to 'promote equal economic opportunity for Canadians' and was intended to further several related objectives regarding competitiveness, sustainable environmental development, and better consultation on internal trade matters.

The agreement also reaffirms that nothing in it alters the legislative or other authority of Parliament or the legislatures of the provinces under the constitution of Canada. In short, the AIT was not an exercise in constitutional change. This was crucial in both the legal and political context of the agreement, although it remains problematic in terms of whether it constitutes, in a certain way, a 'side deal' to the constitution, or, in terms of this paper, a regulatory side deal. The general rules provisions in Part III of the agreement include provisions about reciprocal nondiscrimination, right of entry and exit, and transparency, but they also include provisions concerning 'legitimate objectives.' This latter provision was properly insisted upon by the provinces so as to enable them to practice policies that were legitimate even though they might contradict some or all of the general rules (Lenihan 1995). Such policies would still have to be put in place in such a way that they did not 'impair unduly' the access of economic players, nor could they be 'more trade restrictive than necessary.'

Part IV contains the specific rules of the sectors and areas noted above. Procurement is by far the largest chapter, reflecting its particular sensitivity in the negotiation. It deals of course with the government's own purchases of goods and services and with the extent to which a province can discriminate in favour of its own citizens and firms in its decisions to purchase items with its taxpayer's money. The shortest 'chapter' is on energy, and is in fact a one-line entry, since no agreement was reached. This failure to agree owed largely to regulatory disputes about the transmission or 'wheeling' of electricity across provincial boundaries.

The other sectoral chapters all begin with statements about the extent to which their provisions are an exception from (in whole or part), or governed by, the general rules. With respect to both their content and negotiating processes, these sectors should be seen in two important contexts. First, these chapters were typically negotiated by officials and experts from the other line departments of the governments involved. Second, many of the issues and policy problems they were dealing with had been on their sector's agenda for years. Accordingly, one of the issues of regulatory change is whether the internal trade arena of decision making simply continued the process without much change or whether it altered the dynamics because it was a different political-economic arena for such regulatory decisions.

Parts V and VI of the agreement deal with institutional provisions and dispute settlement and the so-called 'final provisions.' These issues were very much in the hands of the main table of chief negotiators and ultimately of the internal trade ministers as well. The final provisions included politically crucial issues that secured varying kinds of full or partial exemption from the agreement, including regional economic development, aboriginal peoples, culture, national security, taxation, and the financial sector. Many of these policy spheres were included at the behest of the federal government.

The institutional provisions in Chapter 16 of the agreement establish a basis for implementing and building on the deal. A Committee on Internal Trade is established, composed of cabinet-level representation. A jointly funded Internal Trade Secretariat is also established (now based in Winnipeg) as a working party on adjustment, to assess the effects of the agreement on each province in each fiscal year.

Even more important, however, are the agreed provisions regarding dispute resolution procedures, many of which were nominally modelled on international trade dispute settlement practices (Howse 1995, 1996). These cover more than twenty pages of the agreement and were the subject of intense dispute. As Table 14.2 shows, there are procedures for both government-to-government and person-to-government dispute resolution. It was the provisions for private access and the extent to which private access should be available that created the greatest dispute. Under both types of dispute the essence of the process is to enable a sequence of steps to occur. The first resort is the chapter provisions; when these are exhausted, the general dispute resolution provisions should be turned to. Within each stage an aggrieved party or person begins with consultations, then makes a request for assistance, if necessary; finally, a request for a panel may be made, and a panel stage ensues. If a dispute goes to the ultimate panel stage, implementation of the independent panel report will first rely on compliance by the parties or perhaps the influence of adverse publicity. Under prescribed circumstances, retaliatory action can be taken.

The private access procedures contain a screening process to eliminate frivolous complaints and then the same steps apply. An important exception is that a panel report may contain an award of costs of proceeding, but not for damages. Dispute avoidance and settlement steps also vary somewhat among some of the sectoral chapters (Swinton 1995a; 1995b).

TABLE 14.2
The Two Main Internal Trade Dispute Resolution Processes

Government-to-Government	Person-to-Government
– Consultations	– Initiation of proceedings
– Assistance of committee	– Screening
(including ADR processes)	
– Request for panel	– Consultations
– Establishment of panel	– Assistance of committee
– Panel report	(including ADR processes)
– Implementation of report	– Request for panel
– Non-implementation	– Establishment of panel
• Publicity	– Panel report (possible
• Retaliatory action	award of costs of proceedings)
	– Implementation of report
	– Non-implementation
	• Publicity

The analysis that follows allows us to revisit some of the architectural features and fault lines of the AIT. It is important to say at this stage, however, that a regulatory framework does emerge from the AIT from the very fact that many areas are brought together in one composite agreement and that trade-related principles and a rudimentary dispute resolution process anchors it. At the same time, the matrix nature of the pact and the frequent supremacy of the 'sectoral' chapter rules means that a consistent horizontal or framework architecture was politically and practically impossible.

Standards and Regulatory Measures as a Horizontal Issue

Building on earlier discussions from the late 1980s and early 1990s, the AIT negotiators were given several principles by ministers to work from. One of these was that governments 'reconcile standards and regulations to provide for the free movement of people, goods, services and capital within Canada.' In the earlier stages of the AIT negotiations the reconciliation of standards was considered to be in the purview of a separate team on consumer-related measures and standards. However, it was quickly evident that standards crossed many sectoral aspects of the AIT process and needed to be negotiated by a separate group to look at the issue comprehensively. In the final agreement, this produced Article 405 and two annexes (405.1 and 405.2) on standards and standards-related measures and regulatory measures, respectively.

Article 405 enshrines the principle of reconciliation, which the parties agree to support. However, reconciliation, given the need to leave room for legitimate objectives, is deemed to mean many things. It can mean 'mutual recognition,' where the requirements of the provinces are equivalent in purpose and effect. It can also mean harmonization, which itself is seen to be a broad concept ranging from compatibility to full convergence.

In the early stages of negotiations, the federal government pushed for a view that mutual recognition should require all parties to the AIT to accept relevant standards-related measures as equivalent to their own until they can supply a sufficient explanation as to why they should not. Several provinces strongly objected, arguing that such an approach could only work if measures are equivalent in purpose and effect. Many feared that such a concept could ratchet standards in a downward direction and hence harm legitimate objectives. The federal government backed off from its aggressive initial stance, apparently to ensure that a separate annex on regulatory measures could remain in the AIT.

Harmonization was also a contentious concept. The federal government sought harmonization both with international standards and with harmonization obligations in international trade agreements. Within the country, the federal government also tended to see harmonization through the creation of national standards. The provinces were not well disposed to these views and, in particular, viewed harmonization as a reciprocal arrangement between affected provinces.

During the negotiations two other contentious issues emerged. The first was whether the article should or could apply to goods compared to services and investment. Ontario, in particular, saw services and investment as more complex and believed that no single generic concept was sufficient. Both stayed in the agreement – although they are found in separate clauses – since the federal government pressed hard for an encompassing approach to goods, services, and investment.

A second area of contention was whether Article 405 should apply to regulatory measures as well as to standards. Many provinces objected, on the grounds that 'regulatory' measures potentially applied to any measure that a government might introduce and hence would extend too far into provincial jurisdiction. As a result, a separate annex was agreed to which, among other things, commits the provinces to a 'best efforts' approach to address the reconciliation of regulatory measures, including those that do not contain a standard. Annex 405.2 is therefore grounded to a greater extent in a 'consult and cooperate' approach than is Annex 405.1 on standards.

However, Annex 405.1 also reveals the need for compromise, as the negotiators sought to balance trade-centred rules with the legitimate objectives of governance in the Canadian federation.

Thus the annex applies only to those standards included in the scope of the sectoral chapters. Concerns were also raised that private sector standards development organizations might create internal trade barriers. The annex requires governments to make such bodies aware of the governments' obligations under the AIT.

In the discussions over standards there was apparently quick agreement that performance standards rather design standards should be used. In other words, standards should be based on what products or services must be able to do (performance) rather than by specifying how they should be structured or required to operate procedurally (Laplante 1990; Michael 1996). Once again, however, this agreement was not as clear-cut as it seems, in that the provinces could interpret the principle in varied ways. Performance criteria could be used unless it could be demonstrated that they would not achieve a legitimate objective. A performance approach had simply to be considered among many approaches. Or, such an approach could be used to the extent it was felt was appropriate and desirable.

Other provisions of Annex 405.1 centre on the issue of rationales and science-based standards (and regulations). Some parties pressed for a requirement that there must be a scientific or factual basis for a standard. In the end, a 'reasonable' basis for the standard was the chosen requirement. The federal government also sought to include criteria for assessing risk similar to those in GATT and NAFTA (Graham 1995). These criteria were dropped and only a vague 'where appropriate' reminder was left in as an adjunct to the 'reasonable' basis criteria.

Finally, the annex on standards contained provisions on conformity assessment. The intent here was to facilitate reconciliation by assessment of conformity but also to ensure that conformity assessment procedures are not themselves used as disguised trade barriers. Conformity assessment is deemed in the AIT to include a range of obligations, from the use of equivalent conformity assessment bodies, through the recognition that different procedures can produce equivalent results, to the avoidance of multiple testing procedures.

The AIT reflects an effort to supply a general approach to standards and regulatory measures but the negotiations clearly reflected strong differences of view as trade versus governance values and criteria were brought to bear. The standards chapter, moreover, was linked to an array of consumer-related measures, which have not been discussed (Hadfield, Howse, and Trebilcock 1996). But, just as importantly, it was played out in practical terms in several other sectoral regulatory fields, including the two case study chapters/negotiations that we examine below, agriculture and agri-food and labour mobility.

The Agriculture and Food Sector: Framework versus Sectoral Regulatory Tensions

The provisions in Chapter 9 of the AIT cover all agricultural and food goods except fish, fish products, and alcoholic beverages. Article 902 states that the agreement applies 'only to measures identified as technical barriers to trade by the Federal-Provincial Agrifood Inspection Committee.' The technical barrier is defined to be a measure that: (1) involves product characteristics or their related production methods; (2) deals exclusively with terminology, symbols, packaging, marking, or labelling requirements; and (3) involves a sanitary or phytosanitary measure. There is also a provision for the inclusion of such technical measures 'with policy implications' to come within the agreement effective 1 September 1997, after appropriate review.

The sanitary or phytosanitary measures are of course crucial social or 'health and safety' regulatory measures, but the parties are enjoined by the agreement to ensure that when proposing such measures they take into account the implications of those measures for internal trade. The parties also agree that their measures will not 'arbitrarily or unjustifiably' discriminate between parties nor would they constitute a disguised restriction on internal trade.

However, the key regulatory areas left for further review are those which deal with the sensitive issues of supply management and related safety-net programs for agricultural producers. Article 903 commits the parties to 'reduce or eliminate measures that constitute obstacles to internal trade,' but this is to be done in the context of a review with no apparent deadline and of Canadian agri-food policy as a whole. The three areas left in 1994 for further review are the development of sustainable orderly marketing systems in the dairy, poultry, and egg industries; the Western Grain Transportation Act; and federal and provincial agricultural safety-net programs.

The confined health and safety regulatory nature of the agricultural chapter must be seen in the context of the evolution of federal and provincial agricultural and food policies and regulations in the 1970s and 1980s (Skogstad 1987, 1992, 1993), an area of concurrent jurisdiction under the constitution. During the 1970s, the main programs in income and price supports were federal and the federal government had the dominant research expertise (Gilson 1989; Prince 1990). The provincial governments had more limited extension programs but they had also acquired primacy in many areas of technical regulation (Hack, Hughes, and Shapiro 1981). In the early 1980s this pattern changed, primarily through the addition of numerous provincial price and income support programs. By the mid-1980s there was a growing recognition that the internal market in agriculture was quite balkanized. In the latter half of the 1980s, the federal government devoted much of its policy energy into trying to reorder agricultural policy so that there was a greater semblance of a national (as distinct from a federal) policy (Prentice 1994).

However, layered into this policy and regulatory mix was the debate about and the successive negotiations involved in the FTA, NAFTA, and GATT-WTO Uruguay Round. These stretched over the entire 1986 to 1995 period. The FTA, in particular, had a major impact on agriculture (Doern and Tomlin 1991, ch. 5). Its key provisions were the elimination of tariffs over ten years and the prohibition of export subsidies on bilateral trade with the U.S. However, the FTA protected the Canadian supply management system and its various regulatory marketing boards. The FTA was the first trade agreement to subject agriculture to GATT-like rules and it was negotiated amidst considerable tension between primary agricultural producers and food product manufacturers (Skogstad 1995, 1996). The new tensions centred basically on the fact that Canada's food product manufacturers would increasingly have to face competition from American manufacturers whose input costs were lower, largely because the U.S. had a more market-based or nonsupply-managed system. In the FTA, the supply management system was preserved due to the superior political power of the primary producers, but the seeds of major change had nonetheless been planted.

The later NAFTA and WTO agreements extended the trade-based aspects of regulation further into domestic agriculture-food policy and program realms. The changed relationship between the two interests, primary producers versus food products manufacturers, was also reflected in the restructuring of federal ministries in 1993, when Agriculture Canada became Agriculture and Agri-Food Canada.

Earlier reviews had shown that among the eleven governments surveyed there were up to 158 policies and regulations that affected interprovincial trade in agriculture and considerable dispute as to whether and to what extent these may or may not distort interprovincial trade (Federal-Provincial Agricultural Trade Policy Committee 1988).

In terms of basic regulatory politics it is crucial to appreciate that every province had sensitivities and concerns regarding key sectors, especially its provincial poultry, egg, and dairy producers (Skogstad 1990). The provincial horticultural producers and lobbies were also important. These concerns are strengthened by the fact that representation in provincial legislatures is not based strictly on a full 'representation by population' basis, but rather has a 'rural tilt' that affects legislatures and cabinets (Prentice 1994).

The AIT negotiations almost immediately focused on several technical barriers 'with policy implications.' Policy implications simply meant that they were controversial in some major, recognized sense and had been on the agricultural agenda for several years. These technical regulations included provincial regulations on margarine colouring, the reintroduction of the No. 1 Small Potato grade under the CAP Act, standards of butter blends and imitation dairy products, the movement of fruit and vegetables in bulk containers, and provincial regulations for fluid milk production and distribution. Several agriculture ministers did not want to see these issues handed over to, or dominated by, an interprovincial internal trade policy process.

There was also a far larger array of other technical barriers (i.e., those with no, or much less, policy controversy attached to them). Technical barriers involve regulations that require producers from other jurisdictions to change the preparation of their product for sale in the local provincial market, by altering, for instance, grading, labelling, packaging, or the content of ingredients (Prentice 1994). These changes can increase both the cost and the risk of trading for outside producers. The negotiations on technical barriers initially focused on just how fast different provinces felt they could respond and how sensitive particular standards might be to producer groups in their province. The other source of contention in the negotiations centred on the provisions regarding scope and review and hence on what items, if not decided immediately, would have to be decided in the three-year period leading up to 1997.

In the final two meetings of ministers of agriculture, consensus emerged on the provisions described above, especially the elimination of the all the purely technical barriers, but also the inclusion of firm undertakings, with deadlines, to eliminate the technical barriers with policy implications. Importantly, there was also a commitment to a standstill on new barriers.

The agriculture-food negotiations in the AIT also raised the need for national technical standards. As we will see below, in the labour mobility sectoral negotiations, the free trade–internationalization dynamics meant that Canada could not offer ten different sets of technical standards for dozens of agriculture-food products or groupings of products. The provinces accepted that change was inevitable but they did not want national standards to be federal standards.

The choices here were expressed either as harmonization or a mutual recognition of equivalents. A decision was made in favour of harmonization, but this did not eliminate debate or controversy, given sectoral politics and realities. For example, efforts had been mounted to develop a national dairy code but the very notion of a 'code' is that it is not harmonized. In short, it resembles a guideline rather than a rule. Moreover, there are many specific dairy products to accommodate. Similar problems confront the previously mentioned issue of imitation dairy products. Should harmonization be at the level of principles only or actual performance/quality standards? Does one need a special set for subclasses, such as cheese-based products?

Labour Mobility: Harmonization, Mutual Recognition, and the Self-Regulating Professions

Chapter 7 of the AIT deals with the mobility of labour. The agreement's purpose is to enable 'any worker qualified for an occupation ... to be granted access to employment opportunities in that occupation' (Article 701). It applies to measures relating to occupational standards, licensing, certification, registration, and residency requirements. But the chapter does not apply to various social policy measures, such as labour standards and codes, minimum wages, unemployment insurance qualification periods, and social assistance benefits.

Unlike other chapters in the AIT, which could build on and extend recent international trade negotiations, the labour mobility issues had never really been the subject of a full federal-provincial negotiation. In the FTA, NAFTA, and GATT context this was largely because the issue was trade in goods and services and not the free movement of people. Moreover, in the domestic Canadian context full negotiation had never even been attempted. There had certainly been disputes in the labour trades and controversies over professional occupations and their qualifications, but for the negotiators involved, an internal trade negotiation was a new experience and a new arena for dealing with these kinds of regulatory matters.

In the labour mobility negotiations the federal government pressed for a broad, rules-based approach. Several provinces questioned why a rules-based approach was needed, since this was the one chapter that dealt with 'real people.' Rules were not really rules in this case, it was argued, but rather working principles or guidelines. But the provincial opposition to firm rules was rooted in part in principled objections as well as pragmatic ones.

On the principled side, there were concerns about whether provinces could give employment preference to their own inhabitants in job creation policies, especially where there was large-scale unemployment and a need to facilitate adjustment. On the pragmatic side there was the issue of when and how to deal with a very complex array of self-regulating professional occupations, where authority had been legally delegated by the provinces to such bodies. Not only were these groups influential, there were, quite simply, a lot of them to be sorted out, often as many as forty in each province.

In the AIT negotiation process, three basic kinds of barriers were identified: residency requirements, licensing practices, and the recognition of qualifications. The residency issue was quickly agreed to. Article 706 specifies that no party shall require a worker to be resident in its territory as a condition of access to employment opportunities; licensing, certification, or registration relating to the worker's occupation; or eligibility for the worker's occupation.

The issue of qualification was quite divisive. The federal government initially advocated harmonized national standards. This preference emerged from its earlier work, including that of the Canadian Labour Force Development Board, which had strongly recommended that national standards were the way to go. National standards had been suggested even for areas such as tourism, where the labour qualifications were more voluntary in nature. The federal chief negotiator for the chapter pressed hard for standards based on objective performance competencies rather than on paper qualifications.

For the provinces, harmonization was seen as involving too much federal intrusion. Moreover, education was an area of provincial jurisdiction. As a result of this impasse the federal government changed its position and supported the preferred provincial option, which centred on mutual recognition of qualifications. This was, to put it simply, the 'driver's licence' model. Provinces simply accept and recognize the qualifications as certified by the another province. The provinces also cited the example of the European Union, where mutual recognition was the approach taken.

With regard to licensing and the linked issues of professional qualifications, the problems went beyond the harmonized standards versus mutual recognition issue. In labour areas such as the building trades, regulation was directly carried out by the provinces. Hence, programs such as the Red Seal program on the apprentice trades had been worked out to enhance mobility. But, as mentioned, the professions were governed by various kinds of self-regulation (Slayton and Trebilcock 1978; Bayes 1986; Trebilcock 1983). The rationale for self-regulation was that the province would stay out of the way of the professions in terms of expert qualifications provided they behaved in the public interest. But the implications of the labour mobility chapter was that the provinces would be telling them what to do, largely because Ottawa was saying so. Indeed, in some provinces, including Ontario, the pressure in recent years had been to agree to grant self-regulating status to more and more occupational or knowledge groups. But the professions were the main new ground in which the federal government in particular wanted to extend mobility rules-based concepts. Ultimately, the approach taken in the chapter was that an extensive work program was agreed to whereby the provinces would engage in discussions with their various professions with a view to making changes that would enhance mobility.

The chapter also specifies quite a wide range of 'legitimate objectives' ultimately linked to the public interest and trust aspects of services delivered by the professions (Trebilcock 1983). However, these objectives are reined in by the AIT so that they are not done in way that creates disguised restrictions to mobility.

The labour mobility chapter resulted in much more of a federal versus provincial battle than other AIT chapters and the final trade-offs reflected the fact that the federal government led the demand for regulatory change to enhance mobility. The federal government achieved a set of mutually stated obligations, an extended scope to the mobility rules, and a work plan to keep up momentum on the professions. The provinces achieved their preferred mutual recognition approach rather than the harmonized standards approach, with some room reserved for local job initiatives.

Conclusions

As the twentieth century ends, students of Canadian regulatory institutions need to appreciate that the 1994 Agreement on Internal Trade is now a permanent addition to the institutional bridges being built among domestic and international regulatory regimes. The intent of this chapter has not been to examine the AIT in its entirety but to explore the extent to which the agreement is a set of international-trade-modelled 'rules about rules,' and hence a major addition to Canada's regulatory institutions.

A key cross-jurisdictional influence came in the changes in the decision process itself. AIT involved a decision process and negotiation dynamics in which multiple regulatory policy fields were being traded off, forcing governmental departments and negotiators into new regulatory decision-making arenas of a broader, trade-centred kind.

In terms of the overall architecture of the AIT, regulation is equated with governance in a very general way, embracing laws and policies as well as narrower notions of delegated rule making and standards. At this level of aggregation, the AIT deserves to be treated as ground breaking, in part simply because it brings together in one place through one intensive negotiation an agreement that frames important views about rules. This conclusion does not mean that the AIT is not flawed, as critics have pointed out, in respect of its dispute resolution mechanisms and internal contradictions between horizontal versus sectoral chapters (Canadian Chamber of Commerce 1996, Cohen, 1995).

The chapter has also demonstrated that some jurisdictions sought to enshrine international-trade-derived principles for standards through concepts such as mutual recognition, harmonization, performance-based regulation, and science-based regulation. The final agreement shows that, although progress was made in this direction, there is by no means full agreement and indeed, several provinces resisted these concepts when cast in a domestic context and advocated by a federal government whose international and domestic agenda was viewed with suspicion by many provinces.

The two case studies of the agriculture and agri-food and labour mobility sectors and chapters testified to these pressures and partial tensions, as different cross-jurisdictional impacts were debated and negotiated. The agriculture and agri-food negotiations and resultant provisions demonstrate both resistance in the long-standing regulatory issues of marketing boards, but also some breakthrough in technical standards, in part due to the fact that the AIT negotiation brought players under new sets of pressure in the larger negotiating process, and also owing to continued international trade pressure.

The labour mobility area saw fewer gains in framework rule-making per se, in part because it could not draw on earlier international trade experience as readily as was the case in agriculture and agri-food or in the standards debate as a whole. But difficulties in the politics of federalism in dealing with a dense array of self-regulating professions, where the regulation of quality in diverse service realms are problematical and complex, were also significant.

REFERENCES

Agreement on Internal Trade. 1994. Ottawa: Government of Canada.

Appleton, Barry. 1994. *Navigating NAFTA.* Toronto: Carswell.

Bayes, Michael D. 1986. Professional Power and Self-Regulation. *Business and Professional Ethics Journal* 5, no. 2: 26–46.

Canadian Chamber of Commerce. 1996. *The Agreement on Internal Trade and Interprovincial Trade Flows: Building a Strong United Canada.* Toronto: Canadian Chamber of Commerce.

Cohen, David. 1995. The Internal Trade Agreement: Furthering the Canadian Economic Disunion? *Canadian Business Law Journal* 25, no. 2 (July): 257–79.

Doern, G. Bruce. 1998. Mapping Regulatory Institutions in North America and the UK: The Interplay Among Four Regimes. In G. Bruce Doern and Stephen Wilks, eds., *Changing Regulatory Institutions in Britain and North America,* ch. 2. Toronto: University of Toronto Press.

Doern, G. Bruce, and Mark Macdonald. 1999. *Free-Trade Federalism.* Toronto: University of Toronto Press.

Doern, G. Bruce, and Brian Tomlin. 1991. *Faith and Fear: The Free Trade Story*. Toronto: Stoddart.

Federal-Provincial Agricultural Trade Policy Committee. 1988. *Interprovincial Barriers to Trade in Agriculture and Food Products*. Ottawa: Agriculture Canada.

Gilson, J.C. 1989. *World Agricultural Changes: Implications For Canada*. Toronto: C.D. Howe Institute.

Graham, John D., ed. 1995. *Risk Versus Risk: Trade-offs in Protecting Health and Environment*. Cambridge: Harvard University Press.

Hack, R.E., D.R. Hughes, and R.G. Shapiro. 1981. *The Splintered Market: Barriers to Trade in Canadian Agriculture*. Ottawa: Canadian Institute for Economic Policy.

Hadfield, Gillian, R. Howse, and M. Trebilcock. 1996. Rethinking Consumer Protection Policy. Paper prepared for the University of Toronto Roundtable on New Approaches to Consumer Law, Toronto, 20 June 1996 (Revised 28 August 1996).

Howse, Robert. 1995. Between Anarchy and the Rule of Law: Dispute Settlement and Related Implementation Issues in the Agreement on Internal Trade. In Michael Trebilcock and Daniel Schwanen, eds., *Getting There*, 170–95. Toronto: C.D. Howe Institute.

– 1996. Securing the Canadian Economic Union: Legal and Constitutional Options for the Federal Government. *C.D. Howe Institute Commentary*. Commentary No. 81. Toronto: C.D. Howe Institute.

Jacobs, S.H. 1995. Regulatory Cooperation for an Interdependent World: Issues For Government. In OECD (Public Management Service), *Regulatory Cooperation For An Interdependent World*, ch. 1. Paris: OECD.

Laplante, Benoit. 1990. Environmental Regulation: Performance and Design Standards. In G. Bruce Doern, ed., *Getting it Green*, 59–88. Toronto: C.D. Howe Institute.

Lenihan, Donald G. 1995. When a Legitimate Objective Hits An Unnecessary Obstacle: Harmonizing Regulations and Standards in the Agreement on Internal Trade. In Michael J. Trebilcock and Daniel Schwanen, eds., *Getting There*, 98–118. Toronto: C.D. Howe Institute.

Michael, Douglas C. 1996. Cooperative Implementation of Federal Regulations. *Yale Journal of Regulation* 13, no. 2 (Summer): 535–601.

Prentice, Barry E. 1994. *Interprovincial Barriers to Agricultural Trade*. Vancouver: Fraser Institute.

Prince, Michael. 1990. Little Help on The Prairie: Canadian Farm Income Programs and the Western Grain Economy. In Katherine Graham, ed., *How Ottawa Spends: 1990–91*, 137–71. Ottawa: Carleton University Press.

Skogstad, Grace. 1987. *The Politics of Agricultural Policy Making in Canada*. Toronto: University of Toronto Press.

– 1990. The Farm Policy Community in Ontario and Quebec. In William D. Coleman and Grace Skogstad, eds., *Policy Communities and Public Policy in Canada*, 59–90. Toronto: Copp Clark Pitman.

- 1992. The State, Organized Interests and Canadian Agricultural Trade Policy: The Impact of Institutions. *Canadian Journal of Political Science* 25, no. 2: 319–47.
- 1993. Policy Under Siege: Supply Management in Agricultural Marketing. *Canadian Public Administration* 36, no. 1: 1–23.
- 1995. International Trade Agreements and Canadian Supply Management: Can the Systems Survive and Adjust? In G. Coffin, A. Schmitz, and K. Rosaasen, eds., *Regulation and Protectionism under GATT and NAFTA: Case Studies in North American Agriculture*. Boulder, Col.: Westview.
- 1996. Agricultural Policy. In G. Bruce Doern, Les Pal, and Brian Tomlin, eds., *Border Crossings: The Internationalization of Canadian Public Policy*, 143–64. Toronto: Oxford University Press.
Slayton, Phillip, and Michael J. Trebilcock, eds. 1978. *The Professions and Public Policy*. Toronto: University of Toronto Press.
Swinton, Katherine. 1995a. Law, Politics and the Enforcement of the Agreement on Internal Trade. In Michael J. Trebilcock and Daniel Schwanen, eds., *Getting There*, 196–210. Toronto: C.D. Howe Institute.
- 1995b. Courting Our Way to Economic Integration: Judicial Review and the Canadian Economic Union. *Canadian Business Law Journal* 25, no. 2 (July): 280–304.
Trebilcock, Michael J. 1983. Regulating Service Quality in Professional Markets. In Donald Dewees, ed., *The Regulation of Quality*, 83–108. Toronto: Butterworths.
Trebilcock, Michael J., and Daniel Schwanen, eds. 1995. *Getting There: An Assessment of the Agreement on Internal Trade*. Toronto: C.D. Howe Institute.

15

The Myths of NAFTA's Regulatory Power: Rethinking Regionalism as a Vehicle for Deep Economic Integration

ROBERT HOWSE and MICHAEL J. TREBILCOCK

It has become a commonplace that, as tariff barriers have fallen through successive rounds of multilateral trade negotiations, the trade agenda has increasingly focused on domestic policies that are viewed as direct or indirect barriers to free or to 'fair' trade, or both. The range of regulatory fields and instruments at issue has become increasingly broad, ranging from competition policy, consumer protection, food safety, investment, subsidies and government procurement to intellectual property, the regulation of service industries such as telecommunications, labour, and environmental policies.

Although it is sometimes asserted that, until recently, trade agreements have not explicitly addressed barriers created by domestic regulation (Robinson 1993, 334), in fact, the principle that domestic policies must not treat imported products less favourably than like domestic products (the National Treatment obligation in Article III) has been a crucial element in the architecture of international trade law since the 1947 General Agreement on Tariffs and Trade (GATT). Much of the evolution of the treatment of domestic regulation in international trade agreements since then can plausibly be viewed as an expansion, refinement, or application of this principle (for example, agreements on technical barriers to trade). Increasingly, however, the concept of national treatment has been viewed as itself inadequate to manage trade frictions that are connected to regulatory diversity among nations. Some kinds of regulatory diversity have clearly been constrained or limited by the obligation of national treatment, especially given the trend to apply this obligation even to facially neutral policies that have the effect of denying equal competitive opportunities to imports.[1] Nevertheless, what is being called for and to some extent achieved in recent trade agreements amounts to a requirement that even nondiscriminatory policies with trade-restrictive impacts be disciplined or, where the trade-restrictive impact results from regulatory diversity itself, that such policies be harmonized.

Harmonization, as David Leebron has explained, is a concept that has many shades of meaning (Leebron 1996). Its strongest and perhaps crudest form is the replacement of diverse policies or laws with completely identical ones. Another type of harmonization is international minimum standards to which all the parties to an agreement must adhere, even though they remain free to adopt or not, as they please, higher or stricter standards. Alternately, as is the case in the Uruguay Round GATT/WTO Technical Barriers Agreement and the North American Free Trade Agreement (NAFTA) equivalent, parties may be encouraged to adopt standards that are developed by international standard-setting bodies by an obligation to justify any deviation from international standards that has a trade-restricting effect. A further kind of harmonization norm is reflected in the requirement that policy inputs be harmonized – for example, that risk regulation be based upon scientific assessment of risk.[2] Another example of harmonization is an obligation or commitment to increase the compatibility of conformity assessment, licensing, or testing procedures with a view to mutual recognition. While mutual recognition, whereby goods and services may be imported freely if they conform to the domestic requirements of the exporting state, is often characterized as an alternative to harmonization, its premise is in fact almost always a reduction of regulatory diversity or incompatibility through the setting of minimum standards so as to make mutual recognition acceptable, given each country's domestic policy objectives. Finally, where variance in regulatory outcomes appears to derive more from variations in the enforcement of laws and regulations than in differences in the laws and regulations themselves, a harmonizing effect may occur through a requirement that each country effectively enforce its own law (this kind of obligation is embodied in the NAFTA labour and environmental side agreements).

Leebron has provided a thoughtful review of the wide range of normative claims that are often made for harmonization of domestic regulation (Leebron 1996). These include: (1) jurisdictional interface costs, e.g., different railway gauges, telecommunications protocols, or aircraft navigation systems that inhibit mutually beneficial cross-border transactions; (2) externalities ensuing from different regulatory standards, e.g., transborder pollution; (c) leakage and the non-efficacy of unilateral rules, e.g., the undermining of domestic intellectual property protection by the importation of infringing goods; (4) fair competition, e.g., lesser regulatory burdens in one jurisdiction that give producers in that jurisdiction an unfair advantage over foreign producers in international trade; (5) economies of scale, e.g., different technical requirements in various jurisdictions that may prevent manufacturers based in any one jurisdiction from achieving economies of scale from servicing more than one jurisdictional market; (6) political economies of scale, e.g., regulatory requirements that entail marshalling of specialized resources that are beyond the capacity of any single jurisdiction; and (7) transparency, e.g., preventing the adoption of laws or regulations that appear to address legitimate public policy concerns but are in fact disguised restrictions on foreign competition.

However, Leebron also points out that differences between nations may also have value, and that harmonization can only be achieved at the cost of eliminating or reducing differences. He argues that nations can be said to differ in five attributes that affect the laws and policies they adopt: endowments, technologies, preferences, institutions, and coalition formation. If preferences, endowments, and technologies were the only differences between nations, one could perhaps assume that differences in governmental regulation and policy were legitimate determinants of comparative advantage. In cases where differences in policies or legal regimes reflect differences in preferences, harmonization will entail a potential welfare loss for citizens in at least one of the jurisdictions. However, according to Leebron, once differences in institutions and coalition formations are taken into account, the presumptive legitimacy of differences in regulatory choices is less clear.

In other work, we have expressed caution or scepticism about the use of trade liberalization processes as a vehicle for harmonizing domestic regulation (Trebilcock and Howse 1997). One dimension of our scepticism or caution is the lack of institutional capacity in trade institutions to deal legitimately and effectively with regulatory harmonization. Against this perception, the example of the European Union (EU) is often cited in support of the argument that, while multilateral trading arrangements may not have the institutional capacity to move beyond trade rules to integration through harmonization, regional arrangements have this potential. We have suggested that the EU may be regarded, however, as a special case, given the high level of development of all the member states, the historical circumstances surrounding the creation of the community, and the dual hegemonic roles of Germany and France (Trebilcock and Howse 1995, 94–6). In general, most regional trading blocks will not be conducive to deep economic integration, mostly because smaller powers will not be prepared to surrender sovereignty to hegemonic powers, and hegemonic powers in turn will not be willing to surrender sovereignty to federalizing and centralizing supranational institutions of the kind that characterize the EU. However, others take a different position. David Vogel argues that in the environmental area regional trade agreements will be very important (Vogel 1995).

The purpose of this chapter is to discuss and assess the suitability of regional or plurilateral trading arrangements as a means of addressing harmonization-related trade issues through norms and institutions that go beyond the national treatment approach. It examines the experience of the Free Trade Agreement

(FTA) and NAFTA up to the present in moving from a framework of trade rules to an institutional framework for integration through harmonization of domestic regulation.

Many, if not most trade experts today tend to view multilateral and regional/plurilateral processes as complementary rather than conflicting – in part, due to increasing scepticism in the economic literature about the importance of the trade diversion impacts of the tariff preferences that characterize non-multilateral arrangements (Bhagwati 1997). However, even apart from trade diversion and the diffusion of scarce political and bureaucratic capital already alluded to, the proliferation of regional arrangements entails another set of costs. These costs arise from the differences in norms and institutions as between these arrangements, leading to overlap and complexity in the rules with which actors in the system must comply (including firms in many instances) as well as the fora in which those rules are interpreted and evolved.

Interestingly, the view that the FTA and NAFTA are vehicles of deep economic integration is common both to many of the strongest supporters of these arrangements as well as many of the harshest critics. When Ian Robinson, for instance, remarks that NAFTA goes further toward being a framework of full-fledged economic integration than 'any other agreement signed by Canada to date,' he makes a claim that closely resembles the rhetoric surrounding NAFTA in Canadian trade policy circles in the early nineties, even though Robinson is concerned about the effects of economic integration on the capacity to promote values of social justice, democracy, and environmentalism (Robinson 1993, 334).

This chapter proceeds by considering provisions of the FTA and, to a greater extent, NAFTA in a range of areas related to the scope and diversity of domestic regulation, including subsidies; services; intellectual property rights; technical barriers to trade, such as sanitary and phytosanitary measures; competition policy; labour; and the environment. We shall attempt to show that, in a number of these areas, the FTA and NAFTA represented little advance even over the pre-Uruguay Round multilateral legal framework (the GATT), and that, in others, the NAFTA has been overtaken or rivalled by multilateral norms and institutions that have emerged in the Uruguay Round of multilateral trade negotiations.

Technical Barriers to Trade

The FTA contained a number of harmonization-related obligations with respect to technical barriers to trade, extending (at least in theory) well beyond the gloss on national treatment in the GATT Tokyo Round Technical Barriers

Code. In practice, however, these obligations made little difference to the management of Canada-U.S. trade relations. This is dramatically illustrated by the fact that FTA dispute panel rulings that have been concerned with technical barriers, the *Salmon and Herring Landing Requirement, Lobsters*, and *UHT Milk* cases, have relied almost entirely on basic obligations in the 1947 GATT to resolve the disputes in question, and have simply ignored or refused to interpret or at least to make the basis of their legal rulings the supposedly more comprehensive, more extensive, or more detailed rules in the FTA. Indeed, one of these panel rulings, which ironically contains the statement that 'the FTA deals with matters, including standards, which are not specifically dealt with by the GATT, and subjects them to new and more effective discipline, including dispute resolution,'[3] actually had to resort to the vaguest and most general concept of GATT jurisprudence, non-violation nullification and impairment, as the basis of its finding for Canada.

The dispute in this case arose out of insistence by Puerto Rican authorities that Quebec producers of UHT milk be required to adhere to a new American regulatory scheme as a condition of being permitted to continue to import their milk into Puerto Rico. This scheme was known as the National Conference on Interstate Milk Shipments (NCIMS) and its main requirements were embodied in the Pasteurized Milk Ordinance (PMO). The PMO allowed for the importation of foreign milk, where the regulatory scheme of the exporting state was equivalent to that of the PMO itself. However, protracted discussions between Canadian and American officials failed to produce agreement on the timing and parameters of a study of regulatory equivalence. An additional difficulty was the requirement that, even once equivalency was established, the imports be subject to checks by American Food and Drug Administration-certified inspectors.

Canada invoked specific provisions of the FTA, including Article 708.1, which committed the parties to harmonize their 'respective technical regulatory requirements and inspection procedures' and 'establish equivalent accreditation procedures for inspection systems and inspectors.' The panel found that these provisions of Article 708.1 were merely 'best efforts' commitments, and, in effect, not justiciable obligations. With respect to Article 708.2, and in particular the obligation not merely to work toward but to prevent the introduction of new measures that were arbitrary, unjustifiable, or disguised restrictions on trade, the panel relied on the French version of the text, which put this obligation with respect to new measures in as weak language as the commitment to work toward elimination of existing ones. In effect, the panel chose the version of the obligation with the least teeth, which implies something about its general interpretive assumption concerning whether the parties really did intend the FTA to lead to deep integration.

Furthermore, the panel alluded to 'Puerto Rico's genuine health and safety concerns'(paragraph 5.49), despite the fact that not a shred of evidence was ever adduced about a health and safety problem concerning UHT milk even after many years of importation. Nor for that matter was any evidence ever presented that Canada's or Quebec's standards and inspection procedures were inadequate.

The panel did, in the end, find for Canada but not based upon any 'new era' provision of the FTA concerning harmonization of standards, equivalency, or conformity assessment. Rather, the panel held that, while not violating any obligation of the FTA, the United State's actions constituted non-violation nullification and impairment, based upon Canada's long-standing expectation that Quebec milk would have access to the Puerto Rican market. It was only in employing this venerable GATT device (explicitly incorporated into the FTA) that the panel managed to allude to the general spirit of the FTA as an agreement aimed at removing regulatory barriers to free trade.

Finally, it should be noted that the NAFTA provisions on technical barriers do not go substantially beyond the FTA in supplementing national treatment with obligations to harmonize. In most relevant respects, as Sykes notes, the NAFTA provisions are in any case largely identical to those in the Uruguay Round GATT Technical Barriers and Sanitary and Phytosanitary Measures Agreements, in requiring the use of international standards wherever possible and appropriate and that national regulations be based on risk assessment and scientific evidence (Sykes 1995, 108–9).

Environment

It is in the areas of environment and labour that the NAFTA, although not its predecessor, the FTA, appears to move much farther down the path of trade-linked harmonization than other trade agreements, including the Uruguay Round GATT/WTO. How far has been a matter of some controversy among experts.[4]

In addition to general provisions on technical barriers to trade, there are several specific provisions in NAFTA that relate to harmonization issues in the environmental area. First of all, Article 104 states that in the event of an 'inconsistency' between the NAFTA and the trade provisions of several major environmental treaties, including the endangered species convention (CITES), the provisions of the environmental treaty shall prevail. This clearly facilitates transnational environmental regulation, allowing trade sanctions otherwise inconsistent with NAFTA to be a part of the compliance and enforcement regimes for international environmental norms. It is unclear, however, whether this provision also applies to the parties' pre-NAFTA GATT obligations. If not, then there may be little effect, since the trade sanctions in question might well still be considered in violation of GATT, given existing interpretations by GATT panels of the environmentally related exceptions in Article 20 of GATT (Howse and Trebilcock 1996).

Secondly, in the investment chapter of NAFTA there is a provision that states that a party 'should not' relax domestic environmental (or health and safety) standards in order to encourage foreign investment (Article 1114). This provision was clearly aimed at addressing concerns about a 'race to the bottom' with respect to environmental standards. There are a number of reasons why one may expect it to have little impact on regulatory diversity: (1) the provision essentially creates a baseline that accepts the existing degree of regulatory diversity between the NAFTA parties as legitimate; (2) making a causal link between a given change in regulation or its enforcement and the encouragement of investment will likely be difficult; (3) the expression 'should not' is weaker than the obligatory language found in most parts of NAFTA, and, as was already seen in the *UHT Milk* case, any deviation from the strongest expression of obligation may be a basis for viewing a provision as merely a 'best efforts' commitment that is largely nonjusticiable.

The NAFTA environmental side-agreement, the North American Agreement on Environmental Cooperation (NAAEC), contains a number of important harmonization-related provisions. First of all, the agreement is somewhat schizophrenic about harmonization, or regulatory rapprochement as such. Article 3 states that 'each Party shall ensure that its laws and regulations provide for high levels of environmental protection and shall strive to continue to improve those laws and regulations.' Article 3 also recognizes, however, 'the right of each Party to establish its own levels of environmental protection.' Of course, one way of reconciling these two provisions would be to conceptualize the harmonization required as that of meeting 'high' minimum standards, with each party free to deviate upward from those minimum standards.

This being said, the only obligation in the NAAEC that can be enforced as 'hard trade law,' with possible monetary penalties for non-compliance, is the obligation to enforce effectively one's own domestic environmental law. Nevertheless, such an obligation could potentially have a significant harmonizing effect, if many of the trade-impacting regulatory divergences with respect to environment are due to variations in enforcement.

Perhaps of greatest potential significance, however, is the set of institutions that the NAAEC establishes for environmental cooperation, including not only two political-level institutions, the commission and council, but also an expert secretariat and a Joint Public Advisory Council (JPAC). This last institution is linked to a consultative process with NGOs within each NAFTA member country. The NAAEC permits NGOs to make submissions that a party is not enforcing its own environmental law, although for such a complaint to be taken to formal dispute settlement it would have to be advanced by a party (i.e., a NAFTA government).

Writing shortly after the NAAEC had been concluded, we suggested that 'at least as much emphasis should be placed on the broader institutional framework it establishes as on the rather limited enforceable legal obligations that it contains' (Trebilcock and Howse 1996, 357). This assessment is proving to be rather accurate: although there has yet to be a formal complaint or dispute panel under the legal obligations established by NAAEC, it does seem to have given birth to a set of active, if only partly effective, institutions. The secretariat has, for example, developed a concrete work program of co-operation in areas such as ecological mapping to determine pollution flows across North America, the development of consistent laboratory procedures for assessing environmental risk, assessment of environmental training needs, and co-operation in conservation of biodiversity and forest ecosystems (Eco Region 1995).

One achievement of the commission is an agreement on the phase-out or reduction of certain toxic substances throughout North American – PCBs, DDT, chlordane, and mercury. However, specific action plans on these substances are yet to be developed, so the agreement is really a resolution or agreement in principle only (CEC Press Release 1996).

To date the secretariat has received several submissions from NGOs concerning possible violations of the obligation of a NAFTA party to enforce its own environmental laws. The first submission, filed in June 1995 by, among other NGOs, the Biodiversity Legal Foundation, alleged that fiscal restraint legislation in the U.S. that prohibited the Fish and Wildlife Service from making final determinations for species or critical habitat designations for the remainder of fiscal year 1995 and cutting its budget had the effect of a failure to enforce the American Endangered Species Act.[5] In its reply to this submission, the secretariat refused to take the matter further, finding that 'the alleged failure to enforce environmental law results from competing legislative mandates, and not from other action or inaction taken by agencies or officials.'[6] This establishes a fundamental limitation on the obligation of each country to enforce its own environmental law – such an obligation does not extend to a requirement that nonenvironmental legislation not frustrate such enforcement.

The second complaint made to the commission, by the Sierra Club, also concerned a legislative derogation from existing American framework environmental law. In this case the measure was a 'rider' on an American budget-cutting statute that essentially eliminated the possibility of review of salvage timber sales for environmental effects.[7] This complaint was not taken further by the secretariat on the same basis as it invoked with respect to the first complaint, i.e., that 'the Secretariat cannot ... characterize the application of a new legal regime as a failure to enforce an old one.'[8] In this second determination the secretariat also stressed the importance of a factual record showing that nonenforcement was actually occurring, thereby suggesting that even if the 'rider' had been in regulations not legislation, it would have been essential to show that it resulted in an actual pattern of nonenforcement of the relevant environmental framework law.

Another complaint was filed by Mexican NGOs with respect to nonenforcement of Mexican environmental law.[9] This complaint alleged that during the evaluation of a project for a cruise terminal on Cozumel Island a range of Mexican environmental laws had not been effectively enforced, and that two coral reefs were being endangered by the project. Here, for the first time, the secretariat found that there was a justification for requesting a response from Mexico, which was provided in late March of this year – the response is apparently not yet publicly available, but it contains a blanket denial of the petitioners' claims.[10] There is at least one other complaint in the process, but none so far has proceeded to the stage of dispute settlement.

Finally, under the NAAEC, NGOs may also make submissions on matters not directly related to the issue of a NAFTA party's enforcement of its environmental law. One such submission has actually become the subject of a secretariat report. The submission concerned the death of migratory birds at the Silva Reservoir in Mexico. The secretariat struck a panel of scientific experts to investigate the matter, which found that the death of the birds was related to high levels of toxins in the area.[11] The secretariat suggested a number of options for dealing with the problem, including that the reservoir be monitored for waterbird mortality, that the reservoir be drained if there is evidence of a waterbird mortality problem, that birds be kept off the reservoir, or that the topography of the reservoir be altered to make it less susceptible to these problems. However, the formal recommendations that the Council made to Mexico were limited essentially to the recommendation that the Mexican government conduct a comprehensive evaluation of the problem and possible solutions to it. The panel of scientific experts had, by contrast, made some very specific suggestions as to the environmental measures needed to remedy the source of the problem, including proper treatment of raw-discharge municipal wastes and large industrial waste sources. When the experts' work was filtered up the institutional hierarchy of the NAAEC, however, what was proposed largely amounted to further study and more 'best efforts.'

While it is probably too early to make an overall evaluation of the harmonizing impact of the NAAEC, the character and level of its activity to date suggests that this will be modest, although to its credit the secretariat has managed to develop a set of concrete initiatives and to press NAFTA parties to support these initiatives, albeit with mixed success. There has been some useful building of understanding between domestic regulators and a transnational network of NGOs and regulators has been enabled through these institutions, which may eventually lead to the knowledge and trust required for more concrete steps toward more ambitious regulatory co-operation. However, this may be due to the relative autonomy of the institutions in question from the trade diplomacy-dominated main NAFTA regime, allowing the building of transnational links without constant threat of interference from trade and foreign affairs ministries.

Labour

The NAFTA Labour Side Agreement, the North American Agreement on Labour Cooperation (NAALC), much like the NAAEC, exhibits an ambivalent approach to harmonization. Each party is to ensure that its labour standards are 'high' and consistent with 'high quality and productivity workforces,' and yet each party is also free to establish its own domestic labour standards (Article 2). As with NAAEC, the only obligation that constitutes hard law that can be brought before a dispute panel is the obligation to effectively enforce domestic labour laws (Article 3). An institutional framework is provided not unlike that for the NAAEC.

A major difference with the NAAEC is the process whereby complaints may proceed from a non-governmental actor to the trinational dispute resolution process. This occurs through initial consideration of the complaint by a National Administrative Office (NAO). This mechanism is not fully operational in Canada, largely due to the problem of provincial jurisdiction over most labour law. The initial work program of the secretariat, which consists of fifteen persons, has been on technical issues related to occupational health and safety regulation. This has involved a series of seminars and workshops, but little else (Morpaw 1995).

So far there have been a handful of complaints about Mexican labour practices to the American NAO and at least one complaint about American practices before the Mexican NAO, which was subsequently withdrawn (Varaleau 1995). The first two complaints were against Honeywell and General Electric; in both cases it was alleged that Mexican labour laws guaranteeing the right to organize an independent union were not being enforced with respect to the companies' plants in Mexico. The complaints alleged that Mexican law had not been enforced so as to prevent the firing of workers for actively promoting membership in an independent union. The complaints were dismissed by the

NAO on the grounds that the workers had voluntarily accepted severance pay and had been prepared in return to waive their rights under Mexican law. However, it was arguable that they had little choice but to accept the settlement if they were to survive, especially given the long delay and small possibility of success in pressing their claims before the Mexican labour tribunal. The NAO did, however, make the rather anaemic recommendation that there be a government-to-government conference on freedom of association issues and related subsequent meetings involving unions and industry.[12]

Another complaint to the American NAO concerned suppression of efforts to organize an independent trade union at a number of Sony plants in Mexico (the workers were already members of the official government-connected trade union). Here dismissals in retaliation for organizing were involved, but there were also other claims of wrongdoing, including irregularities in union elections. The NAO recommended in this case that the matter be the subject of consultations at the political level between the NAFTA parties, but largely on the grounds that the Mexican Arbitration and Conciliation Commission had refused to register a new union on questionable legal grounds. The result of these consultations was an agreement between ministers, concluded on 26 June 1995, calling for more consultation and study at the technical level.

A further complaint, lodged with the Mexican NAO, concerning suppression of a unionization initiative by workers at an American Sprint facility near the Mexican-U.S. border, also entailed dismissal of workers attempting to organize a union local. Although the workers in question had not exhausted all avenues of appeal within the domestic American legal system, the NAO nevertheless found that there was a serious basis for concern and recommended ministerial consultations.

None of these complaints even came near approaching formal dispute resolution between NAFTA parties. However, in each case public hearings were held and a factual record was established, putting in question the practices of the employer. From the perspective of public opinion, it may not be insignificant that each of these employers was a major multinational corporation, perhaps susceptible to embarrassment by this kind of proceeding. For this reason, even in the absence of formal enforcement, the adverse publicity might have some effect on the future behaviour of these kinds of employers.

As well, the National Administrative Offices and related mechanisms have at least begun to create a meaningful regulatory dialogue across boundaries, for example, on child labour. While a diplomatic culture appears to exist in which the appearance of frontal challenge to any country's regulations or administration of them is avoided, at least a transnational network of regulators, NGOs, and labour lawyers is being developed, in at least some degree of isolation from the pressures of day-to-day trade and other foreign policy politics. But, as with environment, this may reflect the fact that the institutional structure in question has been separated from NAFTA as a trade agreement. As well, one wonders, given the resurgence of activity at the International Labour Organization, whether initiatives on some of these issues at both the regional and multilateral level might dissipate resources and complicate transnational cooperation, rather than result in mutually reinforcing processes. However, this issue is now explicitly on the table, due to a recent complaint raising the issue of the relation of ILO Conventions to the domestic labour law of Mexico – consideration of this complaint will provide an occasion to reflect on the interrelationship between the domestic, regional, and multilateral levels of labour regulation in a systematic fashion.

Competition Policy, Dumping, and Subsidies

Under the Canada-U.S. Free Trade Agreement, no provisions were included that specifically entailed the harmonization of the two countries' competition laws or their integrated administration and enforcement. However, under Articles 1906 and 1907, the agreement contemplated the creation of a working group to develop a substitute system of rules in both countries for antidumping and countervailing duties as applied to their bilateral trade within a period of five to seven years after the entry into force of the agreement. In the event of failure to implement a new regime at the end of this period, either country would be entitled to terminate the entire agreement on six months' notice. In the preface to Chapter 19 in the Canadian government's official version of the agreement, it is stated that 'the goal of any new regime will be to obviate the need for border remedies, as are now sanctioned by the GATT antidumping and subsidies codes, for example, by developing new rules on subsidy practices and relying on domestic competition law.' The North American Free Trade Agreement (NAFTA) which, in 1993, largely superseded the FTA, contains somewhat weaker commitments in this respect. Under Article 1504, the Trilateral Trade Commission shall establish a working group on trade and competition to make recommendations to the commission within five years of the date of entry into force of the agreement on 'relevant issues concerning the relationship between competition laws and policies and trade in the free trade area.' Under Article 1907(2), the parties further agree to consult on (a) the potential to develop more effective rules and disciplines concerning the use of government subsidies, and (b) the potential for reliance on a substitute system of rules for dealing with unfair transborder or pricing practices and government subsidization. Under a Side Accord to NAFTA signed by the three parties in

December 1993, following the election of a new federal government in Canada, the working group commitment under Articles 1906 and 1907 of the FTA has been reinstated, with the group to report within two years of the coming into force of NAFTA. These negotiations have reportedly led to minimal consensus.

Beyond these provisions, NAFTA contains a short chapter (Chapter 15) on competition policy, monopolies, and state enterprises. Under this chapter, each party commits itself to adopting and maintaining measures to proscribe anticompetitive business conduct and to take appropriate action with respect thereto. Pursuant to this commitment, Mexico has recently enacted a comprehensive competition law. The parties also commit themselves to co-operating on issues of competition law enforcement policy, including mutual legal assistance, notification, consultation, and exchange of information relating to the enforcement of competition laws in the free trade area. However, no party may have recourse to dispute settlement under the agreement in the foregoing matters. In the case of monopolies and state enterprises, each party commits itself to ensuring that state-sanctioned monopolies will minimize or eliminate any nullification or impairment of benefits anticipated under the agreement and that in the case of both privately owned and government-owned monopolies they will act solely in accordance with commercial considerations in the purchase or sale of goods or services in the relevant market and provide nondiscriminatory treatment to investments of investors, and to goods and service providers of another party.

A recent report of the Task Force of the Anti-Trust Section of the American Bar Association on the Competition Dimension of the North American Free Trade Agreement (American Bar Association 1995) suggests a number of framework principles for developing the competition dimensions of NAFTA, the first of which is 'identifying a barrier-free and distortion-free North America as a fundamental goal' (American Bar Association 1995, 2). The task force is critical of the statement of the objectives of NAFTA in Article 102, which include promoting conditions of fair competition in the free trade area. The task force proposes instead that 'the Antitrust Working Group, in consultation with the member governments, should consider proposals to incorporate within NAFTA a clear statement identifying the creation of an integrated North American market based on free competition as the fundamental objective of the Agreement' (American Bar Association 1995, 80). The task force is also critical of the competition provisions in Chapter 15 of NAFTA: 'No NAFTA provision attempts to define the areas in which a party may designate a monopoly or state enterprise, nor to specify principles (such as market failure or compelling need) limiting such designation. Indeed NAFTA contains only an off-handed recognition of competition as a fundamental means to attain its broad economic objectives (in the Preamble). Similarly, there are no limitations whatever on competition-distorting government aids or subsidies' (American Bar Association 1995, 62). Comparing NAFTA with the European Union, the task force states: 'NAFTA's statement of the market integration objective is comparatively ambiguous and diffuse. Moreover, NAFTA fails to assign any explicit role to free market competition in the overall legal conception of the Agreement. Provisions analogous to the statement of the market-integration objective contained in Article 2 of the Treaty of Rome and the identification of competition as the fundamental means of organizing economic activity within NAFTA, analogous to Article 3(f) should be considered for adoption as part of NAFTA' (American Bar Association 1995, 79). The task force then proposes that the Working Group on Trade and Competition to be established under Article 1504 of NAFTA 'should consider proposals for NAFTA provisions to control state aids in a manner analogous to Articles 92–94 of the Treaty of Rome' and 'proposals for NAFTA provisions to control state enterprise and private and public monopolies in a manner analogous to Articles 92–94 of the Treaty of Rome' (American Bar Association 1995, 80–1). In contrast to its proposals on the central objectives of NAFTA and on monopolies and subsidies, the task force's proposals on substantive harmonization of competition laws (Chapter 7) are surprisingly modest and brief. However, to date, efforts by the working group under Article 1504 to develop proposals either to harmonize domestic competition laws or to create some form of supranational review process for anticompetitive business practices suggest very modest progress.

Beyond these proposed competition policy innovations, the historical origins of the tension between competition law and international trade policy in North America require serious attention to the remaining protectionist elements in international trade policy, particularly trade remedy regimes such as antidumping and countervailing duty regimes, which are largely lacking in normative coherence and which constrain the operation of international competitive forces far more than do any aspect of current domestic competition policy regimes (Trebilcock and Howse 1995, chs. 5 and 6; Boddez and Trebilcock 1995). But again, despite the precedent of the EU, where antidumping and countervailing duty actions have been abolished between member states, and despite the claim by the Canadian government in FTA negotiations that relief from American trade remedy laws was a primary objective of the negotiations, little or no progress has been made on these issues. Progress within the working group under Article 1907(2) on substantive reform of domestic antidumping and countervailing duty laws appears to have been minimal. The only constraint on antidumping and countervailing duty actions specific to the FTA or NAFTA is the binational panel review process contained in Chapter 19 of both agreements.

While Chapter 19 does not contain any substantive rules that would aid the resolution of disputes over subsidies and dumping,it does permit the review of domestic agency determinations for compliance with the domestic law that the agency purports to be applying, including basic administrative law norms. The FTA/NAFTA binational panel review has been widely utilized and has resulted in a high incidence of panel remands (Mercury 1995). Where Canada has pursued a trade dispute through both the GATT process and the FTA/NAFTA process, e.g., the *Pork* and *Softwood Lumber* matters, it has been able to advance a number of claims through the FTA process that would not have been easy to place before a GATT panel, since they are not directly related to any specific GATT violation, but rather to the manner in which the American authorities have interpreted American law. In respect of all the FTA/NAFTA panel decisions to date where Canada has won favourable legal rulings, these rulings have been based at least in part on arguments that a specific American statute or regulation was misapplied by the American authorities or that general requirements of American administrative law concerning the rationality and evidentiary basis for administrative rulings were not met.

Delays between an initial complaint against an agency determination and the final legal resolution through a remand determination acceptable to a binational panel are not significantly shorter or longer than those involved in the GATT process. However, the costs that Canadian producer interests face are of a much greater magnitude with respect to the FTA/NAFTA process. First, they must pay the costs of representation with respect to the initial panel hearing, then, once they have secured partial or full legal victory in that proceeding, they must be prepared to pay the costs of rearguing the remanded parts of the case before the American authorities a second time. In a number of FTA cases, the determination on remand has involved a whole new series of methodological issues, as the ITA or ITC attempts to find a new basis on which to justify imposition of duties or an injury determination that is consistent with the panel's ruling. This in turn may give rise either to a new agency determination that violates the panel's requirements or reimposition of duties on different grounds. In either case, a further panel decision will be required, and again new costs will have to be born. This further panel decision may ultimately dispose of the matter by a more definitive set of instructions to the agency in question or it may result in a further set of remands, which in turn may give rise to yet another panel review, further increasing legal costs. Finally, in some instances, American interests may attempt an extraordinary challenge to a panel ruling, thereby requiring reargument on appeal to the Extraordinary Challenge Panel.

In several cases, of which *Pork*, *Swine*, and *Softwood Lumber* are the most notorious, it has taken numerous panels and remands to get to the point where the Canadian industry actually obtained remedial action from the American authorities. Although Canada, for example, has been fairly successful in securing, at the end of the process, both positive legal outcomes and some remedial satisfaction, as the *Pork* case well illustrates the result of millions of dollars of legal costs and a substantial victory on the law may well be a very modest reduction of duties that does not substantially restore the competitive position of the Canadian industry in the American market. It must be emphasized that, unlike the normal rule for civil litigation in Canada, the victorious side must pay its own legal costs in any FTA/NAFTA proceedings. And as the ultimate outcome of *Softwood Lumber* demonstrates, it is possible to consistently succeed in the dispute settlement process but, at the end of the day, still have to pay the price for regulatory diversity, because of the politics of trade law. Since there is no requirement for harmonizing the substantive trade remedy law of the NAFTA parties, it is always possible to respond to an unfavourable panel ruling by changing the law, as the U.S. Congress did in the wake of *Softwood Lumber*. The real constraints on changing the law are actually multilateral – it must conform to the WTO Agreements on Subsidies and Countervailing Duties and on Dumping.

Under NAFTA, the defects of the FTA process are not only not corrected, but new defects are created. Most importantly, the grounds of appeal to an Extraordinary Challenge Panel have been extended to include the application of an inappropriate standard of review by the panel. This provision reflects in large part American complaints that the American side has lost many panel cases because the panels have not been sufficiently deferential to American agency determinations – or not as deferential as the American courts had been prior to the transfer of the appeal function to the panels.

The result of the NAFTA provision will be that the losing side in a panel determination will often be able to pursue a rearguard action, thereby further increasing the legal costs and delays associated with the dispute settlement process. Another provision of NAFTA that may represent a setback with respect to what Canada secured under the FTA is the requirement that, wherever possible, panellists be retired or serving judges, i.e., as opposed to the trade law experts who are now extensively used as panellists. Many of the arguments that Canada has been making about the defects in the details of the methodologies employed by the American authorities in their interpretations may have been harder to sustain if they had been made before generalist judges unlikely to have had any prior exposure to these issues, rather than before trade experts.

Moreover, while, under the FTA, a party's options as to whether to pursue a matter at the GATT or through the FTA process, or both, was unconstrained by procedural rules, under NAFTA, depending upon whether the provisions on GATT dispute settlement in Chapter 20 are interpreted to apply to Chapter 19 as well, there would be a fairly strict set of constraints requiring an either/or choice between the GATT or the NAFTA process and, in some circumstances (e.g., where environmental matters are at issue), requiring that the NAFTA process alone be used.

In light of the Uruguay Round Subsidies Agreement, it is possible to conclude that, in fact, the multilateral process has been much more successful in achieving some degree of rules-based order in domestic trade law regimes than either FTA or NAFTA. First of all, the agreement reflects a consensus that certain types of subsidies, including certain regional, environmental, and R & D subsidies, represent legitimate domestic policy choices and should not be countervailable. Secondly, the agreement incorporates the concept of specificity as a precondition for countervailability of subsidies under domestic trade remedy laws, and it defines specificity. This will place a brake on the manipulation of the concept by the U.S. Commerce Department, rightly deplored by the binational panel in two of its rulings in *Softwood Lumber*. It will now be possible to bring a complaint to the WTO DSB, where countervailing duties have been imposed on the basis of a concept of specificity that is unsupported by the criteria contained in the Subsidies Agreement. In some real sense, then, the WTO Agreement has, at least with respect to countervailing duty complaints (which raise important issues concerning regulatory diversity), overtaken the increasingly troubled Chapter 19 binational review process.

Investment, Services, and Intellectual Property Rights

In extending certain basic disciplines to the areas of services and investment, areas where many harmonization-related issues arise with respect to free market access among countries, the FTA may appear at first glance to have been considerably in advance of the GATT prior to the Uruguay Round, and inasmuch as in the case of investment and services the disciplines in the NAFTA are more broadly based in certain ways than those in the post-Uruguay Round GATT/WTO, there would seem at first glance to be a prima facie case that, at least with respect to these 'new era' areas, regional arrangements may well produce a more integrating result. In fact, however, the FTA did little more than extend, with certain reservations and exceptions, the national treatment and MFN approach toward trade in goods embodied in the 1947 GATT to trade in services and a range of investment measures. This approach, as discussed at the outset of this paper, essentially rejects harmonization, permitting as much regulatory diversity as is consistent with nondiscrimination against foreigners.

Certainly, inasmuch as the Uruguay Round Trade-Related Investment Measures (TRIMs) Agreement applies only to a relatively small subset of investment measures that affect trade in goods directly (such as domestic sourcing requirements) and largely affirms the existing GATT provisions in the same area, the FTA and NAFTA extension of national treatment to investors and investments themselves appears a major advance. But the range of measures to which the national treatment obligation applies does not include subsidies or most kinds of investment incentives.

One area where the FTA/NAFTA investment provisions would appear to go beyond national treatment and to move toward harmonization is in the requirement that the investment of another party not be expropriated without compensation. However, given the broad character of these provisions and the lack of consensus on the meaning of expropriation (with the domestic American jurisprudence extending the concept of a 'taking' to regulatory change that merely affects the value of an asset), as Pierre Sauvé notes, the end result may be the creation of new kinds of litigious harassment and new harmonization-related trade disputes: 'Already the NAFTA has shown that the combination of a sweeping definition of investment, strong provisions on expropriation-related matters and the possibility of investor-state dispute settlement form a very potent cocktail. Indeed, there is every sign that the potential for policy harassment embodied in such a combination of provisions may amount to yet another full-employment bill for trade lawyers!' (Sauvé 1995a, 12).

Here, along the lines of Sauvé's observation, it is important to distinguish between harmonizing provisions of trade agreements that can reduce trade friction due to regulatory diversity and thereby serve a trade-liberalizing purpose and those (like the FTA/NAFTA expropriation provisions) that may simply be creating new kinds of trade complaints based upon supposedly 'unfair' domestic policies while not enunciating a consensus-based supranational standard.

In the case of services, NAFTA appears to go beyond the GATS in applying the national treatment obligation to all trade in services, whereas in GATS this obligation only applies to service sectors mentioned in members' specific schedules of commitments. In the case of many countries, these schedules have far from comprehensive coverage. At the same time, there are a wide range of reservations and exceptions to national treatment in NAFTA with respect to specific sectors, and a general reservation now for existing state and provincial measures. One reservation in particular that will limit the impact of

NAFTA on the shape of regulation is the reservation taken with respect to any privatization-related measures, meaning that a post-privatization regulatory framework arguably need not conform to key trade norms, including national treatment.

Indeed, in an important respect, GATS may be further along the spectrum toward harmonization, since it requires a set of further disciplines to ensure that a wide range of nondiscriminatory barriers to trade in services, including those that are not explicitly discriminatory, do not constitute 'unnecessary barriers to trade in services' (Article 6, 4–5). These provisions of the GATS actually apply to services generally, not just to sectors listed in member's schedules. By contrast, the comparable NAFTA provision applies only to licences and certification agreements (Article 1210).

One area where NAFTA may appear to move further toward addressing regulatory barriers to market access is professional services, where various provisions call for a process to facilitate cross-boundary provision of professional services through a combination of harmonization (establishment of the equivalency of professional credentials, etc.) and mutual recognition (Sauvé, 1995b). However, the success of these initiatives entails coordination of negotiations between the parties to NAFTA (national governments), subnational governments (who, in both Canada and the United States, regulate many of the professions) and non-governmental professional bodies. NAFTA simply does not create the kind of strong institutional framework needed for the success of such complicated, multilevel negotiations. In some sense, it offers the worst of all worlds; on the one hand, failing to provide strong transnational institutions of the EU kind, while on the other encumbering informal co-operative links between the relevant domestic regulators with an extra layer of bureaucracy, that of central government trade ministries and related authorities, who are quite removed from the ground-level technical issues to be resolved. Finally, the recent proposals before the U.S. Congress on control of the Canada-U.S. border are a reminder that changes in immigration requirements can easily undermine otherwise promising efforts at harmonization or mutual recognition with a view to transboundary delivery of services. Here, clearly, an economic and political union, such as the EU (with a common passport and significant progress toward abolition of border formalities within the EU for holders of that passport), can provide a more solid framework for liberalization of trade in professional services – although even there progress in some areas (accountancy) has been much greater than in others (law).

Finally, Trade-related Intellectual Property rights (TRIPs) is the one area where NAFTA, although not the FTA, displays what might be called the full-blown harmonization approach – specifying the substantive rights and obligations that must be built into domestic intellectual property laws and eliminating a large amount of regulatory diversity.[13] However, not all the harmonization observable in changes to Mexican and Canadian intellectual property law can be attributed to NAFTA. In Mexico, attracting foreign investment and technology transfer has been a major reason for overhauling its IP regime (Callary and Casada 1993), and in Canada, the abolition of the compulsory licensing scheme for pharmaceuticals may be as much attributable to the relationship between the previous government and the patent drug industry as to the legal requirements of the NAFTA TRIPs provisions, since the latter do permit case-by-case compulsory licensing where certain criteria are met.

In any event, perhaps the most fundamental point is that the WTO TRIPs agreement contains largely identical requirements for harmonization with respect to most forms of intellectual property. There are, to be sure, a number of differences in detail that may have important consequences for certain industries. But overall, it is impossible to conclude that the regional process has generated a significantly more harmonizing or more deeply integrating outcome than the multilateral one.

Institutional Mechanisms and Initiatives Addressing Trade Dimensions of Regulatory Diversity[14]

It is sometimes said that it is unfair to judge the regulatory impact of NAFTA on the basis of the existing legal text. Rather, one should consider the longer-term potential evident in the various institutional mechanisms and processes that are harmonization-related. Thirty-five to forty committees and/or working groups have been established to date under the auspices of the NAFTA agreement, of which a number were originally constituted under the FTA.

A few of these committees have indeed been active in harmonization-related activities, but focusing usually on very technical or rather peripheral matters, in contrast to their often quite grandiose mandates. Bringing Mexico, which is obviously a developing country with limited technical resources in most of these areas, into active harmonization-related technical work has been time- and resource-consuming, again suggesting a structural constraint on the NAFTA formula for regional integration.

Among the most active and apparently successful groups and committees are the Land Transportation Subcommittee and related subcommittees on Driver/Vehicle Compliance, Vehicle Dimensions, Highway Signage, Railway Safety, and Dangerous Goods, many of which meet several times annually. The Vehicle Dimensions subcommittee has to identify core vehicle configurations with a target date. Another active committee is the Telecommunications Standards Subcommittee mandated in Chapter 9 (the technical barriers chapter of NAFTA). The original intention of this committee was to pass its work on to private sector groups that would form a consensus on technical standards and pass recommendations back to the committee. However, industry groups deadlocked and the committee has found itself in the position of having to develop the standards (the committee does rely on industry groups in setting these standards). It has already made decisions on mandatory standards. The Committee on Sanitary and Phytosanitary Measures has apparently been successful in addressing some harmonization-related trade irritants, for instance, the entry of Canadian Seed Potatoes into Mexico and issues related to swine fever. Other committees with apparently crucial harmonization-related mandates, such as the Committee on Services and Investment, have rarely met and do not appear to have made any concrete harmonization-related decisions.

In general, the various institutional mechanisms established by the FTA and the NAFTA with harmonization-related mandates have done some useful technical work (for example, on the transportation of hazardous substances) and solved some peripheral trade irritants (for example, in the agricultural area), but they do not constitute an institutional fabric at all equal to their often very ambitious mandates. Certainly, and this is a relevant qualification to the overall thesis of this paper, in matters such as land transportation-related standards in a contiguous region, there is a certain elemental geographical logic in conducting harmonization exercises on a regional basis. But in an area like telecommunications, it is easy to imagine the admittedly valuable work of the NAFTA-based committee being overtaken by WTO-based processes. However, it must be remarked it is 'early days' for these committees and the participants themselves show some optimism.

Even, however, in areas such as land transportation, it is questionable whether a trade-agreement-driven process – that has to pass decision making on detailed technical regulations through the bureaucratic channels of trade diplomacy – advances or frustrates cooperation between working-level officials.

Conclusions

A survey of FTA and NAFTA provisions and processes concerning harmonization-related trade issues suggests that regional trading arrangements in North America do not have any greater capacity to cope with harmonization-related trade issues than the GATT/WTO multilateral process. This is not to suggest that regional arrangements have not played, or may not play, a kind of stopgap function until multilateral rules evolve, or that they may not provide laboratories for experiments with new kinds of trade disciplines connected to harmonization-related issues.[15] But regional arrangements like FTA or NAFTA are not necessarily likely to lead in the longer run to more 'deep integration' than multilateral regimes.

This observation should, however, be placed in the broader context of the trend toward globalization of regulation. While this trend is driven in significant part by trade opportunities and pressures, at the same time processes of international harmonization or regulatory rapprochement may quite appropriately occur in institutions that have a separate, specialized focus – whether one thinks of the ISO in the case of voluntary standards, the Codex Alimentarius process in the case of food safety, or the International Labour Organization (ILO) in the case of labour standards. These institutions, as well as the plurilateral but obviously not regional institution of the OECD, are designed for discussion, debate, and rapprochement of domestic policy differences. The link to trade law disciplines comes through obligations that encourage the adoption of those harmonized norms or standards developed in these relatively autonomous international processes.

More generally, it is arguable that excessive attention has been paid to trade agreements or negotiations as vehicles of harmonization or motors of regulatory convergence and insufficient attention has been given to what Anne-Marie Slaughter refers to as a 'new transgovernmental order' – built not so much by trade agreements but by the networking of regulators themselves across national boundaries. Slaughter argues:

The state is not disappearing but it is disaggregating into its separate, functionally distinct parts. These parts – courts, regulatory agencies, executives and even legislatures – are networking with their counterparts abroad, creating a dense web of relations that constitutes a new, transgovernmental order. Today's international problems – terrorism, organized crime, environmental degradation, money laundering, bank failure, and securities fraud – created and sustain these relations. While political scientists Robert Keohane and Joseph Nye first observed its emergence in the 1970s, transgovernmentalism is rapidly becoming the most widespread and effective mode of international governance' (Slaughter 1997).

An intervening layer of regional trade law arguably does little to advance these kinds of processes and may simply burden them with greater complexity, dissipating the time and resources of regulators in trade-driven institutions that are unlikely to produce effective transgovernmentalism, with regionalism excluding or marginalizing important transnational actors who have an important stake in regulatory cooperation but fall outside the limits of the region, whether NGOs in an areas such as environment, who have a global focus, or international regulatory organisms that have a genuinely multilateral character. The goal of integration through trade-linked regulatory rapprochement may be much better served through clarification of the relationship between, for instance, WTO norms and processes and transgovernmental regulatory processes. If regional cooperation is appropriate, as with geographically specific challenges, then a separate process for trade negotiations as such is probably preferable; the increasing understanding and interaction among domestic regulators, NGO, and other actors that has been the main valuable outcome of the Environmental and Labour Side-Agreements may be connected precisely to the separate character of these regimes, with institutions with at least some measure of autonomy from the high politics of trade diplomacy.

NOTES

We are grateful to Petrus van Bork for research assistance on this paper and to Pierre Sauvé for comments on an earlier draft. An earlier version of the paper was presented at a conference on NAFTA at the Centre for International Affairs at Harvard University in May 1996 and we are grateful to participants of the conference for useful suggestions and criticisms, especially Dan Treffler and Kalypso Nicolaidis. The usual disclaimer applies.

1 See especially the ruling of a GATT panel in 'Canada-Import, Distribution and Sale of Alcoholic Drinks by Provincial Marketing Agencies,' (1992) BISD 39th Supp. 27, where an identical minimum price requirement imposed on both imported and domestic beer sales was held to violate the national treatment obligation, because it denied equal competitive opportunities to imported beer that could be supplied below this price (the minimum price had been set by reference to the prices of domestic product); see also the Salmon and Herring Landing F.T.A. Panel Decision.
2 These last two kinds of harmonization requirement are present in the Uruguay Round Agreement on Sanitary and Phytosanitary Measures (SPMs).
3 'In the Matter of Puerto Rico Regulations on the Import, Distribution and Sale of U.H.T. Milk From Quebec,' Final Report of the Panel, 3 June 1993, para. 5.60. Of course, the panel's statement that the GATT does not deal with standards, or somehow does not allow for dispute resolution for standards-related disputes, is on its own terms entirely erroneous.
4 On the environment, for instance, at one extreme David Vogel takes the view that 'thanks to the provisions of the environmental side agreement and the much larger size of its domestic market, NAFTA has the provided the United States with the potential to play a role in strengthening Mexican regulatory policies analogous to

Germany's role in strengthening European regulatory standards' (Vogel (1996), 246–7). For contrasting views, see Charnowitz (1994) and Atik (1995).
5 Submission No. SEM-95-001, 30 June 1995.
6 Determination of the Secretariat, 21 September 1995, 3.
7 Submission no. SEM-95-002, 31 August 1995.
8 Determination of the secretariat concerning submission SEM-95-002, 8 December 1995, p. 3.
9 Submission no. SEM-96-001, 18 January 1996.
10 CEC Press Release, 'Mexico Responds to Citizen Petition Alleging Failure to Effective Enforce Environmental Law,' 28 March 1996.
11 CEC Secretariat Report on the Death of Migratory Birds at the Silva Reservoir, October 1995.
12 *Public Report of Review: NAO Submission # 9400001 and NAO Submission #940002*, Bureau of International Labour Affairs, U.S. Dept. of Labour, 12 Oct. 1994.
13 And, indeed, we have argued, particularly with respect to patent protection, the elimination of regulatory diversity may actually be largely unjustified on trade theory or, more generally, economic theory grounds (Trebilcock and Howse (1995), ch. 10).
14 The following observations are based upon a survey of the work to date of these various mechanisms, prepared by Petrus van Bork. We appreciate the co-operation of various Canadian government officials affiliated with the committees and working groups, who have provided information on their activities. However, the judgments about their performance are entirely our own.
15 As Paul Sauvé, for example, has often suggested.

REFERENCES

American Bar Association. 1995. *Report of the Task Force of the Anti-Trust Section on the Competition Dimension of the North American Free Trade Agreement.* Washington, D.C.: American Bar Association.
Atik, J. 1995. Environmental Standards within NAFTA: Difference by Design and the Retreat from Harmonization. *Indiana Journal of Global Legal Studies* 81: 81–103.
Bhagwati, Jagdish. 1997. Essay in the *Economist*, 18–25 October.
Boddez, Thomas, and Michael J. Trebilcock. 1995. The Case for Liberalizing North American Trade Remedy Laws. *Minnesota Journal of Global Trade* 4:1–41.
Callary, S.J., and Y.H. Casada. 1993. State Control of Technology Transfer in Latin America. Faculty of Law, University of Ottawa, November.
CEC Press Release. 1996. Three Additional Chemicals Targeted for Joint Action by Canada, The U.S. and Mexico.

Charnowitz, Steven. 1994. The NAFTA Environmental Side-Agreement: Implications for Environmental Cooperation, Trade Policy, and American Treatymaking. *Temple International and Comparative Law Journal* 8:257–314.

Eco Region. 1995. Newsletter of the Secretariat of the Commission for Environmental Cooperation. 1, no. 1.

Howse, Robert, and Michael J. Trebilcock. 1996. The Fair Trade–Free Trade Debate: Trade, Labour and The Environment. *International Review of Law and Economics.* 16:61–79.

Leebron, D. 1996. Lying Down With Procustes: An Analysis of Harmonization Claims. In Jagdish Bhagwati and Robert Hudec, eds., *Fair Trade and Harmonization: Pre-requisites For Free Trade?* Cambridge, Mass.: MIT Press.

Mercury, John. 1995. Chapter 19 of the U.S.-Canada Free Trade Agreement 1989–96: A Check on Administered Protection. *Northwestern Journal of International Law and Business* 15:525–605.

Morppaw, M. 1995. The North American Agreement on Labour Cooperation (NAALC): Its Impact on Canada and Mexico. Paper prepared for the Lawyers for Canada-Mexico Cooperation Conference, Mexico City, January.

Robinson, Ian. 1993. The NAFTA, Democracy and Continental Economic Integration: Trade Policy as if Democracy Mattered. In Susan Phillips, ed., *How Ottawa Spends 1993–94*, 333–70. Ottawa: Carleton University Press.

Sauvé, Paul. 1995a. Market Access Through Market Presence: New Directions in Investment Rule-Making. Paper presented to the Canadian Economics Association, 3 June.

– 1995b. The Long and Winding Road: NAFTA and the Professions. In OECD, *Liberalized of Trade in Professional Services*, 61–7. Paris: OECD.

Slaughter, A.-M. 1997. The Real New World Order. *Foreign Affairs* 76:183–97.

Sykes, A.O. 1995. *Product Standards for Internationally Integrated Goods Markets.* Washington, D.C.: Brookings Institution.

Trebilcock, Michael J., and Robert Howse. 1995. *The Regulation of International Trade.* London: Routledge.

– 1998. Trade Liberalization and Regulatory Diversity: Reconciling Competitive Markets with Competitive Politics. *European Journal of Law and Economics* 6:5–37.

Varaleau, D. 1995. Dispute Resolution Under the NAFTA Labour Side Agreement: Will Canadian Procedures Make a Difference? Student paper, Faculty of Law, University of Toronto.

Vogel, David. 1995. *Trading Up: Consumer and Environmental Regulation in a Global Economy.* Cambridge, Mass.: Harvard University Press.

16

The Globalization of Finance and the Regulation of the Canadian Financial Services Industry

STEPHEN L. HARRIS

The purpose of this chapter is to review the events – those of both a substantive and process character – that have altered the way in which the Canadian financial services industry is regulated and conducts its business. The industry has undergone a major transformation over the course of the past thirty years or so. The system has evolved from one characterized by an intrusive state that extended beyond activities of prudential supervision. Exchange rates were fixed or managed, coincident with the Bretton Woods Agreement, ceilings on bank lending rates were mandatory, and there was a strict separation of powers between financial and market intermediaries. All of these factors impaired competition in the Canadian financial system. Canada, however, was not alone in this regard, as the financial services industry in most other OECD countries, including the United States, had even more limitations placed upon it.

With an easing of state intrusion in financial market decision making, the blurring of the functional powers of financial and market intermediaries, and the creation of financial 'conglomerates' with wide-ranging ownership powers, a more competitive and open financial system subsequently evolved in Canada. At times Canada was in the forefront of this liberalization, while at other times she lagged behind, as issues of economic nationalism took precedence over values of efficiency and competition. It is worth emphasizing that the liberalization that occurred in Canada and elsewhere in the industrialized world affected institutional powers and market access and involved measures that allowed markets rather than bureaucratic hierarchies to determine interest rates and allocate credit. There was little scope to liberalize prudential supervision. On balance, regulations of a prudential character were probably tightened while the apparatus for regulating financial services has been restructured and enhanced in response to the changed configuration of the Canadian financial landscape.

Canada's financial services industry comprises a number of so-called pillars (institutional types):

- The chartered banks (financial intermediaries) – the major deposit-taking institutions in Canada and traditionally the providers of short-term credit to households and businesses.
- The trust and mortgage loan companies (financial intermediaries), both of which engage in deposit taking from and mortgage lending to individuals and businesses. The former institutions also engage in trustee activities, which include funds management and estate management.
- The co-operative movement (financial intermediaries), whose roots are in collecting the savings of individuals and lending to the household sector. The co-operatives have expanded dramatically over the past thirty years and today, as full financial service providers, they are an important competitive force in the Canadian financial system and occupy a pre-eminent position in Quebec.
- The insurance companies (financial intermediaries), the largest of which are the life insurers. These latter institutions are also engaged in selling annuity instruments and manage substantial portfolios of financial assets. Property and casualty insurance companies insure against all sorts of risks to persons, buildings, and transportation equipment and manage large financial portfolios.
- The investment dealers (market intermediaries), who bring together borrowers and lenders of funds in the financial markets (stock, bond, money, and foreign exchange markets), but who typically are not principals but only agents in the transactions between borrowers and lenders.
- A miscellaneous group of intermediaries such as mutual funds, which pool savings of individuals for investment in money market, bond, and equity instruments; hedge funds, which carry out similar activities for wealthy individuals in risky types of operations; leasing companies – the largest of which are affiliated with large manufacturing companies in transportation and heavy machinery – which borrow on the wholesale capital market and lend to businesses in order to finance the purchase of their parent companies' products.

The process of reaching the point of an open and competitive financial system was circuitous and lengthy. The system evolved in an incremental manner. The Canadian state, broadly defined, had no long-term plan to create such an open and competitive regime – although the *1964 Report of the Royal Commission on Banking and Finance* (the Porter Commission) attempted to chart such a course. The enduring objectives throughout this gradual journey were not only an efficient and competitive financial system, but also a sound (solvent and stable) one.

Basic international developments in the financial services industry and rationales for the regulation of financial services are described below. The financial services policy process is then examined and the key regulatory reform developments of the past thirty years, which have worked to restructure the financial services industry in Canada, are outlined.

International Developments in Financial Services

Considerable liberalization in the financial services industry in the industrialized democracies has occurred since the mid-1960s. A particular impetus to the liberalization process was Regulation Q in the United States, which imposed a ceiling on the rates that financial institutions could pay on deposits. This constraint, together with the development of the Eurodollar market in London, as former 'East Bloc' countries moved their U.S. dollar deposits out of the United States to London, spurred American banks to become involved in that market, where regulatory constraints of the sort that they faced at home were absent. More generally, institutions from many countries found themselves undertaking in the London market activities that they were prohibited from engaging in at home (Harris and Pigott 1997, 41; Reinicke 1995).

This development initiated the globalization of financial markets from which there has been no turning back. It gave rise to an iterative process of competitive liberalization across the industrialized democracies. National authorities were fearful that if they did not respond to the emerging international phenomenon their indigenous financial centres would become backwaters, with important negative externalities for their economies.

The first stage in the liberalization process consisted of an easing of the restrictions on foreign exchange transactions in many European countries. An easing of limitations on banks' borrowing and lending, to allow market hierarchies rather than bureaucratic hierarchies to determine equilibria, followed. Finally, there was a convergence of financial services structures across the industrial democracies.

There were two aspects to this convergence: the first was the convergence toward the universal bank structure – or 'one-stop shopping' for financial services. This phenomenon was characteristic of continental European arrangements, while in the Anglo-Saxon countries and Japan, investment and commercial banking (as well as insurance) were traditionally separated, for seemingly prudential reasons. The second aspect of this convergence related to markets, where American practices and culture have become the norm. The convergence ranged from the way in which monetary policy is implemented (the use of market-based instruments is of increasing importance); the manner in which governments sell their debt (via auctions, as opposed to the use of less transparent syndicates appointed by the debt managers); the influence of financial engineering on market activity (the development of derivatives); and the sensitivity of market reactions to political and economic events (market volatility).

The main reason for the convergence of practice was the pervasive presence of American institutions in foreign markets and the resultant migration of practices, which were imposed on countries without any clear recognition of what was happening or why. The convergence of structure, on the other hand, occurred largely as a consequence of competition among the various types of institutions and a blurring of the activities in which they were involved. In the United States, even the intrusive Glass-Steagall arrangements, which separated commercial and investment banking activities, have been eroded dramatically in the past fifteen years, while prohibitions on interstate banking are rapidly receding in that country (Harris and Pigott 1997, 45). In addition, there was an easing of entry and ownership into the domestic financial services industry, as well as an easing of foreign ownership restrictions in many countries.

It is important to point out once again that most of these changes had a liberalizing effect on financial services and that they were industry led in one way or another. However, in the financial services industries in those countries in which there was a separation of 'pillars,' not all of the pillars spoke with one voice. Each component of the industry wanted to protect its turf. The investment banking industries in the UK, the U.S., Canada, and, more recently, Japan, were strident in the attempts to protect their turf, most notably in the case of fixed commissions for stock exchange transactions and entry into the industry by banks and other nonindustry participants. In continental Europe, however, states were reluctant to surrender their intrusive activities in financial services until the European Union's (EU) Second Banking Directive (SBD) was implemented. The SBD was designed to create a single market for banking services in the EU (Harris and Pigott 1997, 47–8).[1]

The Rationale for Regulating Financial Services

A number of perspectives are relevant in considering the assertion that 'financial regulation is indispensable' (Harris and Pigott 1997, 32–5). The first, and perhaps the most common argument made, is that prudential supervision is necessary in order to achieve the desirable objective of a 'safe and sound' financial system (Dixon 1996). The second concerns entry and ownership in the financial services industry: the degree of international trade in financial services that should be allowed, and the degree of intermingling of banking, securities, and other financial services that should be tolerated (Canada 1985a; Freedman 1996; Harris 1995, 1996b; Kirsch 1997). The third argument made with regard to the necessity of financial regulation is the concept of 'regulatory planning' (Schultz 1982), where the state provides guidance in order to preserve its own strength, to promote national champions, and for distributive purposes. The strength of this notion has all but evaporated in most Western industrial nations, with France and Germany being notable exceptions (Harris 1997, 2).

In order for a capitalist economic system to function effectively, it is necessary for the economic actors to have confidence in the financial system. It is not a sufficient condition for success, but it is a necessary condition. Confidence in the financial system means that those who lend funds to the financial institution will receive what is due to them on maturity; banks who participate in the daily cheque-clearing process have confidence that they will receive what is due to them at the end of every day; and corporate governance structures in financial institutions will ensure that those institutions conduct their business in the interests of their clients and not in their own interests.

Regulations to preserve 'safety and soundness' take the form of capital adequacy ratios, liquidity and risk management system requirements, prohibitions on self-dealing and conflicts of interest transactions, and disclosure requirements (Harris and Pigott 1997, 32–5). Prudential supervision in the past included direct controls on borrowing and lending rates at banks and on other prices in the financial system. It also comprised intended and unintended obstacles to the introduction of new products and other innovations, the institutional separation of banking type activities, and limitations on who could engage in securities underwriting and trading, insurance, and trustee activities.

Enduring objectives of financial services regulatory policy in Canada have been maintaining a competitive financial system, efficient markets and institutions, and a safe and sound system, and protecting the consumer. Nonetheless, the objectives of financial regulation are contextually driven and depend on the state of the economic conjuncture (Reinicke 1995). In the aftermath of the Porter Commission Report, for example, financial services regulatory policy concentrated on enhancing the competitiveness of the Canadian financial system. For a long time prior to this period the focus of the regulatory authorities was on prudential supervision and planning. This was evidenced by the 6 per cent interest rate ceilings on bank lending, fixed commissions on stock exchange transactions, and portfolio allocation requirements for most financial intermediaries. In the 1970s and early 1980s the focus was extended to include solvency in addition to competition in markets and among institutions. With rapid globalization and the unsustainable price pressures experienced in Canada through the late-1970s to mid-1980s period, portfolio excesses among financial intermediaries became common and threatened many institutions. Consequently, solvency again became foremost on the financial sector policy agenda. While of little comfort, it should be noted that Canada was not alone in experiencing banking and related institutional difficulties. Similar problems occurred in the United States, the Nordic countries, Japan, and the United Kingdom.

What we have witnessed over time is a trade-off between regulatory objectives – competition and efficiency versus safety and soundness. There is yet another trade-off, that between economic efficiency and political efficiency. Politically efficient decisions are those which seem 'doable' from the political decision makers' perspective without affecting the level of safety and soundness of the financial system. We will see examples of both as this analysis progresses.

The Financial Services Regulatory and Policy Process

State-Industry Relationships

Building on the path set by the Porter Commission (Canada 1964) numerous formal inquiries, consultative papers, and parliamentary hearings have marked the policy process in Canada's financial services industry over the course of the past thirty years. Such a process is consistent with transparency in the policy-decision-making process of a democratic society and can therefore be applauded. However, there is also another reason for the numerous consultative activities of policy makers. It relates to the capacity of the state to understand the complexity of the financial system and thus to develop structural policies that will be beneficial rather than harmful to public welfare. Thus, this striving to get policy 'right' should also be cheered.

However, one of the major shortcomings of the process is that it can give rise to regulatory capture and/or to indecision. The regulatory capture arises as a consequence of the asymmetric distribution of information between the financial services industry and the state. Historically, the state has had to rely on the financial services industry for suggestions for policy change and for the evaluation of the impact of a potential policy change. The financial services industry recognizes its comparative advantage and attempts to maximize its potential usefulness.[2] Proposals by the state that do not meet the needs/demands of the industry are portrayed in a negative fashion by the industry. Historically, the state is not well placed to counter the arguments of the industry, because its knowledge of the industry is often inadequate. This process gives rise to regulatory capture.

At the federal level it is not unusual for the Department of Finance to ask one of the major banks to second one of their officers to assist with the development of financial policies. The individual would return to the bank when the task was completed. Given the baggage such individuals would bring to the task, it is not difficult to envisage either the character of advice that the department would be given or the character of the proposals it would receive from the competitors of that individual's home institution. Such a practice is not conducive to independence in the policy process.[3]

There is also a close and unique relationship between the elites in the financial services sector and those in the state (whether political or bureaucratic). Presidents of banks and securities firms are only a phone call away from ministers, deputy ministers, governors, and superintendents. There is a constant exchange of visits between bureaucrats at lower levels in the hierarchies and commercial and investment bankers, institutional portfolio managers, and presidents of industry associations. Consumers' associations, on the other hand, wait in the background for formal invitations from the state to present their briefs. There is clearly unequal access of 'ordinary' citizens, compared to financial services industry representatives, to the state's decision makers.

In the securities industry, the chair of the Ontario Securities Commission is typically seconded from one of the influential Bay Street law firms for a two-to-three-year period and then returns to the law firm at the end of the term. These chairs have typically made their careers in private law practice serving the needs of the financial services industry. The consequence of such revolving-door appointments for regulatory capture are well documented in the American literature but have not received the same degree of attention in Canada (Harris 1995).

Political elites also depend on financial elites for 'political' support and thus are reluctant to supply policies that would be contrary to the wishes of the financial services industry. This phenomenon partly explains the extensive delays in changing financial services legislation and regulations. At times, however, the state is put into the position of acting as arbiter among the various components of the financial services industry. This was the case for the liberalization of the securities industry in 1986 (Harris 1995), and, more recently, when the federal government decided that the chartered banks could not engage in selling insurance services through their individual branches, but only though subsidiaries (Canada 1996a).

Indeed, in preparing for the most recent round of proposed changes (1996–7) in financial services regulations, the industry was unusually critical of the capacity of the Department of Finance to carry out its analytical function, with respect to its understanding of the character of the changes that were required in Canada. Part of the problem of the department's capacity, according to industry participants, related to the fact that it had lost a good deal of its expertise. This was attributable to the federal government's downsizing exercise, resignations at the senior level of the bureaucracy, and the fact that the senior staff that was available had been preoccupied with the negotiations on the General Agreement on Trade in Services (GATS) and not with the domestic legislative agenda.[4]

The phenomenon of capture has been more clearly apparent in the securities industry regulation. Historically, the securities commissions have been short-staffed and largely populated by lawyers, not analytical social scientists, and thus not well placed to analyse either the state of the securities industry or the likely impact of proposed policy changes. Indeed, the regulators have been subject to the kindness of the industry for assessments of policy changes. It is not very difficult to determine whose interests will be taken care of in such a regime. Similar circumstances helped the Canadian securities industry to insulate itself from the vagaries of enhanced market competition, from banks, and from non-resident firms over the 1969–86 period (Harris 1995).

The National Policy Process

Historically, at the federal level, the major legislation in question is the Bank Act. This statute is subjected to a legal decennial revision – a 'sunset clause.' Thus, there is a formal motivation for implementing the process of regulatory change. In the case of the securities regulation, the stimulus has for the most part come from outside the formal bureaucracies and institutions – from the industry itself or from offshore developments.

As the ten-year anniversary of the Bank Act approaches, the federal government typically begins the call for submissions from interested parties on proposals for change – perhaps preceded by a 'coloured' paper. At the same time the Senate Banking and House of Commons Finance Committees would call witnesses to testify about proposed changes. In the case of the 1997 revisions, the government issued a discussion paper (Canada 1994); and in the case of the 1992 amendments a 'rainbow of coloured papers' flowed from the federal bureaucracy.

Since 1992, at the federal level, there has been a Senior Advisory Committee (SAC) dealing with changes in the regulatory regime. This committee comprises representatives of the key agencies involved in the oversight of the financial services industry. Its main focus is on structural issues – the ways in which overarching legislation should be reformed in order to meet the objectives of financial services policy. The Department of Finance chairs this committee because it has primary responsibility for framing the overarching legislation. The other members are the Office of the Superintendent of Financial Institutions (OSFI) – the financial services regulator – the Canada Deposit Insurance Corporation (CDIC), and the Bank of Canada. The SAC typically meets at the CEO level, but representatives from the same institutions would meet at lower levels.

The Department of Finance works to balance the interests among the agencies involved. It has also been suggested that the department looks after the interests of 'consumers.'[5] The Bank of Canada's role has been characterized as the 'honest broker' in the deliberation process. 'The Bank looks at the logic of proposals and their arguments. How do the proposals fit together? How do the proposals fit with the regime that is already in existence? The Bank is seen in Ottawa as having a broad perspective and is less susceptible to political influence or pressures.'[6] Moreover, the 'Bank of Canada always brings the laissez-faire point of view' to the table.[7] The Department of Finance sees its mandate as providing the overarching framework for changes in the financial services regime and it sees that of the OSFI as concerned with the technical and operational issues of oversight. Department of Finance officials think that they 'bring an unbiased and analytical perspective' to the table. However, because of the change in resources at the Department of Finance alluded to above, which has weakened its policy capacity, the OSFI, with its enhanced policy capacity,[8] has attempted to expropriate the department's prerogative in this area.[9]

Together, the OSFI and CDIC worry about the technical issues and oversight processes. In this regard, there is a certain tension between the two agencies over which one takes the lead role in the policy-making sphere. Also, there has at times been concern about the over-lapping responsibilities of OSFI and the CDIC (Canada 1995).

With respect to the technical issues associated with regulatory oversight in banking, the Office of the Superintendent of Financial Institutions and, from time to time, the Bank of Canada, will suggest changes of a technical nature that may be hampering the oversight process or interfering with the smooth functioning of the financial market. The major changes to the financial services legislation that are of a structural or systemic character are typically played out among the interests with a stake in the issues.

Dating from 1992, there has been a formal apparatus at the bureaucratic level to deal with what are essentially supervisory issues – the Financial Institutions Supervisory Committee (FISC). The FISC comprises the same members as the SAC but is chaired by the OSFI. 'This interagency committee is meant to ensure consultation and information exchange on supervisory matters that have implications for solvency, last-resort lending and the risk of deposit insurance payout ... The FISC is intended to give the Superintendent, who is responsible for judgments pertaining to the viability and solvency of federal institutions, the full benefit of views from the deposit insurer and the lender-of-last-resort when making supervisory decisions' (Daniel, Freedman and Goodlet 1992–3, 41–2).

Policy Process at the Provincial Level

The policy process for financial services reform at the provincial level varies. In Ontario, in the case of the securities industry, the industry itself takes the hegemonic position, while in the case of financial intermediaries the process is similar to the federal one. In Quebec, on the other hand, the state takes the hegemonic position, partly for historic reasons – the weakness of the indigenous financial services industry – and partly for reasons related to economic planning and economic nationalism (Harris 1995).

In the case of the securities industry in Ontario, over the period of the late 1960s to the late 1980s, when the major framework laws were changed, the policy process pattern was quite clear. The industry would take the lead in examining an issue that was of concern, by convening a 'joint committee' comprising all members of the established SROs in Canada. Small groups of industry elites would form working committees to consider the issues and draft reports for consideration by the Ontario Securities Commission (OSC) in the context of a full-blown commission hearing. The OSC would prepare a report, to which another joint industry committee would draft a rejoinder. Such a process, in the case of the liberalization of the securities industry ownership question, persisted for almost twenty years before it was resolved (Harris 1995). Similar patterns of activity have persisted since.

While the process dealing with entry and ownership in the securities industry was not any shorter in Quebec, it was the provincial government, via its own civil servants and sponsored commissions or boards of inquiry (often chaired by a senior civil servant), which steered the process. Consultation would take place with private interests but, as noted earlier, the process was driven by the political objectives of the government and not by those of the financial market participants.

In the time interval noted above, Ontario and Quebec were locked in a struggle over which city, Toronto or Montreal, would ultimately have pre-eminence in the securities business. This war of hegemony in the investment banking industry helped to prolong the emergence of a resolution about who could participate in this business (Harris 1995).

In the case of reforms related to financial intermediaries, the process in both provinces was rather similar to the one pursued in the federal government. The typical vehicle used to examine these broader questions was the Royal Commission-type of apparatus, which encompassed invitations for formal submissions by interested parties, formal hearings, and, finally, a report with recommendations (Ontario 1985; Quebec 1988).

Canadian Regulatory Reform: A Thirty-Year Perspective

With the developments described above as context, we can now examine more specifically key regulatory changes over a thirty-year period in which international forces were always entwined with domestic factors. Five areas of change are explored.

The Removal of Lending and Deposit Rate Ceilings

Between the mid-1960s and the early 1970s a number of OECD countries began a program of removing bank lending and/or deposit rate ceilings (Harris and Pigott 1997, 42). In Canada, the 1967 amendments to the Bank Act eliminated the 6 per cent interest rate ceiling on chartered bank loans, permitting the banks to engage in mortgage-lending activity for the first time in many years. While this action partly reflected developments elsewhere in the OECD area, the main impetus for change was that the chartered banks found themselves disadvantaged compared to the trust and mortgage loan companies and other nonbank financial intermediaries. Indeed, the interest rate ceiling began to impinge on the rates the banks could offer on their deposits liabilities because of the limits on what they could earn on their assets. In the period between 1963 and 1967, the share of chartered bank assets of all financial institutions' assets declined (Canada 1976, 9).

An additional amendment to the Bank Act, which served to enhance the competitive position of the banks, was the lowering of their required cash-reserve ratio. This had the effect of lowering their average costs of deposits – but not as low as the near-banks, which were not required to hold any statutory cash reserves. The federal government was 'forced' to respond to the eroding position of the chartered banks. As alluded to earlier, all of these matters were noted in the Porter Commission Report (Canada 1964).

Gradual Related Measures to Enhance Competition

The 1980 Bank Act amendments continued the uncompleted legacy of the Porter Commission recommendations. The focus continued to be one of ensuring competition in the Canadian financial services industry while concerns about solvency remained on the 'back burner.' Part of this continuing concern for competitiveness and contestable markets, that is, easy entry and exit, related to the fact the globalization phenomenon was continuing to encroach on the Canadian financial system. More particularly, however, the restrictions on entry of foreign banks in Canada, the remnants of the policies of economic nationalism from the 1960s, had the American banks demanding reciprocity. In the absence of reciprocity there was a real risk that the American legislators would diminish the access that Canadian institutions had to the American market.

With respect to enhancing competition within the domestic financial services industry the federal government moved on a number of fronts:

- Entry into the banking industry for Canadian-owned entities was made easier. In the past, in order for a Canadian bank to obtain a charter, a private members' bill had to be passed in the House of Commons. This was a lengthy and uncertain process, which inhibited entry (Canada 1984, 32). The 1980 changes gave the minister of finance the power to issue a bank operating licence.
- At the same time, the government established the Canadian Payments Association. The power to operate the clearing system was taken away from the Canadian Bankers' Association, as had been recommended by Porter, and was given to this new organization comprising those institutions involved in the Canadian payments system – banks and nonbank financial intermediaries (NBFIs). In the past, the NBFIs were obliged to clear their customers' payment items through one of the chartered banks. The new regime would allow the near-banks the opportunity to participate directly in the new system and to be full participants in its evolution.
- The federal government, in the new legislation, distinguished between widely held banks (Schedule A banks) – the existing big five banks – and closely held banks (Schedule B banks). Schedule A banks had to be Canadian controlled; one shareholder could not own more than 10 per cent of the voting shares; and non-residents in total were only permitted to own up to 25 per cent of the voting shares. The concept of the closely held institution was introduced in order to permit foreign commercial banks to establish full banking entities in Canada (Shearer, Chant, and Bond 1984, 374–5). The provisions surrounding the Schedule B concept would also permit NBFIs (mainly trust companies) to convert themselves into banks without immediately divesting ownership in order to comply with the Schedule A provisions. The roots of this ownership policy lay also in the analysis and recommendations contained in the Porter Report.

- The government again reduced the level of required reserves on demand and term deposits of the banks, which further enhanced the banks' capacity to compete with the NBFIs (Shearer, Chant, and Bond 1984, 372–3).
- Finally, the government allowed the banks to get into the factoring and leasing businesses through subsidiaries (Shearer, Chant, and Bond 1984, 372).

One of the problems of regulatory change generally, but particularly in the case of the financial services industry, is governments' inability to take sufficient account of the spillovers or linkages (or what economists characterize as externalities) of policy changes (Harris and Pigott 1997, 72–4). This has been the history of changes in financial services regulation throughout the OECD area. In Canada, the federal government appeared to have dramatically enhanced the capacity of the Canadian-owned chartered banks to compete with the NBFIs in the areas of deposit taking, mortgage, and other consumer lending, in addition to their strength in the commercial lending field. The powers of the NBFIs were enhanced somewhat, but not nearly to the same extent as for the banks. As will be seen, one of the consequences was to ensure that financial activity became more concentrated in the hands of the banking system. More than that, the prime credits located themselves in the sphere of the banks, while the lesser credit-worthy customers found themselves migrating to the NBFIs – particularly to the trust companies – thus undermining the 'balance sheet quality' of these institutions.[10]

The consequences of this public policy decision making in the sphere of financial services regulation set the stage for a shift to a more balanced consideration of the issues in the next round of revisions to the relevant legislation, which were implemented in 1992. The focus was on both financial system solvency and financial system structure.

The Liberalization of Stock Market Commissions

Toronto Stock Exchange (TSE) commissions were liberalized in June 1982 after an attempt six years earlier had been rejected by the OSC as a result of the intense lobbying by the Ontario-based securities industry. The delays associated with realizing a more liberal regime in Ontario were similar to those experienced in the United States some seven years earlier. One of the factors, which ultimately brought the deliberations to a conclusion, was the fact that Canadian investors were trading cross-listed equities on the New York Stock Exchange (NYSE), thus depriving the TSE of revenue-producing business. This latter development, plus the influence of the federal competition authorities, combined to persuade the OSC that the rents being gleaned by the domestic securities industry in Canada were not justified (Harris 1995, ch. 3). It is noteworthy that four years after the OSC action, in 1986, the restructuring of the London financial markets occurred (Mayer 1995, 138–59; Harris 1995, ch. 3; Harris and Pigott 1997, 42–3).

It is interesting to note the remarkable similarity in the features of these episodes and of the policy process in each of the U.S., Canada, and the UK:

- Monopoly rents were being gleaned by the securities industries as a consequence of the fixed commissions on the three stock exchanges;
- the regulatory authorities fought lengthy battles with the entrenched interests of the industry;
- the intellectual influence of the competition authorities was important in influencing the primary regulators and SROs;
- there was recognition by both the authorities and the national industries that unless the resistance to change evaporated, the respective indigenous industries could suffer a serious hollowing out (of course, national authorities and the industry participants themselves wanted to avoid such a circumstance); and
- the competitive deregulation that occurred reflected the convergence of interests in each of the national markets and a clear convergence, as well, at the international plane.

Ontario Liberalization of Ownership of the Investment Dealer Industry

In 1986 the Ontario government liberalized the entry into and ownership of the investment dealer industry – which means that banks and foreigners were permitted to own, in whole or in part, firms in the securities industry. This was the first formal sanctioning of the blurring of the pillars of the Canadian financial services industry (Harris 1995). It was a long and circuitous journey, beginning in 1969, when Merrill Lynch, the largest investment dealer in the world, took over Royal Securities, a large Canadian dealer with Bank of Canada 'jobber' status. This policy drama pitted Ontario and Quebec against one another, the Ontario-based firms against Quebec-based firms, and Ontario firms against foreign-owned entities. An important, and complicating, dimension in this process of liberalization of the securities business was Canadian federalism and the lack of a coherent Canadian voice in these matters. Indeed, just as there was an important competitive element at the international level for liberalization of financial services, there was the same pressure to stay one step ahead in the Canadian market. Quebec was always at least one step ahead of Ontario (see Harris (1995)).

1992 Financial Services Legislation

As had been the case in the past, the 1992 financial services legislation took some eight years to realize. The first cut at the changes were contained in a paper titled *The Regulation of Canadian Financial Institutions: Proposals for Discussion* (Canada 1985a).[11] This document was prepared under the direction of Barbara McDougall, the minister of state (finance). In December 1986, Ms McDougall's successor, Thomas Hockin, released a revised policy proposal entitled *New Directions for the Financial Sector: Executive Summary* (Canada 1986c). The almost two years that elapsed between the two papers reflects the change in the scope of the proposed reforms. Finally, in late 1990, yet another minister of state (finance), M. Gilles Loisell, released the government's last proposition in the form of a White Paper (its predecessors were respectively Green and Blue) titled *Reform of Federal Financial Institutions Legislation: Overview of Proposals* (Canada 1990).

The government's inaugural proposal, put forward in 1984 (the Green Paper) was the first recognition by a Canadian government of the need for a major change in the way the Canadian financial services industry was structured. With respect to the form of the structure, there were few models within the sphere of the industrialized democracies upon which the government could draw. The choice was only between the existing four-pillars regime, which was eroding as a consequence of the globalization of markets, and the universal bank model, where financial institutions would be permitted to undertake all financial activities and offer all financial services to their customers (Freedman 1996).

However, it was not easy for the federal government, its advisers, and the financial services industry itself to let go of the four-pillars model. The Green Paper fashioned a complicated set of proposals that would have allowed the chartered banks, the trust and mortgage loan companies (TMLs), and the insurance companies to engage in each other's business through the umbrella of a financial holding company. This was not the 'ideal universal bank model' but it did recognize the overlap among financial institutions and financial products that had emerged in Canada and elsewhere. More precisely, a holding company would be permitted to have a bank, a TML, and an insurance company and the shares of an investment dealer in its portfolio. The bank, however, would be a Schedule C bank (closely held). The purpose of this financial holding company regime was to broaden the powers of existing four-pillar institutions without having to abandon the basic structural model. Thus, a trust company whose powers were limited in the commercial lending field could be a full participant in this activity if it formed a holding company and established a Schedule C bank. An insurance company that wished to be involved in the fiduciary business could establish a holding company and then a trust company. The proposals would not apply to the existing Schedule A and B banks, which were already well established in the commercial lending field. In addition, the government proposed to permit networking among financial institutions – but only among the NBFIs and the Schedule C banks (Canada 1985b, 70–2). The implication appeared to be that Schedule C banks would be permitted to sell insurance through their branches and engage as well in the leasing business generally. The existing Schedule A and B banks would not be permitted to network to the same extent, if at all.

The idea of networking gained support across the financial services industry (Canada 1985d, 68) and particularly appealed to the smaller institutions, because it would allow them to provide their clients with a wider range of services than would otherwise be possible. The networking proposal, however, reflected the inability of the federal policy makers to decide if they wanted to maintain the separation of the pillars or to adopt the universal bank model.

This proposal by the federal government regarding ownership arose because there was no legislation in Canada that limited the share of TMLs and insurance companies that could be held by commercial organizations or individuals. Indeed, 'with the takeover of the Canada Trust Company by the Genstar Financial Corporation, all major trust companies and a substantial number of stock life insurance companies [were] now closely held with a significant number also being cross-owned through holding company structures.' The authors of the Green Paper concluded that it would be disruptive to roll back the current ownership regime to meet the precepts of the chartered bank widely held ownership regime. Thus, they fashioned the ownership proposal to accommodate the existing ownership arrangements in the trust and life insurance industries (Canada 1985d, 52).

The concerns about widely held and closely held financial institutions in Canada related to prudential considerations: the former arrangements have traditionally been viewed in Canada as a deterrent for self-dealing transactions, whereas in the closely held arrangement the owners 'could have undue influence' on the institution and thus undermine its financial strength (Canada 1985d, 53).

The House of Commons Finance Committee was opposed to committing to the holding company structure as a way to ensure diversification of the financial services industry. The committee was of the view that the state should be neutral vis-à-vis financial services structure and thus favoured the subsidiary route as the vehicle for financial institutions to expand the scope of their operations (Canada 1985d, 65).

The Senate Committee also 'rejected the proposal that trust companies be required to conduct all additional commercial lending through a holding company and a Schedule C bank. In large measure this was because [the committee] believed that the expansion of in-house commercial lending powers was not only more appropriate but, as well, consistent with regulatory concerns' (Canada 1986b, 83).

On the question of self-dealing, most of those institutions that appeared before the Commons Finance Committee 'favored a partial rather than a general ban of this activity because a general ban could perhaps defeat the overarching purpose of allowing financial institutions to integrate their operations' (Canada 1985d, 71–2).

The Green Paper's proposal of the Schedule C bank was rejected by virtually all of the 'near-bank' financial institutions that presented testimony to the Finance Committee. They favoured 'direct in-house expansion of commercial lending powers' (Canada 1985d, 67).

The major concern in the financial sector about the government's proposal for diversifying the industry was the fact that it imposed a particular corporate structure on those institutions wishing to broaden the scope of their activities. Thus, those institutions that did not want to become part of a holding company would be limited in their activities and moreover could put smaller institutions in a relatively disadvantageous position compared to their larger competitors. There was also a concern among the banks that their powers would not be reviewed until 1990 (the scheduled date for the decennial review of the Bank Act) and in the interim they would be at a competitive disadvantage relative to the near-banks (Canada 1985d, 87).

The House of Commons Finance Committee, in searching for a compromise to the dilemma, saw two alternatives (Canada 1985d, 88):

- broaden the scope of in-house powers of financial institutions without altering the existing institutional structure; or
- permit financial institutions to broaden the scope of their activities through the route of either subsidiaries or holding companies.

The bottom line of the government's initial proposal to restructure the financial system was well summarized by the House Committee: 'Of the one hundred thirty seven submissions received by the Committee, only four groups endorsed the concept of a Schedule C bank. Furthermore, only one of the four groups was a non-bank institution. The most important reason for the non-acceptance of the Schedule C proposal lies in its impracticality. In addition to the high cost of establishing a bank, one of the intended beneficiaries of this proposal, namely trust companies, would have to duplicate their existing deposit-taking function. The combination of these two factors would effectively eliminate small trust companies from competing in the commercial lending market' (Canada 1985d, 94).

Between 1981 and 1984 there had been some fifteen failures of TMLs and insurance companies (Canada 1985a, 11). This gave rise to concerns within the government and regulatory apparatus about measures that could be enacted to reduce the risks of insolvency among financial institutions and thus reduce the threat of financial system failure. The Green Paper consequently contained proposals to prohibit self-dealing[12] and conflicts of interest.[13] At the same time, given that the government was proposing a move toward the universal bank model, it saw a need to strengthen the regulatory and oversight provisions in the financial institutions' legislation. This resulted in a proposal to consider merging the regulatory functions of the Superintendent of Insurance and the Office of the Inspector General of Banks into a comprehensive supervisory body. As well, the government indicated that it would consider expanding the powers of the financial institutions' supervisor to more effectively carry out its responsibilities.

In the ensuing thirty months or so, the financial system – both domestically and globally – continued to change. Domestic market activities among those institutions comprising the Canadian pillars continued to blur while, at the same time, domestic markets continued to be pulled (dragged) into the international arena. In response to the regulatory failures noted above the government sponsored two inquiries – the Estey Commission into the Northland and CCB collapses and a review of the inspector general's office by the accounting firm of Coopers and Lybrand (Canada 1986a). In addition, there had earlier been a study of the Canada Deposit Insurance Corporation (Canada 1985c). Thus, there were many crosscurrents pressing upon the government in its deliberations about the financial services legislation. At the end of this difficult thirty-month period the new minister of state for finance, Thomas Hockin, issued a new rendering of the government's position on this important legislation (Canada 1986c).

The Hockin policy paper followed the broad thrust of the proposals that had been put forward by his predecessor. The proposals would permit the move toward the universal bank model by permitting the integration of the pillars through the vehicle of common ownership. In addition, TMLs would be given much greater consumer and commercial lending powers, banks and insurance companies would be allowed to engage in fiduciary activities, and banks with less than $750 million of capital could be closely held as long as there were no significant owners of voting shares with commercial links. If the capital base of such banks should subsequently exceed this threshold level, they would have five years to have at least 35 per cent of the outstanding shares widely held.

Against the background of the institutional solvency and regulatory problems, the Hockin paper moved decisively to strengthen the federal prudential oversight regime. In addition to the efforts to restrain self-dealing and conflicts of interest there were proposals to tighten corporate governance of financial institutions, including the requirement for independent directors to sit on board committees examining transactions that might involve conflicts of interest, and the enhanced flow of information between auditors, directors, and regulators. All of these details reflect points that had been raised in the Porter Commission Report.

This issue of governance is important because, as noted earlier, the capacity of the regulator to appreciate and understand the microdetails of each institutions' operations is limited. The owners of the institutions, or their representatives, have a clear responsibility to act in the interests of their clients and not in their own interests. Directors would be accountable for the governance of their institutions.

It was also proposed that the regulatory apparatus should be strengthened. Along with the integration of the institutions, it was proposed that the two regulators – the superintendent of insurance and the inspector general of banks – would be merged into one office. The power of the new superintendent of financial institutions to assume control of institutions experiencing solvency problems was reinforced, a committee of technical experts with a broad mandate to assist in the development of both an early warning system for solvency problems and guidelines for financial accounting would be established, and at the federal level there would at least be better management and coordination of oversight policies through the proposed establishment of the FISC.

The government's last word on the plan for the 1992 financial services reform was published as a White Paper (Canada 1990). The basic thrust of the policy proposals, sponsored this time by Minister of State (Finance) Gilles Loiselle, was that 'banks and federally incorporated trust, loan and insurance companies generally have the opportunity to offer a similar range of services and compete in markets that were previously not open to them. This will enhance choices available to consumers. The expansion of powers will take place directly or through financial institution subsidiaries' (Canada 1990, 3).

It is interesting to note that the powers of financial institutions were dampened somewhat from that proposal in the preceding two papers published by the government. First, TMLs would only be granted full powers to lend to consumers and businesses if they had a minimum capital base of $25 million and after satisfying the regulators that they had the appropriate staff and controls in place to undertake such credit-granting activities. Those institutions not meeting these requirements would have their commercial loan portfolio limited. Both banks and loan companies would be permitted to offer portfolio management and investment services, but banks could only obtain trust powers by owning a trust company. As well, all FIs would be permitted to network financial services offered by other FIs, including affiliates; however, banks and TMLs would be prohibited from selling insurance services and offering car leasing services. There were also strict rules on the ability of FIs to invest in commercial downstream companies except those with a clear financial services bias. The prudential safeguards that were proposed were similar to those contained in the predecessor documents. The White Paper also contained the suggestion to eliminate chartered banks reserve requirements over a two-year period. It was this modified proposal that carried the day and created an environment for the major restructuring of financial services in Canada.

In addition, the supervisory capacity of the state was enhanced through the establishment of a super-regulator and a statutory interdepartmental coordinating committee to ensure that prudential issues would not get lost in the bureaucratic machinery of the state. However, securities regulation remained fragmented in the hands of the provincial authorities.

The Financial Services Legislation Review

The 1992 financial services legislation, because of the extensive nature of the changes, contained a 'sunset clause' requiring a formal review within five years. In anticipation of the 1996–7 review, in September 1994, the Department of Finance issued a discussion paper, *Developments in the Financial Services Industry Since Financial Sector Legislation Reform* (Canada 1994). Following consultation with the financial services industry and hearings before the relevant Senate and House of Commons Committees, a White Paper was published. It contained a number of proposed changes, which were minor in character when compared to the 1992 rewriting of the financial services legislation. The Department of Finance expressed the view that 'the new legislation is working reasonably well in practice and is perhaps working very well if one takes into account the extent of the revisions that were made. The Department has been generally satisfied with the direction taken in 1992 and does not expect that there will be a need for major revisions in 1997' (Canada 1994a, 1).

In the period following the release of the Discussion Paper and leading up to the publication of the White Paper proposals, the issues of bank powers immediately surfaced at the top of the financial services policy agenda. The main issue was whether the banks would be permitted to engage in direct selling of insurance products and leasing of motor vehicles. The banks argued strongly for such powers, but the insurance industry mounted an intense grass roots campaign – engaging the lobbying efforts of the individual insurance agents – in opposition to enhancing the scope of the banks' powers. In this process, the Canadian automotive dealers association – which was opposed to the banks getting involved in motor vehicle leasing because it would impinge on a profitable activity for the existing dealers – collaborated with the insurance agents ultimately to defeat the banks' project (Toulin 1996). Curiously, the minister of finance announced the government's decision not to include a recommendation expanding the power of banks in the forthcoming White Paper during the course of his 1996 Budget speech in the House of Commons. This decision, and arrangements for its announcement, surprised all of the actors in the policy process, including the minister of state (international financial institutions), Doug Peters, who was responsible for the review.[14] Minister Peters commented on the policy process this way: 'Some stakeholders took what I found to be a very narrow view on issues ... In particular, I believe that the concerns of Canadian consumers must be the focal point of future reviews. I care much less about which financial institution gets which piece of the pie than I do about the effect of these decisions on people, on consumers, on clients ... Unfortunately, in my view, consumer concerns have been all but lost in the consultation process ... Rather, we have witnessed intensive behind the scenes lobbying, largely by industry-based forces that seem focused solely on protecting and expanding their turf (Peters 1996).'

The White Paper, published in June 1996, about six months later than had been expected, dealt with the following broad topics (Canada 1996b, 7–10):

- Strengthening consumer protection, which encompassed issues such as privacy safeguards, the costs of financial services, the universal availability of basic financial services, tied selling, and the right to prepay mortgages.
- Easing the regulatory burden, comprising the harmonization of federal and provincial regulations, streamlining the self-dealing prohibitions, a deposit insurance opt-out for wholesale banks, and reducing the regulatory burden for entry of foreign banks – but not eliminating the prohibition of foreign bank branching.
- Fine-tuning the legislation, including strengthening the corporate governance regime, providing flexibility for banks to engage in joint ventures and to enhance mutual insurance companies' access to capital.

• There was also a proposal to establish an advisory committee to study the payments system and to deal with some technical amendments to the Bank of Canada Act.

The more fundamental issues, such as the scope of banks' activities, as well as more general questions about the future of the financial services at the turn of the century, were left to a Task Force on Financial Institutions. It is expected to report in the fall of 1998. James Baillie, a veteran Bay Street lawyer, was appointed the first chair of the task force in December 1996. He had been involved in virtually every major financial services reform in Canada since the early 1960s, including advising the securities industry on its anticompetitive stance during much of the 1969–85 period[15] and advising the Bank of Nova Scotia on its decision to establish Scotia Securities in Quebec. This had the effect of blowing open the whole issue of dealer ownership and universal banking in Canada (Harris 1995). Baillie was subsequently found to be in a conflict of interest, acting again on behalf of the Bank of Nova Scotia while concurrently occupying the chair's post, and was succeeded by Harold McKay, a prominent Regina lawyer with a strong connection to the federal Liberal Party (Canada 1997b).

The task force was asked to

inquire into public policies affecting the financial services sector and make recommendations to enhance:
(i) the contribution of the sector to job creation, economic growth, and the new economy;
(ii) competition, efficiency, and innovation within the sector;
(iii) the international competitiveness of the sector in light of the globalization of financial services, while at the same time maintaining strong, vibrant domestic financial institutions;
(iv) the ability of the sector to take full advantage of technological advances as they occur and to meet the competitive challenges resulting from the introduction of new technologies; and
(v) the contribution of the sector to the best interest of Canadian consumers (Canada 1996c).

In February 1997 the federal government introduced legislation that essentially mirrored the proposals contained in the White Paper. The clear exception was provisions relating to foreign bank entry. The key provisions in this regard were:

(i) 'Regulated foreign banks' which own a Schedule II bank will no longer be required to own other financial institution subsidiaries through the Schedule II bank.

(ii) 'Near banks' which have received approval under the Bank Act to enter the Canadian market will no longer need to seek further approvals, provided that their activities do not include taking deposits.

(iii) 'Near banks' will be permitted to own any non-bank financial institution (Canada 1997a).

At the same time, the government announced that it would develop a new framework for foreign bank entry as branches (Canada 1997a). This move was long awaited by Canada's trading partners. Canada was the only G-7 member to have prohibited foreign bank branching and was among very few members of the OECD to have taken a reservation to the OECD Codes in respect of this matter.[16] In addition, the American trade authorities had been pressing the federal government to liberalize this component of its financial services regulatory policy.[17]

It is not clear why the federal government had not responded sooner to the demands of both the domestic and international banking communities for access to the Canadian market via the route of branches as opposed to incorporated entities. Establishing a foreign bank branch is simpler (less 'red tape') and cheaper (no requirement for segregated capital) than is the case for an incorporated Canadian entity. It can be hypothesized that the large Canadian banks supported foreign branching in the Canadian market when they appeared before the parliamentary committees because they needed an anchor for future arguments to support mergers among them. Presumably, the large Canadian banks could argue that as a consequence of the enhanced competition emanating from the foreign banks, competition in the banking sector would not be undermined in the event of a merger of two large banks. Also, there would be no danger of a 'merged' bank using its dominant position to undermine the competitive position of the rest of the system (Partridge 1997, Schuettler 1996).[18] The Canadian banks were becoming concerned that their international competitiveness would be eroded if they could not maintain their rankings in the international banking tables. Particularly, they were concerned that the interstate banking restrictions in the U.S. were evaporating and 'mega-mergers' of banks in that country were beginning to emerge. In addition, similar kinds of mergers were beginning to occur in Europe and Asia.

Conclusions

The purpose of this chapter has been to explain the evolution of the regulation of the financial services industry in Canada over the course of the past thirty years. The analysis has shown that international factors have been of growing importance, but also that they have always been a key part of the regulation of financial services. Domestic factors and interests have likewise been crucial. Indeed, the financial services sector shows that it is difficult to separate global and national forces. Each component is somehow connected to every other component. Indeed, achieving equilibrium in financial services regulatory reform is a delicate balancing act to ensure that the changes are welfare improving without undermining the important oversight precepts of safety and soundness.

In its approach to regulation, the state has consulted with interested participants, some with more flexible state access than others and some with more influence than others. The state considered the key factors as they seemed appropriate – prudence, competition, solvency, and efficiency, as revealed internationally and nationally. Not surprisingly, these objectives have varied in importance over time. The financial services industry does not stand still, money does not stand still, and ideas about 'how to do financial services' change every day.

Given these dynamics it is not surprising that the state's capacity to keep up is impaired. Fortunately, financial services regulators recognize this shortcoming.[19] More importantly, national regulators are not alone in dealing with these issues. International cooperation is strengthening – perhaps more so than it is in the Canadian confederation itself.

The history of regulatory reform in financial services in Canada reflects incrementalism at work. Despite the frequent use of terms such as 'Big Bang' in this industry, no regulators, policy planners, or politicians have been sufficiently clairvoyant to have prescribed and carried a fully rational reform of the financial services sector. There has been no grand plan.

NOTES

The author is a staff member of the Financial Affairs Division in the Secretariat of the Organization for Economic Cooperation and Development (OECD). The views expressed in this paper are strictly those of the author and not those of the OECD, its secretariat, or its member countries. The author is grateful to Michael Andrews, William Coleman, Margaret M. Hill, Raymond Hudon, and Stephen Wilks for their comments on an earlier version of the paper.

1 Home country control means that primary responsibility for oversight of banking institutions resides with the institutions' home country supervisors.
2 The authors of the *1964 Report of the Royal Commission on Banking and Finance* warned policy makers that 'competition is an uneasy state and that, however much they may thrive under it, businessmen have an inclination to protect themselves

against it. We must therefore be alert to developments which would lessen
competition or threaten its vigor' (Canada 1964, 369).

3 Based on confidential interviews.

4 Based on confidential interviews.

5 Based on confidential interviews.

6 Based on confidential interviews.

7 Based on confidential interviews.

8 As a consequence of the appointment of a deputy superintendent for policy matters.
Based on confidential interviews.

9 Based on confidential interviews.

10 Observations made in a confidential interview.

11 This was accompanied by a Technical Supplement entitled *The Regulation of
Financial Institutions: Proposals for Discussion* (Canada 1985b).

12 The Green Paper (Canada 1985a, 16) defined self-dealing as a non-arm's length
transaction. This would involve any transactions between the financial institution
and its principals.

13 Whenever a financial institution finds itself in a situation where it must choose
between its own interests and those of a client for whom it is acting, the financial
institution finds itself in a conflict of interest (Canada 1985a, 17).

14 Based on confidential interviews.

15 Baillie was chair of the Ontario Securities Commission in the 1978–80 period.

16 The newer members have pointed to Canada's reservation to the OECD Codes as a
rationale for not allowing foreign branching in their countries.

17 Based on confidential interviews.

18 The merger of two large Canadian banks has not yet surfaced as a major public
policy issue. A number of bankers have bemoaned the fact that Canadian banks
have slipped in the international rankings over the past fifteen to twenty years or
so. As well, there have been a number of 'mega-bank' mergers in the U.S., Japan
and Europe. This has apparently made some of the large Canadian banks nervous
about their ability to compete in international markets and thus provide the
requisite global services to their Canadian clients. Undoubtedly, this will be an
issue that the Task Force will examine.

19 Based on confidential interviews.

REFERENCES

Canada. 1964. *Report of the Royal Commission on Banking and Finance*. Ottawa:
Queen's Printer.

Canada. 1976. Economic Council of Canada. *Efficiency and Regulation: A Study of
Deposit Institutions*. Ottawa: Supply and Services Canada.

Canada. 1984. Department of Finance, Capital Markets Division. Canadian Financial
  Institutions: Trends and Policy Perspectives. In *Background Working Papers on
  Financial Institutions Issues*. Ottawa: Minister of Supply and Services.
Canada. 1985a. Department of Finance. *The Regulation of Canadian Financial
  Institutions: Proposals for Discussion*. Ottawa: Minister of Supply and Services.
Canada. 1985b. Department of Finance. *The Regulation of Canadian Financial
  Institutions: Proposals for Discussion (Technical Supplement)*. Ottawa: Minister of
  Supply and Services.
Canada. 1985c. Department of Finance. *Final Report of the Working Committee on the
  Canada Deposit Insurance Corporation (CDIC): Submitted to the Honourable
  Barbara McDougall, Minister of State (Finance)*. Ottawa: Minister of Supply and
  Services.
Canada. 1985d. House of Commons, Standing Committee on Finance, Trade and
  Economic Affairs. *Canadian Financial Institutions, Report of the Standing
  Committee on Finance, Trade and Economic Affairs*. Ottawa: Queen's Printer.
Canada. 1986a. Department of Finance. *A Study to Assess the Current Mandate and
  Operations of the Office of the Inspector General of Banks: Submitted to the
  Honourable Barbara McDougall, Minister of State (Finance) by Coopers &
  Lybrand*. Ottawa: Minister of Supply and Services.
Canada. 1986b. Senate. *Towards a More Competitive Financial Environment*. Ottawa:
  Minister of Supply and Services.
Canada. 1986c. Department of Finance, *New Directions for the Financial Sector
  Institutions: Executive Summary*. Ottawa: Minister of Supply and Services.
Canada. 1990. Department of Finance. *Reform of Federal Financial Institutions
  Legislation: Overview of Legislative Proposals*. Ottawa: Minister of Supply and
  Services.
Canada. 1994. Department of Finance. *Developments in the Financial Services
  Industry Since Financial Sector Legislative Reform: Background document
  prepared by the Department of Finance for the Senate Committee on Banking,
  Trade and Commerce*. Ottawa: Minister of Supply and Services.
Canada. 1995. Canada Deposit Insurance Corporation. *Annual Report, 1994–1995*.
  Ottawa: Minister of Supply and Services.
Canada. 1996a. Department of Finance. *Budget Speech*. The Honourable Paul Martin
  P.C., M.P., Minister of Finance, March 6.
Canada. 1996b. Department of Finance. *1997 Review of Financial Sector Legislation:
  Proposals for Changes*. Ottawa: Minister of Supply and Services.
Canada. 1996c. Department of Finance. Announces Details of Task Force on the
  Future of the Canadian Financial Services Sector. Ottawa: Department of Finance
  New Release 96–101, 19 December.

Canada. 1996d. Senate Standing Committee on Banking, Trade and Commerce. 1997
    Financial Institution Reform: Lowering the Barriers to Foreign Banks. Ottawa:
    Senate of Canada.
Canada. 1997a. Department of Finance. Government Introduces New Legislation for
    Financial Institutions and Announces Decision to Allow Foreign Bank Branching.
    Press Release, Ottawa, 14 February.
Canada. 1997b. Department of Finance. Government Names New Task Force Chair
    from Western Canada. *Press Release*, Ottawa, 21 July.
Daniel, Fred, Charles Freedman, and Clyde Goodlet. 1992–3. Restructuring the
    Canadian Financial Industry. *Bank of Canada Review* (Winter): 21–45.
Dixon, Huw. 1996. Controversy: Should We Regulate the Financial System?
    A Symposium in *The Economic Journal* 106, no. 436 (May): 133–44.
Freedman, Charles. 1996. How Should Universal Banks Be Regulated? In Anthony
    Saunders and Ingo Walter, eds., *Universal Banking: Financial System Design
    Reconsidered*, 724–36. Chicago: Irwin Professional Publishing.
Harris, Stephen L. 1995. The Political Economy of the Liberalization of Entry and
    Ownership in the Canadian Investment Dealer Industry. PhD thesis, Carleton
    University.
– 1996a. The Politics of Financial Market Liberalization: The Case of the Canadian
    Investment Dealer Industry. A paper presented to the 1996 Annual Meeting of the
    American Political Science Association, San Francisco Hilton, San Francisco,
    California, 29 August – 1 September. Forthcoming, *Policy Studies Journal* (Fall
    1997).
– 1996b. Public Policy and Financial Market Access in the Global Economy. Mimeo,
    Organization for Economic Cooperation and Development, 29 October.
Harris, Stephen L., and Charles Pigott. 1997. Regulatory Reform in the Financial
    Services Industry: Where Have We Been? Where Are We Going? *Financial Market
    Trends* 67:31–96.
Kirsch, Clifford E., ed. 1997. *The Financial Services Revolution: Understanding the
    Changing Roles of Banks, Mutual Funds and Insurance Companies*. Chicago: Irwin
    Professional Publishing.
Mayer, Colin. 1995. The Regulation of Financial Services: Lessons from the UK for
    1992. In Matthew Bishop, John Kay, and Colin Mayer, eds., *The Regulatory
    Challenge*, 138–59. Oxford: Oxford University Press.
Ontario. 1985. *Ontario Task Force on Financial Institutions: Final Report, A Report to
    the Honourable Monty Kwinter, Minister of Consumer and Commercial Relations*.
    Toronto: Government of Ontario.
Partridge, John. 1997. TD Bank assails rivals for inviting industry mergers. *Globe and
    Mail*, 23 January.

388   Stephen L. Harris

Peters, Doug. 1996. Notes for remarks by the Honourable Doug Peters, Secretary of
State for International Financial Institutions, to the Annual General Meeting of the
Canadian Life and Health Insurance Association. Ottawa, 30 May.

Quebec. 1988. *Reform of Financial Institutions in Quebec: Intermediaries*. Quebec:
Office of the Associate Minister for Finance and Privatization.

Reinicke, Wolfgang H. 1995. *Banking, Politics and Global Finance: American
Commercial Banks and Regulatory Change, 1980–1990*. Aldershot: Edward Elgar
Publishing Limited.

Schuettler, Darren. 1996. Canada's leading banks lobby for right to merge. *New York
Journal of Commerce*, 10 June.

Schultz, Richard J. 1982. Regulatory Agencies and the Dilemmas of Delegation. In
O.P. Dwivedi, ed., *The Administrative State in Canada*, 89–106. Toronto: University of Toronto Press.

Shearer, Ronald A., John F. Chant, and David E. Bond. 1984. *The Economics of the
Canadian Financial System: Theory, Policy and Institutions*. Scarborough:
Prentice-Hall.

Toulin, Alan. 1996. Welcome mat laid out for foreign banks. *Financial Post*,
2 October.

17

Conclusions

G. BRUCE DOERN, MARGARET M. HILL, MICHAEL J. PRINCE, and RICHARD J. SCHULTZ

The preceding chapters have examined regulatory institutions, processes, and reforms in Canada over the past twenty years. In the introduction, we presented a general framework for the analysis of the regulatory state based on four regimes: Regime I, the sectoral regulators; Regime II, the horizontal or framework regulators; Regime III, the cabinet or executive arena for making and managing regulations; and Regime IV, the international field of regulation. We suggested that the four regimes have distinct enough attributes to permit a separate analysis of each. Nonetheless, we also recognized that the four regimes are fundamentally interconnected. The modern regulatory state, in our view, is therefore best seen as the resultant interplay of convergences and collisions among the four regimes.

One of the key contentions of the book is that regulation is best understood in very broad terms. It must be understood to include not only delegated legislation, but also constitutional provisions, intergovernmental agreements, codes of conduct, standards, guidelines, and procedures. Furthermore, we must not limit our analysis of regulation to the rules governing the marketplace. Equally important, as various chapters have shown, are the rules pertaining to morality, the community, families, and the welfare state, as well as the regulators themselves and the regulatory state they oversee. Last but certainly not least, the four-regime framework underscores that the modern Canadian regulatory state is much more than an ad hoc arrangement of independent regulatory agencies. The analysis of Regimes III and IV, in particular, is intended to show some of the issues involved when the state regulates itself and manages its rule-making activities, while at the same time having to accommodate international systems, the rules of which are crossing borders in ever more complex ways.

The investigation of Canadian regulatory regimes and institutions presented in this collection of essays establishes a foundation for stocktaking. After more than two decades of study and regulatory developments, this exercise is more than appropriate. The analysis in this last chapter first takes stock of what we have learned, particularly as seen from the standpoint of the four-regime framework. We then step back from the book's individual chapters and consider what they suggest, in an overall sense, about the capacity of the Canadian regulatory state to formulate, manage, and implement regulation and about Canada's national style of regulation.

Taking Stock

In a review of the literature on Canadian regulation in the early 1980s, one of the editors of this collection concluded that 'the academic study of regulation, particularly that in political science and public administration, is very much in its early stages' in Canada (Schultz 1982). Indeed, *The Regulatory Process in Canada* (Doern 1978), a collection of essays on five selected regulatory agencies, was the first significant new contribution to the field since John Willis's 1941 classic, *Canadian Boards at Work*. Key knowledge gaps remained, however. As Schultz noted, there was still much to discover about the full range of regulatory processes and techniques, the origins and evolution of regulatory agencies, the collegial nature of decision making by collective boards, regulation by government departments, the relationships between regulatory bodies and other public sector organizations in given policy areas, and regulation in the provinces. Schultz implied that addressing these gaps in our knowledge would require going beyond the valuable baseline of research established by government organizations (most notably the Economic Council of Canada, the Law Reform Commission of Canada, and the Science Council of Canada) and encouraging a new generation of research activity, both inside and outside government.

In large measure, many of the weaknesses and gaps identified by Schultz have been addressed over the past years. The profile of regulation has increased not only among students of political science and public administration, but also among those studying law and economics. Inside the state, too, regulation is far more visible as a result of efforts at regulatory planning and priority setting, the establishment of central units for regulatory review, and the development of techniques for regulatory analysis.

Over the past twenty years the agenda for research and practice has moved beyond its original preoccupation with the emerging regulatory Leviathan toward a much fuller appreciation for deregulation, regulatory reform, and, most recently, re-regulation and regulatory management. Work appeared that drew attention to regulation as a governing instrument embedded in and shaped by policy structures and processes and the dynamics of resource allocation. Regulation also figured prominently in the research studies done for the Macdonald Royal Commission on the Economic Union and Development Prospects of Canada. These included Schultz and Alexandroff's analysis of federalism and regulation; a series of reports coordinated by Bernier and Lajoie (1985) on law, society, and the economy, regulations and administrative tribunals, family law and social welfare law, consumer protection and environmental law, and labour law and urban law; and two studies coordinated by Cuming (1985) on the harmonization of laws in Canada.

Much of the progress that has been made over the past two decades in closing the gaps in our knowledge is the result of case studies. Case studies have been undertaken on everything from energy regulation to the airline, broadcasting, and telecommunications industries; trade and industrial policy; environmental regulation and pollution control; and the regulation of financial institutions and services. While the limits of case studies are well known, it is equally important to recognize that detailed analyses of Canada's experiences with regulation, deregulation, and regulatory reform have gone a long way toward addressing the substantive gaps in knowledge identified by Schultz in the early 1980s.

It is equally important, as we take stock of the past two decades, to recognize the broadening of the research community. Significant contributions to regulatory research have come from Canada's policy think tanks. The Institute for Research on Public Policy, the Fraser Institute, the Conference Board of Canada, and the C.D. Howe Institute have published reports mixing analysis and advocacy on a range of regulatory issues. These include cultural regulation, divorce, rent control, minimum wage laws, and the regulation of Canada's telecommunications and transport sectors. Scholars have lately observed a general rise in the influence of think tanks in shaping the policy agenda. At least in Canada, this new influence seems to apply to the regulatory area as well.

Key Themes and Debates: Where Lessons Have Been Learned

A number of recurring issues and themes can be noted over the past twenty years. The venerable 'old' topics of the impact of regulation of economic efficiency and the accountability of regulators, especially regulatory agencies, to governments continue to be studied. In some instances, the old issues have taken on slightly new guises in the 1990s. This is perhaps best illustrated by the concern today with the benefits and costs of regulation from the standpoint of Canada's ability to compete in the global marketplace.

But in addition to putting 'new wine in old bottles,' important new insights have been gleaned, often related to new aspects of the Canadian regulatory state. Some of these insights have been noted in the preceding section. Here we focus on lessons learned in four areas: organizational forms for regulation, the accountability and autonomy of regulatory agencies, experiences with deregulation, and regulatory implementation.

Diversity of Organizational Arrangements for Regulation

On the organization of regulation, the literature has expanded its focus from agencies, boards, commissions, and tribunals to an examination of the regulatory activities of government departments/ministries, professional bodies, marketing boards, trade agreements, and the courts. Significant institutional additions to the Canadian regulatory state have taken place, including the Canadian Charter of Rights and Freedoms in 1982, the 1988 Canada–United States Free Trade Agreement, the 1993 North American Free Trade Agreement, and the 1994 Agreement on Internal Trade (AIT). These additions were examined in previous chapters. The Harris chapter on financial services regulation also refers to the General Agreement on Trade in Services as a liberalizing influence on regulatory policy in Canada. Any map of the regulatory terrain today must include these new major landmarks. The trade agreements illustrate the internationalization of regulation policies and politics in Canada, while the Charter, AIT, and recent reforms to the Canadian financial services industry emphasize the continuing importance of domestic influences on rule making.

Diversity is also evident inside the Canadian regulatory state. Within the executive arena, cabinet committees and central agency units charged with responsibility for regulatory affairs have been formed. Within the legislative arena, regulators of the state itself have increased in numbers, with the formation of privacy and conflict of interest commissions. Auditors' and ombudspersons' offices have also seen their mandates expanded. Furthermore, the number of occupations and professions granted self-regulatory powers by provincial governments has increased over recent decades, with as many as forty self-regulating groups in some larger provinces. We have come to better appreciate that so-called regulatory agencies are usually more than that, possessing policy advisory, research, granting and/or adjudicative responsibilities. They also constitute bases of knowledge and influence.

Within particular sectors of the economy, the nature of regulation has shifted from the policing role to a promoting and or planning mode, and back again in some cases. Margaret Hill's chapter on the federal transport regulatory system traces the change in federal transportation regulation over the last thirty years, showing that the role has shifted from planning and promoting regulatory functions to a role informed more by a market paradigm and focused more on classical policing regulation of the air and rail sectors.

Accountability and Autonomy

One of the key insights of the past two decades is that the concept of 'independent agencies' and the political theory of 'clientele capture,' both prominent in the American literature, are inadequate general characterizations of regulatory agencies and processes in Canada. This is most obviously due to our distinct mixture of federal and provincial public enterprises in the economy, the dominance of cabinets in our parliamentary system of government, and the dispersal of power under Canadian federalism. It also, however, reflects more subtle debate about the appropriate division of responsibility over policy and regulatory administration. As chapters by Doern and Hill show, the National Energy Board and the Canadian Transport Commission, once the dominant policy actors in their sectors, have seen their power and autonomy decline vis-à-vis the federal bureaucracy and government over the last decade. By contrast, Schultz argues that the CRTC is still standing tall, having effectively resisted challenges to its stature as the lead actor in the communications regulatory field. The 1991 Broadcasting Act and 1993 Telecommunications Act, Schultz predicts, will do little to alter the policy relationship between the political authorities and the regulatory agency.

In general, we have come to realize that the autonomy and accountability of a regulatory agency are not absolutes but rather relational processes and that numerous formal and informal devices are at play in shaping the actual status of a given agency. Our understanding of accountability systems has been enriched, for example, by research calling attention to the role of an administrative culture shared by officials in central agencies of government and in regulatory agencies. We have concluded that regulatory agencies should no longer be depicted as 'structural heretics' but seen as regular, front-line organizations in the Canadian state. Moreover, through their public hearings and consultative processes, Canada's regulatory agencies strive to be responsive and accountable, just as their departmental counterparts do.

The phrase 'statutory regulatory agency' unfortunately sometimes still makes an appearance in the regulatory literature. The term was coined by research staff for the Regulation Reference of the Economic Council in the late 1970s as a substitute for the American term, 'independent regulatory agency.' The idea was to avoid debates over the nature and merits of independence and, more positively, to highlight the legislative basis and accountability of agencies in the Canadian context. The term '*statutory* regulatory agency,' however, is a redundancy. All regulatory agencies, as distinct from our notion of regimes, operate under the rule of law and are created by statute.

The Deregulation Experience

From the political rhetoric to the practical reality of deregulation initiatives in Canada, a paradox has been revealed. Deregulation in Canada has resulted in a more focused and likely more robust regulatory role by government. Case studies of deregulation in various sectors show that major deregulatory actions have been accompanied by refinements and creations of new regulatory instruments. Schultz's (1994) evaluation of deregulatory efforts in transportation and energy found that deregulation in Canada has not led to a fundamental downsizing of the state; instead, there has been a recasting of public policy objectives, with some regulatory tools and processes being replaced by others. In this book, Waters and Stanbury find a similar phenomenon but refer to it, as we have seen, as 'regulatory shift.' Regulatory shift takes several forms. It can entail the reimposition of rules (re-regulation); the creation of new economic rules; the substitution of new regulatory techniques for old ones; and the introduction of user fees in the sector. The largest component of regulatory shift in Canada, according to Waters and Stanbury, has been the generation of substantially more social regulations.

This pattern of regulatory reform is also reflected in the chapter by Stephen Harris. The liberalization of financial services regulation in Canada has dealt with institutional powers, market access, and measures for determining interest rates, but at the same time regulations of a prudential character were tightened and the overall regulatory apparatus for this sector was restructured. The goals of efficient and competitive markets have been weighed against goals of solvency of the industry and protection of consumers.

The conclusion that follows from Schultz, Waters and Stanbury, and Harris is that rolling back the state is too simplistic a metaphor. It does not capture the nuances and complexities of the regulatory reforms that have been implemented in Canada. The regulatory state has been redesigned over the past two decades, not rolled back.

Regulatory Implementation

The literature has gone beyond estimating, at a macrolevel, the share of the Canadian economy subject to some form of direct regulation, to examining, at the microlevel, the actual implementation of regulations. Case studies of enforcing laws and rules expose as a myth the image of state organizations as enforcement machines responding automatically to perceived infractions in a consistently hard and inflexible manner.

Commenting on the Canadian regulatory state in the 1970s, Gilles Paquet (1978) observed a change from ruling to gaming, a drift of regulatory processes into a negotiating or bargaining style. In the fields of anti-inflation controls, competition policy, and foreign investment, Paquet noted that broad discretionary powers were explicitly granted to regulators to consult and bargain with outside interests, and that private sector players were seeking guidance from regulators about how they might respond to planned private sector activities. Paquet hypothesized that this emphasis on flexibility, information sharing, and learning enabled faster strategic decisions, thus improving the workings of the economy.

Several chapters in this book have described regulatory implementation as persuasion and negotiation. The analysis of environmental regulation by Kathryn Harrison in Chapter 6 showed the role of bilateral company-to-government department agreements, guidelines rather than fixed standards, and the phase-in of compliance schedules. Hudson Janisch's analysis, in Chapter 5, of federal competition policy notes that considerable discretion is built into the 1986 Competition Act, and in the implementation strategies of the Bureau of Competition Policy and the Competition Tribunal. Doern's examination of the 1994 Agreement on Internal Trade between the federal government and the provincial and territorial governments shows that the agreement itself was the result of hard bargaining at the level of executive federalism, and that the agreed provisions for trade dispute resolution involve a series of steps, including interpretation of the relevant chapters in the agreement, consultations, and information exchange. In Chapter 9, by Michael Prince, human rights were discussed, a field in which civic regulation in Canada has occurred through negotiation, not as a result of drift but as deliberate public policy and administrative practice for over thirty years. As well as educating the public about rights and duties, federal and provincial human rights commissions investigate complaints and decide whether complaints should be dismissed, referred to a more appropriate agency, resolved by mediation, or go to a tribunal hearing for a decision. Only a minority of complaints typically end up in a formal hearing; more customary approaches are conciliation and mediation. Similarly, in Chapter 13, Colin Bennett's analysis of the implementation of information and privacy protection laws across Canada demonstrates the key role of organizational learning, flexibility, and mutual adaptation between information and privacy commissions and government departments and central agencies.

Regulatory implementation, then, is usually a political dialogue, a process of bargaining within governments, between governments, and between a government and outside economic or social interests. We have come to more fully appreciate Geoffrey Vickers's view of regulation as a continual and mutual transaction between governors and the governed.

The widespread practice of regulation by negotiation, mediation, and softer compliance approaches certainly has the attraction of being adaptive, noncoercive, and often effective. This practice raises concerns, however, about the accountability of governments and regulators for the development, implementation, and adjudication of public laws, especially when regulatory bargains are made in private. Such arrangements are usually inaccessible and invisible to the public, parliamentarians, and the press. When matters of regulatory policy and administration are concealed, third parties are unable to influence the process. Moreover, it is unclear how regulators' activities are to be evaluated and what means of redress are available. Perceptions of bias or capture of the regulators can arise. If trade-offs are negotiated and implemented on a decentralized basis, then the initial aims of the legislation may go astray, resulting in inconsistent and unintended applications of laws and rules (Grabosky 1995).

Emerging Issues

The Canadian Regulatory State: Both Declining and Enhanced Capacity

Taken together, the chapters shed different rays of light on the issue of the capacity of the regulatory state in contemporary Canada. Initially, the concept of state capacity was used by political scientists to discuss and assess the relative autonomy of democratic states within capitalist societies. Frequently, the question is asked whether the rule-making powers of the Canadian state have been weakened as a result of international agreements like NAFTA, deregulation measures, and general government restraint.

For our purposes, state capacity refers to the ability of government agencies to formulate policies and implement regulations that address public issues, affect economic, organizational, and social relations and thus advance in some way policy objectives. This ability is a function of the availability of a mandate and governing instruments, financial and personnel resources, expertise, societal mobilization, and political will. In speaking of state capacity, we need to ask, capacity of which part and level of the state, to do what? As various chapters demonstrate, state capacity is a multidimensional phenomenon and the authors' analyses yield an array of findings and insights.

One form of state capacity is evident in efforts to structure regulatory management inside the federal and some provincial governments. Over the last decade, Ottawa and many of the provinces have developed policy frameworks governing the making and evaluating of new and existing regulations. These frameworks include instituting centralized regulatory review processes, annual planning cycles, and mandatory impact assessments. Across jurisdictions, most departments have formal and informal means for consulting the public, especially client groups who may be affected.

State capacity is also manifested in relations between regulatory bodies and their surrounding communities of interest. The capacity of interest groups like the Consumers' Association of Canada and social movements such as environmentalism to influence the regulatory agenda and actions of the federal government has gradually declined. In the case of the former organization, the source of funding was important. The influence of environmental groups fluctuated in line with levels of public attention to environmental or trade issues. Public interest groups were involved in the processes around the Canada-U.S. Free Trade Agreement and the NAFTA, but the AIT was more a closed process of policy discussion and negotiation. Business and industrial interests, on the other hand, wield relatively greater leverage with policy makers in adopting market-oriented approaches to regulating and in striking bargains during the implementation stage of regulatory processes. Consider, for example, the CRTC and telecommunications regulation, the subject of Chapters 2, 7, and 8. Pollster Angus Reid (1997, 40) reports that opinion surveys show 'Canadians no longer regard the CRTC as a guardian of Canadian culture, but as a protector of corporate interests.' Reid adds that the CRTC is perceived to be 'little more than an arbiter between powerful communications empires seeking bigger pieces of the marketplace.' In Chapter 7, Waters and Stanbury cite the CRTC in its role as broadcasting regulator as perhaps the best example of a regulator protecting incumbents against real and potential rivals entering the sector.

The chapters on the NEB, CTC, and the Privacy Commissioner's Office illustrate the ability of one part of the federal state, the cabinet, to effectively exert control over other segments of the federal public sector. These are cases where the political executive, over the last ten to fifteen years, has further regulated the regulators and administrators. In comparison, the chapter on the CRTC highlighted the commission's capacity to successfully maintain its autonomy in relation to the cabinet and the public service bureaucracy.

The capacity of governments to regulate the economy, at a federal or provincial level, has no doubt been constrained by the introduction of NAFTA and the AIT, among other accords on trade. By definition, deregulation initiatives also reduce governments' abilities to control or constrain economic behaviour in the marketplace. While deregulation as applied in Canada has significantly altered certain regulatory regimes, in all cases it has been a partial removal of rules, resulting in a continuing regulatory role by government using some traditional and new forms of controls. Moreover, as Stephen Harris notes of the regulation of financial services, the state's capacity to keep up is hindered somewhat given that the structure and practices of the industry constantly change and that money does not stand still in a global economy. At the same time, though, international co-operation among states can serve to bolster a national government's ability to deal with issues of trade and multinational corporations.

One aim of this book has been to widen the perspective of both academics and practitioners as to the nature of government regulation and hence on issues of capacity and political power. Chapter 9 in particular looked at 'civic regulation', bringing civil society and the social union explicitly into the study of the regulatory state. Whether in the realm of moral and sexual regulation, human rights, criminal justice, or social programming, civic regulation is probably expanding in scope and significance. Both a demand for and capacity to intervene in these realms with rules is apparent in the Canadian political community. In keeping with predictions made in the early 1980s, we know that federal and provincial governments, faced with serious fiscal pressures, have resorted to the regulatory instrument because its public budgetary consequences are fairly small, vested interests often wish to maintain particular rules, and regulating is a supple, multipurpose governing instrument. As a result of expenditure cuts, restructuring and regionalizing services, and contracting out program delivery, governments are moving away from their role as direct provider of benefits and services to the role of regulator of benefits and services provided by others. The welfare state is becoming the regulatory state.

National Styles of Regulation; Canada's Precarious Pluralism and Regulatory Gradualism

Like all other industrial states, Canada's is a regulatory state with a complex apparatus of public, quasi-governmental, and private organizations making and enforcing societal rules. Regulating is an inescapable part of governing and public administration (Majone 1994). It is a distinct policy instrument of government with its own political, social, economic, and administrative dynamics. This allows us to think of styles of regulation.

In concert with most OECD countries, Canada has experimented with regulatory reform agendas and, more recently, regulatory management systems, policy, and administrative trends discussed in Chapter 11. And like many nations, Canada has enacted competition, environmental, and trade liberalization laws, among others. Several chapters underscore the growing importance of international agreements and globalization in shaping domestic regulation. More specifically, Canada shares with other 'Anglo-Saxon' states a cultural legacy that gives prominence to market solutions, citizen independence, and the autonomy of groups and corporations in the mixed economy and civil society (Doern and Wilks 1998). Thus, Canada, Britain, and the United States have embraced more competition-oriented goals and market-based instruments in economic regulation, and certain industrial sectors have undergone deregulation in one form or another. They have also seen expanded regulation in several framework realms. Indeed, on an overall basis the UK has had to invent an entire set of utility regulators in the wake of its massive Thatcherite privatization program (Doern and Wilks 1998).

Beyond these common features and general trends of convergence in regulation, nations may exhibit distinctive regulatory styles. In an analysis of regulation in Britain and the United States, Vogel (1986) determined that each country had a characteristic approach to regulation. American regulation tended to be formalized and rule oriented, so as to fetter the discretion of government officials, with comparatively more prosecutions and conflict as a result. British regulation was more informal, flexible, and discretionary, placing greater reliance on persuasion and negotiation than on prosecution for regulatory compliance. Vogel (1986, 25) found also that: 'Many of Britain's regulatory policies are formulated and implemented through mechanisms of interest-group representation that are essentially corporatist. By contrast, both the making and the implementation of government regulation in the United States take place in a large number of highly visible, publicly accessible, and relatively adversarial forums: America's mode of interest group representation tends to be more pluralist than Britain's.'

What of Canadian regulation? Hoberg's (1993) examination of environmental policy, drawing on the work of Vogel and others, and extended here by Harrison's chapter, argues that important changes have taken place since the 1970s in the policy style of this sector. Hoberg describes Canada's traditional regulatory style as based on a bargaining process that is 'closed, informal and co-operative' between governments and business, including a predisposition for delegation and strong ministerial discretion. Over the last two decades, Hoberg suggests that, at least for environmental policy, the regulatory process has become significantly more open than before, with additional societal interests involved; increasingly formal, with the introduction of socio-economic impact assessments; and, somewhat more legalistic and adversarial due, in part, to the addition of the Canadian Charter of Rights and Freedoms to the constitution.

Several chapters in this book offer evidence of these trends. The elaboration and hence politicization of policy communities is apparent across many regulatory fields and regimes. In Chapter 4, Hill described the expansion of actors and interests in the air and rail policy communities. Waters and Stanbury, in Chapter 7, noted that within the federal transportation policy sector legislative provisions now deal with issues of access for persons with disabilities. In Chapter 8, Schultz traced the evolution of the telecommunications regulatory system from being consensual, closed, and nonconfrontational to a more open, participatory, and adversarial process. In Chapter 13, Bennett pointed to the formation of a new policy sector with the creation of data protection laws by the federal and provincial governments as well as by other nation states. The AIT, examined in Chapter 14, brought together two different policy communities, that of trade and that of federal-provincial relations, each with their own values, vocabularies, and track records. This politicization of policy communities has meant, in some cases, that the role of the state has shifted from representing the 'public interest' to refereeing public interests or negotiating among various state interests. Though old policy communities have enlarged, some collided, and new ones formed, Chapters 6 and 8 show that gaining access to a previously closed process does not guarantee influence over regulatory decisions. Viewed over a twenty- to twenty-five-year time frame, interest group representation in Canada's regulatory institutions appears to have grown but been effective in a cyclical way. Perhaps the Canadian manner of interest politics in regulation is best described as precarious pluralism. At root, pluralism in regulatory policy communities tends to be weak and unstable because of the significant inequality of power and legitimacy between producer groups such as businesses, banks, and professions, on the one hand, and public interest groups such as consumers, environmentalists, and feminists on the other. Moreover, decision processes are not always agreed on or as transparent and accountable as may be wished by certain groups.

Canadian regulatory institutions have a number of arrangements and techniques that make up a national style spanning the four regimes. One feature is the rich mix of organizational modes of regulation used in Canada, a mix that may well be greater than in either Britain or the United States. A second feature is that Canadian legislative mandates commonly confer multiple functions and enormous discretionary powers on regulatory authorities over policy, duties, and procedures. The multifunctionality is like American agencies, whereas the wide discretion is more like British regulatory practice. Regulation in Canada has also been used a proxy for regional and social policy through the cross-subsidization of services. The 'nation building' mandates of key regulators such as the CRTC, NEB, and CTC, have been sharply curtailed in recent years. A third characteristic, noted in Chapter 1, is that it is rare for only one regulatory body to control the entire system in a given policy field. In many sectors of Canadian society and the economy, Crown corporations and other governments as well as private firms and community groups are part of the regulatory policy community of agencies and departmemts. Consequently, many regulatory bodies are dependent on other public and private organizations for information, resources and implementation.

Federalism is a fourth factor. Like the United States but distinct from Britain (until legislative assemblies are formed in Scotland and Wales), federalism in Canada requires the striking of bargains between regulation making and the enforcement of rules between the federal and provincial levels. The criminal justice system is a major example of this division between the formulation and the implementation of laws.

A fifth feature is that, with a parliamentary system of government, the political executive in Canada is inherently more integrated and dominant than is the American executive branch in relation to the regulatory process. This is apparent in the traditional concerns of control and accountability up to ministers and, through them, to Parliament, and in the institutionalization of regulatory management in the federal government. Relatively more screening of regulatory initiatives now takes place within Canadian departments and central agencies, though departments retain considerable discretion in the actual nature of these reviews. Chapter 10 cautioned against attributing too great an influence on Canadian politics and policy to the Charter. True, the courts are more involved in policy issues today and Charter decisions have had a significant impact, on criminal law especially, but on the whole neither private legal rights nor social rights claims have been as extensively expanded as in the United States (Doern and Wilks 1998; Sunstein 1990).

Another measure of a nation's regulatory style is the degree, direction, and pace of change in laws and rules. In terms of the degree of change, this book has shown that great changes have occurred in Canadian regulatory institutions. A range of constitutional reforms as well as organizational and policy innovations have been surveyed. In terms of the direction of change, despite the deregulation of certain key economic sectors, the overall density and extent of rule making by government has increased, including regulation of the state by the state and the whole field of civic regulation. In terms of the pace of change, while significant remodelling of the regulatory state has been accomplished, many of these profound changes have unfolded over the long term. Regulation is still growing in the 1990s, although at a slower rate than in the 1970s. From earlier chapters as well as from other published sources, we can identify a number of trends that reflect this pace, which can be called a style of regulatory gradualism.

Given that incrementalism probably characterizes most decision making in most public organizations, a gradualist approach to regulatory implementation and reform should not be altogether surprising. This is especially so in areas clearly governed by the rule of law. The theory and practice of incrementalism, however, has been equated most often in the policy literature with budgeting and the expenditure process. Regulatory gradualism is an instrument-specific manifestation of incremental public policy making. What is noteworthy, we believe, is that despite efforts in recent decades to introduce other policy styles to regulatory institutions – rational microeconomic choice, legalism, or multi-stakeholder bargaining – the gradualist approach widely persists. Examples of this style include the following:

- The reliance on selective compliance methods and flexible implementation rather than strict enforcement for achieving regulatory goals.
- Regulatory shift: the adoption of partial forms of deregulation in certain sectors, usually supplemented by other kinds of government oversight and intervention.
- The mixed record of successes and setbacks for interest groups and social movements in influencing regulatory processes and decisions.
- Transitional regulations: the establishment of new rules to manage the transition from a regulated monopoly to greater competition in industries long subject to economic regulation, such as telecommunications.
- The patchy execution of regulatory impact assessments by departments within the federal government.
- In social assistance reform, a preference by most provinces to date for voluntary employability enhancement programs, with expectations of improving skills and seeking work, rather than mandatory workfare schemes that compel a would-be recipient to do work in order to receive basic income support.
- Regulatory reform of the financial services industry in Canada over the past thirty years as 'incrementalism at work,' with successive governments consulting different interests and juggling competing values in the absence of a grand plan.

- Federal-provincial negotiations over labour mobility as part of the AIT involved very different opening positions between the two orders of government and resulted in trade-offs, with both Ottawa and the provinces achieving some of their goals but yielding on others.
- Even the Canadian Charter of Rights and Freedoms, in its first fifteen years, has not produced the 'rights revolution' that its critics feared and many of its supporters desired. The Charter has been grafted onto the Canadian constitution, adding some new rights to those already in effect, respecting the division of powers between the federal and provincial governments, and only slightly constraining the supremacy of Parliament in policy making.

Several factors are at play in shaping and reflecting this style of regulatory gradualism – the dominance of liberal values in Canadian society and political culture; the divided jurisdiction of federalism; and the common law tradition of Canada's legal culture are certainly fundamental factors. The limited space for regulatory changes on the policy agenda of any given government's mandate further limits the scope and pace of change. Following after American regulatory debates and reforms, moreover, has afforded Canadian policy makers the opportunity to draw lessons from American policy successes and failures. Other contextual factors include the exacting politics of moral and sexual regulation, and the era of restraint in the 1980s and 1990s, with governments reducing staff and budgets and regulators having to operate with less. Finally, the self-restraint of the Canadian Supreme Court, for the most part, in interpreting Charter rights and applying them to the public policies of governments and other public sector institutions has reinforced a gradual approach to reforming regulations. A few of these factors are contextual in nature, but most are more permanent structural features that will continue to influence the choices and changes made by the regulatory state.

Regulatory gradualism has certain implications for policy, management, and politics. In the short term, most existing regulations are taken as given by stakeholders and or remain hidden from public and academic attention. Reforms frequently occur step-by-step at the margins of a regulatory system. As the chapter by Fazil Mihlar shows, systematic evaluation methods tend to have a modest influence, at best, on rule making and review within governments. Proposals to eliminate or drastically alter established rules and laws typically provoke resistance by vested interests. In addition, regulatory officials prefer negotiation and persuasion as implementation tools. Yet, over the longer term, a series of marginal changes in several sectors and across the four regimes have transformed the regulatory state, altering economic and social relations and modifying public expectations and policy communities. A central message of this book is that Canadians have found many ways to significantly change the rules of a complex economy and society.

Beyond Economic Liberalism

Economic liberalism has been the dominant idea in regulatory reform but, in the real world, ideas and practices are more varied and complex. For example, definitional diversity over the meaning of key concepts persists. Conceptions of what is regulation vary, as is evident across the chapters in this book, from conventional notions of regulation as delegated rule making to wider notions that see regulation as rules that govern the economy and society, as a key element in managing governance, or as something that individuals, communities, and businesses either demand or need. Similarly, deregulation may refer to the loosening of economic rules, to reducing the actual number of rules, or to the total removal of government restrictions on activities in specific sectors. Different definitions yield different benchmarks against which to assess regulatory reforms and these, in turn, are likely to lead to different conclusions about the efficacy of any reforms that are implemented.

Academics and practitioners need to rethink the recently dominant liberal economic paradigms of regulation. By and large, regulation is seen as an inherently limiting and constraining policy instrument in relation to private sector economic behaviour. This is neo-classical economic thinking, based on the idea of the 'free' market economy, in principle self-regulating, so that government action of almost any kind is cast as interventionist and restrictive. However, it is also a unidimensional conception of economic regulation, focusing on the policing function. What it ignores is that regulation is, in fact, multifunctional and may perform promoting and planning purposes as well, although whether it should be so employed is a subject of ongoing debate.

Regulation can protect and promote the interests of actors in the economy, polity, and larger society. The chapters by Waters and Stanbury on telecommunications and transportation, Bennett on privacy legislation, Hill on managing the regulatory state, and Prince on civic regulation all call attention to rationales and domains for regulation that lie outside the traditional view of government regulation. Beyond economic values, social and political values serve as important arguments for government regulation. On this, the distinguished economist Richard Lipsey (1984, 16) has commented: 'Laws against gambling, prostitution, drugs, pornography, certain sexual practices, and a host of other activities thought to be immoral, probably owe their public support to these desires. Such motives are ruled out by economists' utilitarian theories of consumer behaviour but they are potent social forces revealing what economic theory denies: that consumption has a social as well as a private dimension. Economists will get nowhere by denying this.'

On matters of moral and sexual regulation or the Criminal Code of Canada, for example, Lipsey suggests that economists can and should contribute to research and policy discussions by estimating and publicizing the costs and benefits of regulatory measures. The expanded conception of regulation presented in this volume points to the need for multidisciplinary approaches to the study and practice of regulation, and Lipsey's remarks call for each discipline to recognize its limitations and potential contributions.

In conclusion, the state of regulatory analysis in the late 1990s, compared to twenty years ago, is characterized by far more academic studies generated by a still modestly sized research community, relatively fewer governmental studies on regulatory processes or performance, but relatively more studies by assorted think tanks. Using our framework of four regulatory regimes, we observe that much of the literature continues to consist of economic and policy analyses of Regime I sectoral regulatory agencies and practices in the fields of energy, telecommunications, and transportation. In contrast, little work has been done on health-and-science-related regulators. Over the 1980s and 1990s, a considerable literature has been produced on some Regime II horizontal regulatory agencies involved with competition policy and the environment, but little on others, such as intellectual property and other marketplace framework rules. Comparatively speaking, Regime III has risen in prominence, with various reforms made to structures and processes within the executive arena of governments to enhance the management of regulation, as has Regime IV, with the establishment of trade agreements both within Canada and between Canada and the United States and Mexico. For policy makers and practitioners, regulation continues to be linked to government agendas in terms of how rule-making agencies and processes can be altered to contribute to the priorities of downsizing, economic growth, harmonizing rules, and lowering or eliminating barriers to trade across jurisdictions. Federal and provincial government officials have persisted, although with less fanfare than in the 1980s perhaps, with various reforms for managing regulatory systems and reviewing regulations.

Much work remains to be done on the institutional features of most regulatory agencies. What is required, to advance our understanding of regulatory practice, we believe, is more integrated studies of regulatory organizations – agencies, departments, and self-regulating occupations – informed by theory that links their internal governance structures and processes as well as their external economic and political environments.

REFERENCES

Bernier, Ivan, and Andrée Lajoie, eds. 1985. *Law, Society and the Economy*. Toronto: University of Toronto Press.

Cuming, Ronald C.C., ed. 1985. *Perspectives on the Harmonization of Law in Canada*. Toronto: University of Toronto.

Doern, G. Bruce. 1978. *The Regulatory Process in Canada*. Toronto: Macmillan.

Doern, G. Bruce, and Stephen Wilks, eds. 1998. *Changing Regulatory Institutions in Britain and North America*. Toronto: University of Toronto Press.

Grabosky, Peter N. 1995. Using Non-Governmental Resources to Foster Compliance. *Governance* 8, no. 4: 527–50.

Hoberg, George. 1993. Environmental Policy: Alternative Styles. In Michael Atkinson, ed. *Governing Canada*. Toronto: Harcourt Brace Jovanovich.

Lipsey, Richard G. 1984. Can the Market Economy Survive? In George Lermer, ed., *Probing Leviathan: An Investigation of Government in the Economy*, ch. 1. Vancouver: Fraser Institute.

Majone, G. 1994. The Rise of the Regulatory State. *West European Politics* 17, no. 3 (July): 77–101.

Paquet, Gilles. 1978. The Regulatory Process and Economic Performance, 34–67. In G. Bruce Doern, ed., *The Regulatory Process in Canada*. Toronto: Macmillan.

Reid, Angus. 1997. *Shakedown: How the New Economy Is Changing Our Lives*. Toronto: Seal Books.

Schultz, Richard J. 1982. Regulation and Public Administration. *Canadian Public Administration* 25, no. 4: 638–52.

– 1994. Deregulation Canadian-Style, State Reduction or Recasting? In Robert Bernier and James Iain Gow, eds., *Un État Reduit? A Down-sized State?*, ch. 6. Ste-Foy: Presses de l'Université du Québec.

Sunstein, C. 1990. *After The Rights Revolution: Reconceiving the Regulatory State*. Cambridge, Mass.: Harvard University Press.

Vogel, D. 1986. *National Styles of Regulation: Environmental Policy in Britian and the United States*. Ithaca: Cornell University Press.

Contributors

Colin J. Bennett is an associate professor of political science at the University of Victoria. He is the author of *Regulating Privacy: Data Protection and Public Policy in Europe and the United States* (1992) and *Implementing Privacy Codes of Practice* (1995), as well as several articles on comparative and Canadian data protection regulation.

G. Bruce Doern is a professor in the School of Public Administration, Carleton University and holds a joint chair in public policy in the Politics Department, University of Exeter. His recent books include *Changing Regulatory Institutions in Britain and North America* (1998, with Stephen Wilks), *Comparative Competition Policy* (1996, co-edited with Stephen Wilks), *Border Crossings: The Internationalization of Canadian Public Policy* (1996, co-edited with Brian Tomlin and Leslie Pal), and *The Greening of Canada* (1994, co-authored with Tom Conway).

Stephen L. Harris is an economist and political scientist who is presently a policy analyst at the Organization for Economic Cooperation Development (OECD) in Paris. He was for several years an economist at the Bank of Canada. The author of several articles and studies on financial regulation, he has also been a visiting professor in the School of Public Administration at Carleton University.

Margaret M. Hill is a visiting professor in the School of Public Administration, Carleton University and was formerly a lecturer in comparative public policy and public administration at the Politics Department, University of Exeter. She is the author of several articles and reports on comparative and Canadian regulation. She has also worked as a consultant and adviser to

several federal departments and regulatory bodies in Canada and is presently a
senior policy adviser at Environment Canada.

Kathryn Harrison is a professor in the Department of Political Science,
University of British Columbia. She is the author of *Passing the Buck:
Federalism and Canadian Environmental Policy* (1996) and *Risk, Science and
Politics* (1994, with George Hoberg), as well as numerous journal articles on
social regulation.

Robert Howse is an associate professor in the Faculty of Law, University of
Toronto, and associate director of the Centre for the Study of State and
Market. He is the author of *The Regulation of International Trade* (1995, with
Michael Trebilcock) as well as numerous articles on related trade law issues,
including internal trade in Canada and the constitution.

Hudson Janisch is a professor of law in the Faculty of Law at the University
of Toronto. He is the author of studies such as *Freedom to Compete: Reforming the Canadian Telecommunications Regulatory System* (1993, with Richard
Schultz) and numerous articles dealing with key aspects of regulation and
administrative justice, including discretion, accountability, and regulatory
forbearance in several regulatory fields.

Fazil Mihlar is a senior policy analyst at the Fraser Institute. He is the author
of *Regulatory Overkill: The Cost of Regulation in Canada* (1996) and *Unions
and Right-to-Work Laws* (1997). His articles have appeared in several
newspapers, including the *Globe and Mail, Financial Post, Calgary Herald,*
and *Vancouver Sun.*

Michael J. Prince is Lansdowne Professor of Social Policy, University of
Victoria. He is the author or editor of several books on Canadian public
policy, including: *How Ottawa Spends* (1986, 1987), *Federal and Provincial
Budgeting* (1985, with Allan Maslove and Bruce Doern), *Public Budgeting in
Canada* (1988, with Allan Maslove and Bruce Doern), and *The Origins of
Public Enterprise in the Canadian Mineral Sector* (1985, with Bruce Doern).

Richard J. Schultz is a professor of political science at McGill University
and formerly director of the Centre for the Study of Regulated Industries at
McGill. He is the author of several books, including *Economic Regulation and
the Federal System* (1985, with Alan Alexandroff) and *Federalism, Bureau-*

cracy and Public Policy (1980) and has written numerous articles on telecommunications policy and regulation.

W.T. Stanbury is UPS Foundation Professor of Regulation and Competition Policy, Faculty of Commerce and Business Administration, University of British Columbia. He is the author of many books on various areas of regulation, economics, and public policy, including *Perspectives on the New Economics and Regulation of Telecommunications* (1996), *The Future of Telecommunications Policy in Canada* (1995, with Stephen Globerman and Thomas A. Wilson), *Reforming the Federal Regulatory Process in Canada, 1971–1992* (1992), and *Business-Government Relations in Canada* (1993).

Michael J. Trebilcock is a professor of law and director of the Centre for the Study of State and Market at the University of Toronto. His numerous publications include *The Regulation of International Trade* (1995, with Robert Howse), *Unfinished Business: Reforming Trade Remedy Laws in North America* (1993), and *Trade and Transitions: A Comparative Analysis of Adjustment Policies* (1990).

W.G. Waters II is a professor in the Faculty of Business Administration and Commerce at the University of British Columbia. An economist, he is the author of several articles on the transportation industry and on the regulation of transportation.